GABRIELLE PETIT

GABRIELLE PETIT

THE DEATH AND LIFE OF A FEMALE SPY IN THE FIRST WORLD WAR

Sophie De Schaepdrijver

Bloomsbury Academic
An imprint of Bloomsbury Publishing Plc

B L O O M S B U R Y
LONDON · NEW DELHI · NEW YORK · SYDNEY

Bloomsbury Academic

An imprint of Bloomsbury Publishing Plc

50 Bedford Square	1385 Broadway
London	New York
WC1B 3DP	NY 10018
UK	USA

www.bloomsbury.com

BLOOMSBURY and the Diana logo are trademarks of Bloomsbury Publishing Plc

First published 2015

British Library Cataloguing-in-Publication Data

A catalogue record for this book is available from the British Library.

ISBN: HB: 978-1-4725-9087-9
        PB: 978-1-4725-9086-2
     ePDF: 978-1-4725-9088-6
     ePub: 978-1-4725-9089-3

Library of Congress Cataloging-in-Publication Data

Schaepdrijver, Sophie de.
Gabrielle Petit : the death and life of a female spy in the First World War / Sophie De Schaepdrijver.
pages cm
Includes bibliographical references and index.
ISBN 978-1-4725-9086-2 — ISBN 978-1-4725-9088-6 (ePDF) — ISBN 978-1-4725-9089-3 (ePub) 1. Petit, Gabrielle, 1893-1916. 2. World War, 1914-1918—Secret service—Belgium. 3. World War, 1914-1918—Secret service—Great Britain. 4. World War, 1914-1918—Underground movements. 5. Women spies—Belgium—Biography. 6. Spies—Belgium—Biography. I. Title.
D639.S8P487 2015
940.4'86493092—dc23
[B]
2014031167

Typeset by RefineCatch Limited, Bungay, Suffolk
Printed and bound in Great Britain

To Ronnie Po-chia Hsia

CONTENTS

ILLUSTRATIONS

All illustrations copyright Royal Army Museum, Brussels.

MAPS

ACKNOWLEDGMENTS

This book has been long in the making and my debt to all of those who helped me and stood by me is enormous. Since archivist-historians are a girl's best friend, my first thanks go to them: at the Belgian State Archives, Michaël Amara, Pierre-Alain Tallier, Luc Vandeweyer, and Luc Janssen who provided crucial help with the judicial files. My thanks, also, to Gerd De Prins at the Belgian War Victims administration, to Jean Houssiau at the City Archives in Brussels, who helped me search a hundred boxes for one elusive document, and to Sven Steffens who gave me access to the municipal archives in Molenbeek.

Digital access to the Belgian press was still fledgling when I conducted this research; my thanks to Marc d'Hoore and his staff at the periodicals section at the Royal Library in Brussels, especially to Joz Sterken. Thanks to Jacques Bredael for helping me track down a 1964 documentary; at the Cinematek in Brussels, thanks to Clémentine De Blick and Francis Malfliet. Thanks to An Coucke, the associate director of Saint-Gilles prison, for guiding me around the building in 2012, and to the prison's director, Ralf Bas, for making this visit possible. Thanks to Nicole Demaret at the Musée du Folklore in Tournai; to Gustaaf Janssens, formerly of the Royal Palace Archives in Brussels; to Jeroen Huygelier at the Belgian Army Archives in Evere (Brussels); to Florence Loriaux at the Centre d'Animation et de Recherche en Histoire Ouvrière et Populaire in Brussels; and to Robert Van Hee at the University of Antwerp. Further thanks to Guillaume Baclin, Rudi De Groot, Luc De Munck, Robin de Salle, Paul Delforge, Clive Emsley, Alison Fell, Emmanuel Gerard, Ann Kelders, Nicole Leclercq, Anna Luyten, Muriel Hanot, Peter Heyrman, Françoise Quattrus, and the late Roger Vranken.

A very warm word of thanks to fellow historians who went out of their way to answer questions, discuss issues, and help me access documentation. I am in especial debt to espionage experts Jim Beach, Emmanuel Debruyne, Keith Jeffery, and Jan Van der Fraenen, who have been extremely generous. So has Isabel Hull, who not only read chapters and provided vital comments, but also helped me decipher signatures of German Foreign Office personnel. I also owe a great deal to Martin Conway's comments on the "memory" chapters. Rebecca Scott generously sent me press clippings from the Bibliothèque Marguerite Durand in Paris, and, in conversation, provided me with inspiring ideas. Sincerest thanks to Monsieur Pierre Ronvaux for kindly sharing his insights and research—even, one memorable afternoon, helping me find a crucial source—and for showing me around the former orphanage where Gabrielle Petit grew up. Rob Troubleyn of the Royal Army Museum in Brussels provided essential help with the sources and illustrations. My thanks, also, to Helga Boeye for drawing the maps. An enthusiastic thanks for their collegial help and their ideas to fellow grandeguerristes James Connolly, Aurore François, Leen Engelen, Rainer Hiltermann, Benoît Majerus,

Christoph Roolf, Andreas Toppe, Antoon Vrints, and Thomas Weber. In addition, I gained much insight from conversations and correspondence with Stéphane Audoin-Rouzeau, Annette Becker, Gita Deneckere, Bruno De Wever, Anne Duménil, Jonathan Gumz, John Horne, Heather Jones, Chantal Kesteloot, Alan Kramer, Christophe Prochasson, Tammy Proctor, Anne Rasmussen, Hubert Roland, Pierre Schoentjes, Jens Thiel, Christine Van Everbroeck, David Van Reybrouck, Kaat Wils, Lode Wils, Jay Winter, and fellow traveler Laurence Van Ypersele. Finally, sincerest thanks to the anonymous readers of this manuscript for their inspired and inspiring comments. Of course, all mistakes and misinterpretations in this book are my own.

At Penn State, my thanks to the Department of History and the College of the Liberal Arts for their trust and support; to the Institute for the Arts and Humanities, where a Resident Fellowship in the Fall of 2012 gave me some much-needed time; at Penn State University Libraries, to Eric Novotny, History librarian, to Heather Ross at the Donald W. Hamer Map Library, and the spendid staff at the interlibrary loan department; and, finally, to my smart and generous colleagues.

Without time and surroundedness, this book would have remained a fond project. That I could take the time to research and write it I owe to the ones who surround me. As ever, I want to thank my mother, Claudine Spitaels, the warmest and sharpest of great minds, the most present of presences: where we would be without her, I cannot think. My thanks to our children, Mathilde Hsia and Eduard Hsia, for giving their parents so much joy and for commenting on Gabrielle Petit, which, given her book's demands on their mother's attention, is typically generous of them.

Finally, my greatest gratitude goes to the most brilliant historian I know—my husband, Ronnie Po-chia Hsia, who saw this book, and so much else, to fruition. His profound insights, his time, his love are in here; it is fitting that this book should be dedicated to him.

INTRODUCTION

In a provincial town in Belgium, behind a church dating back to Norman times, stands a monument that celebrates secular martyrdom in the twentieth century. It represents a young woman in an austere dress, striding forward, her hands by her side, clenched into fists. She gazes upward, presenting her chest. The pose is bold and chaste, with no hint of the erotic. A rather more sensuously rendered angel embraces the young woman tenderly, one elegant arm gesturing to the sky. The monument dates from 1924. Today, its dramatic intensity seems lost on its surroundings. Many here have given up. On the benches surrounding the monument, men slouch, drinking beer from cans. Across the street, a store called *Mike's Reptipark* sells snakes for pets, as well as rodents and "accessories."

The monument is not an allegory. It is a memorial to a young woman, who was born in this town—Tournai, on the Belgian-French border, sixty miles west of Brussels—in 1893. Her name was Gabrielle Petit. She spied for the British army behind the Western Front during the First World War. In 1916, she was executed on orders of a German military court; she was twenty-three. Petit's death went almost unnoticed, unlike that of the English nurse Edith Cavell, whose execution in 1915 had caused a worldwide uproar. As the war ended, Petit lay unremembered in an unmarked grave at the execution-grounds in Brussels. But after the Armistice, her remains and her story were exhumed. She became a modern Joan of Arc insistently held up for the admiration of her contemporaries.

This book is both a biography of Gabrielle Petit and a study of the way she was commemorated. Some recent scholarship on national heroes and heroines and on the process of "heroization" has concentrated fruitfully on memory, not biography.[1] Other scholars have chosen to study both the lives and the legends of heroes (or antiheroes).[2] So have I, for reasons I will explain below. The first, biographical panel of this book is an exercise in documenting an obscure life; for, in spite of Petit's status as heroine, there are not all that many traces. Not that Petit's trajectory must be told completely through contextual information, as is the life of the unsung French clog-maker Louis-François Pinagot so heroically reconstituted by the French historian Alain Corbin.[3] Personal testimonies about Petit do exist; and one sporadically hears her own voice. Still, the corpus of authenticated sources documenting her life and work is modest, and parts of her brief existence can barely be described at all; in spite of her posthumous fame, she is never more than a few steps removed from anonymity. Reconstituting her life also serves to shed light on the society and culture surrounding it. Before the war, Petit lived, successively, in the world of the struggling petite bourgeoisie in provincial Belgium in the late nineteenth century; in the closed universe of Catholic educational institutions; and in the precarious world of service workers in *belle époque* Brussels. From the summer of 1914, her trajectory meshed with the collective experience of military mobilization, invasion, the establishment of an occupation regime, and the creation of networks of civilian resistance; and it ended in the closed universe created by German military justice. Through it all, even if the sources about Petit are rare and sometimes opaque, the contours of her own individual story can be traced. That story is the story of an ambition, intermittently visible but unmistakably present; an ambition that was very much a part of the increased claims to distinction that had percolated, over the preceding century, down to the mass of ordinary citizens.

In the second part of the book, that single story is replaced by the many strands of Petit's memory. Even as Petit's elevation to the status of national heroine symbolically untangled *one* thread out of the knotted experience of Belgium's war, her memory was itself multi-stranded. Private memories of the young woman were at odds with public ones; vernacular commemoration and professional document-gathering efforts proceeded along separate paths; and Petit rose to the status of heroine in various quarters, with variable accents. Retracing the creation of such memories casts light on societies as they came out of war. For one thing, the sheer extent of the commemorative endeavor is striking. As the historians Jay Winter and Emmanuel Sivan have pointed out a decade and a half ago, "the effort to create artifacts or ceremonies in the aftermath of war has been so widespread that it is time to consider them . . . as a set of profound and evanescent expressions of the force of civil society itself."[4] So it is with Petit's memory. It was certainly fleeting: it was past its zenith five years after the Armistice, though it would be another four decades before it entered what one could call its afterlife. But it had mobilized a considerable effort from many quarters in civil society, and it had found receptive audiences. Petit's memory was both an evanescent and a profound "expression of the force of civil society itself" as it came out of the war.

What war experience did Petit's memory address? What story was it meant to tell? To answer this question, let us return to her monument in Tournai, as well as contemplate her monument in Brussels, which was built the year before, in 1923, and stands on an elegant square in the center of the capital. Both monuments are bronze statues that depict Petit standing bold upright, facing execution. Both pedestals carry her alleged, defiant last words: "*I will show them how a Belgian woman knows how to die.*" Both, then, are conceived as *tableaux vivants* in which the presence of the firing-squad is implied, and they condense her narrative into one significant moment: the drama of a young woman facing her imminent end. The inscriptions on the pedestals form the exegesis of the frozen scene. They point to a transcendent horizon, linking Petit's end to the cause of the nation. What is commemorated here is the acceptance of death for the common good.

As the monuments to Petit were unveiled, so were tens of thousands of monuments commemorating the death of young men from 1914 to 1918. Some thirty thousand local memorials went up in France, and Belgium's 2,636 communes all built one (or more than one). Memorials ranged from simple stelae to elaborate sculptures representing soldiers in various poses, sometimes accompanied by wingèd Victories or grieving Pietàs. All, of course, listed the names of the dead. Indeed, the very idea of a monument as "a place for the pure display of names" emerged out of the First World War, as Thomas Laqueur has pointed out.[5] Those ubiquitous monuments, built at considerable cost, expressed a wish to permanently hold up to public contemplation the fact that so many men had died and to give this massive fact a space forever demarcated from the profane. Whatever one thought of the war—slaughter or sacrifice—no-one disputed that the fallen possessed, *qua* fallen, unassailable authority.[6]

Seen from this angle, the monuments to Gabrielle Petit have everything in common with the monuments to the dead of the early 1920s. Both commemorated the death of young people; both portrayed their memory as hallowed. But there is a difference. Petit's statues depict Petit—albeit under the traits of the sculptors' models—and no-one else. By contrast, the statues of soldiers on the monuments to the dead, even if some were modeled on the likenesses of actual men, never represent any man in particular. Individual fallen men were certainly commemorated—airmen, soldiers who had been the first to be killed in one theater or another, volunteers of particular valor—but not in public monuments in the center of cities.[7] The "commemorative hyper-nominalism" of First World War memory did not take individual soldiers out of the mass; and the only individual soldier to be publicly commemorated in the heart of the city was an anonymous Everyman: the Unknown Soldier.[8] The uniform, it seems, precluded the dead from being represented individually.

Public statues *were* built, in the interwar years, to individual men in uniform. But these did not commemorate the dead; they glorified leaders. The squares and avenues of interwar Paris, to give the most striking example, went abristle with statues of military commanders and allied monarchs, from Galliéni in 1926, over Peter I of Serbia and his son Alexander I of Yugoslavia, to Joffre in 1939. This proliferation of authority-glorifying statuary was, in fact, a massive throwback. As the art historian June Hargrove writes, such "messianic adulation of the 'artisans of victory'" broke with the prewar Third Republic habit of building statues for exemplary fellow citizens instead of for generals and kings.[9] Indeed, between 1870 and 1914, the Third Republic had decorated Paris with a veritable "outdoor Pantheon" of monuments (Hargrove's term) to citizens of merit from past and present. These men (and a very few women) exemplified Progress—science, the arts, civic devotion, charity. Most were remembered for their exemplary endeavors; some for their sacrifice on behalf of the greater good (or what was remembered as such). Nineteenth- and early twentieth-century Belgian culture, too, exhibited what contemporaries made fond fun of as "statue-mania" (*statuomanie*). Plentiful public contracts kept a guild of distinguished *statuaires* in steady work. In Tournai, for instance, three major monuments went up between the mid-1860s and the mid-1890s: an 1863 bronze statue of Christine de Lalaing, the princess d'Espinoy, alleged to have organized the defense of the city against Spanish troops in 1581; and two monuments to contemporaries: a marble memorial to a distinguished local scientist and newspaperman (1883), and a bronze statue of an internationally famous history painter born in Tournai (1896). The bronze pageant of exemplary historic figures and contemporaries also featured those who had met a significant death. In notably anticlerical Brussels, for instance, these ranged, in chronological order, from an 1864 monument to the dukes of Egmont and Horne, beheaded on orders of the Duke of Alva in 1568, to a remarkable homage to a contemporary: a monument to the Catalan free-thinker and anarchist Francesc (Francisco) Ferrer, unveiled in 1911, two years after Ferrer's execution by royalist troops in Barcelona.[10]

The monuments to Gabrielle Petit belong to this prewar tradition: they highlight individual citizens' contribution to the common good. But they were conceived in the immediate wake of a threat to the nation's survival; and, far from evincing the prewar monuments' serene confidence in Progress, they represent the shock of death in the midst of the community and in very recent memory. This brings them closer again to the monuments to the fallen, with their urgent message to remember sacrifice.

The memorials to Petit, then, stand at the intersection of two types of public monument—the monuments to the war dead, and the monuments to exemplary individual citizens. They are not the only ones. In the two decades following the Armistice, this intersection was populated (so to speak) by a small group of people, all commemorated because they lost their lives in similar circumstances: they were civilians, men and women, who had been executed on orders of the German military regime in occupied Belgium and northern France. A modest pantheon of civilian heroes emerged from the occupation; several were commemorated in monuments. Only those civilians who had lost their lives through chosen action qualified as heroes; civilian *victims* did not. The memory of the six thousand people killed in a series of massacres in Belgium and northern France during the 1914 invasion was enshrined in aggregate monuments, which listed names and presented allegorical images, like those of the fallen. But individual memorials were reserved for *agents*. In the Belgian village of Marchienne-au-Pont (Hainaut), for instance, there is a monument to the dead that commemorates the local fallen of 1914–1918 together with the victims of the local 1914 massacre. Close by stands an individual monument. It commemorates a girl of ten, Yvonne Vieslet, who was shot by a German sentry in 1918 for having handed her school-issue sandwich to a French prisoner of war. Though a child, she is remembered as a heroine, not a victim: the monument shows her proudly proffering her precious *couque scolaire*; it does not show her gruesome death. Indeed, representations of civilian agents as victims were sure to draw protest. In Lille, the 1929 monument to five intelligence agents who had been shot in 1915 depicted four of them standing upright, with the fifth—the Belgian teenager Léon Trulin—lying face down. Some, including his family, took offense; in response, a bronze statue went up in 1934—a rather awkward affair, which in its eagerness to show Trulin facing death courageously, practically had him smirking. The same motif of defiance marks the 1923 monument erected by the mining town of La Louvière in Hainaut to Omer Lefèvre, an intelligence agent shot in 1916. This grandiose group composition stages grieving Belgium, the army (in the guise of a uniformed soldier), the civilian population (in the guise of an elderly man), and the enemy (in the guise of a rapacious eagle); Lefèvre, standing tall and presenting his bare chest, is the only individual. The monument was inaugurated in 1923 before a fifty-thousand-strong audience including Queen Elisabeth.[11] What all of this means is that chosen endeavor alone conferred the right to be represented individually. And it may well be that civilians were felt to represent chosen endeavor more than men in uniform.[12] In uniform, even actions of exceptional valor ultimately occurred within a cadre; this made the army as a whole heroic, but not the individual soldier. That is why civilians facing the execution squad could be elevated to individual hero status in a way soldiers were not. Moreover, like the exemplary individuals glorified before the war, they represented individual ambition, up to and including self-immolation. And theirs was felt to be an endeavor that emerged out of civilian society. Postwar audiences might feel ambivalent about the desirability of putting an entire generation in uniform ever again. But the exemplariness of civilian endeavor was beyond dispute.

Moreover, it was civilian endeavor in the service of a worthy cause: resisting an occupying power. The men and women thus glorified represented the "Republican" view of the civilian in wartime, to use the definition coined by the scholar of occupation Karma Nabulsi.[13] In this "Republican" view, it is civilians' right and duty to defend the invaded fatherland with the methods they have. (By contrast, the "Martian" view denies that the unarmed and vanquished have rights; and the "Grotian" view proclaims that civilians have a right to protection, but must stay out of the fray.) This "Republican" view had its prewar champions—including in Belgium. A recent article by Jonathan Gumz draws attention to the passionate defense by Auguste Beernaert, the Belgian delegate to the 1899 Hague conference on the laws of war, of civilians' right to defend their invaded nation. Beernaert's view broadened the remit of mobilization for war to include civilian volunteers. He justified this on the grounds that protesting military occupations was morally formative, whereas acquiescing in such an "abuse of force" would sap the "powerful mainspring of patriotism" and condemn the citizenry to political regression and even moral corruption. Encouraging civilians to remain "mere spectators . . . in the struggles in which the fate of their country is at stake" would deepen "that baneful indifference which is perhaps one of the gravest evils from which our times suffer."[14] In other words, occupied populations' willingness to accommodate themselves to military occupations was every bit as harmful as those occupations themselves. Accommodation would corrupt the body politic, weaken moral fiber, enthrone egotism, and, worst of all, lead to a lack of purpose (what the French called *veulerie*[15]) both in the individual and in the collective—an object of obsessive fear in the modern West, where concerns over encroaching slackness generated urgent reflections on the proper cultivation of energy.[16] Beernaert's take on civilian engagement under military occupation was exceptional among commentators on war, as Gumz has pointed out; most agreed that limiting war's potential damage meant limiting civilians' right to resistance. At the same time, Beernaert's insistence on collective purpose and his exhortation to national energy meshed with much wider turn-of-the-century concerns.

This very theme of energetic endeavor was central to the postwar commemoration of civilian resisters. Remembering them expressed a quest for honor on the part of societies that had been invaded and had experienced the war under a military occupation regime.[17] Liberating these lands had been an Entente war aim; the ten million occupied in the West, specifically, had carried great symbolic significance. But at the same time, they were portrayed as helpless victims; worse, some suspected them of connivance with the enemy. After liberation, fervent remembrance of how some civilians had faced death without flinching was a way for liberated civilians to assert their society's own contribution to the war effort vis-à-vis their uniformed liberators. (Some of whom rather relished throwing their weight around: half a century later, one veteran gleefully recalled how he and his companions had in January 1919 chased "civilian" engineering students out of their lecture hall at the University of Liège and claimed sole rights to higher education for those who had been at the front.[18]) The highlighting of civilian valor was a way to state that the occupied territories had been fronts as well.

And so they had been. But they had also been areas of porosity and compromise. Women, especially, came to represent the permeability of occupied society. After liberation, the return to a prewar order—or, rather, the *effort* to return to a prewar order—was marked by outbursts of ritualized popular rage, much of it directed at women suspected of intimacy with the enemy. They were subjected to public humiliations—beaten, stripped, shorn, sometimes even branded with hot irons. In some cases, returned soldiers initiated these retributions; everywhere, crowds partook eagerly, keen on claiming honor by dissociating themselves from those who had allowed the body of the nation to be penetrated, or so the essence of the charge went. These cruel events may go some way towards explaining why women figured so prominently in the exaltation of civilian valor after the war (next to the tangible fact that women *had* played a major role in resistance work). As a foil against the images of permeability, corruption and degradation presented by the "shorn women" stood the image of the heroine—forming an impenetrable front, unsullied, standing tall. (A foil not just to the degraded, but to the undistinguished masses overall: in May 1919, a Belgian poet called for a "lofty statue" to Edith Cavell in Brussels that would "soar high above the chatter below."[19]) There were other symbolic reasons for postwar heroinism. First, women could represent civilian valor more unproblematically than men, since they, unlike male civilians, did not face charges of having shirked front-line duty. Second, the existence of female patriots—willing to give their all in spite of their subordinate position—seemed to prove that patriotism was a primeval force. Third, women's images traditionally served as allegories of the nation.

Women, then, figured more prominently in the pantheon of civilian heroes. Or, to be more precise—for not all executed women were remembered—those civilian heroes most intensely remembered were women. Of course men were commemorated too, some grandiosely so. But none generated anywhere near the same fervor that developed around three heroines in particular: Edith Cavell, Gabrielle Petit, and Louise de Bettignies. These three women had all stood trial before a German military tribunal in Brussels, the largest occupied city of the First World War. Cavell and Petit had both been executed in Brussels. De Bettignies, a Frenchwoman who led a resistance network, was pardoned, but she died in a Cologne prison in 1918. The memory of all three heroines generated memorial explosion over a wide variety of media—prose, poetry, drama, music compositions, postcards, movies. And all three were commemorated in major monuments. In 1920, Edith Cavell monuments went up in Paris, London, and Brussels. The Paris monument, a bas-relief in the Tuileries Gardens, was demolished by the Wehrmacht in 1940, but the one in London still stands.[20] George Frampton's austere statue in white marble set against a lofty pillar of gray granite stands close to the National Portrait Gallery and to Nelson's column, highlighting Cavell's place in the grand narrative of British heroes. (As to the 1920 Brussels monument, it commemorates Cavell together with another civilian heroine, Marie Depage, a Belgian nurse who died aboard the *Lusitania* on a fund-raising journey.) In 1927, Cavell was also represented in a bas-relief on a monument for Louise de Bettignies. This one stands in De Bettignies' home town of Lille, fifteen miles east of Tournai, across the border in France. A work by the very prestigious Maxime Real del Sarte, it represents De Bettignies upright; a kneeling French soldier kisses her hand in gratitude. He represents the entire French army, but she, though channeling collective courage ("To Louise de Bettignies and all the heroic women of the invaded country, A Grateful France," the inscription reads), is an individual, not an allegory.[21]

Unlike male heroes of the occupation, whose memory always remained local, the three heroines acquired wider prominence. Cavell's posthumous renown was worldwide. She is still remembered today; in 2007, Cavell was one of British Prime Minister Gordon Brown's "portraits" of courage.[22] To some extent Petit and De Bettignies were glorified as the Belgian and French "responses" to Cavell. As with other commemorative achievements of the First World War—cemeteries, poetry, poppies—the sheer discursive *oomph* of British war culture provided a hard-to-resist template. This does not mean that the other two commemorations were somehow derivative; rather, First World War heroism constituted what one might call a text—one with multiple internal references. And of course the "heroizations" of De Bettignies and Petit were commemorative endeavors in their own right, carrying accents of their own, surrounded with public emotion, and reaching well beyond the local. De Bettignies' glory encompassed all of occupied France. As to Gabrielle Petit, it is no coincidence that the monument in Brussels predated the one in her home town; by the spring of 1919, she was anointed the "national heroine" of Belgium. This assertion, as I will show, clashed with local claims to her memory; still, it means that Petit's memory resonated beyond the local, alone among Belgian *fusillé(e)s*.

How Petit became a national heroine in post-occupation Belgium is a story worth telling. She was one of very few heroes of the war (and the only civilian) whose memory crossed the linguistic divide, which meant that she symbolized all of Belgium. Belgium, as the war broke out, was a somewhat loose nation-state by Western European standards, a place of fiercely defended local priorities and particularistic interests, its linguistic duality only one axis of centrifugality among several. Military duties did not weigh heavily upon its citizens: conscription was only generalized in 1912 and even then allowed for wide exemptions. Yet the notion of national defense was potent enough. In August 1914, Belgium became an Entente symbol of resistance: invoking the principle of neutrality, its government had denied the German armies the right of passage to France, and the citizenry had overwhelmingly accepted this decision. The German invasion and civilian massacres burnished the image of "Gallant Little Belgium," both to the Belgians themselves and to liberal public opinion internationally. But this moment of fervor was followed by a war experience different from that of other belligerents: because most of

Belgium's territory was occupied, only a minority of service-age men had been mobilized. This war experience was discredited in a postwar Europe that defined "sacrifice"—the central trope of wartime—exclusively as front-line service.

It was in the aftermath of these bewildering experiences that the conceit of Petit as a national heroine emerged. The Petit cult responded to Belgium's loss of international prestige. It also helped make sense of the past occupation. It expressed a striving to suspend the profane, to hold on to the idea that there were lessons to be learned from the war. Observers hoped that an unbroken willingness to commemorate would unite and elevate the citizenry, whereas, they gloomily predicted—for anxious exhortations, too, formed part of memory discourse—forgetting and ingratitude would fatally coarsen it.

The wish to exhume Petit, then, tells us something about her contemporaries, just as it sheds light more generally on imagined communities' "exits from war" after 1918 (a subject of renewed scholarly interest[23]). The case of Petit is particularly instructive, since her exhumation required so much more of a deliberate effort than did that of other civilian heroes. Other *fusillé(e)s* had backgrounds, families, friends, professional identities; Petit was opaque. Cavell had been a highly esteemed professional in her late forties who left a legacy of students and correspondence. De Bettignies, thirty-eight years old when she died, was of patrician (if penniless) background, well-educated, well-traveled and well-surrounded. Petit, who had just turned twenty-three at the time of her execution, was not, as she would come to be remembered, a working-class woman; she came from a provincial middle-class background, but her family had fallen apart and she had been abandoned. In the years before the war, she had eked out a living in a succession of short-lived pink-collar jobs, and her employers barely remembered her, or did not care to. She was largely estranged from what remained of her family, did not have a wide circle of friends, drifted between rented rooms, and left little in writing. Her wartime activity remained largely unknown even after the war; she worked, as I will show, in relative isolation, whereas most agents were embedded in tight networks. Even Petit's last writings offer little clue; they are terse, almost businesslike instructions, very different from the effusive last letters of other executed men and women, widely circulated after the war.

Could it be that contemporaries commemorated her strictly as a symbol? As a kind of national allegory because of her gender and her youth (and, possibly, because she was the only Belgian woman to have been executed in the national capital, Brussels)? Certainly, efforts to actually document her life and work started late and were never systematic. Still, Petit was never an abstract allegory. Contemporaries might not have known more than the bare bones of her life's story, but it was her story that struck them. Whether they commemorated her solely for her heroic death or included a heroic sense of her entire life—her determination in spite of a lowly start—she struck them as an epitome of *striving*. And, in this, neither her hagiographers nor their audience were mistaken. Petit's elevation to the status of national heroine was, of course, a conceit, as such elevations always are. The cries of ardent patriotism ascribed to her were largely (though not entirely) apocryphal; and she was not the saintly figure of lore. But her life story, as it emerges from the dispersed evidence—another exhumation—really does hint at that very fixity of purpose so admired, both before and after the First World War, as the essence of the exemplary life—or the exemplary death. Through the bits and pieces of evidence loom the contours of a bruised, self-absorbed and fiercely ambitious personality, that of a young woman who would find, in war, the opportunity for distinction that had eluded her all her life, and whose vaulting ambition encompassed her defiant death.

That is why this book is not just about Petit's memory, but also about her life. It is a study of an individual trajectory, how this trajectory intersected with the war of 1914, and what this war meant to those who found themselves in demand for the first time in their lives. Petit's war engagement affords a view of the reach of "Republican" ideas about civilians' duty in wartime. But her example also shows how such strivings could merge with private strivings for distinction, social status and financial independence. In mapping out Petit's war, I will touch on life under occupation, on secret intelligence work, and on the occupation regime's military justice; on endeavor, danger, and death in civilian life during the First World War. I will then go on to consider how fellow citizens' war actions and their deaths were made sense of, after the war, by contemporaries. Lastly, the book offers a brief view of what happens to such a *lieu de mémoire* over time—how it becomes a repository for layers of meanings, while retaining its recognizability and urgency through another world war, before finally retreating into the folkloric, the irrelevant, or the postmodern. But without ever disappearing altogether, as if stories of individual endeavor, even the failed and tragic ones—*especially* the failed and tragic ones—never quite relinquish their hold on the modern imagination.

The book is structured as follows. A prologue flashes forward to Petit's exhumation and state funeral in May 1919, as her legend was first created. The next five chapters deal with Petit's life. Chapter One traces her childhood between 1893 and 1908—a story of a child's abandonment as a family slid down the social ladder—and the prewar years spent drifting between service jobs and rented rooms in booming *belle époque* Brussels (1908–1914). Chapter Two depicts the outbreak of the war, the never-quite-elucidated circumstances of Petit's parting from her fiancé, a career NCO in the Belgian army, her departure from the occupied country and her engagement as an agent for the British War Office. Chapter Three is an account of her war work compiling reports on German troop movements in the Belgian-French border zone, from August 1915, when she crossed the border into occupied Belgium after her briefing in London and the Netherlands, to her arrest in February 1916. Chapter Four is about the circumstances of her arrest and trial and the much-strengthened German police and military-justice apparatus. Chapter Five reconstructs Petit's last month in prison and her end. It analyses the refusal to commute her death sentence; and it charts Belgians' reactions to the execution against the backdrop of a changing dynamic between occupiers and occupied and within the occupied population.

The second part of the book deals with Petit's memory in three chapters. Chapter Six, "Memory Agents," explains how she became a household name to Belgians coming out of the war; it depicts the exalted exit from occupation, the return of government and army, and the recasting of bourgeois Belgium amidst the advent of generalized male suffrage. This chapter examines the forces of civil society that made for Petit's emergence as "national heroine"—for this was not, as I will show, a state-led effort at all. Chapter Seven, "National Heroine," paints Petit's commemoration at its zenith, from the discursive explosion following her May 1919 funeral to the unveiling of her Brussels monument in 1923, shortly after the publication of her first serious biography. That book ended the stream of Petit hagiography, while the monument 'set' her image. Both the book and the monument, each in their own way, signified an end to the live stream of Petit discourse. They also coincided with the start of what historians have called the "pacifist turn,"[24] a turning-away from the heroic and sacrificial image of the past war.

Still, as I indicate in Chapter Eight, "Palimpsest," Petit remained an icon of sacrifice through the 1920s and 1930s and the most recognizable face of resistance in the Second World War and its aftermath. From the 1960s, Petit faded as a symbol of sacrifice, as the entire notion of war mobilization in Western Europe became obsolete; and by the early twenty-first century, her memory had retreated into the local, the victimized, or the ironic. Not only was she no longer considered a national heroine, there no longer was any space—and, in the functionalized Brussels of the second half of the twentieth century, the term "space" must be taken quite literally—for the very idea of national heroism.

In this way, Petit's life and the long arc of her memory illuminate a century's worth of mobilization and demobilization in Western Europe.[25] They also illuminate the democratic impulse. The fact that a young woman of no social distinction, a contemporary, could be the object of such commemorative fervor for what was arguably the first time in European history, shows a force at work; the same force that underlay Petit's own lifelong, if scattershot, striving. Petit's story illuminates these issues at a modest level; the history told in this book—both that of her life and of her memory—is a marginal affair. But one of the purposes of this book is precisely to chart political and social imaginaries as they manifested themselves in obscure, provincial, and hard-to-reconstruct endeavors.

PROLOGUE: EXHUMATION

At eight o'clock in the evening of May 27, 1919, a small group of people stood at the former execution-grounds of the German occupation army—a rifle-range at the outskirts of Brussels. The executed had been buried there. As the group watched, two bodies were dug up. One was that of Mathieu "Pitje" Bodson, an invalided soldier from the Belgian army. Condemned for having helped British soldiers and Belgian volunteers escape occupied Belgium, Bodson had been shot in September 1916. The other corpse was that of Gabrielle Petit. Like Bodson, she had been executed one month after her twenty-third birthday. Her grave was opened first. The diggers found her body clad in a long blue overcoat, pierced by bullets at the heart. The newspapers wrote that her remains were "perfectly recognizable." They were not, as her sister, who was present, later said; but, then, the bodies of martyrs and heroes were commonly imagined as incorruptible.[1]

And Petit was by now a heroine. *Le Soir*, Belgium's most widely read French-language daily, ran a reverent report on the "touching ceremony" with all the details—how diggers had brought the disintegrating pinewood casket to the surface, how Petit's sister had fainted, how the body was transferred to an oak casket in preparation for the state funeral. Belgium's largest Flemish daily, *Het Laatste Nieuws*, did likewise.[2] The reports marveled at how a humble, forgotten example of the heroism of occupation times was finally reaching the light.

Indeed it had taken half a year after the Armistice for Petit to become a name. May 1919 was the month when nationwide commemorative fervor suddenly, massively, coalesced around her image. Her funeral, on May 29, Ascension Day, was a very prestigious event. It took place in Schaarbeek, the largest and wealthiest borough of Greater Brussels. Petit was laid to rest together with Mathieu Bodson and another executed patriot, the intelligence agent Aimé Smekens, shot in July 1917 at the age of forty-eight. The idea behind this triple state funeral was to surround Petit, made to symbolize the entire nation, with emblems of regional valor: Smekens, a Fleming, and Bodson, a Walloon. Both men formed "glorious apostrophes around the name of Gabrielle Petit."[3]

Petit was first declared Belgium's national heroine on May 1, 1919. *Le Drapeau* [The Flag], a new patriotic magazine, ran a front-page article declaring that

> Belgium must offer to Gabrielle Petit the homage of admiration that is her due. She is one of ours; she is our NATIONAL HEROINE. She . . . offered up her youth on the altar of the Fatherland. . . . She faced the German bullets with the bravery of a patriot . . . [and] fell like a soldier, on the field of honor. . . . Love for the Fatherland rendered this humble working-girl sublime![4]

High expectations surrounded the funeral of the "greatest of all the executed." Papers predicted "princely" honors.[5] The ceremony benefited from perfect weather, drew vast crowds, and did not disappoint. The decorations, the music, the speeches, the pageantry, the lavish, theatrical backdrop of Brussels' *belle époque* public architecture, all combined to produce "a funeral that was sumptuous, and, if we may say so, international in character."[6] Film footage shows crowds massed in front of Schaarbeek City Hall, a vast neo-renaissance building.[7] Inside, a funerary chapel was laid out in the lofty entrance hall, with Petit's coffin on a catafalque in between those of Bodson and Smekens. From an adjacent hall came the sound of muted funeral marches. People filed past the caskets for an hour, many in tears. Before a packed and silent hall, Prime Minister Léon Delacroix gave a speech, followed by a local dignitary and by a former political prisoner. Then, Queen Elisabeth made a dramatic surprise entrance. Dressed in white, visibly touched, she bowed before the caskets and pinned decorations to the flags covering them. "Intense emotion" surrounded this brief ceremony, the press reported; the Queen was then at the height of the aura she had gained in the war. Amidst profound silence, she exchanged a few whispered words with Petit's relatives, bowed once more before the caskets, and left. It was four o'clock. Under clarion calls, the caskets were carried outside and hoisted onto gun carriages draped with the Belgian tricolor and the Union Jack.

Meanwhile, the crowd in front of City Hall and all along the one-kilometer trajectory of the funeral cortège—from one end to the other of the stately *Rue Royale Sainte-Marie*— had steadily grown and was now overflowing the sidewalks; people thronged the street and were massed on top of newspaper stalls, on window ledges, on cornices. School-children, members of patriotic associations, and boy scouts stood to attention on City Hall plaza before arranging themselves in a cortège that spanned the entire length of the trajectory. Bands played solemn tunes as the procession advanced; the caskets were preceded by a military picket and followed by the relatives; behind them marched representatives of the royal court, dignitaries, and delegations of societies. In Royal Saint Mary's Church, a strangely affecting neo-Byzantine edifice, the head of the Catholic Church in Belgium, Cardinal Mercier, now world-famous for his defiance of the occupation regime during the war, spoke the eulogy. Choirs sang the national hymn. After Mass, the procession marched to Schaarbeek cemetery, two and a half kilometers eastward. The embankment of the road to the cemetery was crowded with onlookers. An elaborate stone bridge flanked by monumental staircases offered a kind of open-air balcony; hundreds of people gathered at this belvedere to take in "the admirable view offered on the sunlit street below: those pickets of soldiers, the funereal chariots draped with national colors, that multitude of wreaths and banners, gave the procession a majestic allure."[8] The cemetery, decorated with the slogan "Honor to the Heroes," was, as photographs show, heaving with people; clusters of onlookers perched on the walls, on nearby roofs, some even on top of grave monuments. There were more speeches. At six-thirty, the funeral was over.

That day, vendors had done a brisk business selling Petit's portrait for the benefit of a veterans' charity.[9] A booklet entitled *Gabrielle Petit: National Heroine* was equally popular, for, as a journalist exclaimed, "who, today, does not want to know the sublime end of she whom people already like to compare to the great Joan of Arc?"[10] The booklet portrayed Petit as the ultimate embodiment of sacrifice. It opened with solemn staccato sentences:

> Gabrielle Petit was executed for the Fatherland on April 1, 1916.
> She was barely 23 years old.
> She fought and died as a heroine.
> . . .
> The Belgians will never forget her.

The booklet then offered a succession of dramatic scenes that stressed her bravura. When war broke out, Petit became a nurse. When her soldier fiancé was wounded in the glorious battle of Liège, she nursed him back to health, then guided him across the danger-strewn border. Meanwhile she had joined secret intelligence, though her recruiters had warned her of "torture and death." As a spy, she took on disguises, shook off German snoops in the winding streets of old Brussels, prankishly planted the underground paper *La Libre Belgique* on the Governor-General's desk, and ran her own network: "extraordinary sight— a girl of twenty-two, poor, isolated, setting up an organization stretching from Brussels to Lille." But she was betrayed by a mole and arrested. Though in solitary confinement and, once, "mercilessly beaten," she remained silent. At her trial, her judges taunted her by saying that the King of Belgium was a "puppet." She bit back that King Albert was "in the trenches with his soldiers, while your Emperor is in the back with his courtiers." She hotly defended her engagement: "I am not a spy like your spies. I spied on you in my country . . ., whereas you are here unrightfully . . . You have no right to condemn me. All you are is brute force. You will kill me. Make it quick." Asked what she would do if pardoned, Petit said she would resume her work. Again she refused to name names: "Ugh! Don't insult me." Condemned to death, she lived another, agonizing month. Resorting to graffiti to strengthen her resolve, she wrote on the walls of her cell that "I refuse to appeal to show my enemy that I don't give a damn." And she inscribed her credo: "it's the humble ones that make unknown heroes." When finally the execution order was read out to her, she remained calm and even consoled her relatives on their last visit. "*I* seemed to be the one who had to die," her sister said. Her last words to her godmother before she disappeared at the end of the long prison corridor were: "You know, no blindfold! Adieu!" On her last night, her atheist German warden rather undelicately told her that there was no eternal life. In response, "she spoke of the soul's immortality, of the existence of God, whom she would see face to face a few hours later . . . She added that she prayed to God for her jailer and would remember him high above." She then calmly wrote her last messages, distributed her modest belongings, asked the guard to cut off a lock of her hair to give to her nearest, took communion from the German chaplain, and left prison, reciting the Rosary, raising her voice at the end of each *Ave Maria* at the words "now *and in the hour of our death.*" At the execution-grounds, as she left the carriage, a soldier offered to support her, but she politely declined: "Thank you, Sir, but I do not need your help, you will see how a Belgian girl knows how to die." She strode to the stake with alert step and refused to be blindfolded; as someone tried to force her, she violently pushed him away, telling him to "at least respect the last wish of a woman about to die," and no further attempt was made. As the commanding officer shouted his orders, Petit cried out "Long live Belgium, long live the . . .!"—her last word cut off by the shots. She was buried on the spot. "And her soul soared into immortality."[11]

Gabrielle Petit: National Heroine made Petit's name. The booklet was mass-distributed; blinded veterans received a free Braille version. It was extensively excerpted in the daily press, even on the front page of the Socialist *Le Peuple*.[12] Petit was granted the Order of Leopold, a Belgian award, in words that condensed the booklet's narrative:

> True national heroine whose humble existence is crowned with glory. After having, at great risk, crossed the border with her fiancé who goes on to the front, she returns to Belgium to take up intelligence service. In fulfilling her dangerous task, she shows remarkable intelligence and manly courage. Once arrested, she astonishes her torturers by her spiritual strength; condemned to death, she takes the secret, on which so many lives depend, with her. On the eve of her death, she confounds the enemy with her calm and elevated thoughts. She falls at the age of twenty-two [*sic*], having refused the blindfold, standing proudly upright, with the cry of "Long Live Belgium! Long live the . . ."[13]

Petit became the embodiment of a defiance welling up naturally from the depths of Belgian society. Speakers at her funeral called her a "childlike soul", a "brave and noble child," a "simple heart," and a "lily-like child (*liliale enfant*)." She personified unsullied patriotic sacrifice as a "pure heroine" showing her compatriots "radiant heights of honor and glory."[14]

A few weeks later, a Senator asked the government what it planned to do to keep Petit's memory alive. He made a lengthy speech of it. Petit should serve, he stated, as an example to the next generation that might be called upon to "defend our liberty and independence against an invader." It was up to her fellow Belgians to ensure that her motto "it is the humble ones that make obscure heroes" would be a self-denying prophecy: "humble, yes; obscure heroine, no, no!" His speech ended on a grand statement–

> "France has Joan of Arc.
> Belgium has Gabrielle Petit.
> It's a draw. We have no need to envy our neighbors!"
>
> (*Très bien! Très bien!* from all benches).[15]

One thing Petit certainly had in common with the Maid of Orleans: little was known about her, even though she, unlike Joan, was a contemporary. This did not detract from Petit's aura—quite the contrary. "Her chivalrous death belongs to the realm of the marvelous, not that of the real," the Senator exclaimed. This drive to remember a contemporary in legendary terms indicates postwar Belgians' desire for an icon—abstract, hieratic—to personify civilian valor.

But, of course, Petit's death had not occurred in legendary circumstances at all; and neither had her life.

PART I
LIFE

CHAPTER 1
DISINHERITANCE, 1893–1914

The Senator who championed Petit's memory thought the state should purchase the house where she was born—a minor expense, he was sure: "a child of the people, she was probably born in a modest craftsman's dwelling." That she had popular roots was part of Petit's fond myth. But she was not a "child of the people". She was a child of the bourgeoisie—a disinherited child. This, more than anything else, explains what drove her.

Petit came from the provincial bourgeoisie of Tournai, a town of some 35,000 inhabitants—which made it medium-size by the standards of late-nineteenth-century Belgium—close to the French border. Tournai's economy was flagging, but its middle class, if small, was still prosperous enough.[1] Both her father's and her mother's families were established in trade and civil service. Great-great-grandfather Petit was a grain merchant; his son and grandson were customs officers.[2] There were some prestigious connections. Great-grandfather Petit had married Caroline Bara, the daughter of a Tournai doctor, whose brother, Jules Bara, a star of the Liberal party, twice served as Minister of Justice.[3] Their son, Gabrielle's grandfather, had even married a baroness. The Ségard family, on Gabrielle's mother's side, owned glassware businesses in the center of town. Her maternal grandfather Barthélémy Ségard, a customs officer like the Petits, was already on the voters' lists in 1877, when suffrage still depended on sizable assets; his son Eugène Ségard was a surgeon in Antwerp.[4] But bourgeois status was never given. Gabrielle's parents slid down the social scale like people in a Balzac novel.[5] And, like in a Balzac novel, Petit's fierce lifelong ambition would be to recover lost social ground.

Early Childhood, 1893–1902

The sources on Petit's early years paint a picture of a gifted child, the second of three siblings in a very fraught household. Her parents' marriage was bitterly unhappy. Her mother, Aline Ségard, regularly sought refuge at the house of her parents, who lived with her unmarried younger sister Hélène, Gabrielle's godmother. Hélène Ségard would recall her sister's exasperation towards her willful second child, and Gabrielle's stoicism under harsh treatment. Once, when she was four, her mother—whose younger daughter, Louise, had just died aged one—beat her particularly hard. "Gabrielle came downstairs . . .; we could see that she had cried, but she was smiling . . . and kissed us all in turn, sat down and ate with great gusto; my father couldn't believe his eyes. We acted as if nothing had happened, she kissed us again and went off to school." Barthélémy Ségard berated his daughter, pointing out that Gabrielle, with her "precocious intelligence," was receptive to reason and defied force.[6] As Hélène Ségard recalled it, her sister then adapted a more conciliatory manner, which "worked wonders." A year later, Aline told her father he had been right and that Gabrielle had become quite indispensable to her—"my right hand." She was five.

By then, Aline Ségard had another child—a boy, Jules, born in November 1897—and the marriage continued to disintegrate. Time and again, the doorbell rang at the grandparents': it was Gabrielle, cheerfully declaring, "standing to attention on her little legs, with her hands behind her back: 'My dad has said like that to my mum, go back home with your children [sic], well here we are.'" Aline Ségard, "meek and resigned," followed with little Jules. (These anecdotes never mention the eldest child, a girl also called Hélène, who was one year older than Gabrielle and was not raised at home; more about her later.) Money was a source of constant tension. Jules Petit, a commercial traveler dabbling fruitlessly in mechanical inventions, failed to provide for his family. At school, Gabrielle's classmates asked her what her father did for a living; she declared that "my father does nothing, and when he's at home, he's always in bed." She repeated this at her grandparents'. "My sister went red in the face," wrote Hélène Ségard; "we knew the child was telling the truth."[7] Jules Petit's in-laws were not alone in finding fault with him; his sister reported after the war that their mother, the baroness, had cut off all contact.[8] The nuns who educated Gabrielle remembered him as an "unworthy father": brutal, profligate, and pretentious, a "braggart" who "liked to live it up." His debts forced his wife to scrimp and save on household necessities, "and even so she was unable to make ends meet." Behind her back, he sold housewares. As a result, Gabrielle and her siblings grew up in "an atmosphere of physical and moral squalor. No money came in and the family eked out a living in a state of need close to destitution; and the children suffered from the perpetual strife between a profligate father and a long-suffering mother."[9] The resulting social humiliation was not lost on the child. When still in day school, she ate the school lunch, considered a form of charity. After a put-down on that score by one of the nuns ("Miss Petit eats here, but doesn't find the food to her taste"), Gabrielle refused to eat. She grew pale and prone to fainting, but refused to tell her mother. She finally told her godmother, stressing how mortified she had been at the jibe, made in front of her classmates. Her grandfather called her pride "a good sign."[10]

When she was seven, she lost the shelter of her grandparents' home: in April 1900, her father took the household to live in Ath, a small town twenty miles east of Tournai, to her mother's "great grief." Her godmother said the move was the father's idea, but another source states that both sets of grandparents, wary of social scandal, forced the drifting household to leave Tournai, "and that is the origin of the striking isolation in which Gabrielle grew up."[11] In Ath, Jules Petit rented a house too large for his vacillating means and too far from school so Gabrielle often missed class. Aline, an accomplished pianist, gave music lessons at home to supplement the income. Gabrielle had by now become her mother's "confidante" and swore to her grandfather that "if papa were to beat maman, I would jump on his back and tear his hair out." By the time she was eight, as her mother's health failed, Gabrielle attempted to help raise her little brother: "she reasoned like a grown-up, you had to admire her," wrote her godmother, who now only saw the child on holidays.[12]

In a desperate attempt to provide the household with a steady income, Aline studied to qualify as a piano teacher at the Music Academy of Ath, although she suffered—among other things—from stomach ulcers.[13] After one exam, she had a hemorrhage and was carried home. She told her sister how afraid she was for Gabrielle: "what is to become of her? ... Such a young child, it's such a pity, and yet I cannot do without her, she is my friend, she understands, young as she is, and she worries about her little brother wanting for anything." The nuns at the hospital, too, would recall Aline Ségard worrying about Gabrielle incessantly. She underwent surgery in Ath—whether for heart or respiratory troubles is unclear[14]—where, thanks to generous friends, she did not lie in a charity ward but received "all the consideration owed her rank and her misfortunes." Aline, resigned and pious, in tune with class dignity never spoke ill of her husband, which deeply impressed the nuns.[15] Meanwhile, the children were in social free fall. "No-one in this little town ignored the state of things in that household." Jules Petit had moved out of the house and sold his wife's piano, which greatly upset Aline, since it was a gift from her parents to both her and her sister. She made Gabrielle promise to reimburse her godmother if she ever came into money—rather a burden to place on a child so young. Gabrielle was now living with her father and little Jules in rented rooms, where their poverty had ceased even to be genteel. One report described, in indignation-dotted sentences, how after the war people in Ath well remembered "seeing the girl in shops, a pint in hand, buying beer ... on credit ..." yet she "energetically" refused to give in to sadness and shame.[16] Hélène Ségard too recalled that "poor little Gabrielle was a sorry sight, but she did not cry. Maman will come back, she said." By then, the child had been placed in boarding school. She went to visit her mother in Ath hospital shortly before the surgery and came back distraught, telling her godmother:

Marraine, mother is so thin, and they cut off her hair. She asked me how I was and if I was good, and I said, yes Mother, but father pinched my arm, and I showed her the bruise, Mother cried so. Oh, how bad I have been, Marraine, to make my sick mother cry, yes, yes, I have been bad,' she repeated, and this memory, which she often mentioned to me, haunted her throughout her short existence.

The intervention was not successful, and the young woman was transported to Saint John's Hospital in Brussels for a more invasive procedure. And there she died, after a two-hour surgery, on July 6, 1902, at the age of thirty-three.[17]

Inexplicably, Gabrielle does not seem to have been told of her mother's death until much later. "We kept the news from her for a year," her godmother later said, "and she only found out at the time of her communion. She bravely withstood this scalding grief, but talked always of her mother, whose memory was a cult to her." But Hélène Ségard's recollection of family events becomes, at this point, quite confused. Gabrielle's communion took place not one but two years after her mother's death, in 1904; and it remains unclear how such news could have been kept from a child for so long. The confusion and secrecy show that the family was falling apart. In September 1901, after the death of her maternal grandmother, Gabrielle was sent to a nuns' boarding school in Mons, twenty-five miles southeast of Ath. The "cruel separation" from her ailing mother took its toll. Eighty years later, a classmate recalled her as difficult and "strange." Abandoned and acting out, Gabrielle was accused of stealing and expelled at the end of the school year 1902. Although the nuns at Mons never made this information public, their memories of their former pupil were ambivalent enough that the congregation refused to have a statue of the 'national heroine' put up in the school's courtyard after the war.[18]

At the age of nine, then, Gabrielle was no longer surrounded by protective adults. Her mother, in Ath hospital, had mentioned to the nuns how afraid she was that after her death her child would be shunted around one arrangement after another; and Aline had made a last attempt to see Gabrielle fostered in a "good home" and receive a solid education.[19]

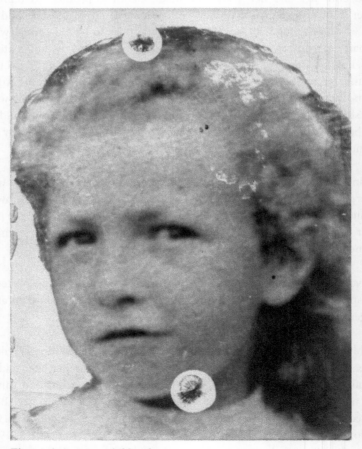

Figure 1 Petit as a child, n.d.
Brussels, Royal Army Museum, Prints Cabinet

The Orphanage, 1902–1908

In the event, the child was to remain in an institution. Three months after her mother's death, her father had her placed in the orphanage of the Sisters of the Child Jesus at Brugelette, a village five miles southeast of Ath.[20]

After the war, Petit's first actual biographer Arthur Deloge would write that the move from the posh boarding school in Mons to the orphanage in rural Brugelette, close to the Borinage mine fields, was a downgrade: "the child's very refined nature was . . . painfully struck by her new environment's obvious educational inferiority." He based this in reminiscences by Gabrielle's older sister Hélène, who also spent time in the orphanage.[21] In reality, there was no such social shift. In 1994, the local historian Pierre Ronvaux demonstrated that, at Mons, she was not registered in the tony part of the school, but in a branch reserved for girls of modest backgrounds.[22] In 1923, Sister Marie-Walthère, a teacher at Brugelette, indignantly defended the school's reputation. Hélène Petit painted her sister Gabrielle (and, by implication, herself as well) as "a kind of princess" surrounded by an adoring throng of little pale-faced proletarians; this showed, the nun sternly stated, "a desire to make oneself look better."[23] (Hélène Petit did have social pretentions; she would claim all her life, for instance, that her father had been an engineer.[24]) In fact, there was a social mix at the orphanage, Sister Marie-Walthère wrote. Among its charges—a little under three hundred girls in Petit's time—were some local girls from "excellent families" whose parents wanted to save on boarding-school fees; the nun proudly listed them. What she did not mention was that they were a minority; more than nine out of ten girls were working class.[25] Many were miners' children, several of them orphaned by mining accidents.[26] In other words, the orphanage at Brugelette stood at the very edge of what was still, in turn-of-the-century Belgium, a universe of abysmal poverty and exploitation. (Only in 1911 did it become illegal to send boys younger than twelve down the pit.[27]) Moreover, the bourgeois girls eventually transferred to the regular boarding school, also located at Brugelette, whereas Gabrielle did not.[28] She lived under the orphanage regime: she scrubbed the long corridors, swept floors, spent up to an hour in the kitchen peeling potatoes every day, worked in the laundry-room, and waited at table on the students of the teachers' college. "The principle of the orphanage," Sister Marie-Walthère wrote, "is to teach the children all that is done in petit bourgeois families." She did not clarify whether "all that is done" referred to the lady of the house, or to the maid-of-all-work. She did not need to.[29]

Gabrielle also lived in an orphanage regime in the sense of being quite neglected by her relatives. Her godmother saw so little of her that she was compelled, after the war, to write to the Mother Superior to ask for "some information as to [Gabrielle's] character etc. during the years she stayed at your school."[30] Self-servingly, she would claim that this was for the girl's own good: because the nuns thought that she was "without benefit of family affection", they nurtured her all the more warmly.[31] In late 1904, Gabrielle's father left Ath with little Jules to live in Ostend; a year later, he moved to Brussels; soon after, to Mechelen (Malines) between Brussels and Antwerp. Throughout, he was a very infrequent visitor at Brugelette. "Again and again, ten times in a row, that fine gentleman would promise to visit, before finally showing up," wrote Sister Marie-Walthère. He did pay Gabrielle's board (200 francs a year, plus incidentals such as shoe repairs, dentists' fees, and the occasional pinafore), as the school's ledger shows. He probably received help from his grand-uncle Charles Bara, Gabrielle's godfather.[32] Gabrielle wrote to Bara, calling him her "Benefactor," and talked to the nuns about him. But Bara never wrote back or visited.[33]

Hélène Petit would bitterly recall their shared years as neglected children:

> Gabrielle Petit's childhood was a very sad one, as was that of her sister Hélène. . . . Hélène and Gaby were abandoned and none of their relatives cared for them. . . . While classmates would receive visits from their families, Gaby never saw anyone; she was never called to the visiting-room, no-one ever sent her the smallest parcel of sweets; she never went on holiday. Indeed where would she have gone? Who would have welcomed her? . . . So the holidays were spent with the good sisters, who did everything they could to make the dear little one forget her abandonment.[34]

Hélène's own childhood bears out the girls' neglect very starkly. She lived at Brugelette too, in 1904–1905. In the spring of 1904—she was then twelve and raised at an institution in Brussels—she received two days' leave to attend her little sister's communion. This favor was granted because none of Gabrielle's adult relatives planned to come. Even at an orphanage, such a thing was considered unusual enough that Gabrielle was allowed to invite her sister. No-one expected the father to be there; Charles Bara paid Gabrielle no personal attention; grandfather Ségard had died in January 1904; and Hélène Ségard, though Gabrielle's godmother, did not plan to make the trip. She thereby broke a promise she had made to her dying sister, as she would admit later, saying in her own defense that the deaths of her mother, sister, and father in such close succession had exhausted her.[35]

Hélène Petit was only meant to stay for a brief visit, but the two children pleaded with the nuns not to separate them, and so she was registered at the orphanage. Not for long: she left a year and a half later, in the summer of 1905. Sister Marie-Walthère described her as "sulky, of bad disposition, and quick to complain; she often had to be reprimanded."[36] There was a reason for the girl's "bad disposition." Even more than Gabrielle, Hélène Petit was a neglected child, given little space even within the household, and soon shunted around from institution to institution. She does not figure in her aunt's memories of the Tournai years because she was sent away as a small child to make space for the younger children; and in 1900—she was then eight—she did not join the household in Ath; she lived at the Sisters of Providence Institute in Tournai.[37] When she was fourteen, her aunt Hélène Ségard claimed, this school expelled her because she kept trying to run away to her uncle Eugène Ségard, the Antwerp surgeon, who was her godfather. As he refused to take her in because she was too difficult, both sets of grandparents then decided to send her to Brugelette.[38] This account makes no sense at all. Hélène Petit turned fourteen in early 1906; by then she had left Brugelette, as the orphanage ledger shows. When she arrived there in the spring of 1904, three of her grandparents had died, and nothing indicates that her paternal grandmother, the baroness, took any interest in her estranged son's children. Hélène Ségard's confusion of dates expresses neglect, and even her hazy account spells out the dynamics of abandonment: the troubled child, the distant parent, the exasperated relatives, the rejection by the regular school. Sister Marie-Walthère's notes confirm this abandonment with a crucial and damning fact. When Hélène Petit, twelve years old, entered the orphanage in 1904, she did not come from the genteel Sisters of Providence school in Tournai. She came from an institution in Brussels, "where her family had placed her because she was resisting discipline." The nun only referred to this institution as "the establishment in the rue Terneuve," with the clarification (which she later crossed out) "a kind of home for wayward children [*maison de préservation*]."[39] There was indeed such an "establishment" in the rue Terre-Neuve in Brussels. This was the "Refuge Sainte-Madeleine," run by the sisters of the Sacred Heart of Jesus since 1828. It was, as the name indicates, a Magdalen asylum—an institution for teenage single mothers and for "strayed" young women arriving there from brothels, hospitals, and prisons having "contracted the habit of vice." It also took in younger girls (on paper, from the age of thirteen), who, as a 1904 publication had it, were "not yet completely lost," to re-educate them through needlework and domestic chores.[40] At the turn of the century, the Refuge was packed.[41] That it was a place of unspeakable squalor, which treated its charges very badly and where babies died in horrendous numbers, did not come out until after the war. The resulting scandal, in 1920, spelled the end of the Refuge Sainte-Madeleine.[42] It seems inconceivable that a girl of eleven, of a bourgeois family, could have been relegated to such a dismal place. Yet, as the historian of childhood Aurore François has confirmed to me, it was perfectly possible. Families' right to institutionalize "difficult" children—the so-called "paternal correction right"—was enshrined in Belgian law until it was handed to juvenile courts in 1912. In that year, the Refuge still housed twenty-one girls sent there by their families.[43] Some of them may indeed have been very young: the Refuge's Protestant counterpart in Brussels took in girls as young as ten who were feared to have "bad instincts,"[44] and the Refuge probably did so too. That Hélène Petit was consigned to a place like this, shows extreme, almost punitive neglect. The following years would only deepen her status as a "morally abandoned" child (as the term went). Jules Petit never paid his eldest daughter's board at the orphanage. "The father," wrote Sister Marie-Walthère, "thought he could leave her here without paying, as was his habit, but the Directress did not see things this way. As the child was of bad disposition, and a bad influence on the others, the Directress sent her back to her Uncle, who had raised her."[45] If parents were unable to pay their children's board, the orphanage might waive it or look for donations. But in this case, the parent was not destitute but unwilling to pay, and the girl was at any rate unwanted at Brugelette. And so Hélène was sent away. This was in July 1905; she was then thirteen and a half. Her uncle Eugène Ségard had no intention to take care of her, and neither did her father, and so she landed in a home for "morally abandoned" children in Mons.[46] She eventually rejoined her family, but the reunion was not a success: Jules Petit, tired of his eldest daughter's "persistent insubordination," packed her off to Brussels to fend for herself.[47] Hélène Petit must have been very young still when she made this inauspicious entry into the world; made, as the

1919 memoir based on her testimony stated, if not in her own words then certainly expressing her own bitter feelings, "to make her own living from day to day, with no advice and no support, like so many of those orphan girls that the world will always be indifferent to."[48]

The two sisters were not close. Gabrielle, as both her godmother and the nuns asserted, did not like her elder sister all that much; but she always took Hélène's side.[49] Family anecdotes underscored this—while stressing Hélène's malice. One anecdote had Gabrielle, then eight, standing on a chair to play orator. Her sister deliberately overturned the chair and Gabrielle broke her elbow. She remained stoic and refused to tell her father who the culprit was, although several children had seen it happen.[50] The nuns at Brugelette reported that "Gabrielle felt she had to defend [her sister] against all comers," even though they did not get along.[51] Overall, Petit as a child was described as sweet, stoic, and exceptionally self-willed all at once. "Even then, she was not ordinary," her godmother wrote. "She never apologized ..., and never complained, being very proud." When she entered the orphanage, she was, the nuns remembered, "intelligent and sensitive, of delicate sentiments, but also self-willed and strangely bold for her age. Nothing, it would seem, intimidated her."[52] Someone asked her why she did not cry; she said it would be no use, since she had to stay at the orphanage anyway.[53] (This precocious matter-of-factness, wrote her 1922 biographer Deloge, "might seem normal in an American child"; for a Belgian girl of nine, it was exceptional.[54]) Gifted and bereft, she had developed a habit of "hostile defiance against authority, that of the Father to start with, and for good reason," Sister Marie-Walthère wrote. Conversely, she was inclined to take the side of the suffering. By the time she entered Brugelette, "her mother ... [had] shown her what is good and just in oppressed vulnerability; by contrast, force [for her] meant brutality, injustice, dishonesty and selfishness. The child was intelligent and delicate enough to see and feel everything. Such were the lessons of her life [by then]."[55] Gabrielle dedicated what her godmother called "a cult" to her mother's memory, calling her, the nuns remembered, "my saintly mother," and remembering her "with deep admiration and tenderness."[56]

But she had not inherited her mother's lauded meekness, as some orphanage anecdotes show. Once, her father on a rare visit gave her some fine cotton; she decided to crochet a cover for the altar in the convent's chapel. Told to craft something more useful for herself, she persisted, telling the nun she wanted to give her "a keepsake." Soon after, during evening Mass, she proudly pointed to the altar where her work was displayed. That the nuns remembered this small feat of ambition, if fondly, as "mischief," says something about the sheer degree of conformity they expected from their charges.[57] Petit also showed her pride by making fun of her neglect. The orphanage girls kept their families' gifts of sweets in a storage room called, bluntly, "l'avoir" ("the having"); once a day, they were allowed to retrieve a treat. Girls without stock were excluded. For a joke, Gabrielle would stand outside the room, hand held out, asking for "Charity!"[58]

But she was also prone to despondency. One higher-grade teacher later recalled how her eyes were often red from weeping at night; "I did not understand then what was going on, but I do now."[59] She would veer from utter loneliness—spending playtimes all by herself, turning round and round on one foot—to a kind of frenzied leadership, goading her classmates into small feats of subversion which, though innocuous enough by later standards, did not endear her to all but the most comprehending teachers.[60] Petit alternated between despondency and exuberance all her life, and, as one of her last letters shows, was well aware of it.

In December 1905, Jules Petit, now forty, remarried without telling his new bride, a waitress of twenty named Bernardine Degros, that he had children. Two months later, eight-year-old Jules, who had been farmed out to a family in West Flanders, joined the couple in Mechelen. Sometime in mid-1907, during an argument with his stepmother, the boy revealed that he had two elder sisters.[61] By then the couple had a daughter, Marthe, born in April 1907. Forced to inform Gabrielle of his new family, Jules Petit wrote her a letter. It has not survived, but her answer did.

To: Monsieur Jules Petit, 30, Arsenal Street, Mechelen.
Brugelette, June 12, 1907.

Dear father,

I received your letter, which you wrote would cause me certain emotions. Yes, I was upset and I cried a lot when I read that you had remarried; but, since you have done it for our good, I resign myself to it. If our stepmother is good with us and likes us well, I will like her too, as well as my new little sister. . . . Since you ask me how I use my time, this is my schedule: first, we rise at 5 . . . At 6 we go to Mass, followed by breakfast. We do household chores until 8.30, then classes start until 11.30. At 11.30 dinner and recess until quarter past one. Then classes start again until 3.30, then an afternoon snack and recess, after which we do needlework until six-thirty, then evening prayers, dinner and recess until 8.30, then rest.

On another topic, you ask me what I have done with the prayer-book you gave me in remembrance of my first and regretted little Mother; I have it and I use it; as to the one you gave me for my communion, it was not solid, I dropped it once and the cover and bindings came loose; the pages got lost one by one and now the book is gone. As to the one you sent me now, I am perfectly satisfied with it and will show it to you when I see you again. I will . . . show exemplary conduct . . . [to] deserve my holidays.

Now, Dear Father, I say goodbye to you and embrace you with all my heart.
Your child who loves you,

Gabrielle.

P.S. Give Hélène, little Jules and the whole dear family a big kiss from me.

I would be happy if you would reply to me as soon as possible and . . . if you would take a photograph of the whole family and send it to me. I would be very glad of it.

Don't forget to reply to me, please Father![62]

Sister Marie-Walthère, who read the letter in its published form after the war, noted how it expressed abandonment. The girl told her father her schedule in such detail because he had no idea of how she lived at the orphanage; and his queries about her prayer-book were typically "the kind of questions asked by a faithless person who wants to rekindle some rare memories after a long absence." She found Gabrielle's repeated injunctions not to forget her "extremely revealing." While rejoicing "in having 'recovered' her Father," she knew it would not last.[63]

Gabrielle was then fourteen. That August, she was granted two weeks' vacation with her father and his family. Holidays were not automatic for the orphan girls at Brugelette: the girls had to "deserve" them, their families had to request them, and the families had to be "respectable."[64] These two weeks in August 1907 were probably Gabrielle's only holiday away from the orphanage in six years. When she found her father in Mechelen, Jules Petit had, finally (if not perhaps permanently), made good. He worked as a sales representative in industrial equipment.[65] He lived in a smart neighborhood, wore velvet jackets, kept a horse-drawn carriage, and—the necessary condition of bourgeois status—employed servants, including a nanny for his little daughter Marthe. Marthe would, decades later, tell Pierre Ronvaux that her father liked to "live large" and exhibited "gentleman's airs." She was not yet ten when her father died and would in her old age remember him rather more favorably than her eldest half-sister Hélène. But she did not hide his authoritarian nature, calling him "very harsh" and "choleric." His own sister too reported that he was domineering and had a violent streak; and everybody knew that his daughters from his first marriage, Hélène and Gabrielle, bore the brunt of his temper.[66]

The holidays were not a success. When Gabrielle returned, the nuns saw that her sadness had deepened. It did not help that Jules Petit liked to play the piano on Sunday, imposing total silence on the rest of the household, whereas Gabrielle could not bear the sound of piano-playing, which reminded her of her mother.[67] Having found her father once more wanting, "the poor child suffered from being so alone, but her very proud soul straightened up under the sorrow, she shut up her heart and hid her tears ... This gave her demeanor something rigid and cutting, and gave an exaggerated and fake air to her gaiety, her follies." As an adolescent, she became brittle, mocking, defiant. She liked to play class clown, which entertained her classmates and irritated the teachers. "Only those who knew the child ... guessed what she was hiding, and tried to calm her down."[68] The nun who oversaw laundry duty recalled telling her one morning to accept her lot with more humility; hiding one's grief behind a rigid exterior was a sign of self-importance. (Clearly, the nun saw these things differently from Gabrielle's late grandfather: she used the term *orgueil*, vanity; he had called it *fierté*, pride.[69]) "There is sorrow and shame in all families. Yet you can see for yourself that your classmates do not ridicule everything the way you do ..."[70] Others were less comprehending, with far-reaching results.

While, according to one source, her lack of discipline precluded her from using her intelligence fully,[71] all sources describe her as very sharp. Her godmother praised her quick wit. Her sister Hélène recalled that a school inspector had once been so impressed by Gabrielle's bright remarks that he gave her his calling-card and told her to contact him if she needed support pursuing her education.[72] Sister Marie-Walthère, echoing her *consoeurs'* memories, wrote that the girl had "an intellect fit for study" and could focus fiercely if she put her mind to it.[73] When she entered the orphanage, aged nine, she was placed in second grade because her education had been badly neglected, but her native aptitude soon showed. When goaded, she would spring into action; once, in middle school, told that she would receive poor grades if she did not apply herself, she set to work and within the semester was placed among the top of her class.[74] Little class chores such as cleaning the blackboard and putting the room to rights gave her a sense of importance; she relished them, but also "liked to tweak the tasks to her own liking, occasionally refusing to do exactly as she was told"—though always politely, for an insolent answer would have earned her "a good smack in the face" from the principal.[75] Like many gifted children, she was both self-willed and receptive to the notion of sacrifice; which of course is no paradox at all. In an undated note to her father, Gabrielle repented of having written a "nasty letter" (possibly with complaints about the orphanage) for which she had almost been expelled. She would be forgiven, she wrote, on condition of forgoing her holidays home, "and I accept this penitence with all my heart, I will make this sacrifice to the good Lord. This year, I will set to work with all my heart, I am growing up now and this time it is for real."[76]

At fourteen and fifteen, Gabrielle was, by several accounts, greatly influenced by her higher-grade teacher. The somewhat unfortunately named Charlotte Cludtz, in religion Sister Félicité (1851–1929), was a squat, nearsighted, energetic woman with an unregimented teaching style and a passionately patriotic outlook—two things that were quite rare in *belle époque* Belgium. She taught a small class of fifteen girls and employed the brightest ones as teaching assistants, including Gabrielle. She delighted in her position, leaving and entering the classroom like a teacher in her own right, enjoying a familiar rapport with the Reverend Sister, and correcting her classmates' dictations and drawings during her breaks, which she was allowed to spend in the quiet, companionable classroom.[77] Sister Félicité was, as Sister Marie-Walthère recalled, an indefatigable champion of King Leopold II; she ardently sang the monarch's praises "*at a time of almost universal denigration of what people called Leopold II's crazy projects.*"[78] Belgians did indeed show very little enthusiasm for Leopold II's "Congo Free State", less for its murderously exploitative regime than because they considered it a reckless venture. When the state took over the territory in 1908, Belgium entered the era of imperialism with public misgivings and indifference.[79] At the same time, as the historian David Van Reybrouck observes, colonial dreams of glory, action, and mission swayed many lower middle-class youths in the provinces.[80] The classroom at Brugelette is a case in point. Sister Félicité's "interminable ramblings" (as her *consoeur* described them, with unexpected tartness) were received "hungrily, avidly" by her teaching assistant. "At such moments, [Gabrielle] sat transfixed, as if she were the only one who understood." As a result, the girl became "patriotic at a time when this sentiment was not fashionable at all."[81]

She also started to harbor ambitions. Once, her beloved Sister Félicité admonished her that she would not go far if she remained so undisciplined; she replied that she would "be better than you think."[82] She even had a very precise idea of what she wanted: to attend teaching college at Brugelette. But she was turned away. Only in 1940 did Sister Marie-Walthère bring herself to commit this fact to paper, admitting that "one was so much in the dark as to what direction her life would take that the Directress of the teaching college, an eminently level-headed person, thought it best to turn her away when the question of her continued education came up. Among the students, the presence of someone who would have disturbed the order and provoked authority could not be countenanced."[83] This rejection would alter the girl's life irretrievably, closing off the possibility of a life of independence. She would remain painfully aware of the road not taken. In 1909, she would beseech Charles Bara to lend her money to continue her education.

By then, she had left the orphanage, in typically unhappy circumstances. She later told her godmother what had happened. Her father had, for once, sent some sweets. Since she was punished for one or the other misdemeanor, "as usual," this was kept from her. A classmate saw the gift in the visiting-room and told her relatives, who told Gabrielle's father. In a huff, Jules Petit wrote to the Mother Superior and accused the nuns of pocketing his gift. She, in turn, summoned the unsuspecting Gabrielle to accuse her of complaining to her father and to demand she name her classmate. (This girl, according to the stern rules of the orphanage, had committed a serious faux pas: communication with the outside world was strictly controlled.) In Gabrielle's words (as relayed by her godmother),

> I was not going to betray my classmate. So I asked for a leave to talk things out [with my father]. "If you go," the Mother Superior said to me, "you cannot come back." "All right," I said, "then I leave." "Tell your esteemed father that we do not steal from children here, we punish them." All of a sudden, I understood [what had happened], but I did not want to go back on my decision.[84]

The school ledger bears the note "Gabrielle Petit—left on August 14, 1908."[85] She was fifteen and a half years old and was never again to receive any formal education. She owed this jarring end to her school days to circumstances beyond her control: like many orphans, she found herself caught between conflicting loyalties to clashing powers—in her case, the orphanage, and her father—that both placed their own pride before her well-being. Gabrielle's own impetuousness did the rest. She would regret it for the rest of her life. "You don't think clearly at that age," she told her godmother. Her father took it more lightly: as far as Jules Petit was concerned, his daughter had received all the education she would ever need, and it was time she came home, where there was enough for her to do.[86]

Adrift in the *Belle Époque*, 1908–1911

A teenager not surrounded by family, with no social connections, bearing the burden of a bereft childhood, with little talent for meekness, possessing enough education to be unhappy but not enough to aspire to a higher level, perched in between social classes, and too intelligent for the positions open to her, Petit was ill-equipped to make her way in a world offering the likes of her few chances to begin with. And indeed the years between her departure from the orphanage and the outbreak of the war were marked by restiveness, poverty, and despair. She did have her share of enjoyment: that which came with being striking and witty—like Louise de Bettignies, Petit was described as a slender, petite blonde with a keen sense of repartee—as well as receptive to romantic reverie.[87] Relatives and friends described her to Arthur Deloge, her 1922 biographer, as fond of dancing and flirting. Tellingly, Deloge wrote that she liked to *"courir le guilledou,"* an archaic expression usually translated as "womanizing" or even "wenching"—in other words, that refers to a kind of sexual freedom reserved for men. Such boldness would have set Petit apart from typical bourgeois daughters of the era, adding to her status in between social classes (even if young women of the Belgian petite bourgeoisie were not on as tight a leash as their counterparts elsewhere).[88] It certainly caused a violent clash with her father. In his new incarnation as a solid bourgeois, and with his authoritarian temper, Jules Petit senior did not welcome the estranged, undisciplined daughters from his first marriage. Hélène Petit had spent very little time under his roof. And, despite Gabrielle's affectionate letters from the orphanage, the attempt at reunion fared little better in her case. In a letter to his brother Georges, a senior bank administrator in Brussels, Jules Petit mentioned giving Gabrielle "a severe correction" (i.e., a beating), adding that "she's no more use than Hélène."[89] She herself wrote in mid-1909 that she was ill-treated and unwelcome in her father's house.[90]

By then, she had left home. From Mechelen, she had contacted her sister about employment opportunities in Brussels. Belgium was then the most densely populated country in the world, but had no very large cities. Still the capital was growing fast: from half a million inhabitants in 1890 to three-quarters of a million in 1910.[91] Its booming service sector offered many entry-level jobs for young women, especially those from the Walloon provinces whose native language was French.[92] Hélène knew of an attorney's household, the Limage family, that was looking for help with the children. Jules Petit urged his daughter to take the job. Gabrielle wrote to Hélène that "Father has said that it is something respectable . . . He would like for me to take it. But he leaves the choice to me."[93] She took the job and liked it at first. As she wrote to her father in early 1909, "I am really comfortable here." Her employers were friendly, their children very polite, her duties (looking after the children, making the beds, waiting at table and mending clothes) light and pleasant, and she had ample time to herself. In short, "it's nice!!" She asked her father for clean clothes, her savings-book, and her school certificate, inquired after the growing family's well-being, and ended on a note of intense affection: "My best to all, and kisses to you in particular. Your daughter who loves you, Gabrielle."[94]

But less than two weeks later, her mood had completely changed. Her father had still not sent her things. If he persisted, she defied him: "well then I will remain like this, with my linen black as coal." She demanded her savings-book (with money given by her godfather Charles Bara), and her school certificate. "As to the rest, frankly, you can keep it. If my own family refuses me my belongings, I will ask help from strangers." It is not clear what caused the crisis. Did Jules Petit refuse to send his daughter's belongings because he wanted to assert his authority? Did he need her back home because his health was bad and there was a new baby in the house (Marthe's little brother, Emile)? Or had Gabrielle changed her mind about her job? She mentioned that someone had told her it was better to work in a shop than to become a servant. She might have started to chafe at the constraints of domestic service. (As might her sister: a note from Jules Petit to his eldest daughter, written around that same time, recommended Hélène, who was probably in service herself, to be "above all <u>very respectful</u>" towards her employers.[95]) She certainly felt unjustly treated by her family and vehemently rejected them in turn. In a furiously written note in the margin—"I cannot write any better than this, I am too upset and angry"—she declared that she would not write to any of her relatives anymore, "it is the only way to avoid trouble."[96]

Another letter, salvaged by the greatest of coincidences in 1940 and unknown until 1994, throws even sharper light on Petit's feelings at the time. It is undated, but written during her time at the Limages to her "benefactor" Charles Bara. She implored him to help.

> I have been placed [here] as a governess . . . [but] I don't work as a governess at all, I am considered a nanny and a chambermaid and do a chambermaid's work. I cannot reconcile myself to such a life. For six years now I have had in my mind the unsinkable [*sic*] desire to study, but there is no money for that and I feel that if I cannot study, life for me will be nothing but misery.

She pleaded for money to attend "the teachers' college of your choice." She did not mention Brugelette, where she had, after all, been turned away—and also, possibly, because the Baras were known Liberals. With considerable practicality, she named the exact sum, which was hefty: 2,400 francs for four years' tuition, room and board, plus 100 to 150 francs for clothes and other necessities upon entering college. "Oh! Dear Benefactor," she wrote, "if you knew my anguish, you would not refuse me this, especially since you have my <u>formal</u> promise that after this time I will . . . pay you back." To prove her sincerity, she pledged to have the money deducted from her future salary as a teacher. He would never regret his largesse: her prospects would be "brilliant", her conduct "exemplary."[97]

Clearly, she felt trapped. It was true that she had more or less freely chosen the job—she was not "placed" in service—and her first letter to her father summed up quite precisely the tasks of a nanny and chambermaid, which at the time seemed acceptable enough to her. Chambermaids did the lighter housework—tidy, make beds, dust, wait at table, and mend linen. A professional family like the Limages probably employed a general housemaid for the rough work, such as scrubbing floors and doing laundry. They probably were not able to afford the rarefied services of a full-time governess. And if they had, they would not have hired a teenager from a provincial orphanage; the typical Brussels governess was a well-educated foreign woman in her twenties or thirties. But whether or not Petit's expectations were realistic, she must have suddenly realized her dead-end position. Brussels nannies—most of them, like Petit, provincial teenagers, some as young as thirteen—received paltry pay, enjoyed little status (even well-meaning reformers enjoined them to treat their charges, however young, as their social superiors[98]) and usually doubled as chambermaid.[99] Petit probably asked for her school certificate because she hoped to make use of her education, but it was of no use in her present job. She had neither the leisure nor the money to complete her education; the sum she asked of Bara represented a decade's worth of her entire earnings.[100] In short, she saw her future life and she was in a panic.

We do not know whether Charles Bara ever did lend his god-daughter the scholarship funds; the Baras never went public about their contacts with Petit and the family papers are lost. But money was certainly sent. On January 8, 1910, Petit thanked her "dear Benefactor" for "showering me once more with an unforgettable act of kindness." He had, judging from her letter, sent her a check. "Be assured that the moment I will have the joy of satisfying my sole wish, I will prove my gratitude to you," she wrote.[101] That "sole wish" seems to refer to her ambition to become a teacher. But Petit never went back to school. It is unclear what happened. Certainly, even if Bara did send her money for her education, pursuing it would have been a struggle for a sixteen-year-old who lacked personal support and was prone to despondency. At any rate, we shall never know how her quest to pursue her education fared; none of the documents gives a clue, and her 1922 biographer, who might have questioned people who knew her, had no idea she harbored this ambition.

At the time of her thank-you note to Bara, in January 1910, she had long left her job with the Limages. In late October 1909, she was working at a fashion store in an affluent quarter. She had let her father know that she was "very happy there," or so, at least, Jules Petit told his brother Georges. Her employer, one Madame Carçan, however, would after the war remember her teenage help in "frankly bad" terms. She described Petit as slovenly; she had arrived without a change of underclothes and would not mend the ones she had.[102] (This glimpse into Petit's life points to the live-in help's lack of privacy.[103]) By contrast, her godmother described her as very fastidious, and Sister Marie-Walthère, reading this description, protested that Gabrielle had been too well taught at Brugelette to be slovenly. If she was letting herself go in Brussels, the nun wrote, it was out of despondency—"her heart must not have been in it."[104]

This is probably true. Left to herself in the opulent, indifferent city, Petit protested against her father's lack of support by neglecting her appearance. But as a result, she lost what assistance her middle-class relatives in the city might have given her. She was no longer welcome in her Uncle George's house, nor in that of her aunt Louise Pilatte, née Petit, her father's sister.[105] At sixteen in the city, she was now quite alone. Hélène Petit's hazy, rosy description of Gabrielle's life in those years ("Gaby was placed by her sister as a private teacher in a family. She did admirable work. She later worked as a laundry overseer in a large establishment") indicates that they did not see much of each other.[106] Nor does she seem to have been in contact with her godmother, though Hélène Ségard had by then moved to Brussels; she lived with a cousin, another middle-aged single woman, in a modest neighborhood in the center of town, and occasionally visited Gabrielle's uncle Georges Petit.[107] It is unclear whether Ségard made any attempt to contact her teenage god-daughter. She claimed after the war that they had been close in those years, but in secret, because Petit did not want her father to know.[108] Others swore that Petit and her godmother only met again during the war.[109] Gabrielle had no contact whatever with her younger brother Jules or with any of her other relatives.[110] Her godfather Charles Bara never replied to her letters, keeping her at arm's length and in some funds through his accountant, who sent her money and received her on her occasional visits to the Bara château near the Hainaut hamlet of Bauffe (where she did not stay; she lodged with a school friend nearby).[111] In other words, Petit now had as good as no family support.

In early 1910, she was on her third job in a pastry-store in the affluent borough of Ixelles; she rented a room around the corner from the shop. She had changed jobs without telling her father; and, now seventeen, she was living on her own for the first time, more a shop assistant than a live-in household help.[112] This may point to a certain degree of emancipation. As the urban historian Valérie Piette has shown, *belle époque* Brussels saw a movement in women's service work from a logic of personal servitude to one of salaried service. Saleswomen and workers in cafés and hotels were redefined (and redefined themselves) as commercial employees, not servants. They benefited, if intermittently, from changes in labor law—such as the right to sit down on the job and the right to free Sundays—that excluded servants. Ever fewer *demoiselles de magasin* lived with their employers.[113] Their livelihoods remained precarious (in some ways, more so than those of live-in maids) and the boundaries with servanthood were porous in practice. But the symbolic advances were significant, including that of the conscious definition of shared interests: unlike domestic servants, *demoiselles de magasin* and other sales personnel unionized and launched their own press.[114] Like thousands of other young provincial women in the capital's service sector, Gabrielle Petit partook of this first, modest shift in expectations. That said, her circumstances remained wretched enough. In February 1910, she sent a curt, bitter note to her father who still had not sent her belongings and savings. "Here I am, running around with nothing, and my things are at home," she wrote. "I don't understand why I have to plead so much, I have always been so very ill-treated."[115] In subsequent months, Petit befriended a young woman named Julia Lallemand, who after the war would be an important witness to this period in her life. They met at the World's Fair, which was held in Brussels from late April to mid-August 1910. It was a cheap outing: young working women received free tickets. But the Fair's opulence must have contrasted starkly with their lives. Julia recalled that she had found Gabrielle living in an unheated garret, badly dressed, sleeping out of doors when the rent money was lacking, and often going without food for days. She herself married around this time and was able to help out her friend with gifts of clothes—once, a pair of shoes—and meals. Several times, Julia told Deloge, she went with Gabrielle to her Uncle George Petit's house to seek help, but the two young women were turned away.

Deloge hinted, without disclosing his sources, that the reasons for Gabrielle's family's estrangement were "very serious ones, we know." Their niece was disheveled, angry, and undisciplined, and had stopped going to church. There was worse: in extremely veiled terms, Deloge hinted at sexual misbehavior. He wrapped this disclosure in an indictment of what young women working in the city were facing: "Well-off people [*les personnes du monde*] who have no idea of the ceaseless money troubles that most single young girls have to contend with, will say that Gabrielle had no excuse ... When an honest girl claims a living wage, [she is told], 'Do as your colleagues, Miss. They have such pretty dresses.' And Gabrielle, who breathed that toxic air, who did not have the antidote of family life, was expected to emerge unscathed from that asphyxiating cloud?"[116] It is unclear what Deloge's hint at sexual misconduct referred to. One wartime document had it that Petit was an occasional prostitute. (I will return to this in Chapter Five.) Certainly early-twentieth-century Brussels, a town with booming luxury commerce, an expanding bourgeoisie, Haussmannesque boulevards and cafés, and an increasing number of tourists, generated a growing demand for sexually available young women at diverse levels of prostitution, from the dwindling number living in officially sanctioned brothels, over the occasionally available working poor (women as well as men), to rich men's mistresses.[117] But it is more likely that Petit's sexual misbehavior—or what passed for it in that era—had nothing to do with prostitution. Deloge hinted that at some point, she fell in love with a foreman at a construction company; when she discovered that he was married with children, "Gabrielle broke up with him, but too late, alas!"—a discreet hint that she had already slept with the man.[118] In fact, this episode in Petit's life was far more substantial. She lived with her lover—a divorced man—for over a year, from the spring or summer of 1910 until the summer of 1911, when he left her. That liaison may be the reason her relatives refused to see her.

Little Molenbeek, 1911–1914

This information comes from a woman who was Petit's neighbor in 1911–1916, took her in when she was out of work, and, during the war, helped her in her secret intelligence work and was arrested and tried together with her. Marie Collet née Sauvage was born in 1854; like Petit, she was from Tournai. A faded picture in Deloge's book shows her in her mid-sixties: a kindly-looking, dignified woman with tired traits and wavy white hair. Petit had come to live in a garret above the Collets' apartment in the summer of 1911, after the misadventure with the foreman.[119] This was in a working-class area northwest of central Brussels, a section of the industrial borough of Molenbeek known as 'Little Molenbeek.' In Flemish, the area was called De Kassei (the Chaussée), after the Chaussée d'Anvers, the ancient cobblestoned highway that ran through it. On this Chaussée d'Anvers, the Collets rented a "humble workingman's apartment" (Deloge) on the third floor of an old building, above a baker's shop; above theirs was a small furnished garret that overlooked the inner courtyard and rented for two francs a week. There, Gabrielle landed, at eighteen, having lived with her lover (who worked for a construction company on that same Chaussée) in a nearby street. Little Molenbeek would be her neighborhood, off and on, until her arrest by the German police in February 1916.[120] The location gives some indication of her life. The area was both central and marginal. Located right outside the boulevards that surrounded the city center, it was a short walk's distance from its prestigious shopping areas. At the same time, it was a liminal quarter, situated in between an industrial canal and what remained of Brussels' "river", the unprepossessing Senne. (Which had already been vaulted out of sight in the Haussmannized center of town.) In the later twentieth century, Little Molenbeek, very much the kind of neighborhood considered expendable by urban planners, would fall prey to high modernism. Slated for partial destruction from at least the 1930s, it lost many inhabitants and became a place for transients, including many refugees from the countryside during the Second World War. Little Molenbeek was completely razed in successive waves from the 1950s through the 1970s.[121] But in the *belle époque*, its population was at its densest; it was a lively area of small shops and businesses, housing—among other people—many service workers who welcomed the cheap rents and the easy commute from the commerces of central Brussels.[122] Julia Lallemand, who had married a waiter, lived here too.[123] So did, from March 1914, Hélène Ségard—another indication that the former Tournai bourgeoise had come down in the world.[124] Although the two women now lived around the corner from each other, Gabrielle may not have known of her godmother's presence in the area until the war. As with so many young women of precarious means in the modern city, Petit's network of support was not one of kin. She was more or less taken in by the Collet family. Michel Collet was a journeyman cobbler; the couple, both widowed, had teenage sons from earlier marriages.[125] Their support of their hapless young neighbor was a case of "the poor helping the poor," as Deloge wrote. He described the Collet home—"that hovel of happiness, where everything breathed valiance and honesty" as a haven: "a home, at eighteen! A soft voice that was not that of the seducer, a heart unlike the heart of stone . . . of the employer who does not care about his employees' welfare! . . . From that moment onward, the orphan had a father and a mother."[126] But as Marie Collet, Julia Lallemand, and other people who knew her would recall, Petit remained prone to bouts of despondency, bitterly inveighing against her relatives.[127]

While still living with her lover, Petit had left the pastry shop to work as a saleswoman's assistant at a fur store in central Brussels in the shadow of the gothic church of Saints Michael and Gudula. She made two francs a day—a relatively decent salary—plus meals. She kept this, her fourth known job, until the end of 1912.[128] Two years at one employers' was a long time by her standards, and the fur store, "À L'Ours Noir" (*The Black Bear*), was an elegant establishment. But that did not mean Petit asserted herself professionally and socially. In 1920, her employer, Laure Butin (who also worked for secret intelligence during the war), tersely stated that "Miss Petit has worked for me as a saleswoman [*demoiselle de magasin*] for two years," adding nothing further.[129] This concision may indicate the extent to which (as Deloge observed, with his Christian Democrat's keen eye for the injuries of class) employers simply did not perceive their hired help as individuals. Petit's frequent changes of work were not exceptional: job uncertainty and turnover were high in Brussels' service sector. But Laure Butin's terse tone, *and* the fact that none of Petit's other employers stepped forward to reminisce about her except Madame Carçan who had nothing positive to say, may also indicate how much of a misfit she was. Her friend Julia Lallemand would recall how Petit's resourcefulness in her spy work astonished her, "since she was so very helpless in ordinary life."[130] To boot, she was quick to take offense: at Butin's, she came to blows with a clerk who ordered her about, and was said to have left one of her jobs because her employers failed to address her with the respectful "Mademoiselle."[131] Petit shared this alertness to slights—and for that matter the very experience of slights—with the other resistance heroine, Louise de Bettignies. De Bettignies' work in service was played out at a higher level—well-educated and of impeccable patrician background, she worked as a governess for affluent families and traveled around Europe with them—but it yielded its own snubs, none of which she forgot.[132] As the life of Edith Cavell, the third heroine, well demonstrates, the only path to independence for intelligent women with scant family means was that of formal education and recognized expertise. Petit knew this very well and that is why she wanted to become a teacher. The road not taken or not offered closed off the possibility of a life of self-reliance. The rest was fruitless struggle: the systemic harshness of Brussels' service labor market combined with Petit's personal problems made for a "career" that did not add up structurally. Her move towards autonomy, from domestic service to wage work, while significant, did not amount to actual promotion: she built up neither expertise nor seniority, and her means of existence remained precarious. Awareness of her dim prospects deepened her despondency. Marie Collet mentioned a suicide attempt in 1912: after an altercation at work, she took oxalic acid, a bleaching agent. In a self-dramatizing flourish, she had dispatched a message beforehand to the local police station to blame her father for having abandoned her. Taken by panic, Gabrielle then dragged herself to Marie Collet's, who administered first aid. When, on the next morning, the police commissar went to enquire, she had already left for work; "he summoned [Gabrielle] to the station to berate her; she said she had done it to show her father."[133]

In late 1912, Gabrielle left Butin's employ, apparently after an argument.[134] She then found a job at a department store in central Brussels. She lived on the premises. The population registers listed her as "saleswoman" (*demoiselle de magasin*), but Collet said she worked as a household help.[135] (She also said Petit was a servant at Butin's, whereas Butin herself, and the population registers, list her as a saleswoman. This inconsistency shows, at the very least, that the boundary between sales work and domestic work remained porous.) Gabrielle apparently lost the department store job after only two months, and, remaining unemployed for months—a common experience for saleswomen—became quite destitute and moved in with the Collets.[136] In December 1913, she found a job as a laundry supervisor in a hotel near the Stock Exchange, again living on the premises.[137] She was in poor health that year. She asked Bara for help in paying her medical bills; his accountant assured her that money was on its way—"you should not get so alarmed, Miss"—and accused her of hypochondria, if in kindly terms: "I am sure that you worry about your health too much. One should not wax despondent like this. Come on now, Miss, take heart and get back on your feet."[138]

Her pharmacist, too, would recall how she fretted over her health.[139] She suffered migraines and had heart problems, for which she took digitalis medicine; once, at Collet's, a doctor warned her she might die young.[140] Bara paid the medical bills, at least up to a point: his accountant informed Gabrielle that "Monsieur Bara has agreed to intervene, within a certain limit." And for the New Year 1914, he sent a hundred-franc check. Petit also used his money to help the Collets with their medical bills, since Michel Collet was ailing.[141]

After three months, she left her laundry overseers' job near the Stock Exchange, and, "led astray by bad girlfriends," as Marie Collet said, went to work as a waitress in a café near the Gare du Midi, a less than respectable occupation.[142] In late March 1914, her dignified demeanor caught the attention of one of the customers. This was a young man of Petit's age, Maurice Gobert, an army sergeant stationed at a Brussels garrison and studying for his second-lieutenant's exam.[143] The two struck up a conversation; Gobert was impressed (he later told Deloge) by the young woman's distinction.[144] (Gabrielle, her godmother insisted, was "well-taught, educated, distinguished-looking . . . and nobody would ever have mistaken her for a common working-class girl."[145]) Both were from Hainaut; Gobert, a skilled metal technician before joining the army in 1912, was from the small industrial town of Fontaine-l'Évêque near Charleroi. They discovered that they had a link through Brugelette; one of Gobert's aunts, a nun, belonged to the congregation there. "She looked intelligent and educated to me," Gobert later told Deloge. "I went to see her a few times afterward and she promised me she would leave that place [the café, SdS] as soon as possible." In Marie Collet's words, Gobert, "seeing that Gabrielle was not the type of girl used to that kind of life, [suggested] to her she quit this job which was not for her, and become his girlfriend."[146]

Gobert was an example of upward endeavor himself: a young man working his way up through education, offered by an institution clamoring for men like him. The Belgian army, in full reform, had become a career option even for Catholic skilled workers like Gobert, who, one generation earlier, would have rejected the army because of its hostility to religious practice and its record of ferociously repressing popular protest. Gobert served with the First Carabineers, a choice unit lodged in a prestigious new *caserne* in Brussels and benefiting from an excellent regimental school, located in the little town of Wavre south of Brussels. Besides education, the school offered amenities not generally available to recruits in the rather miserly Belgian army, conveying the message that the young men were considered assets and that their development mattered: good food, a library, sports (gymnastics and soccer, especially), showers—and, another innovation, the mandatory use of toothbrushes.[147] In this achievement-friendly environment, Gobert quickly rose through the ranks: having entered the career army in October 1912, he was promoted to corporal in November of that year, made sergeant in December 1913, and was preparing to rise higher when Petit met him. Gobert, then, represented exactly the kind of "energy" so praised in those years, an aspiration in which education, upward mobility, respectability, and national service merged. Deloge, who met him after the war, described him as the epitome of vigor: "a type of man one does not forget. Dark hair, olive skin. Of medium length [his military file lists Gobert as 5 foot 6 inches, SdS], very fine-featured, he leaves an indelible memory on all who meet him, as I can attest."[148] Falling in love with Petit had not been part of the plan. Young men studying at regimental schools were received in "good families" and had opportunities for useful encounters.[149] From a family strategy point of view, Gobert could have done better for himself than to have met a penniless orphan working as a waitress in a Brussels café. He said later that he had fretted over having to confess to his family "the rather strange encounter I had made." But Petit's distinction and charm, and a shared link to Catholic respectability, made the difference. Gobert does not seem to have considered the liaison temporary: "loving each other very much," as he told Deloge, "we exchanged promises."[150]

Deloge, who considered Petit's encounter with Gobert decisive, quoted Marie Collet as saying that "Mister Maurice" had lifted Gabrielle out of her despondency. He showered praise on a picture of Petit, taken in that time, which Collet lent him. It is reproduced in Deloge's book; the original is lost. It shows her looking demure and serene, with flattened hair, a half-smile and a milder look than in the two other photographs that exist of her. Gobert, it seems, represented the possibility of enduring affection—and also of shared respectability and social aspiration. Gobert told Deloge that Petit was no longer a practicing Catholic when they met, and mocked him for his faith, but that he won her over and they started attending Sunday Mass together, which was also a way to see more of each other (the young recruits were only free on Sunday afternoon, but if they went to church they had Sunday morning off as well[151]). Deloge quotes Marie Collet as telling him that Gabrielle looked radiantly happy when her fiancé came to fetch her of a Sunday. By contrast, Collet's own postwar statement was rather more terse: after meeting Maurice, she said, Gabrielle "kept herself out of trouble." (Hélène Ségard claimed that Petit talked a great deal about her fiancé but was ambivalent: "she said to me, 'I don't think I will be happy in marriage.'")[152]

At any rate, aspiration meant a return to dependency. At Gobert's insistence, Petit quit her waitress job and went to live with the Collets again. They gladly took her back in. In Marie Collet's words, "I let her know that my door had never been closed to her, that she could come back when she wanted and that she had caused me much pain by being gone for so long without letting me know where she was."[153] Gobert was, as he told Deloge, "pleased by her goodwill in following my advice, since it meant leaving a well-paid job."[154] But as a result she was jobless from April through June 1914 and had to depend on the old couple's generosity, much to her embarrassment. To make ends meet, she occasionally waited tables, to Gobert's displeasure.[155] In July, she found a proper job in the laundry-room of a hotel near the Gare du Nord; not a long-term prospect, since the stifling air aggravated her heart troubles. She was still working there when the war broke out.

Another picture, taken in these same months, may also be proof that the encounter with Gobert lifted her out of despondency—or it may show Petit's native resilience. She sent it to a school-friend in Hainaut on June 27, 1914. "How are you?" she wrote. "As for me, as you can see from this card, I look pretty much the same as always." The picture shows her bold upright, hand on hip, the picture of chic simplicity in a dark tight skirt and a sleek white blouse.[156] (Petit seems generally to have been averse to the era's sartorial ideal of high femininity, preferring simple clothes and a simple hairdo, like her namesake Gabrielle "Coco" Chanel, who—perhaps no coincidence—had also grown up penniless and motherless, had been raised in a nuns' orphanage, and started out in life fiercely determined to make her own way.[157]) The blouse gave her a "very harsh expression," wrote Deloge, who preferred the softer look in Marie Collet's picture. But her expression is not harsh at all. It is, rather, self-assured, if slightly weary, and a little amused. At the risk of reading too much into this photo, one might say that it shows a young woman ready to seize opportunity.

Figure 2 Petit in June 1914.
Brussels, Royal Army Museum, Prints Cabinet

CHAPTER 2
ENGAGEMENT, AUGUST 1914–AUGUST 1915

Mobilization

Although the newspaper-reading public in Belgium had greeted the mounting international tension of 1913–1914 with a kind of roller-coaster anxiety, most people believed that Belgium's neutral status would shield it, give or take the need to preventively mount guard at the borders. The Sarajevo murder raised some worries in late June 1914, but these were fleeting. The Austrian ultimatum to Serbia, and Serbia's answer, caused keener fears. Customers stormed banks to change notes into gold. On the 29th, the Socialist International convened in Brussels, voicing ideas for last-minute arbitration, but in fact accepting the inevitable. That evening, Berlin's ultimatum to Belgium arrived at the German legation in Brussels in a sealed envelope with instructions not to open it. Two days on, with the German government still refusing to answer Belgian requests for assurances, the Belgian government sent out the order to mobilize. It was seven o'clock in the evening of July 31, 1914.[1]

In barracks, the First Carabineers prepared for departure from Brussels. From her place of work, Gabrielle wrote to Maurice on August 1:

My very dear boyfriend,
   I am so very afraid that you will have to depart suddenly. I love you so much! I trust you so much more than I used to; I feel you love me sincerely. As to you, you couldn't possibly doubt any more, could you? It would be refusing to accept the obvious. ... Say, my little Maurice, if ever danger arrived, I would try to enlist in your regiment's Red Cross unit. ... [S]wear to me ... that you will not leave me without news and that you will be brave. I know you to be a loyal and generous soul; once you will have given your promise, I will no longer fear. I am convinced that you will come out victorious whatever post they place you in, resolute and brave as you are. ... [I]t is your good and sublime behavior towards others that makes me love you so passionately. Sometimes I dream that I sit next to you. I have a heart attack and I die. Then I would ask God—since I am becoming pious again—to take you as well, and all those I love. Aren't I bad to talk like this? I can't help it, it's stronger than me. I am so afraid that my baby, the fiancé I respect and love with all my soul, will be taken from me. ... Papa's state remains the same, he is almost completely paralyzed. [Michel Collet was dying after a stroke, SdS.] ... How sad it is and what a sight to have before one's eyes.

I must stop, since the housekeeper's stately bulk will appear any moment now. And then, you see, there would be recriminations, and now is hardly the time for those.

Your loving and faithful little fiancée,

GABY.[2]

This letter, which Gobert showed Deloge after the war, expresses profound anxiety over losing a new-found pillar in a fragile support and emotional network. It hints at mutual doubts, apparently recently overcome. It shows Petit's possessiveness—and her penchant for drama, obvious in her image of a perfect union in death. Its priorities are of a purely private nature. Although Petit praised her fiancé's sense of duty, there is no reference to public issues. But, then, on August 1, few people expected Belgium to be involved in the war.

On August 3, Maurice's regiment left to take up positions twenty miles southeast of Brussels. "It was all I could do to prevent Gaby from following me."[3] By then, Belgium was facing war directly. At seven o'clock in the evening of August 2, the Belgian minister of Foreign Affairs was handed the ultimatum from Berlin. It demanded the right of free passage on pain of hostilities. ("Should Belgium oppose the German troops . . . the eventual adjustment of the relations between the two States must be left to the decision of arms.") The Cabinet and King Albert had convened in the night and decided to defend Belgium's neutrality. At seven in the morning on August 3, the ultimatum's deadline, the Belgian government made it known that

[t]his note has made a deep and painful impression . . . The attack upon [Belgium's] independence with which the German Government threatens her constitutes a flagrant violation of international law. No strategic interest justifies such a violation of law. The Belgian Government, if they were to accept the proposals submitted to them, would sacrifice the honor of the nation and betray their duty towards Europe. . . . [T]he Belgian Government are firmly resolved to repel, by all the means in their power, every attack upon their rights.[4]

On Monday morning, August 3, then, the Belgians found themselves facing a war for which little had prepared them; for, in spite of the much-stepped-up defense efforts of the past year, Belgium had remained a lightly mobilized nation by continental European standards. Up until 1909, the Belgian state had held off on introducing personal military service. A lottery system allowed affluent young men who drew a bad ticket to pay substitutes to serve in their place. As a result, to quote a memoir of 1906–1908, "the Belgian army consisted exclusively of the sons of the small people."[5] But the old system proved untenable. A heterogeneous protest coalition ranging from the dying King Leopold II to the Socialists (who condemned the unjust distribution of the "blood tax") mounted an assault on the replacement scheme, and it was abolished in late 1909. The personal military service regime then introduced (at the rate of one son per household) made for a conscript-to-population ratio, in 1911, of no more than 1 in 400, as against 1 in 170 in France, 1 in 243 in the German states, and 1 in 262 even in the neutral

Netherlands. Generalized military service was introduced in August 1913. It still allowed for wide exemptions. Belgian voters were more reluctant to see the army as a salutary school of the nation than were their counterparts in France or Germany; few bourgeois sons coveted reserve officer status; neutrality was believed to be a secure shield; and the Catholic middle classes trusted the Wilhelmine Empire. (They trusted France less, but thought it too frivolous for aggression.)

Yet, at the same time, the campaign for army reform had effected (or revealed) some changes in mentalities towards the idea of the nation in arms and away from the belief that the bourgeoisie paid its dues to the common good in the form of taxes. While many still saw Belgium's neutrality as a shield, guaranteed by the great powers, behind which the nation enjoyed peace, the idea gained traction that this neutrality was a part of international law, worthy of active defense. Among the educated middle classes, a sense of heightened national prestige—a thriving economy, colonial-power status, the 1911 Nobel Prize in literature, and other achievements—made for greater receptiveness to the idea of national defense. Moreover, the army offered avenues of upward mobility for ambitious sons of the skilled working class or lower middle class, Maurice Gobert being a case in point.[6]

This shift explains something about the Belgian public's reaction before the colossal *fait accompli* of imminent war on August 3. Eyewitnesses described a state of shock and anxiety, indignation over the brutality of the German demand, with a measure of resolve thrown in, as well as pride in the government's dignified answer. Neutrality, an apparently technical issue, assumed acute emotional, or, to be more precise, moral importance. Scattered skepticism over the wisdom of rejecting the ultimatum did not cohere into organized protest. Socialists and Flemish militants rallied with some zeal—precisely *as* Socialists and Flemish militants. Belgium, then, in spite of its belated preparation for war, its long history of laissez-faire government, and foreign observers' doubts over what it would do when war broke out, was no exception to the wider West European pattern of August 1914. The image of "mindless crowds . . . cheering their nations on to catastrophe" was, as scholarship on France, Germany, and Britain has shown, a postwar myth. The mood was not marked by euphoria so much as by resolve to engage in what was very widely seen as legitimate self-defense. As invasions followed upon invasions, "nations and empires seemed threatened in their essence." In addition to the summer crisis, there was, as John Horne has pointed out, a longer-term process at work: "the war galvanized the sense of national community and involvement in politics that had been growing in the previous half-century."[7] The same happened in Belgium. The historian Henri Pirenne later described August 3 as a day passed "in a kind of delirium made of anger, worry, and resolve." He observed this in the city of Ghent.[8] Though witnesses reported similar sentiments in the countryside, public displays of resolve were most visible and audible in the big cities. Brussels, especially, became a theater for electrified feelings of national belonging, complete with attacks on "enemy" foreigners and long lines of volunteers.[9] Again, Belgium was no exception: the "intense ritualization of the passage from peace to war" across belligerent Europe was most intense in the cities, and again at its most intense in the national capitals.[10] One of the most dramatic, and still most mystifying, aspects of the First World War is the suddenness of populations' entry into war—and into what historians have called a "war culture," viz., into a perspective defining national defense as the ultimate priority and transforming death in its service into "sacrifice." This suddenness presents a sharp contrast to the exit from war and war culture from the Armistice onward, a process that was much slower, as well as uneven, and in some cases would take another war to run its course.[11] In Brussels, this sudden entry into resolve is well expressed by the diaries of one inhabitant who lived a short walk—though many worlds—away from Petit, the middle-aged novelist Georges Eekhoud. On August 3, Eekhoud first wrote of his fear of war "with its train of horrors!" But then a fellow author came to bring him "the good but also grave and tragic news that we have rejected the ultimatum!" And the two men communed in a spirit of "fine patriotism."[12]

On the next day, August 4, the Belgian Parliament convened. The Senate was filled to the rafters. King Albert gave a short speech calling for "tenacious resistance." The head of cabinet, Charles de Broqueville, then read the text of the German ultimatum and the government's rejection, ending on the words "vanquished, maybe; subjected, never!" under the thunderous cheers of the assembly, many by now weeping openly. This display of resolve was followed by the order of the day: votes for war credits, allocations for soldiers' families and other practical matters. During the discussions, De Broqueville was handed a message. He read it and, shaken, told the assembly that the German armies had crossed the border.

War

The Brussels mood of effusive resolve mixed with dread persisted for a fortnight.[13] On August 5, Eekhoud and three fellow *littérateurs* spent the evening at a sidewalk café in the center of town. "We wax quite enthusiastic, lyrical, effusive. We overflow with patriotic pride . . ." The first wounded brought in from Liège were "received with a truly maternal fervor," Eekhoud wrote on August 7.[14] Petit (out of a job and living on money Bara had sent) was one of many to tend to the wounded as best she could; she enrolled as a fund collector for the Red Cross and worked back-to-back shifts well into the night. "Much [money] is needed to take care of our wounded (they are carried in triumph here)," she wrote to Gobert on August 11, "and let me tell you, I do excellent business." But she wished she could do more: "If I could, I would join your regiment and stand by your side; I am sure I would make a tough machine gunner in no time. If only one could act as one wanted!" Meanwhile, life had been sad at home. Michel Collet had died on August 9, only fifty years old. Marie Collet, at sixty, was now twice-widowed.[15]

Meanwhile, the Germans had taken the city of Liège. Gobert's company, stationed with the bulk of the Belgian army in central Belgium, had not yet seen action. He wrote to his fiancée, describing the heat, hunger and thirst; she wrote back to say how not being able to help him "tormented" her. Sometime after August 11, she met up with Gobert's brother and one of his sisters—it was her first meeting with her in-laws—and the three, traveling on her Red Cross pass, managed to locate Maurice at Néthen, southeast of

Brussels. No description of the encounter survives. Eventually, Gobert's company retreated with the rest of the surviving army, to the "national redoubt" of Antwerp, while the advancing German armies clashed with Entente forces in Hainaut. From Antwerp, the Belgians effected sorties to cut German communications lines. Gobert's machine-gun company was in the center of the first sortie, advancing towards Elewijt, south of Mechelen, on August 25. As they took the village of Hofstade at dawn, Gobert, in the vanguard, was badly wounded in the right thigh and the left knee. (The sortie was called off on the next day, as the Entente armies were retreating into France; it had been ill-coordinated and cost the small Belgian army an estimated four thousand wounded, missing, and dead. While it had tied down German troops before Antwerp, it had also exasperated them into brutal retaliations against civilians in that area.)[16]

Gobert was evacuated back to Antwerp; from hospital, he wrote to Petit on September 3, asking her to inform his family. By now, his fiancée was living in an occupied city; Brussels had been taken on August 20. People were allowed to leave the city, except in the direction of Antwerp and the coast, and so Petit decided to travel to Fontaine-l'Évêque, a 70-kilometer trip south of Brussels through territory that had seen violent clashes between the German and Entente armies just days before. "The poor little one" then had to tramp back to Brussels on foot (as Gobert described it) to find an empty house: the Collets had joined the throng of refugees out of Brussels. Quite without support, she wrote to Maurice's family and they took her in.[17] If this meant she was once more dependent on the kindness of strangers, she nevertheless sounded upbeat, and quite pleased with herself, in an October 2 letter to Gobert:

My dear little boyfriend,

I have received your letter of 3 September, telling me you had been wounded in both legs; I immediately went to announce the news here. Now listen: as your girlfriend I would like you to ... tell me <u>exactly</u> what is wrong with you, whether you suffer much and what you will have to do once you are mended. If anything serious is the matter, I will keep it to myself, I promise. But by all means do not imagine that I must be spared, <u>I want to know!</u> Is your nurse taking good care of you? What a pity that one cannot take service, or I would never entrust you to a stranger's care. Tell me also what the effects of your wounds will be. Whatever happens, I am yours and will forever be, do not forget that. But you understand, since I do not know for sure, I imagine all kinds of things. I am more mischievous than ever and I have put on weight here. ... Your mum has her hands full with me; she will lecture you about me when you return, but you know what I am like. ... I have received the key to your study (I am the only one to have it, you know), and I ... was deeply touched by the notes you took from my letters. I take care of your things ... but you will have to give me a hand to put everything back to its original order ... My dear little fiancé, be brave, think of us all, write as soon as you can and rest assured on our account. As for me, I feel so at home here that it seems to me I have never lived anywhere else.

Your Gaby for life.[18]

Clearly, she feared that her fiancé might have become an invalid, though she assured him it would make no difference. The letter shows that she was not exactly a self-effacing house guest bent on pleasing her prospective mother-in-law. She took a rather regal attitude towards Gobert, noting with satisfaction that he had treated her letters reverently, and announcing grandly that, as the sole possessor of the key to his study, she was taking care of his things—though apparently in such a way that the study would need tidying. Even from this brief glimpse, one infers that she was not exactly suited to the role of spousal helpmeet, as she herself would acknowledge later.

In contrast to Gobert's picture of helplessness, Petit's godmother portrayed her niece during this period as having a dashing time in the Red Cross, traveling freely. According to Ségard, she now worked as a nurse. This is probably true: Petit's papers contain a note from a physician stating that "Mademoiselle Gabrielle Petit has shown all of the qualities required of a good nurse in a field hospital," and a permit entitling her to travel by automobile. Both documents place her in Brussels, Fontaine-l'Évêque, and Antwerp.[19] Did she manage to reach Gobert at the hospital in Antwerp? He himself did not mention seeing her there. As he told the story, he managed to leave the hospital on October 9, as the city fell after a massive bombardment. Still in bad shape, he went into hiding with friends so as not to be taken prisoner. On October 25, his sister Nelly came to take him back to Fontaine.[20] But on December 4, he received word that "the Boches had heard from the neighbors" that he was home, and were on their way to arrest him. (One source states that Gobert, during his convalescence, "made himself useful," possibly helping army volunteers leave the country. This would explain why the neighbors wanted him taken prisoner: the district commanders took hostages to prevent local men from joining the Belgian army.[21]) Still far from mended and walking on crutches, Gobert went into hiding among ruins left by the Battle of Mons. To deflect the curious, Petit, who was at Fontaine, left for Brussels on the same day. She knew of Gobert's hiding-place and promised to write.[22]

Suspicions

According to Hélène Ségard, the fiancés kept in touch, and, once Gobert was healed, Petit persuaded him to join the Belgian army on the Yser front. Through her connections with escape networks, she helped him cross into the neutral Netherlands; she herself followed soon after.[23] Postwar legend had the fiancés cross the border together: the 1928 film *Femme belge* shows Gabrielle guiding Maurice through the Campine heath; the tragic couple then stoically part.

Gobert's own account painted a less sublime picture. He did not hear from Petit at all for four months; she finally wrote in March, deploring not being able to see him. This forced separation quite suited Gobert's parents. His fiancée had, at first, charmed the family "by her intelligence, her cheerfulness ... and her audacity," but her peremptory tone wore out their sympathies. His mother, especially, came to resent Petit's possessiveness towards Maurice. The atmosphere grew tense and Gobert was made to feel (as he stated after the war) that he had to choose between his fiancée and his family. Meanwhile, still in hiding, he slowly regained as much leg function as he would ever recover. In April and May 1915, he made three failed attempts to cross the border and rejoin his regiment. In late May, his parents agreed to let him leave for Brussels, where he hoped to find help; he went into hiding at a friend's, growing a beard and wearing glasses. Thus camouflaged, he went to the Collets' twice to look up Gabrielle. Told Petit was out, he gave Marie Collet the letters he had written during his days in hiding. On his second attempt, a female neighbor told him that he "should not see that woman anymore. She has been leading a shady life for months, going out to cafés and coming home at impossible hours." Gobert eventually, with all the circumspection that his situation necessitated, managed to see Petit again, demanded to know how she had been spending her time, and confronted her for having avoided him—for he now knew that she had actually been home when he came to visit. He had intended to break up with her, but she, as he later said, charmed him into starting over. He made her promise to find a job, which she did. (If this account is correct, it is unclear how she was making a living up until then. Service work had shrunk desperately.)

But Petit and Gobert were to break up again, this time for good. They both left occupied Belgium in June 1915, but not together, and in circumstances that left Gobert with doubts about Petit's loyalty so grave he broke off all contact. As he told Deloge after the war, Gobert announced to his fiancée that he wanted to escape the occupied country; she wanted to find work in France or England and save, so they could get married. "Both of us, each on our end, then went to look for that one precious tip [on how to get out of the country, SdS]."[24] Interestingly, Gobert defined Petit's wish to leave in purely private terms, as a family strategy befitting a spouse-to-be—whereas postwar lore showed an ardently patriotic Petit taking the initiative to leave, winning over a hesitant fiancé.

At any rate, leaving Belgium was by now very difficult. In the Fall of 1914, after the Western Front had set, British and French soldiers had found themselves trapped in northern France and western Belgium. Locals helped them survive; eventually, networks of helpers guided these men, as well as Belgians and Frenchmen who wished to volunteer, across the occupied country to different crossing-points along the Dutch-Belgian border.[25] Belgian men who had managed to get across, placed coded ads in the Dutch newspaper *De Nieuwe Rotterdamsche Courant*, which was not (usually) banned by the German censors.[26] For the patriotic-minded in the occupied country, war efforts converged around these escapes; help arrived from different quarters and in different forms—false identity papers, food, clothing, medical care, safe houses, help in escorting the men to the border or even crossing together with them, and money to pay smugglers in the border zone. "People are wonderfully generous with their loyal help," wrote Edith Cavell in her diary on April 27. Her nursing school in Brussels was a major safe house and she provided the men with guides to the border. But she also wrote about increasing difficulties in crossing the border.[27] German surveillance had increased. From January, all men aged sixteen through forty were banned from the border zone, all escape helpers were threatened with punishment "according to the laws of war," and plans were announced to close off the Dutch-Belgian border by way of an electric fence. This fantastic-sounding scheme became reality, to the astonishment of the occupied: in April, German engineers descended on the border region to lay out the route and install the generators and poles. In May, the first wires were strung. Eventually, most of the border was closed off by August 1915, with remaining gaps filled in by the summer of 1916.[28] As a further deterrent, the occupation authorities circulated pictures of the mutilated corpses of Belgians electrocuted at the wire.[29] Yet there were still escapes, enthusiastically relayed in patriotic circles, such as that of three young men from Brussels who in early June 1915, guided by a smuggler, had managed to make their way out through a sewerage tunnel underneath the Campine Canal.[30] By then, the occupied civilians were aware of the increased presence of the German secret police.[31] Police Department B, which specialized in dismantling escape organizations, was closing in on Edith Cavell's network. She expected to be arrested any day. (In the event, she was not arrested until August 5, since the *Polizei* wanted to strike wide and not arouse suspicion with separate arrests.)[32]

It was in these tense days that Gobert was planning his escape. Around June 10, a friend put him in contact with a well-connected organizer of an escape network, an "ardent patriot" in his mid-sixties named Franz Merjay, who promised to help him cross the border. (Merjay would be executed in May 1917.[33]) Elated, Gobert told Petit of his success. On June 14, he was summoned to a rendezvous; suspicious, he had the summons shown to Merjay, who declared it was not his and advised Gobert to move and await *his* summons. Gobert shaved his beard and was taken to another safe house. That evening, his sister Nelly, who was in touch with the Merjay network, came to tell him that the German military police headquarters at Fontaine had received word that their parents had hidden him for months. They had heard this from a friend who worked as an interpreter for the Germans. The friend had also said that the denunciation letter was signed Gabrielle. Gobert, as he later recalled, was stunned. He did not question his sister's account; and promptly suspected that Petit had also sent a fake summons to have him arrested. "It was beyond doubt; I had to acknowledge now that my fiancée wanted to harm me, though I had no idea why." But there was no time to fret; Gobert received Merjay's summons, met the designated guide, managed to reach the Netherlands on June 16, wrote to let a friend know he had crossed, and, as his military file shows, rejoined his division's depot in France on June 28. "I left with a heavy heart," he later said, "knowing that I left my good, sensible parents to what looked like a grim fate. I swore to my sister that I would never have any truck with that Gabrielle again." As it happened, the first summons delivered to Gobert at his hiding-place in Brussels was indeed Petit's; it was delivered by one of Marie Collet's sons. It was completely above board: she had simply gotten hold of her own escape tip for her fiancé.[34] But Gobert did not know this, and later events only served to burnish his suspicion. His parents' house was perquisitioned twice; on July 9, they were arrested and interrogated together with his sister Nelly. Asking to see who had accused them, Nelly Gobert saw that the denunciation letter was signed Gabrielle. In revenge, she told the *Polizei* that Petit had, in fact, helped Maurice to escape— a highly punishable offense—and gave them Petit's address in Brussels, where she was arrested on the next day. The Goberts were released for lack of proof on July 12, but this in no way diminished their suspicion of Petit, nor Maurice's.[35] (In reality, as a friend and network agent later testified, Gobert himself was to blame for his family's interrogation: he had sent his message from the Netherlands by regular mail, which was the height of imprudence. That the Goberts' denunciation was signed Gabrielle meant nothing: anyone could have signed with that name.[36] Everybody in the occupied country knew that letters of denunciation were almost always anonymous: in May 1915, a German poster had even urged Belgians—in vain—to *sign* the information they wanted to share with the police.[37] The *Polizei*, incidentally, were deluged with anonymous letters: an estimated 371,000 by September 1917, according to one source. Most of them were useless.[38])

As to Petit, she was arrested late in the evening of July 10, and taken to the Brussels *Kommandantur* at 11.00 p.m.[39] Marie Collet reported that the policemen told her she would be taken to prison in Germany; she retorted that over there, at least, she would see Belgian soldiers, "whereas all I see here is trash." Warned that she would shed tears before long, she bit back: "not for you lot. Anyway, stop the fuss and take me away." In the stairway, she gave a shaken Collet her brooch containing a portrait of King Albert (a trinket much in vogue under the occupation, although it was forbidden to display patriotic symbols openly), grandly declaring that "I do not want my King to have to spend the night at the *Kommandantur*."[40] She returned home two days later to find all of her papers confiscated, including the letters Gobert had written to her at his hiding-place in Hainaut. These could serve to incriminate network agents in Fontaine and in Brussels—and add to the Goberts' mistrust of Petit. In these times of mounting mutual misgivings—"people are irritable, spiteful, suspicious of each other," noted Eekhoud[41]—the Goberts, in attempting to make sense of what was happening to them, were probably all too eager to blame Petit, the interloper. Her volatile temperament and the fact that she had no family to vouch for her respectability probably led her in-laws, and, ultimately, her fiancé to conclude that she must also be a bad citizen—a conclusion easily reached in the mistrust-laden fog of occupation.

And yet, as Marie Collet would recall, Petit loathed the occupation regime; the word "*patrie*" entered her vocabulary, and she told Collet that she had up until then quite ignored the very idea of the fatherland, but since the invasion felt surrounded by it everywhere—in the streets of Brussels, in the government buildings, and in those around her, whom she now saw as fellow citizens.[42] Petit's feelings—and her prized King Albert brooch—fit in with a description of the mood in occupied Brussels in 1915 given by the expressionist poet Gottfried Benn (who served as a physician in the military administration). The denizens of "the beautiful, impulsive, edgy, hate-filled capital," Benn wrote, were "full of absolutely blatant hostility, [wearing] the national colors large as saucers on hats, buttonholes, umbrellas and cravats."[43]

"Done Being Useless"

Gabrielle was released in the evening of July 12. She had meanwhile arranged for her own travel, on a regular passport for the Netherlands through her Red Cross connections, and she left occupied Belgium during the following week. (Her bread ration card shows that she picked up her last loaf on July 15.[44]) She had no intention yet of enrolling in the intelligence service; she wanted to join Gobert. At least she wrote as much to Gobert's younger sister, Eva, who with her little son Théo was living in a refugee camp in Harderwijk, the Netherlands, close to her husband, who was interned in a Belgian soldiers' camp. (Belgian troops who had crossed over into the Netherlands after the fall of Antwerp were interned for the duration of the war; their families were allowed to live close by, albeit in makeshift circumstances. A family camp had been built near Harderwijk, a small town on the Zuiderzee coast.[45]) In a note written from The Hague on July 20, Petit mentioned the paperwork needed to travel from the Netherlands to France via Britain: "Such formalities! Such errands!" Gobert, during his brief stay in the Netherlands, had told his sister of their estrangement, but Petit did not know this: "Maurice sends kisses," she wrote. Her note, written in a warm tone that suggested mutual sympathy, consoled the family for their dispiriting circumstances ("Be brave and take heart, and consider that little Théo is happy with his ships . . ."). Petit intended to be reunited with the man she still thought of as her fiancé: she announced that she would sail on the 22nd and rather dreaded becoming seasick—but, "ah well! At the end of the trek, there will be Maurice."[46]

It was not to happen. On July 24, she sent Maurice a note, written from Folkestone.

Very dear fiancé,

I was going to rejoin you, dear and good fiancé, only I have been offered something else. Later on, you will know and you will approve of me. We will be separated for the same cause.

All of my best kisses and with God's grace.

GABY.[47]

What had happened? On board the SS *Copenhagen* en route to Folkestone, Petit had been approached by a recruiter for British intelligence, probably Joseph Ide, a tall, handsome 27-year-old law graduate from Antwerp who had been working for British intelligence in different capacities since the Fall of 1914.[48] Belgians from the occupied country, smart and daring enough to return there and gather military information, were in high demand. Occupied Belgium provided the Entente armies with great opportunities: it was that rarity, a friendly hinterland to an enemy army. Since the end of mobile warfare, occupied Belgium had become a formidably defended hinterland to a large section of the German front in the West. It was an area of rest, of first aid to the wounded, and of training. It was buttressed with airfields, anti-aircraft gun emplacements, a submarine base at Bruges, the inland harbor of which had been connected to the coast since 1907, garrisons and camps, munitions dépôts, and layers of in-depth defense. Through occupied Belgium flowed reinforcements in men and *matériel*, sent via the Belgian railways (now run by and for the German military). A lot could be gleaned from close observation of the goings-on in this hinterland. Spies in Belgium could help the Allied armies stuck on the other side of the impenetrable Western Front see what was going on. Moreover, Belgium bordered the unoccupied Netherlands; reports and people could still get out across the electric fence, if at enormous risk.

There was no unified Allied intelligence bureau: Belgian, French, and British services worked side by side, occasionally getting in each other's way. Belgian and French services had been very active in the first months of the war, but lack of organization and funds quickly sapped them. By the time Petit was approached, in July 1915, the British services were already occupying most of the terrain; they would quite dominate it during the second half of the war.[49] Not that British intelligence was unified. The War Office and General Headquarters (GHQ) each had their own bureaux.[50] Both chased information coming out of occupied Belgium. Petit was recruited by GHQ intelligence. In November 1914, GHQ had opened a bureau in Folkestone to recruit agents and collect information from among the French and Belgian refugees arriving there. It was headed by Major Cecil Cameron who reported to Colonel Walter Kirke, GHQ intelligence head in Saint-Omer in northern France.[51] In early 1915, GHQ opened a second bureau at the instigation of Sigismund Payne Best, a second lieutenant who had served in France with the GHQ Intelligence Corps before being invalided back to London at Christmas 1914. While in France, the polyglot and energetic Payne Best had hit upon the idea of organizing an intelligence service in occupied Belgium; back in England, he had started to interrogate Belgian refugees. Eventually, he persuaded Kirke to let him set up an organization of his own. This new organization was led by an invalided officer, Major Ernest Wallinger, who had lost a foot at the battle of Le Cateau in August 1914.[52] GHQ, then, possessed two bureaux: Cameron's and Wallinger's. Both men served as titular heads only, since they were artillery officers with no expertise in intelligence work. The Wallinger bureau was effectively run by Payne Best. His closest associate was Joseph Ide, Petit's probable recruiter. Payne Best and Ide had met in 1914, as both were reconnoitering the German advance through Belgium. Payne Best did so in an official capacity as a member of the Intelligence Corps, though this denomination covered a great deal of improvisation: the intelligence historian Jim Beach has qualified the Intelligence Corps officers as "the untidy, the unmilitary, the unusual, the eccentric, and the lateral thinkers." Payne Best himself, in a memoir written shortly before his death in 1978 at age ninety-three, wrote that "my work from the start was of a bumbling nature. You see I had no rules to go on. I had no one who told me what to do. There was in fact no one who had any idea of what could be done. I just had to use my brains and go on with trial and error."[53] Ide for his part was barely institutionally established at all: a volunteer in the Belgian army, he was first enrolled in a reconnaissance capacity, then transferred to an infantry regiment, from which he had become separated after the fall of Antwerp. He had then started collecting information on the German advance on his own, so coming in contact with Payne Best, who had relayed his information to GHQ. Ide then made his way to Britain, where, to make his status with the British forces official, Wallinger eventually enlisted him as interpreter for the Intelligence Corps.[54] Ide, who spoke Dutch, helped Payne Best interrogate Flemish passengers from the ferry and recruit those who seemed promising.[55] Ide also recruited through other channels. In London, early in 1915, he met an acquaintance from Antwerp, a dashing architect in his early thirties named Jozef Baeckelmans, an ardent patriot; Ide persuaded him to return to occupied Belgium and run a railway-observation service. Baeckelmans left London in February 1915, received rudimentary instruction in the Netherlands, and, back in Belgium, started operations in March.[56] Although Baeckelmans and Petit never met—in spite of postwar legend—he would play a major role in Petit's war work.

In Folkestone, Petit sent a telegram to London to let the Wallinger bureau know she had arrived. On July 24, she sent word to Eva Gobert and her family to say that "I don't know if I will see Maurice any time soon. I have been offered something more useful than what I had in mind. Ah well! We will be separated, but he will be very pleased with me when he finds out." She told them how to get in touch with Maurice, who had, she wrote, left Folkestone for France on June 27. (This was correct.) "Many kisses to the two of you, especially to little Théo, and take heart."[57] And with that, she left for London, where, as Ide wrote to her, she was eagerly awaited at the Empire Hotel in St. Martin's Lane, Holborn; she was invited to take a taxi and submit all travel expenses.[58]

Payne Best's superior at GHQ, Walter Kirke, noted in his diaries that the Wallinger bureau "seems to be employing a good class of agent exclusively," in contrast to Cameron's organization, or that of the War Office. By this, he meant people with patriotic motives, who were more likely to do conscientious work.[59] Kirke even seems to have mentioned Petit specifically, noting in his diary a few months later that "Mademoiselle Petit ... helps us from [motives of revenge]," since her French fiancé had been shot at Mons by the Germans.[60] If this does indeed refer to Gabrielle Petit, it is unclear how Kirke came by this story. At any rate, Petit was counted among those who took the engagement for other than material reasons. And she applied herself zealously. At the Wallinger bureau in Basil Street, Knightsbridge, she took a fortnight's instruction. Ide, who was in charge, told Deloge after the war that he had never met a woman who was "more intelligent and more keen to learn."[61] Petit's papers include notes taken during her time of instruction in London—notes on military units and insignias, on troop trains and the like.[62] After her return to Brussels, she proudly told her godmother of her "military instruction," and how she had, as she put it, "passed her spy levels"; the requirements were a minimum age of twenty-one, the capacity to draw up intelligence reports, and courage—"in other words, being able to sacrifice yourself usefully."[63]

She probably found the proposition attractive. Like other Belgians recruited by British intelligence officers, she may have been charmed by their dash. Wallinger, for one, established in style with his butler in a flat above the Knightsbridge offices, was "a great big man, very good-looking and extremely pleasant," in Payne Best's words.[64] Moreover, serving with British intelligence was a major step up for Petit in many ways. It was a brilliant opportunity to use her intelligence and daring bent, further her education, make money, be independent, meet people and garner social capital, and, as she thought, gain her fiancé's esteem. She wasted no time divesting herself of her lowly patronym and—not altogether prudently—chose the opposite nom de guerre Miss Legrand.[65]

But she was aware of the risk. She wrote to Gobert on July 28:

Dearest, best fiancé,

As you can see, I get around quite a bit: first at Folkestone, now in London. I await orders from my superior. I will not enroll at the field hospital, I have something much more useful to do; later on, you will know everything; I will have done my duty well, you will be most pleased. But do pray that nothing bad will happen to me. Still, do not get upset; there is danger everywhere. . . . If I succeed in my endeavor, I will ask my superiors to obtain a leave for you, which I will spend with you. . . . Dearest fiancé, be very brave, very prudent, and pray for us. . . .

Forever your faithful fiancée,

GABY.[66]

She wrote again on July 30 to tell Gobert that he had escaped Brussels in the nick of time, since the Boches were chasing him.

Not finding you, they came to my place, in hopes of making me confess; oh, what a hard time I gave them! I have shown them exemplary rudeness and astonishing arrogance. . . . The officer took one of my photos; I asked him why. He went all cagey. "When you'll return to Sauerkrautland," I told him, "do show that picture around: it shows a Belgian woman who has guts." The effect was immediate; I wonder if he got over the insult. . . . So you see, dear little fiancé, that I have followed close upon your heels. Unfortunately, it might be two or three months before I see you again. . . . I will ask my major [Wallinger, SdS] to look after our correspondence, yours and mine; he is so good and so sweet that he will grant me my wish. . . . For now, all you can do for me is not to forget about me, to love me more than before, if that were possible, and to pray for me and for my safety. I am almost done being useless [she used the expression "échantillon sans valeur", a postal expression meaning "sample of no commercial value," SdS]; we will build our future with no-one's help.

I am set to pass a little exam on Monday, 2 August and to leave London on the 3d. Some patience, and you will be able to congratulate me a lot. Be good, be brave, be loyal; be prudent, danger lurks everywhere; in whichever manner one serves one's country, one is always exposed to danger.

Dearest fiancé, I must sign off now, I have to study; more news in a day or two. When you have the means to write to me, make me a journal and send it to me in a closed envelope; the censor will open it and seal it afterward. These are our allies, after all!

My good and dear little one, be brave, think of she who aspires to see you again and who kisses you with all her soul,

Your faithful and devoted fiancée,

GABY.[67]

Departures

Urging Gobert over and over again to write, Petit may have hoped that the break-up was temporary. In her notebook, she copied wistful poetry; and, on a more combative note, reminded herself, in bold lettering, of the proverb "*à bon chat, bon rat,*" meaning that attacker and attacked both grow stronger from finding new ways to outwit each other.[68] (After her return to occupied Brussels, she wrote to her sister that her fiancé would "probably be furious" when he heard she had come back, but that the quarrel would make the reconciliation all the sweeter. Out of caution, she gave no indication that she knew that Gobert had left Belgium, writing instead that "I am very busy, I don't have time for anything . . ., not even for my fiancé."[69]) But Gobert, as he stated after the war, had no intention to reconcile; he remained unconvinced by Petit's description of her defiant behavior at the *Kommandantur,* and unimpressed—in spite of what she, poignantly, thought—by her engagement in secret intelligence, which he may have dismissed as being of a piece with her self-dramatizing and reckless character. "Instead of joining me [once she had reached the Netherlands], she enrolled in a special service in England," Gobert indignantly told Deloge after the war.[70] Her choice once more demonstrated that she was not inclined to put her future husband first. Gobert never contacted Petit again. He served at the front for over a year, before being transferred to the Belgian munitions works at Le Havre in August 1916. There, in February 1918, he married a young Frenchwoman, Julienne Deschamps.[71]

Meanwhile, Petit prepared herself for her mission. She left London on August 3 and spent two weeks in Flushing, the Netherlands, receiving further instruction from Wallinger's network chief in the Netherlands, Emmanuel Van Tichelen, an Antwerp man whom Payne Best described as "my most useful and valuable colleague."[72] (Like all intelligence offices, Wallinger's service operated through a base in the Netherlands that sent instructions and funds into Belgium and received reports from Belgium, with couriers going back and forth.[73]) On the morning of August 10, 1915, Petit wrote to Gobert's sister in Harderwijk, in her usual see-what-I'm-capable-of vein:

> Dear all,
>
> I have received your express [message], thank you very much. I am going, come what may! Constant [Eva's husband, SdS] guessed right [about Petit's plans, SdS]; I do not understand why Eva did not immediately realize for herself, for after all, with a character like mine, nothing should come as a surprise. I have been told [when being recruited, SdS]: "It seems to me that you love your fiancé very much; since he makes a sacrifice, do as he does (but as a competitor, put your pride into it)." I said "Yes." Anyway, if I had joined a field hospital, I would have run the same risks and it would not have served me later on, whereas now, I have friends in high places who very much have my best interests in mind. Little Théo . . ., when you say your prayers for Uncle Maurice, add "and for Gaby too." . . . Be brave . . . Kisses to Constant, Eva, and especially little Théo. . . . N.B. Do not write to me any more—the letter wouldn't have the legs to run after me.[74]

A week later, on August 17, the day of her return to occupied Belgium, she wrote two messages to Gobert. The first one, sent from Flushing as she was waiting for her passport, asked him to "pray for me as I pray for you," and was signed "Your future wife who loves you with all her soul." She left that same day for the Dutch border. From there, she sent word that she expected to be on Belgian soil in an hour. "Eva knows why I am returning," she wrote, and promised she would send Eva money to visit her brother at the front and clear up things: "then, you will know for sure, and maybe you will be pleased with me. About time, isn't it, my poor baby?" She beseeched him to be cautious, not to forget her, and to pray "for us and for our future in common." She signed "as ever, your dear fiancée who loves you, Gaby." She wrote a brief post-scriptum, probably meant to dispel what she now knew were his suspicions, and signed it separately with the words "Yours only, for life, G."[75] With that, she crossed the border.

CHAPTER 3
WAR WORK, AUGUST 1915–FEBRUARY 1916

Roaming Agent

In 1929, a breathless German account of spy operations in Belgium during the First World War defined Petit as a "master female spy [*Meisterspionin*]." Two years running, Petit led the German counter-espionage services into a devilish dance, flitting around the occupied country brazenly outfitted in a German officer's uniform, traveling to and from London, handing British intelligence invaluable information and rendering entire German regiments worthless.[1]

The reality was more pedestrian: Petit's war work was of far shorter duration and the day-to-day routine of it involved considerably more drudge-work. But it was not entirely devoid of dash either. Intelligence work, though dangerous and exhausting, gave Petit more of a horizon that she had ever had, and certainly more of one than was allotted most of her compatriots in the occupied country. She managed to roam freely across a country hedged about with military frontiers, no-go border zones, and barrages across streets and highways and fields; a country under military occupation in which most people were confined to the limits of their own locality, the men of Petit's age especially so, since they had to report to the occupation authorities on a regular basis to prove that they had not joined the Belgian army. (The people Petit knew outside of occupied Belgium suffered restricted movement as well: Maurice Gobert was under military authority and Eva Gobert's husband was interned, with Eva herself housed in a "family village," not free to go as she pleased.) To this spatial freedom was added that of being financially independent, even more so, of being able to help others, the same people that in the past had supported her from what little they possessed. This new dignity was enhanced by another leap in status, that of responsibility. Petit, the lowly employee, always on the receiving end of the chain of command, had risen to the status of Mademoiselle Legrand entirely on her own, entrusted with the task of setting up a network of intelligence-gatherers and couriers; for the first time in her life she found herself hiring people. Her observation work allowed her to use her intelligence and initiative to a greater extent than she ever had been called upon to do since her school days. (She who had been "so very helpless" in ordinary life, now astonished her friends by setting up and directing her spying network "in such a cool and clever way."[2]) Importantly, her new mission awarded her masculine freedoms and she knew it. At some point in late 1915, Hélène Ségard, pleading with her god-daughter to give up her dangerous work, told her that inviting men up to her room would damage her reputation and that her beloved grandfather would not have been proud. Ségard later testified that her god-daughter had thought this reproach over for a moment before giving the dignified answer that "it remains to be seen, Marraine, whether he would not have been proud."[3]

Her sister recalled that Gabrielle had thought nothing of playing cards with men during her intelligence-gathering train trips to Tournai and of treating them familiarly, as comrades—in other words, evincing none of the Catholic *jeune fille*'s bashfulness. Someone who knew her in 1916 described her as having "the free bearing of an American woman."[4] In short, in her war work, she owned space more than she ever had: she had been a drifter, now she was a roaming agent, rendering legible the space of the occupied country; she had been disreputable, poor, and dependent, now she had respectability, money to regale her friends, and a place of her own. Before the war, she had passed under the shadow of Brussels' grand buildings "small" and uncomprehending; now they had been usurped, she told Marie Collet, she grasped what they stood for, and felt they were hers as much as anyone else's.[5]

Petit's war work has never really been mapped out. The relevant chapter in Arthur Deloge's thorough 1922 biography is choppy, unchronological, and relegates much information to footnotes to emphasize uncertainty; he complained about the many loose ends he encountered during his research.[6] Ninety years on, many questions must remain unanswered. The documents—scattered over three archive collections, only one of which was collected with the express aim of documenting war work—present imprecisions and contradictions. The history of several intelligence networks can be written through Belgian lawyers' trial reports, but Petit had no Belgian defender before the military court, and no text of her accusation survives. The records of the German counter-espionage police no longer exist. All reconstructions of Petit's war work, then, must be hedged about with caveats. Still, a consistent narrative emerges. It is that of intelligence work undertaken from August 1915 through January 1916 against a backdrop of ever-more-massive German entrenchment in the West. From the start of the year 1915, the German priority had been to free up troops for the East, which meant turning the Western Front into as "passive" a front as feasible. That required defensive build-up in great depth. By the Fall of 1915, the defensive belt on the front had thickened to three miles.[7] And defense meant two more things. The first one was the closing-off of the hinterland, which was occupied and therefore potentially hostile. *In casu* that entailed closing off the Belgian-Dutch border with an electrified fence from April 1915 onward. The second defensive line was the closing-off from hostile interference of the German military arrangements inside the occupied country. This meant control over the all-important railways running between Germany and the front by the *Militär-Generaldirektion der Eisenbahnen* (which answered to the General Staff, not to the Governor-General). It meant imposing restrictions on movement of people, information, and goods by a system of internal frontiers; this comprised a plethora of rules on passes and permits (with the additional advantage of yielding money from fees and fines), including special restrictions on men of military age. It meant combating all hostile action, including fueling a hostile spirit among the citizenry, preventing fellow occupied from offering their services, smuggling information, helping trapped Entente soldiers or new volunteers escape the country—and gathering information about the German armies in the West.

Such information was, needless to say, crucial for the Entente. "How to advance successfully into a hail of death" was, as the historian Michael Occleshaw has written, the "constant tactical problem." Patrolling and reconnaissance were of limited use on a stalemated front. The fog of trench warfare required its own type of operational intelligence. It was no longer enough to merely locate enemy troops. It had become imperative to identify units, so as to determine what division was holding the trenches opposite, and from there surmise "the enemy's movements and deployment ..., so shedding a chink of much-needed light on to his intentions." Moreover, in light of the war of attrition, it was important to know the nature of the reserves (the men's age, for one thing), so as to gauge Germany's resources in manpower; it was also important to find out what state the troops were in regarding equipment and morale. "In the unavoidably rigid conditions imposed by trench warfare and the strategy of attrition ..., staffs cried out for information on enemy units and their whereabouts in a bid to evolve a response to the baffling new warfare." Direct contact with the enemy was the only way to acquire all of this information.[8] This is where civilians came in. It was fortuitous that the German army's hinterland was located in hostile, or at least latently hostile, territory: civilians could be found to aid the liberating armies even at great risk. (Money played a role, but not a decisive one; I will return to this.) Allied intelligence would eventually recruit some 6,400 agents in the occupied West, mainly Belgium. To this must be added the unknown amount of people offering help in different guises and who do not register in postwar tallies. Spying on the Germans behind the Western Front was not a matter of making spectacular single discoveries; the effort had to be cumulative—in this sense, the 'front' that was military intelligence was no different from other fronts in this war. This was especially true of railway observation, which required the continuous and systematic gathering over a long period of time of similar data (schedule, amount of rolling stock, identifying signs) at several points in the railway network.[9]

The German authorities in the occupied West did not intend to lose on this "front" any more than on the others. In June, eight people were shot in Liège for being, as the German poster formulated it, "members of an organization that transmitted to the enemy information regarding movement of German troops on the railways under military control." The executed had been working for Cameron's bureau at British GHQ. They were the first people to be officially condemned to death and shot for spying. At GHQ in Saint-Omer, Walter Kirke, who did not usually dwell on these things, called it a "tragedy."[10] The poster announcing their sentence and execution was affixed across the length and breadth of the Government-General.[11] Meanwhile, the German police were closing in on the network of Jozef Baeckelmans (the architect from Antwerp recruited in London in early 1915) which was operating at the other end of occupied Belgium, mainly at Saint-Ghislain, an important railway junction between Mons and the French border.[12] In Brussels, "Police Bureau A" (*Polizeistelle A*) which focused on dismantling secret intelligence networks, sent out a Dutch-Belgian mole to infiltrate Baeckelmans' operation. This mole, an architect by trade like Baeckelmans, passed himself off as a courier, managed to get hold of reports to be expedited, and had them photographed at the German police headquarters before delivering them to the unsuspecting Van Tichelen, Wallinger's network chief in Flushing.[13] In late July 1915, Baeckelmans was arrested in Brussels.

Petit started her war work, then, under less than propitious circumstances. Some sources assert that she was sent out to complement or take over Baeckelmans' service.[14] It is unclear whether this was true, indeed whether the Wallinger bureau, or GHQ more generally, intended or was able to achieve systematic coverage.[15] No document indicates specific orders given to Petit. Yet the outlines of her intelligence task emerge from the evidence. She was not given a railway observation post to manage, but instead was tasked with observing the German troops and defenses in a particular area as a "roaming agent".[16] Women, who faced fewer restrictions on mobility than men, may have been in special demand for this kind of roaming observation. Louise de Bettignies, aptly code-named "Ramble," proved extremely competent at it. Working for Cameron's bureau at GHQ, she had by August 1915 managed to indicate all of the main German artillery emplacements around Lille.[17] ("If anything happened to her," wrote Kirke in late September, "it would be nothing less than a calamity."[18])

Petit's geographical remit was the Tournai area, striking out further west all the way to Lille, in other words, the westernmost *Etappe* (staging area) and even the Operations Zone of the German Sixth Army. Both Tournai and Lille were, in German operational parlance, "*Ausladeorten*," i.e., ports of discharge where the troops left the trains, and therefore privileged observation posts for troop movements.[19] She was, in all probability, directed to Tournai because it was her native town and she could make contacts there, while her status as resident of Brussels then enabled her to commute back to the capital with her reports ("taking care of internal transmission herself," as the networks' turn of phrase had it), and send the reports to the Netherlands from there (this was referred to as external transmission).[20] Petit had been given instructions in how to recognize units, troop movement, and infrastructure. Among her papers are two pages of her course notes, taken during her time of instruction in London. They listed the identifying colors on headgear and rosettes (a yellow ribbon on the cap meaning uhlans, and so on), the way to assess the strength of units traveling by train (one had to count fifty men to a railway car, or eight horses, or six field guns), and other key facts. It listed what to look out for—aviation fuel depots, powder stores, artillery ("ordinary field guns or howitzers"), units' arrival and departure, and whether the troops were active, reserves, *Landwehr* (second-line reserves), or *Landsturm* (third-line reserves, the oldest draftees at thirty-nine to forty-five years of age). She was also instructed to report upon the state of the troops and their morale.[21]

Petit's intelligence work spans the time from August 26, 1915, the date of her first trip to Tournai, to February 2, 1916, when she was arrested upon a return from Tournai—a stretch of five months and one week. The general context of this stretch was that of the stalemated, though far from static, war in the West, with the German armies further strengthening their entrenchment, extracting resources from the occupied country to do so, all the while managing enormous movement of men between the Western and Eastern fronts. Petit's first trip was made a month before the doomed British offensive at Loos near Lille. Her last trip concluded as the Germans were preparing the attack on the Verdun salient in the Meuse sector, 300 kilometers south-east of Tournai.

Reports

On August 17, 1915, Petit crossed the Belgian-Dutch border at Rosendaal, north of Antwerp. On the next day, she was back at Marie Collet's in Brussels. She trusted her friend enough to enroll her as her first associate, asking her to take delivery of the instructions that couriers would soon bring in from Flushing and to hand these couriers her own—Petit's—reports twice a week.[22] Once more, Marie Collet helped out her young lodger, and this time at enormous risk. But, now, Petit was able to assist financially to thank her for the years of support. Collet recalled Petit as saying that "now that living becomes expensive, your daughter will be able to help you out a little."[23] (Life *had* become expensive. Though the big surge in prices came only in the spring of 1916, chroniclers already noted that "meat has become rare and costly," soap "worrisomely expensive," and train fares exorbitant.[24]) The money sent from the Netherlands would be welcome. Not that engagement was purely a matter of money. Marie Collet (and her sons, who lent a much-needed hand) could have offered their services to the German police, which was the safer and more lucrative option. They probably acted out of conviction. The mood in Brussels was fiercely patriotic: the celebration of the Belgian national holiday on July 21 was a collective enactment of defiance. At the same time, Collet tried to talk Petit out of taking such extreme risks. Everybody knew that people had already been executed for spying on the Germans and that women were not immune: among the eight people shot at Liège in early June had been a young woman named Louise Derache, née Frenay, the mother of a little boy. Petit declared that the risk did not faze her. In London she had committed herself to "total loyalty," she told Marie Collet, and intended to stick to that pledge.[25] She repeated this statement, later on, to her friend Julia Lallemand, who, as danger was closing in, advised her to quit her life of constant anxiety and leave the occupied country to wait out the war in the Netherlands; Petit replied that her mission was not accomplished yet.[26] Hélène Ségard remembered her god-daughter as shrugging off danger with the words "you only die once."[27] In the worst case, Petit told a cousin in Tournai, she would be buried in her home town, close to her grandparents.[28]

Six days after her return, Petit took the train to Tournai. She was henceforth to make this trip once or twice a week.[29] At 100 kilometers, this was long trip even in peacetime. In wartime it would qualify as an extreme commute. The German army was operating the Belgian railways, reducing Belgians to limited space and limited schedules—if they were allowed to ride trains at all, as depending on military needs they often were not. Train tickets had become very expensive—though Petit's remuneration would have covered that. All movement necessitated passes, paperwork, and payment. Like some other intelligence agents, Petit may have secured a pass as a commercial traveler; she ran commercial errands, partly as a cover. One source claims that she had a pass from the relief commission, but this cannot be proven.[30] (Louise de Bettignies and her second-in-command, Marie-Léonie Van Houtte, had no difficulty either getting permits for their frequent train trips between Lille, Tournai and Brussels.[31])

However arduous, the train ride to Tournai was the easiest part of the trip, since it was still within the area of the Government-General. Two-thirds of the occupied country, including Brussels, fell under this military-civilian regime allowing a certain measure of normalcy, certainly during the first half of the war. But the westernmost third of the country was subjected to a purely military regime. This was the so-called *Etappe*, the staging area of the German Fourth and Sixth Armies, where restrictions on civilian life were considerably more severe, and became more so as one approached the Operations Zone. The boundaries between the Operations Zone and the *Etappe*, and between the *Etappe* and the Government-General, shifted in the course of the war. During the entire war, Tournai found itself in a frontier zone between *Etappe* and Government-General; its regime fluctuated with the situation at the front. During the months of Petit's intelligence work, Tournai proper was administered by the Government-General; Greater Tournai sat astride the border with the *Etappe*. Petit, then, did not have to cross a military frontier in traveling from Brussels to Tournai. But from Tournai to Lille, some thirty kilometers further west, she would at some point have had to cross into the *Etappe*, and from there into the Operations Zone, or at least very near it. Moreover, there were barriers to cross at the Belgian-French border. From Tournai, civilians could not travel by train westward.[32] We do not know by what means Petit reached Lille, but her reports indicate that she relied on the tram, which in those days constituted a very dense network crisscrossing the countryside in Belgium and northern France, and that she walked enormous distances along back lanes and country roads. This ease of movement gave her a sense of exhilaration: "I can weave my way through anything," she wrote in a report.

Having enlisted Marie Collet's help, Petit found another close and trusted collaborator at Tournai: a cousin on her mother's side named Georges Delmeule, whose wife ran a glassware business in the center of town. Delmeule was "a helper worth ten people," she told her godmother.[33] He provided her with information about Tournai and surrounding areas; they walked the town together, observing troops and furtively taking notes. When touring the countryside, Petit took Delmeule's ten-year-old son, Georges junior, with her. With the boy by her side "giving her some bearing," she took down details about field hospitals, artillery emplacements, airfields, and the like in a little notebook. (Once, the boy saw her note the number on a military car and told his parents "cousin Gabrielle" must be a spy; his mother told him never to say such a thing again if he did not want his parents shot, and "the child ever after remained absolutely discreet.")[34] She regularly went to Froyennes, a village northwest of Tournai, now a very heavily guarded railway-distribution center in the *Etappe* where troop trains were directed to their front destination.[35] The place boasted a small, elegant spa, in favor with the troops; Petit used its café as her observation post.[36] When she was in Brussels, Delmeule took over surveillance of troop strength ("as precisely as possible"), length of their stay in and around Tournai, regiment numbers, soldiers' ages, and, "after adroit questioning," information about their upcoming moves. Back in Tournai, Petit took down Delmeule's information in what he remembered as some form of shorthand; he then promptly destroyed his own notes. Petit's notes were made on cigarette-paper, which she rolled into cigarettes (she planned to smoke them if caught), or she would crumple them inside a little medallion that she wore around her neck, a memento from her mother. In return, she ran errands for Delmeule and for the extended family on her mother's side (Tournai tradespeople all) when she was in Brussels. Her postcards to the family, written from Brussels, mix routine business information with scattered little codes referring to her war work. "We immediately took to Gabrielle," her cousin said later, "because of her open and cheerful character. She'd tell us about the tricks she played on the Germans. She was always ready to do us a good turn and ran many errands for me in Brussels."

In order to observe troop movements, which happened mainly after nightfall, she stayed at a modest café with occasional lodging opposite Tournai's main station, where she took notes during the night. Petit's first documented stay there was on August 26, 1915; she left on the following day.[37] Presumably, she then pushed onwards to Lille, from where she sent word to her godmother—a terse message saying "I have arrived." Back in Brussels, she told Ségard that she had succeeded where others had not; the men her superiors had sent had not been able to reach even Tournai. She was aware of other efforts in the field and of the fate of those who were caught. In September, Baeckelmans appeared before a German military court in Brussels, together with his helpers and a friend, Alexander Franck, an Antwerp businessman who had operated a network for Wallinger in the Ghent area. Petit was greatly alarmed, calling their capture "a disaster." Ségard recalled her as saying that "one does not replace heroes like that."[38] She met their distraught relatives and even contacted a Belgian lawyer to represent Baeckelmans.[39] But the defense, barely informed of the charges, could do little. Baeckelmans and Frank were condemned to death on September 14 and executed on the 23rd—the first Belgian spies to be shot at the *Tir National*. Their fate caused a stir. Stories circulated of their heroic attitude before the court, where each had tried to take sole blame.[40]

Hélène Ségard recalled her god-daughter as saying that "we must work all the harder now," and establishing new contacts.[41] She filed three reports before September 21. These took a while to reach their destination. A September 23 message from "Cereal Company" (the code name which Van Tichelen continued to use for his operation—rather unwisely so since it could link Petit to Baeckelmans) expressed "great surprise." A courier had come to collect her reports three times, but had not received anything. Petit was instructed to "please give your correspondence to the bearer of the present message; I will otherwise be forced to break off all commercial relations, to my regret."[42] But a message written one day later expressed satisfaction at having finally received Petit's first three "order forms", as the code term went. Still, once again, the courier had said he had been at Petit's three times and had not been handed any report. "But let us hope that things will go much more smoothly from now on." Cereal Company declared itself, in the obligatory cryptic tone, "happy to hear that nothing fatal will happen to our friends." The message promised 100 francs for every report sent and declared Petit's system of reporting "ideal."[43] Petit's first three reports are now lost, but the three subsequent ones, compiled between September 30 and October 17, have been preserved. The first of these, Petit's fourth report, consists of one large thin sheet of paper, tightly filled with notes in a neat hand, covering observations from September 30 through October 4, 1915.[44]

4th Report   Legrand.

Tournai, today 31 September [*sic*]. City and surrounding area free of troops. A
few reservists guard roads, highways, bridges, etc.; barely 300 in barracks. ... [She
then gave information about the hard-to-identify uniforms of the few reservists
guarding bridges and roads, SdS.] By contrast, hospitals, field hospitals, seminary,
even schools full of wounded soldiers. On Sunday 27, Monday 28 and Wednesday
[*sic*] 29 August [*sic*] there was a steady stream of motor-cars with red crosses. Some
Englishmen and Frenchmen among the mutilated <u>boches</u>. They are very badly hurt,
among others, an officer who is cared for at a private house in town has lost his nose,
as well as his right arm and left leg. Today, the 31st [*sic*], after dinner, violent aerial
fight, ending in allied and enemy [pilot] both going off in the direction of the frontier.

Tournai, 1 October. ... 350 to 400 soldiers have arrived from Charleroi, or so they
claim. If that is so, they must just have been dismissed from hospitals, they look
deathly pale. There is infantry, very young boys with gray caps ... [followed by
details about the uniform, SdS]. They are contemptible and if they are meant to
serve as reinforcements, a woman like me for 3 soldiers and in 2 days one would not
find a trace of them. Every day, they send train waggons to Lille full of entire felled
trees and mortars. To make a little money, civilians of Tournai and surroundings go
to help Germans in Lille fill bags, these latter [the mortars] contain gases.

Tournai, 2 October. This morning, I went to Mont-Saint-Aubert [a hilltop
village a few kilometers north of Tournai, SdS]. All the guns and munitions are
gone, as is the observation post near the church. People coming off the tram from
Péruwelz [a town on the French border midway between Tournai and Valenciennes]
said that there, too, apart from the wounded, there is nothing to see. ... [She
reported that the district commander had ordered all train lines leading to Tournai
from the East to remain open, SdS.] What to think of that!!! [*sic*] ...

[On the next day, 3 October, a Sunday, she mentioned that the 300 to 400
infantrymen mentioned earlier had left or were leaving. Soldiers were leaving in
the direction of Lille; others had been overheard saying they were on their way to
Vimy, others to Lens. She noted their very full backpacks and the absence of a
munitions train.] Airplanes fly over Tournai, they are being gunned, it seems as if
the fire comes from Froyennes, we see the shells, people double up, the pilot runs
circles around the clouds of smoke. Never any damage to the enemy unfortunately.
... [A military marching band was giving a concert on a square in town, SdS.] To
bury the dead probably. ...

These were the German dead from the ill-fated British offensive at Loos, which had
started on September 25 after a four-day artillery offensive. In spite of British numerical
superiority, it was a German victory, demonstrating the superiority of defense at the
tragic cost of what the Germans called "*das Leichenfeld von Loos*" (the field of corpses
at Loos)—16,000 British dead for a narrow two-mile-deep salient. Petit's report gives
an indication of what the aftermath looked like on the other side—the casualties
(which were very heavy on the German side too, among others in the Bavarian infantry

regiment where the young Adolf Hitler served as a regimental runner[45]), the movement of German troops, the reinforcements (described in a tone of bravado that may have been more indicative of her state of mind than properly useful to British GHQ), the emplacement of artillery. She noted the material reinforcement of the German front line—wood, sandbags, gas shells—and local civilians' aid in this, voluntary or not. She observed sorties by Allied airplanes and the riposte by anti-aircraft artillery. The locals would come to resent the air attacks which killed and maimed civilians, as did the anti-aircraft artillery.[46] But as yet, the population still welcomed Allied air raids and pinned great hopes on liberation offensives. On the Entente side, the Loos hecatomb did not yet dent belief in the possibility of a successful breakthrough.[47] Nor was the impregnability of German defenses a foregone conclusion for the Germans themselves.[48] In Brussels, in late September 1915, the occupation authorities were nervous. A German police report depicted the *bruxellois* as ready to riot if the imperial armies suffered setbacks on the fronts.[49]

Petit ended her report by mentioning that she was leaving Tournai for Brussels that morning, October 4, that she would write again soon, and that she was writing the report with her thumb and little finger, having injured the other three fingers. (She added, somewhat self-dramatizingly, that "they may have to amputate my middle finger.") Before her trip, writing out an earlier report, she had knocked over a phial of acid meant to mix invisible ink, and badly burned her fingers. She took off for Tournai anyway, "suffering atrociously," as Delmeule later testified; he and his wife took her to see a doctor, who prescribed an ointment, warning her to expect an abscess.[50] On October 5, she wrote from Brussels to tell them that she had punctured (or, as she put it with her usual bravado, "butchered") the abscess herself, and expected to be healed soon.[51]

She set off for Tournai on that same day. Her fifth report, written in acid on thin white paper—a feat of penmanship—covers October 5 to 10, and documents the thickening of German defenses as one traveled westward, but also the interstices in the German presence.[52] She reported that having found nothing new in Tournai, she had left that same evening for Lille. (In fact, as she told her godmother, she had been followed on the train to Tournai by a woman *Polizei* agent, but had managed to shake her off in Tournai and left immediately for Lille.[53]) The rest of the journey "was made in stages, of course." Between Tournai and the village of Templeuve one mile from the border, she noticed some reserve troops, "the same as at Tournai." Further west, as she crossed the Belgian-French border between Templeuve and Roubaix, the region became "gray with uniforms", but she had heard that their presence varied: "One day, there are plenty of them; on the next, no-one." She noticed uhlans, reserve infantry, and a hundred or so cavalry, "between 25 and 35 years old," well outfitted and of good morale. Moving west in the direction of Marcq-en-Baroeul, fifteen kilometers from the front, she observed trenches going in a northeast direction. They were off-limits, but she had heard that they contained munitions and other war *matériel*. From Marcq, she went east again to Wasquehal, where there was an off-limits airfield; she noticed planes on the 7th, but could not give further details. Further on, she noticed a munitions works. On the evening of the 7th, having moved west again, she arrived at Lille: "nothing but soldiers here, of different categories. Cannot give even approximate amount of the troops that are awaiting their departure here." She gave details about their uniforms, such as the "<u>extra-flat</u> caps" of the infantry, worn by "twenty-year olds, real kids [*gamins*], professing much insouciance." She noticed that outfit and morale looked "rather good." She noted machine-guns in the trees of one of Lille's boulevards and on a church tower, gave details about the placement of telegraph installations, and mentioned that munitions were stored at the railway station. Doors and windows shook with explosions. The wounded, who arrived daily, were re-evacuated swiftly. The coming winter threatened famine for the locals; there was "almost no food." On the 8th, passing by Ronchin, south of Lille, she noted that a great many German wounded (from a railway accident on the 6th) had been taken in all over the village. She gave further details about the strengthening of trenches in the region. She was back in Tournai in the afternoon of Sunday, October 10.

She then probably returned to Brussels to write up her report. On the 12th, the day of the execution of Edith Cavell, she was back in Tournai for what seems to have been a fairly grueling reconnaissance trip athwart the Belgian-French border, much of it on foot. This, her sixth report, noted "young infantrymen" arriving from Lille for three days' rest at Tournai before leaving for Ypres. On the 13th, in the afternoon, she observed four Lille-bound munitions trains with ten to fifteen wagons each, though could not give details as the wagons were "carefully covered." An aircraft hangar was going up at Chéreng, over the French border. Tournai's highest-located church, Saint-Brice, now housed an observation-post. The General Staff of Sixth Army had established itself at Froyennes since the 6th. On the 14th, word was that Tournai would return to the *Etappe*. She was unfazed by the possible blockade: "I know the area well." Something seemed afoot: trains and cars departed all night long, officers were roused at night for departure, but she could not indicate where they were sent to. "They are very cautious; inside the stations and on the trains, the military are told not to talk, for fear of providing information to the spies who slip through everywhere." By contrast, on the 15th, there was nothing to observe. The day after, it "rained" arrests of civilians who refused to work for the enemy. (Even though an all-out forced labor regime would not be introduced until the Fall of 1916, more-or-less-coerced work arrangements in the service of the German defense were ubiquitous in the hinterland.) On that day, she walked from Tournai to Orchies across the border in France, so crossing into the *Etappe*; on the way, she made detours past several villages and hamlets southwest of Tournai, noting anti-aircraft machine-gun batteries in the woods. As she made her way southeast towards the village of Rongy on the French-Belgian border, locals alerted her not to go further because the forest down the road was cordoned off with barbed wire. She proceeded to Orchies, where, on the next day, October 17, she noticed 700 to 800 soldiers, ages twenty-five to thirty-five, sporting "good outfits and morale."[54]

"External Transmission"

It was one thing to travel to western Belgium and northern France, weave her way across the border and back again, roam city and countryside, take notes, get herself back to

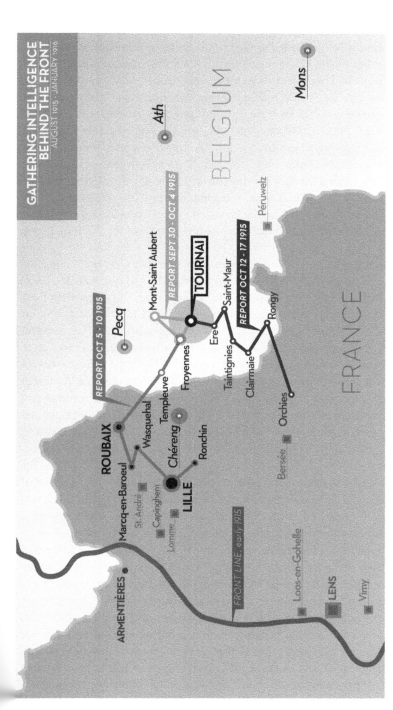

This map is based on an excerpt from the map "Die Westfront bei Beginn des Jahres 1915—Abschnitt der deutschen 4. und 6. Armee," from the postwar series *Der Weltkrieg 1914–1918* (Berlin, Reichsarchiv, 1924). It shows Petit's intelligence-gathering forays behind the German Sixth Army front. The circles indicate places she visited personally. The squares indicate places about which she gathered information without necessarily traveling there.

Map copyright Helga Boeye. Base map: copyright Donald W. Hamer Maps Library at the Pennsylvania State University.

Map 1 Gathering Intelligence Behind the Front, August 1915 to January 1916

Brussels, and write up her findings. It was another thing to get these findings to the Netherlands and receive instructions and funds. Successive messages from Flushing indicate that communications remained arduous. One message from Cereal Company, written between October 14 and 17, expressed surprise that she had not yet received any money, since large sums had been sent—100 francs on October 8 and another 500 on October 14. (Even though the French intelligence services noted that "the English are not nearly as generous as some of their men would have you believe," this was good money—even in the inflated circumstances one year into the war, when, for instance, a kilo of black soap that sold for 40 centimes before the war now cost 1 franc 80.[55] The money was sent in Belgian franc notes, which she asked Delmeule to convert to marks.[56]) The manager—probably Van Tichelen's co-director at Flushing—mentioned that "we now have another conduit who, let us hope, will function regularly"; he meant a new courier, who would bring another 300 francs "to count towards your next order forms. I have received word that [the organization] is satisfied with you; so, continue in the same manner."[57]

The next message from the Netherlands, written sometime after October 17, suggests that Petit had notified Flushing that she had sent the fourth, fifth, and sixth reports. "Dear Miss," Thuysbaert wrote, "we are very happy to hear from you; so, [it is clear then that] you only await our instructions to bravely set to work again." The 100 francs, sent on October 8, had come back; Cereal Company forwarded them to her again "because you are owed them." The 500 francs had to be given up as lost. Thuysbaert did not dwell on it, stating instead that communications were set to improve: "I think we will now have a serious man who will transmit your order forms to us." This courier would present himself twice a week at "number 61 at the chaussée" (meaning Chaussée d'Anvers 61, at Marie Collet's). Thuysbaert added another 100 francs "for encouragement" and reassured Petit that she would receive what she was owed. He ended by wishing her "bon courage" and hoped to receive further "order forms" soon.[58]

All of this shows how hard it was to get reports, instructions, and funds into and out of the occupied country. The Belgian-French border area, though close to the front, was more fluid than the cordoned-off border between occupied Belgium and the neutral Netherlands. External transmission had to rely on specialists of border passage—men recruited among smugglers, a traditional occupation in the border zone. (Kirke had noted in early June that such professional smugglers "have the monopoly and make the necessary arrangements with the sentries."[59]) But since these smugglers were receptive to counter-offers—and the German army paid better—intelligence and escape organizers started to recruit residents of border villages to get messages and people across.[60] The members of these clandestine passage networks were reimbursed for their costs but not much more. (One of them testified after the war that his switch from freelance to patriotic passage work had not been exactly lucrative, and much riskier: he had to pay expenses out of pocket, since his per diem did not suffice, and was badly beaten after his arrest.[61])

Although the Petit documents do not offer much precision about that part of the organization, they seem to evince a similar pattern towards reliance on a border network.

Nothing much is known about the first courier, one Fernand Van Andruel, save that after having transmitted Petit's first reports, he was only able to pick up her reports irregularly, though he was the one who informed the Flushing bureau of her arrest in February 1916.[62] Another intermediary during the first month (or so) of Petit's intelligence work was a Dutchman—no document mentions a name—who operated a riverboat down the Scheldt-Brussels canal. Petit was able to use his services thanks to an old acquaintance: Laure Butin, the owner of the fur store where she had worked between 1910 and 1912. Butin, who worked for British intelligence herself (she received a medal after the war), claimed that she had not contributed much to Petit's service, other than telling her to be prudent, and, importantly, helping Petit smuggle her reports out of the country. Butin had received a crucial tip from a cousin, an engineer named Joseph Dasveld who ran a relief organization for the small town of Kapelle-op-den-Bos, twenty-three kilometers north of Brussels, heavily shelled in the summer of 1914. One day, Dasveld was offered a lift back from Kapelle to Brussels on the canal by a Dutch riverboat captain. The man offered to take reports across the border for pay. Though the bargeman (whose name Butin did not know) "was most often drunk," and his boat was used for transport by occupation troops, it seemed too good an opportunity to pass up. When in Brussels, the boat was moored at a canal around the corner from the Chaussée d'Anvers. Rather ingeniously, Dasveld hid the reports in the wall of the water tank of the ship's toilet. "The Germans who inspected the boat so very thoroughly never thought to take apart the WC, which on Mr. Dasveld's advice was deliberately left in a state of unparalleled filth— moreover, the little room was aired as little as possible so the Germans would not linger." The ploy worked for a while. However, at some point, the captain disappeared; the crew said he had been arrested in the Netherlands for theft. His successor threatened to denounce Butin and Dasveld if they did not hand him 1,000 francs. Pretending to agree, they stayed away on the appointed date and never went near the docks again. They never again heard from their would-be blackmailer.[63]

Thus ended a communications line that was at any rate not very efficient, judging from Cereal Company's messages. At some point in October 1915, it was replaced by another painstakingly assembled transmission arrangement. A new courier appeared; Marie Collet remembered him as a farmer from the Flemish-Dutch border area. She never asked his name and he never volunteered. This man was Theodoor Broeckx, thirty-four, from the small town of Neerpelt, ninety kilometers east of Antwerp, just five kilometers south of the Dutch border and the electric fence. Broeckx served as courier between Brussels and the border region. He had been recruited by a fellow inhabitant of Neerpelt, a 31-year-old baker named Frans Laukens, known for his savvy in getting people and documents across the border. Laukens himself had been tapped for Cereal Company in September 1915 by a Belgian train guard, one Jozef Vandewalle, who lived in Valkenswaard across the border (he had fled to the Netherlands at the start of the war). A "not very commendable" character, according to a postwar report, Vandewalle had in 1915 started to offer his cross-border recruiting services to every imaginable intelligence network "simultaneously or successively," which multiplied the risks of infiltration.[64]

As Marie Collet would later relate it, through the Fall of 1915, twice a week, Broeckx, nicknamed "*den boer*" (the peasant), in his hobnailed boots trudged up the rickety stairs to her apartment to deliver instructions and cigarette-paper from Flushing, and to pick up Petit's reports. After Madame Collet dried his clothes and fed him a meal, one of her sons, Alphonse Anneet, led him out of the house (trying to avoid the curious stares of the baker on the first floor), guided him through Brussels to pick up other reports, and then brought him to safe lodgings in the neighborhood. Broeckx usually departed around six in the morning on the next day, sometimes after having picked up Petit's latest report, written in the night. The reports, written on cigarette-paper, were slid into a matchbox or even in a pipe, re-covered with tobacco. Then, Broeckx went on his way back to Neerpelt, a 110-kilometer haul made along back lanes and with many detours.[65]

At some point that Fall, the pace of Petit's reports for Cereal Company seemed to slacken. Her activities after mid-October are difficult to date with precision. They seem to have been manifold; her friend Julia described her as extremely busy. Aside from her intelligence work, Petit apparently lent a hand where she could; she took on charitable work for prisoners of war, and she still dutifully collected funds for the Red Cross. On November 1, a blustery All Saints' Day, she stayed out collecting at the cemetery all day, Hélène Ségard recalled. (She remembered it because of her dread that her niece had been arrested, and because Petit came back with a bad cold.[66]) On November 24, Petit went to visit her friend Julia. These are the only dated events for November. Not even her bread-ration card shows any activity; its last stamp dates from October 22.[67] Her railway subscription card, which might have shed some light on her comings and goings, was preserved after the war, but may now be lost.[68] There is no trace of Petit's seventh report, written at some point between October 18 and November 29. Her eighth report, covering November 30 and December 1, was far less extensive than the earlier ones, though the document preserved may be a fragment, or even just a draft. It contains terse notes, presumably taken in and around Lille, about the military she saw on the train, the heavy presence of troops in Saint-André (a village north of Lille), and about requisitioning of civilian goods—cotton, bed sheets, horses.[69] This little report was immediately followed by a ninth, covering December 2 through 4, containing observations made in Tournai. She noted troop movements by train, the passing of cars from the *Commission for Relief in Belgium* ("with the [Belgian] national flag on the hood," a sight rare enough that she noted it), the evacuation of wounded to Péruwelz, the departure of a regiment of *Jäger* from Tournai garrison (but she could not indicate where they went), and a westbound trainload of trees felled in the woods east of Tournai. She returned to Brussels on December 4.[70]

Around that time, in early December, she moved out of her sublet at Marie Collet's. The owner of the house evicted her, ostensibly because of overdue rent, possibly out of suspicion over Petit's activities. She took a furnished room nearby, in the rue du Théâtre. Since there was little traffic in this narrow street, couriers would have been too conspicuous, and so Marie Collet's apartment on the busy Chaussée d'Anvers continued to serve as "letter-box."[71] Petit was as busy as ever. On December 16, "in mid-gallop," she wrote to the Delmeules in Tournai to inform them about errands she ran for them in

Brussels. She told them that she would arrive in Tournai on the 20th. Her next trip probably happened as announced. She was back in Brussels on the 22nd, being on duty, as she wrote to the Delmeules, at "Aunt Cunegonda's"—an oblique reference to her superiors at Flushing.[72]

On New Year's Day, 1916, Broeckx picked up the correspondence at Marie Collet's as usual. He was, as she recalled later, "very worried": a companion of his had been arrested the day before.[73] Collet never saw Broeckx again. On January 4, he and Laukens were arrested near Liège. Laukens was able to get away, rather dashingly so: escorted to the border zone by the military police to show where exactly he crossed the fence, he managed to escape, stayed hidden in the bush, then made his way to the Netherlands.[74] Broeckx remained under arrest, and, though he was never formally condemned, spent the rest of the war in captivity: he was sent to prison in Germany without trial and remained imprisoned until shortly before the Armistice, including a year and a half in a forced-labor gang behind the front in France.[75]

The two men were part and parcel of a larger collective effort: that of tunneling clandestine circuits underneath the many frontiers erected by the Germans in Belgium. Such circuits emerged across the occupied country and for a variety of purposes: smuggling correspondence to and from the Belgian army at the front, distributing forbidden publications, helping soldiers and volunteers escape, and gathering and transmitting clandestine military intelligence. The intelligence services were not really dissociated from those other clandestine circuits; many agents engaged in a range of underground activities.[76] Petit was no exception; even if the range of her war work cannot be ascertained, she does not seem to have limited herself to secret intelligence. (Louise de Bettignies too did both intelligence and escape work.) Julia Lallemand would say after the war that Petit "was involved in everything," including the *Mot du soldat,* the clandestine network transmitting messages between families and soldiers in the Belgian army. Julia herself helped Petit gather volunteers to guide across the border. One of them was a son of Marie Collet's, Jean Anneet, who did not get across—he was arrested at the border and sent to a prison camp in Germany.[77] (All three of Collet's sons were involved in resistance activities.) Petit was said to have been arrested on one such occasion and held overnight in Mol, near the border.[78] She also distributed Belgium's most famous clandestine newspaper, *La Libre Belgique,* which worked to keep up Belgians' hopes in liberation. Yet she "did not think she was making herself all that useful in carrying the *Libre Belgique* around," as her godmother later recalled; rather, "she delivered it at the Boches' [probably at the *Kommandantur,* SdS] to be sure that Von Beau-Singe [Von Bissing, a play on words meaning "Pretty Monkey," SdS] gets it, [and she said], if need be I'll bring it myself to make him see red—the Boche detests being made fun of." Petit, in other words, seems to have considered the clandestine press' role in keeping the Belgians' spirits up less important than its capacity to rile the Germans. Her boast that she just might deliver the paper to Von Bissing directly would be a centerpiece in her postwar legend.[79] That she was indeed one of the hundreds of people working for the *Libre Belgique,* is proven.[80] It exposed her to additional risks. On one occasion, in early January

1916, on her way to deliver copies at a distributor's near La Cambre wood in Brussels, she found herself followed, shook off her pursuer by taking a secluded lane through the wood, and delivered the parcel. The distributor went to check on her two days later. An all-out hunt for *Libre Belgique* couriers started in the second week of January.[81] Petit had avoided that trap, at least. She would not remain safe for long.

On January, 9 1916, a new courier presented himself at Marie Collet's. The downstairs neighbor's young daughter gave away Petit's all-too-transparent alias ("I am looking for Miss Legrand"—"There is no Miss Legrand here, but there's a Miss Petit") before Collet could intervene. At that point, her sons had grown worried over the risks she ran and they saw how the incessant comings and goings exhausted her. Alphonse refused to guide couriers around any longer. Petit had agreed to henceforth handle the couriers herself at her own lodgings in the rue du Théâtre. So, Collet, breaking habit, guided the new courier to Petit's lodgings.[82]

After the disappearance of Broeckx, Gabrielle had started to feel ensnared, as Marie Collet and Julia Lallemand later testified; and she did not quite trust the new courier, who insouciantly showed up in broad daylight, unlike the cautious Broeckx. She told Collet, shortly after the encounter, that she regretted having given this new man her reports, or, at least, some of them—she had held back a part of her notes and planned to send those off by another route. Not feeling safe any longer, she intended to make only one or two more journeys. She told her godmother that she mistrusted the new courier because he had asked her not to fold her reports, but roll them up. (She also said that she had mistrusted him for having arrived late and hung over.)[83]

By then, she was also working outside of the Tournai-Lille axis, a part of her observation work hard to map; scattered sources name dates and associates, but these cannot be confirmed. One postwar report mentions that she traveled to the railway hubs of Namur and Mons to gather information.[84] According to her godmother, Petit had received orders not to travel to Tournai and to stay away from Brussels, and from late October 1915 liaised with other intelligence networks active in other sectors; this can neither be proven nor disproven.[85] One message locates her in Antwerp in mid-January 1916 on orders from Flushing. She let the Delmeules know that she was "overburdened with work" and unable to come "visit my native city. This is most annoying, as I was rather hoping for Aunt Anastasia [her superiors] to grant me a little leave & right then she gives me enough [work] to make me catch meningitis. I will shut up from now on, since the more I gripe, the more the work is piled on.... Otherwise, all goes well, as I am being assured every day." She hinted that she was not yet "allowed to return to Tournai."[86] But on the 20th, she notified her cousins—as ever "in mid-gallop"—that she would arrive in Tournai on the 24th, and to let her know if they needed anything from Brussels. On the 24th and 25th, she stayed at her usual pension, possibly pushing on to Lille afterward.[87]

The *Musée du Folklore* in Tournai has Petit's last report, or notes taken for her last report. The barely legible scrawls on a small sheet of cigarette-paper cover the days between January 26 or 27 and the 31st. One of them mentions Allied aviators taking down a Zeppelin near Ath on January 30.[88] On the evening of February 1, she sent the Delmeules word from Brussels that she had found the time to pick up some glassware for them—which she promised to deliver at the end of the week—because "Aunt Catherine" had not shown up (in other words, the courier had not come to collect her report). She expected her "aunt" on the next morning, February 2.[89]

On that day, she was arrested. She had been right in suspecting the new courier; he was a mole. He had transmitted her reports to the German police from the start—he had probably asked her not to fold her reports so they would be easier to photograph—and had been spying on the Chaussée d'Anvers "letter-box." It was unclear at the time who the infiltrator was. The bureau in Flushing was informed of Petit's arrest through Van Andruel, the sometime courier; he gave the name of a Belgian mole. That man (one Wépiar or Wypior, from the village of Ougrée near Liège, a known double agent as it turned out later) was, at the time, unknown at the bureau, and the agents were unable to investigate further. Van Tichelen declared after the war that Wépiar/Wypior could not have been the infiltrator. At some point in 1921, it was established that the mole was a Dutchman from Maastricht named Nikolaas Keurvers, well-known for having infiltrated other networks through 1916.[90]

External transmission was the weak part of any intelligence operation. By the summer of 1916, it had become known in Belgian secret intelligence circles that Maastricht was a hub of German counter-intelligence and that courier moles were launched from there. The German consulate there employed some forty people—over half of them Dutch, ten German and half a dozen Belgian—to infiltrate Allied intelligence networks. Agents also knew by now that "betrayals almost always happened through the couriers." In Liège, an important network working for British GHQ was infiltrated by the same Nikolaas Keurvers; the main agent, Dieudonné Lambrecht, was executed on April 18, 1916.[91] Lambrecht's death cast a long shadow, for it generated a far-reaching renewal of intelligence work. His self-designated successors started a new network, known as *La Dame Blanche* after the legendary white ghost said to herald the end of the Hohenzollern dynasty. It would become arguably the most important secret intelligence operation of the First World War in any theater. The name was the only romantic touch to this network: it was put on a sternly professional footing, with little space for dash and improvisation. Concluding that Lambrecht had done too much himself (including some external transmission tasks), and that too many associates had known him personally, the leaders of the *Dame Blanche* took care not to enter into direct contact with their agents, let alone with their couriers. Agents were instructed not to take on additional tasks—such as work for clandestine newspapers. In addition, the *Dame Blanche* organizers were able to rely on a highly efficient external transmission network set up for them by the British War Office's secret services. But this was not in place until July 1917.[92]

Petit never had that luxury; she had to rely on more haphazard courier services, in the end against her own misgivings. (Ségard recalled that Petit, shortly before her arrestation, had inveighed bitterly against "the ones in Holland who are safe behind the border and betray us and steal from us," contrasting them with the English, "valiant soldiers that one enjoys working with." She remembered her god-daughter as saying that "the English are gentlemen, they are really splendid, are the English—if only I could work with the chiefs directly!"[93]) Nor was she able to follow her own plan to close off her identity and whereabouts from Madame Collet's home (the "letter-box") and hence from the couriers, because the sons Anneet had—quite justifiably, on their end—refused to run further risks and dissuaded their mother. In sum, Petit was done in by a combination of all-too-permeable external transmission, and a flagging of her informal support network.

Counter-espionage

From the Fall of 1915, the clandestine circuits had been running into mounting difficulties while the German police grew in strength.[94] Petit's intelligence work pitted her against three different German police corps: the Secret Field Police, the Military Police, and, most importantly, the Political Police. The Secret Field Police (*Geheime Feldpolizei*) was operating in the Operations Zone, the staging areas (*Etappengebiet*) and the Navy-occupied zone (*Marinegebiet*), in other words, in northern France, westernmost Belgium, and on the Belgian coast. In those areas, which were placed under stricter military authority than was the civilian-military hybrid of the Government-General, the *Geheime Feldpolizei* went after networks of intelligence, escape, and recruitment. Within the Government-General, the largest and most visible German police corps was the Military Police (*Militärpolizei*), 1,000 men strong in Greater Brussels alone by 1917, not counting the 700 troops patrolling the railway stations and tracks. These were all largely *Landwehr* and *Landsturm* reserves. The Military Police kept watch over the German troops stationed in and transiting through Brussels, a city used as a "rest and recreation" area, with much potential for disturbances and desertion. And, of course, the Military Police kept order among the occupied population. After the invasion weeks with their bursts of extreme violence, routine occupation had been established in the Fall of 1914. Violence was now highly contained, at least until the mass deportations of forced laborers from the Fall of 1916. But repression was rampant, in the form of heavy fines, prison sentences for minor offenses, deportation without trial to Germany of recalcitrants, and highly publicized executions of Belgians convicted of war treason. As far as the occupation authorities were concerned, the situation always had the potential to degenerate. In October 1915, Governor-General Von Bissing complained to the Brussels municipal government that he had been obliged to protect the back of the German army during the recent Entente offensives; some weeks later, the *Libre Belgique* gleefully reported that Von Bissing had berated the municipal authorities on the locals' "unjustified hostility" against the military quartered in the city, and had mentioned that "the population of Brussels has in many cases actively aided enemy intelligence." The *bruxellois*' forbidden celebration of the Belgian national holiday on July 21, 1915 had vexed German police circles, as I have mentioned above; in response, the *Militärpolizei* of Greater Brussels strengthened its arsenal, and machine-gun automobiles circulated menacingly through the city on July 21, 1916.[95]

Much less visible was the Political Police (*Politische Polizei*), a much smaller corps (122 agents in mid-1915, 172 in mid-1917), supervised and partly staffed by policing professionals, complemented by Germans with local knowledge and by Belgian, Dutch, and French informers. The Government-General was divided up into political police districts. Specialized units policed passages across the Dutch frontier, the recruitment of volunteers for the Belgian army, the hiding of Entente soldiers, correspondence-smuggling, and the distribution of underground publications. In Brussels, one unit, *Polizeistelle A Brüssels* ("Brussels Bureau A"), concentrated on counter-intelligence; *Polizeistelle B* specialized in dismantling recruitment and escape networks, and contended with secret correspondence and the clandestine press. Similar units operated elsewhere in the Government-General.[96] The Charleroi bureau, for instance, included one particularly competent deputy, an Alsatian whose parents had long been established in Brussels; in 1916, this man managed to contact all of British GHQ's unsuspecting network managers in the Netherlands.[97] One year into the occupation, counter-resistance policing—both the counter-intelligence and the counter-recruitment branches—had been honed to a high level of expertise. This paid off in a spate of arrests and executions during the summer and Fall of 1915. Baeckelmans and Franck were arrested by *Polizeistelle A* in late July 1915 and executed on September 23. Edith Cavell was arrested by *Polizeistelle B* on August 4 and executed, together with Philippe Baucq, on October 12. On October 29, a Brussels police agent, Pierre Poels, was shot for having plotted, in September, to blow up railway lines carrying German troops to the Champagne battlefields. (One may note in passing that the willingness of Poels and others to take on such extreme risks connotes confidence in the final liberation offensive—and that dismantling this plot once more demonstrated German defensive strength.) Overall, the last trimester of 1915 signaled a new harshness, with a total of forty-five executions, including that of Léon Trulin, an intelligence agent for Cameron's bureau, shot in Lille on November 8, 1915; he was sixteen.[98] These trials and executions were the result of a massive police effort, the German internal line of defense. One of the results of this police effort was the "calamity" so feared by Walter Kirke at British GHQ in Saint-Omer: on October 20, his best agent, Louise de Bettignies, was arrested at Froyennes near Tournai. Months of thorough investigation followed; De Bettignies was not put on trial until March 16 of the following year.

Petit's war work, then, was conducted at a time when clandestine networks, whatever the quality of their individual agents, were no match yet for the German police. The railway sabotage plan involving the policeman Poels, for instance (see above), was an ill-conceived scheme, masterminded, if that is the word, by French Intelligence (which was very keen on it: "I hold to this operation enormously and ask you to use all your energy to make it happen," as one bureau chief wrote to a network head in the Netherlands), and infiltrated almost from the start by German counter-intelligence, after which the imprudence of associates in Brussels sealed Poels' fate.[99] He went to his death bravely, yet bitterly regretting his involvement in the plot.[100] Such disproportions struck some as irresponsible, not to say criminal. There *was* something quixotic in occupied civilians' willingness to court extreme danger by working against their occupiers. Certainly this was the opinion of the prominent Brussels lawyer Sadi Kirschen, a naturalized Belgian born in Iași whose brother fought in the Romanian army. Kirschen was one of a small group of Belgian lawyers allowed—under very limiting conditions—to defend many of the accused before the German military tribunals. He covered all of the major cases from that of Edith Cavell and Philippe Baucq (executed in October 1915) to that of Georges Kugé (the son of a German watchmaker in Hainaut, executed in May 1917 for secret intelligence) and saw up close the despair and devastation of civilians trapped in the net of a military power. Consequently, Kirschen was scathing in his condemnation of the network chiefs in the Netherlands, "undisciplined, incompetent tattlers," whose bureaux were easy prey for German counter-espionage, and who from their safe perches thought nothing of putting in danger the lives of civilians. Writing during the second half of the war, Kirschen bitterly predicted that, once the nation would be able to "pay its debt towards its children," the network chiefs would reap the honors, while the field in occupied Belgium would be littered with the executed and with people broken by prison.

To boot, it was all for nothing, or at least for very little, as far as Kirschen was concerned. In his view, military intelligence ought to be gathered by military specialists who knew what they were looking for; sending out civilians only resulted in "derisory reports and ridiculous statistics."[101] Some in secret intelligence circles echoed this assessment: one operative in the Netherlands, for instance, claimed that Baeckelmans' reports had little value because he had received only rudimentary instructions.[102] Yet this operative also claimed that Baeckelmans randomly compiled reports, which was incorrect: he systematically tallied railway traffic along a crucial East-West axis. As the historian of resistance Emmanuel Debruyne has observed, Kirschen may have underestimated the usefulness of the information because the accused would have downplayed it themselves; and he may have overestimated networks' permeability because he only saw the arrested agents.[103] One should note that Kirschen himself established differences, calling Baeckelmans and Franck mere amateurs—albeit heroic ones—compared to some other networks; and that he knew nothing about the vast, effective underground network of the *Dame Blanche*. The German bureaux, for their part, considered the secret intelligence networks in the West effective enough. One German analyst after the war testified to the density of intelligence in occupied Belgium:

> enemy espionage covered the Belgian territories occupied by us with an extremely tight net, and each time we ripped apart some of its links, the holes were immediately filled in. For nowhere, at any time, it seems to me, have people spied more fanatically and with more of a spirit of sacrifice than, precisely, in Belgium.[104]

Admittedly, stressing Belgian spy networks' strength may have been meant to emphasize the enemy's disloyal methods. Still, this appraisal implies that the effectiveness of secret intelligence also consisted in its Hydra-like quality—in the fact that, over and above the failure of separate networks, and in spite of or precisely because of the fate of individual agents, secret intelligence seemed impossible to stamp out. It also suggests the symbolic weight of secret intelligence as an indicator of civilians' determination to reclaim invaded space.

How to gauge the effectiveness of Petit's work? The messages from Cereal Company seem to indicate that she was appreciated by the organizers. A fellow agent, Marthe Doutreligne, a fiercely patriotic mayor's daughter who was Baeckelmans' fiancée and a close friend of Franck's sister, and took over the Franck network after his execution, stated after the war that Petit filed altogether "some fifty reports containing general information" with Cereal Company. (Doutreligne may have itemized Petit's daily messages as separate reports.) She also states that Petit's service had been "a good one."[105] The German military assumed her work was solid. "The condemned woman," as one report, drawn up after her trial, had it, "has been an energetic and, it would seem, successful spy"; another highlighted the praise she received from her network chiefs.[106] In 1931, the German military prosecutor at Petit's trial, Eduard Stoeber, described Petit as a figure worthy of remembrance who stood out among many "unmeritorious and even cowardly" defendants; he stated that she had been, "without a doubt, as the military court concluded, a great spy"—if perhaps not quite so great as postwar descriptions, including German ones (he meant Binder, the author of the fanciful account mentioned above), had it.[107] In 1919, a Belgian journalist lauded the precision of her reports; taken separately, they might look inconsequential, but they were priceless when read in sequence.[108] (During the war, the apparently trifling nature of civilian actions did not stand in the way of patriotic praise. The fact that many civilians, each in their own sphere, mustered their feeble resources to limit the remit of military authority was considered a cause for hope in itself, regardless of efficiency. "Let us admire! Let us admire without reserve!" wrote one provincial councilman in October 1914. "Think of the sheer number of actions undertaken—trifling in appearance, but ennobled by the goal! How they testify to the valor of this country that is determined not to die, that mobilizes all of its resources and bravely resists the boot that wants to crush it!"[109])

Petit was a "roaming" observer, sent out to report on a variety of enemy actions (troop movements, morale, and equipment, the location of airfields, and so on), unlike the static railway observation posts that collected the same kind of information continuously. The Jesuit Henri Philippart, a secret intelligence organizer in the Tournai region, described her work as general reportage.[110] Judging from the praise given to Louise de Bettignies, this method could be very fruitful.

It also offered a symbolic counterpoint to the ever-constricting space in the occupied country. Though hardly as glamorous as postwar accounts would have it, Petit's action had its moments: her cousin Georges Delmeule reported that he had seen her cross a barred bridge over the river Scheldt in Tournai in full view of the sentry, dancing and laughing; on another occasion, in the café near Tournai station where she stayed nights, he witnessed her playfully taking the cap off a German soldier to quickly check the regiment number inside (the numbers on the outside were hidden by a strip of cloth) while keeping up a steady stream of banter. "She knew enough. She had her information." It is perhaps significant that those who knew her in those months described her as capable and upbeat (a mood reflected in her appearance, as Hélène Ségard stressed: "in

Figure 3 Petit in the winter of 1915–1916
Brussels, Royal Army Museum, Prints Cabinet

spite of her hectic life she was always very neat and very soignée"). Julia Lallemand could not get over her friend's new-found resourcefulness, since she remembered Petit's despondent drifting of the prewar years.[111]

Between her intelligence trips, distributing clandestine papers, helping people leave the country, and her work on behalf of POWs, Petit kept up a frantic pace. Her agenda for the better-documented weeks, such as the first week of October 1915, shows a phenomenally busy schedule. Those who knew her, testified to it.

Going on her trips, indefatigable, even in the most bitter cold, in the middle of a thousand dangers that she realized full well, she was always figuring out how to get her reports to destination. Then finding out she had to change everything around, she did not lose heart but thought up a new plan, if this doesn't work then something else will, she said.[112]

Her time out west was equally draining. The sleepless nights spent trainwatching from the window of her dingy lodgings at Tournai exhausted her.[113] The notes sent to the Delmeules—"in between two trains", "triple gallop"—showed pride in this busyness. Though she remained aware of danger: "such a life, such anxiety!" her godmother recalled.[114]

Hélène Ségard insisted after the war that her god-daughter was much more understated than her portrayals had it. On one occasion, she recalled, Petit had gone out of her way to evacuate a Frenchwoman whose husband had been arrested for espionage and who feared for her safety. Ségard had berated her for putting herself at even more risk for the sake of others. "She looked at me, kissed me and did not respond; as I have told you, Gabrielle acted, she gave her all, she talked little."[115] Yet the sometimes vehement and personal tone of her reports (especially of the fourth one, see above) suggests a somewhat more theatrical modus operandi, in tune with her choice of alias. Word among agents was that she talked too much.[116] Philippart—who, admittedly, never worked with Petit and never met her—suggested that she was not real spy material: "full of exuberance, enthusiastic, and deeply generous, she might have lacked the taciturnity needed for such an enterprise. Her family suspected what she was doing, since she did not exactly hide it; but energetic and indomitable as she was, they knew well that she would never betray anyone."[117]

She would not, indeed, name any names during her interrogations. Since she was put on trial virtually alone (see Chapter Four), it is not clear what kind of organization she had built up. Postwar lore had it that hundreds of people worked under her orders. The well-documented Deloge, who generally steered clear of exaggerations, wrote that she "developed her creation [oeuvre], recruited a great many helpers, and finally assembled all of the strands of her organization in Brussels."[118] By contrast, her fellow agents Henri Philippart and Marthe Doutreligne wrote that she worked essentially alone.[119] The archives shed light only—and even that intermittently—on her informal support networks: the Delmeules in Tournai and the Collets in Brussels. Does this mean these were the only people Petit worked with (apart from her "external transmission" couriers, like Broeckx)? Petit's file at the Belgian State Archives seems to have contained a list of agents at some point; it is now lost.[120] It is unclear whether Petit's service was linked to any other.[121] It is, therefore, hard to conclude whether she did indeed work alone. Given her postwar fame, one might have expected collaborators to come forward after the war, and to figure in the dossier that was compiled on her war work in 1920–1921 (see Chapter Seven). On the other hand, the dossier tends to under-report her network: Julia Lallemand, for instance, is barely mentioned.[122] A few figures crop up, both in relation to her intelligence and her escape work, but remain unnamed ("a lady from Lille," "an agent with a large dog in Namur") or cannot be identified.[123] She herself noted, in prison, that she had been arrested together with Marie Collet, two of Collet's sons, and another man—whom I have not been able to identify.[124] It seems safe to conclude that Petit probably had more associates than the sources indicate—but not many more. No vast network remains to be uncovered. But she was not unsurrounded either.

There is a submerged logic to Petit's wartime action. The very informality of her network, and her manifold wartime activities—resistance and other—connote an overall strategy which was not completely war-related. Her new importance as an intelligence agent, with the financial means and the increased mobility that came with it, allowed her to recreate a family circle—she, the orphan who had grown up in such "striking isolation," had then drifted, far from family, and had been rejected by her prospective in-laws. A new possibility now presented itself of recreating a family circle—this time, one created through her work. With the Delmeules, she entered into a mutual agreement: they helped her gather military intelligence and she ran business errands for them in Brussels. These errands in turn helped her pass for a traveling saleswoman, which gave her the mobility she needed for her war work. (Several intelligence agents posed as commercial travelers.) In other words, with her Tournai family, war work and family strategy were indissolubly linked. She also drew closer to her godmother in Brussels, sharing her new—if still very relative—affluence with her mother's sister who had fallen on hard times.[125] Upon her return from London, she had brought her two closest relatives together, inviting her sister to meet at Hélène Ségard's, arguing her busy schedule ("that way, I see you both together on one visit").[126] But she kept her war work from her sister. Marie Collet was adamant: "Hélène [Petit] has never cared about her sister. She has nothing to do with her [war] service."[127]

CHAPTER 4
CONFRONTATION, FEBRUARY 2– MARCH 3, 1916

High Alert

In early 1916, the German police was in a state of high mobilization. In the night of January 7, in the Brussels borough of Schaarbeek, a young Belgian informer working for the Germans was shot dead. His name was Remy Neels; he worked for *Polizeistelle B*, the department that tracked down recruitment for the Allied armies. Neels had helped dismantle Edith Cavell's escape network, which had resulted in the execution of Cavell and of Philippe Baucq on October 12, 1915. After that, he had continued to work as an informer, posing as a conduit for young men who wanted to join the Belgian or Allied armies. Having become a lightning-rod for the pent-up anger of young patriots, he was killed by one of them. It was the first time the Belgian resistance committed a violent act. To the occupying authorities, it seemed to confirm the prediction made in late September 1915, that some among the occupied would be ready to use violence if Germany's military fortunes turned. As it happened, the murder was no harbinger of violence; Belgian resistance was to remain almost completely unarmed. The underground press rejected violent action because it would worsen civilians' vulnerability vis-à-vis the occupying forces—and it would constitute a breach of the unspoken division of labor between civilians and their national army. Clandestine writers condemned Neels' killing as being of a piece with the deterioration of norms wrought by the German armies—the lawlessness, the corrosion of public space, the all-pervasive threat of violence.[1]

In that January night, the first on the murder scene were the local police. They promptly, and to the considerable annoyance of the Germans, leaked the fact that the murder victim had been an informer. As punishment for this indiscretion, the borough police commissar was condemned to a year in prison, Schaarbeek received a 50,000 mark fine, and, for good measure, all of Greater Brussels was fined half a million marks. To avoid further revelations about the German political police, the matter was taken off the hands of the Belgian justice apparatus (which went well outside the occupiers' remit, since the murdered man had been a Belgian).[2] And with that, the *Polizei* quest for Neels' killer was on. "This execution," as one witness later testified (one notes the telling use of the term), "put the entire [German] police on high alert."[3] The quest did not last long. On January 10, German police arrested the killer, a young man named Louis Bril who waited tables in his family's Italian restaurant. Bril had plotted the murder together with some friends and had been aided by Neels' neighbors. On February 9, Bril was condemned to death by a military court. He was executed at dawn on February 11.

By then, Petit was in prison. Her arrest on February 2 took place against the backdrop of a massive rounding-up of Allied intelligence networks. German counter-intelligence was, just then, concluding its investigation into some major cases. De Bettignies had been arrested in October 1915 and would be put on trial in mid-March.[4] In that same month of October, the first arrests were made among members of a highly professional network led by the telegraph operator Charles Parenté. In May 1916, the leaders and main agents of the network—thirty-seven men in all—would appear before a military court. In between were months of police work so meticulous that even Sadi Kirschen, the Belgian defender at the Parenté trial, expressed grudging admiration.[5] The dismantling of the Parenté network led to that of others, in a rolling operation that would end up wiping out four major services, all working for Belgian military intelligence, between October 1915 and May 1917.[6] Petit's arrest, then, happened in a time of great successes for German counter-intelligence. By mid-1916, the activity of all Allied intelligence services on the Western Front had reached a low point. As one agent would later describe it, "At Verdun, German attack followed German attack, and none of the Allies seemed to have a serious intelligence organization left in the field."[7]

Bureau A[8]

Counter-intelligence operations were a major component of German entrenchment in the West. Like other forms of German entrenchment, they came into their own in mid-to-late 1915 and ensconced themselves deeply in the conquered terrain, making adroit use of its features. *Polizeistelle A* (Police Bureau A), a department of the Political Police in Brussels, had started to concentrate exclusively on counter-intelligence in the Fall of 1915. Located in the commandeered offices of a Belgian cabinet ministry in the stately rue de Berlaimont in the Brussels government district, the bureau fielded twenty-one full-time detectives by early 1916, not counting German secret agents and Belgian informers.[9] The bureau was headed by a young infantry lieutenant, Paul Schmitz, in civilian life a commissar of the judiciary police in Düsseldorf.[10] Schmitz' second-in-command, Hans Goldschmidt, who was to play a major role in the Petit investigation, was an attorney from Elberfeld (present-day Wuppertal); mobilized in the Elberfeld *Landwehr*, he had entered the service of the German police in Brussels in March 1915 with the rank of *Kriminalkommissar*.[11]

There are two important sources of documentation on Police Bureau A. The first is a postwar deposition by Goldschmidt's secretary, a young man named Ernest Frédéric "Fritz" Ball. Ball had been born in Belgium of German parents; barely twenty when the war broke out, he worked in a bank in Namur. Offered the choice between joining the German army and the German police, Ball had chosen the latter.[12] The second source is a postwar deposition by a Belgian informer in the service of the Germans, Léopold Wartel, a young salesman from Hainaut.[13] Both Ball and Wartel, in an attempt to regain credit with the Belgian authorities after the war—Ball was abroad and wanted to return to Belgium, and Wartel was in prison—left a detailed description of the personnel at the bureau, including both the German staff and the Belgian associates. These descriptions show that several of the German staff had prewar ties to Belgium. One of the detectives, the highly appreciated Jules Levy, ran a gunpowder factory in Hainaut before the war, together with his brother who possessed Belgian nationality. One of the bureau chiefs, Willy Fay, was an automobile salesman who had been well established in the Brussels area before the war, and divided his time between Brussels and Frankfurt. Like other agents, he cut an elegant figure; Wartel described him as "a man of indeterminate age, of the American type," implying a modern esthetic of male grooming—slender, clean-shaven, with hair slicked back. Some recruits were from Alsace-Lorraine. One of Bureau A's most formidable agents was a *lorrain* in his mid-thirties, the very handsome Jean Burtard, a German military intelligence agent since before the war. (In 1910, by his own account, he had made off with a prototype of a new French machine-gun at the munitions works of Châtellerault.) An established secret intelligence star, Burtard had been recruited by the Brussels *Polizei*—together with his brother Paul—in November 1914, in other words, as soon as the German occupation of Belgium showed signs of permanence.[14]

The German agents at Police Bureau A had the rank of *Kriminalbeamte* (detective). This allowed them to arrest people and set up preliminary trial inquiries. The Belgian informers were defined as "advisers" (*Vertrauensleute*). There were full-time informers as well as occasional ones. Wartel, an informer himself (though he would claim after the war that he had acted as a double agent on behalf of French Intelligence), wrote that there was never a dearth of Belgian associates—and that the pool of helpers for the German police in Brussels widened as misery spread. In 1914, it was the most wretched, people in clogs and rags from the poor *Marolles* district, who came to offer their services and were given the simplest of informers' tasks. By March 1915, the German police could send the proles home, as help was now forthcoming from people in bowler hats and silk cravats: the petite bourgeoisie of commercial travelers and clerks. As the pool widened, the German police could set the bar higher on respectability, language skills, and education.[15] Even though Wartel may (for obvious reasons) have exaggerated the widespread nature of informership, his description certainly qualifies pious postwar statements that only "the dregs of the Belgian population" would lend themselves to such work.[16] (By contrast, neither Wartel's account nor that of Fritz Ball suggest that German counter-intelligence might have been able to take advantage of "ethnic differences"[17] within Belgium. Flemings were not overrepresented among the informers they named; and, conversely, resistance networks of necessity spanned the breadth of the country from the French to the Dutch border.) The most prized among Police Bureau A's Belgian "advisers" were given the rank of detective. One of them was an early middle-class recruit, the engineer Gaston Goffaux. He had had reason to turn against his fellow citizens: at war's outbreak he and his common-law wife, known only as Miss Moeller or Müller, a dactylographer who may or may not have been of German descent, were subject to brutal neighborhood charivari and lost their jobs. The impoverished couple had then joined the German secret police, which paid well and offered generous expense accounts. Moeller was the clandestine *Libre Belgique*'s most effective foe at Police Bureau B. (After the war, from Breslau, she defiantly wrote to a Brussels judge that she was proud of her war service, because it put her on a par with her cousins in the

German army.[18]) Goffaux, at Police Bureau A, was the one who tracked down Neels' killer Louis Bril.

Against counter-intelligence heavyweights like Burtard and Goffaux, Wartel stressed, many resistance operations were defenseless—especially as they were conducted in a dilettantish manner to begin with.[19] Goffaux, for instance, had had a ridiculously easy time of arresting Bril—at the house of Neels' neighbors, to whom Bril was paying a most unwise thank-you visit. Half a year earlier, Burtard had concluded the dismantling of French GHQ's leaky railway-dynamiting scheme (mentioned in Chapter Three) by single-handedly knocking out the Belgian policeman Pierre Poels, one of the main agents. Burtard's dashing tackle of Poels in a Brussels street—a film noir move *avant la lettre*—gave an accurate idea of his less-than-bureaucratic modus operandi, as Fritz Ball observed.[20] It gave an idea of the flavor of German counter-intelligence operations more generally. In some respects the employees of Bureau A were more like characters in a detective novel than like military men or bureaucrats. They inserted themselves in city life smoothly, quite unlike the lumbering Military Police with their unsightly copper badges hanging on chains around their necks, bearing the letters "MP"—giving rise to the play on words "*Marken-Pakkers*" (grabbers of [Reichs]marks)—a reference to their eagerness to write out heavy fines for the slightest offenses.[21] Sartorially, the contrast was striking between the Military Police and "the enemy's elegant secret police," as the *Libre Belgique* called it. Those dapper wardrobes may well have served to mark a certain distance from the military; civilian administrators in the Government-General had fought hard for their right to wear mufti.[22] The office culture at the political police in the swank rue de Berlaimont was considerably more relaxed and urbane than at the heel-clicking military police headquarters (*Kommandantur*). Its display of cosmopolitanism and even of bohème rowdiness did not escape observers. Wartel's introduction to it was a bit of a culture shock; after having met the young and somewhat haughty department head Schmitz (in whom, Wartel wrote, one could recognize the officer even though he wasn't wearing uniform), he was taken to the common office upstairs. On the landing, he was greeted by a great ruckus—a chorus of "Tipperary," its rhythm beaten out with rulers, interspersed with loud talk in excellent French and even Parisian slang. Asking himself if this could really be the German secret police, he warily knocked on the door and went in, finding an impromptu celebration by twelve men in a smoke-filled room, one of them dancing on top of his desk. Asked sternly who he was, Wartel ironically swept off his hat, Versailles-style, and announced himself as "le nouveau!" And with that, he was introduced to room 10, where henceforth he would report twice every day, at 8.30 a.m. and 6.30 p.m., and was initiated into "the little secrets of the service."[23]

This office microculture partook of officer-corps rowdiness; it also had something of the colonial civil service to it, complete with heavy drinking. But it was also, to some extent, an enactment of civilian-ness against what were perceived to be the unpragmatic priorities of the military. As the war wore on, the culture in room 10 would become more conspiratorial; calling themselves "the Bolsheviki," the detectives would use the daily 6.30 p.m. meeting to gripe about the war, as well as about the deportations and forced labor imposed on Belgians and about the executions of Belgian patriots, all the while plotting practical jokes, exchanging office banter, and, eventually, complaining bitterly about the severe cuts in pay (see below).[24]

The personnel at Police Bureau A seem to have been, by and large, polyglot and worldly. Wartel described them as sophisticates, debonair in manner, smartly dressed, who preferred French to German and liked Parisian slang best of all. Goldschmidt, the most senior civilian at Police Bureau A, was described, both by Wartel and by his secretary Ball, as an elegant man of the world. Ball painted his boss, with evident prejudice, as "an eminently intelligent man, who spoke French to perfection—but deceitful, devious, Jewish, and dishonest. You were his friend if you could get him food at a good price, which he would send to Germany—or if you could introduce him to pretty women." Wartel remembered Goldschmidt as exuding an air of weary irony, even cynicism. He described him as very dapper (he wore gold-rimmed glasses and came to the office with a fresh flower in his buttonhole; his young subordinate Ball imitated him) and "still very proud of his appearance, although he was over forty-five."[25] Goldschmidt was responsible for day-to-day contact with Belgians. This entailed the recruiting and handling of counter-espionage agents. His smart attire, which contrasted with the ever-more-disheveled clothes of even the Brussels bourgeoisie, may have had a recruiting influence. Goldschmidt would find recruits in the clandestine *locaux de nuit*, a kind of speakeasies, that had sprung up all over the occupied city: Brussels' status as a rest and recreation area for German troops made for a thriving night-life in an otherwise hamstrung economy. This night-life was a conduit to the underground workings of the city.[26]

There is a more general point to be made here concerning disreputability. The world of louche pleasures that was one face of occupied Brussels allowed the *Polizei* to insert itself into intelligence networks. Petit's nemesis, Nikolaas Keurvers, was said to "enjoy himself into the early hours in Brussels cafés"; an agent mentioned his "red bloated face and small vicious eyes."[27] Petit, it was said after the war, mistrusted Keurvers from the start because he arrived at their first meeting late and hung over from an evening at the Brussels *Folies Bergère*.[28] Such mistrust was not mere prejudice on the part of the respectable. There was real danger in enjoying the night-life. Secret agents who liked to live it up in restaurants and bars could wind up talking too much. Or they could be tempted to partake of the war-profit deals brokered in these places. Nikolaas Keurvers, for one, posed as a Dutch broker in colonial merchandize—including that now rarest and most profitable of commodities, coffee—in order to infiltrate intelligence services by offering agents a cut in business deals. Since these deals were not exactly above ground, the agents thus lured effectively entered into a relationship of shared secrets, which the mole could then further exploit.[29] It was precisely in order to avoid traps like this that, in the second half of the war, *La Dame Blanche*, the most efficient intelligence service of the occupied areas behind the Western Front, would be set up along lines of the strictest respectability. The organizers made a point of recruiting amidst "people of proven valor," whom they knew personally or who had been recommended to them. Respectability meant dependability. In order to keep out mercenaries, their agents were not paid. (Since this excluded people with no means, manual workers made up only 12 percent of the *Dame Blanche*'s effectives.) Because of this waterproof model, the network's rate of arrestations was spectacularly low: an estimated 4 out of 100, as against 40 out of 100 for French and Belgian networks.[30] (By contrast, those who, like Petit, were not part of a solidly middle-class social network, and who needed money to work, were vulnerable to the infiltration of their service.) In addition, respectability signaled a certain self-image. The *Dame Blanche*'s modus operandi of solid, even stolid respectability was also a way to underscore that its agents were not engaged in spying—an activity that connoted deception, disloyalty, and dissipation—so much as in *military observation*, an effort that, like their peacetime lives, was all about discipline and drudgery and unrewarded (but always expected) diligence. One may note in passing that, after the war, Belgian fiction about the occupation would either portray secret intelligence as a *repudiation* of the world of easy night-life pleasure in Brussels, or, conversely, as an *emanation* of it.[31]

Against the respectability of (much of the) Belgian resistance stood the *demi-mondain* hue of the German secret police. Wartel detailed agents' taste for the night-life, most of all that of the *lorrain* agent Burtard, whom Wartel described as dark, blue-eyed, and powerfully-built, indeed "gifted with an uncommon force—which he liked to squander in bars." Though married with children, Burtard had mistresses—with attendant bachelor pads and aliases—all over the city, was known for going on three-day benders (often missing the 8.30 a.m. daily briefing), and would by the end of the war have dilapidated, in the bars, casinos, brothels, and shady little theaters that had sprung up all over occupied Brussels, all of the considerable savings (some 190,000 francs) he had accumulated as a spy before the war, not to mention his lavish pay and allowances during the war. (Remuneration was generous. Wartel claimed that, by 1916, the expense accounts of the agents at Police Bureau A had risen to 3,000 marks per person per month. In 1917 these expense accounts would be very severely curtailed, probably as part of a general cutback of expenses not strictly military.)[32]

Police Bureau A relied heavily on its infiltrators in the Netherlands. Their work allowed detectives to locate secret intelligence agents in the occupied country. The bureau then conducted dragnet operations; if, after a first round of arrests, the commissar in charge of the investigation suspected that not all members of the network had been caught, a "mousetrap" was set up where the suspected network head or main courier lived or received mail. That "mousetrap" was manned permanently, and all visitors were arrested indiscriminately and released only after a tight interrogation. (The resulting intimidation of the neighborhood was decried by the underground press as wanton terrorization.) In other words, once a suspect had been apprehended, Bureau A set traps for other members of the network, leading to further arrests. In Petit's case, the *Polizei*'s first coup was the January 4 arrest, near Liège, of her courier Theodore Broeckx, the 'peasant' from the border area near Holland. In his cell, he managed to eat the documents he carried; and he did not speak under interrogation, though he was most likely beaten. Taken to Brussels, he was walked through Petit's neighborhood in hopes he would give details. He did not—but the foray proved that the police knew by then where to look.[33]

Arrest and Questioning

On Wednesday, February 2, at 1.20 p.m., Collet and two of her sons were arrested at their apartment on the Chaussée d'Anvers. They were taken by automobile to the rue du Théâtre, where Petit was arrested in turn. She was at that moment having coffee with her downstairs neighbor, Auguste Dickmans, the woman she sublet her room from and whom she considered a friend. (This apparently anodyne scene had become, by early 1916, exceptional, not to say extravagant; coffee was a prohibitively expensive black-market item, enjoyed only on the most festive occasions.) Petit opened the door herself and confirmed to Goldschmidt, who led the arresting party, that she was indeed Miss Legrand. The scene, as Dickmans later told Deloge, was terrifying; one of the arresting agents punched Petit in the stomach, and she herself was jostled by Goldschmidt. The arresting party included a Belgian informer, later identified only as "a man from Antwerp," whom Petit wasted no time lambasting: "they are Boches, but you are a Belgian. Really you should be ashamed of yourself!" This was her way of setting the tone: if she was afraid, she would not show it. As the men ransacked Petit's room, at first failing to find incriminating material, she taunted them—"you poor Boches, you can't find anything, how very sad"—and laughed when they found proof of her work. (Rather unwisely, she had made large flashcards with details about German military uniforms.) Shoved across the room, she did not lose countenance, telling Dickmans, who proffered an ashtray to an agent tipping his ashes on the floor, not to bother: "these people feel themselves at home in a stable." Collet, from the back seat of the car, saw Petit being brutally pushed out the front door and almost falling down the steps. Made to sit next to the chauffeur, Petit used this position to loudly cry to passers-by: "I have been arrested by the Boches!" At pains to puncture the terror of the situation, Petit, during the drive, assured Collet that she and her sons would be released that same evening, and invited her to help herself to the provisions she had in her room—a ham among them. The police officer in the back seat scoffed at Petit's ability to buy hams—a very precious commodity in 1916—with the lavish proceeds from her spy work. Collet later remembered the scene: "Gabrielle laughed; the German was furious and said he would hit her if she did not shut the f... [sic] up. She turned around and retorted: 'We'll see about you having the nerve to hit me. One has to be a dirty German like you to dare say this to a woman.' She had already taken her hat-pin to stab him in the eye and I'm sure she would have done it if he had said anything else."[34]

The arrestees were first taken to the *Kommandantur* in central Brussels, and from there to the prison of Saint-Gilles in the south. This model panoptic prison, a neo-Tudor edifice from the 1880s, had been designed to intimidate, with its long radiating corridors and strict isolation of prisoners. (Even in chapel, a circular hall on the top floor of a tower whence they were led via an intricate complex of separate stairs, they heard Mass enclosed in individual cubicles.) Since the start of the occupation, one-third of the cells had been reserved for prisoners of German military justice; that section was managed by a German officer, captain Wilhelm Behrens, a Hamburg banker in civilian life, and described by Belgian commentators as rather a good sort.[35] Behrens' Belgian counterpart, the administrator Xavier Marin, had been deputy director of the prison since 1913. (There is no indication that anyone thought Marin's position during the war compromising; I will return to this.) Saint-Gilles prison, where hundreds of Belgian and French citizens were held, became a focal point of patriotic fervor; built for the edification of the 'dangerous classes' in Benthamite fashion, it had never before housed so many "respectable" folk.[36]

The two women were taken to different cells. They were not to see each other for a month, until their trial on March 2. But even in these circumstances, Petit kept her promise to take care of her friend. Having been handed a sum of 100 francs (money taken from her room, which the *Polizei*, as in all such cases, made a point to scrupulously account for), Petit used it to send Collet some provisions through the guardian. Two days after the arrest, Marie Collet received "two large ham sandwiches and a comb," and more followed in later days—"eggs, cheese, milk, sugar, handkerchiefs, and so on ..."[37] Petit did not forget the women in her support network. On February 7, she sent a letter to her neighbor on rue du Théâtre, Auguste Dickmans, thanking her for a care parcel she had sent, apologizing for the "upset" her arrest had caused, and asking her to look after her things "until I have established certainty about my prospects." Breezily, she gave her address as "Miss Gabrielle Petit, Cell 21, Château Saint-Gilles Prison."[38]

Meanwhile, interrogations started, as they always did within twenty-four hours of an arrest. Collet was interrogated about Petit's actions: "what she did, where she went, whom she saw." Goldschmidt probably questioned Petit himself at first.[39] It is not known whether she was physically mistreated. (Weeks later, on March 22, her sister mentioned seeing her after a renewed interrogation, very upset, and "with one side of her face violently red and swollen."[40]) Physical torture was part of interrogation repertoire—agents reported that their teeth had been knocked out with revolver-butts, others suffered hernias from the beatings; other forms of torture included binding arrestees very tightly to a chair with head bent sharply back—but not systematically as would be the case under the Nazi occupations. Rather, as happened in the colonies, subjects may have been implicitly classified as torturable or otherwise on the basis of status.[41] Gender seems to have mattered, but working-class women were more likely to have been beaten than women of rank like Cavell and De Bettignies. Women (and men) of rank may or may not have been subjected to other third-degree methods such as withholding food, though Hans Goldschmidt, as late as 1937, would vehemently object to his portrayal as De Bettignies' tormentor.[42] Where these patterns left Petit, who was neither a bourgeoise nor working class, we do not know. She herself went out of her way to say that Goldschmidt "is good to me."[43] The German prison chaplain, Leonhard Leyendecker, would claim that Petit was never subjected to third-degree methods, "for she would have thrown it in my face—she was not one to hold back."[44] Still the interrogation period, during which arrestees were kept in complete isolation, was invariably a time of terror that reduced many to despair, some even to suicide. Even the unflappable De Bettignies broke down and briefly confided in a sympathetic cell-mate—in reality, an informer.[45]

Whatever the precise ordeal Petit went through, everything indicates that she named no names. None of her collaborators, specifically the Delmeules in Tournai, were ever much as questioned. Petit's refusal to incriminate Marie Collet, whom she portrayed as absolutely ignorant of everything, would lead to Collet's eventual acquittal for want of proof. Collet's sons were released after two weeks. If Petit's network was connected to others', she did not incriminate those. She was not confronted with Theodore Broeckx, the courier, who for his part had not given anything away either.

Petit had known she was likely to be arrested, and had made up her mind to contain the damage. "Calais is endangered," Hélène Ségard remembered her as saying in December 1915. Jeopardizing Allied intelligence was not an option: "I will be arrested alone; I will be shot alone. . . . Everything must continue; if I fall, I will be replaced."[46] In prison, she buttressed her resolve in a defiant attitude, as testified by the German interpreter at Saint-Gilles, a man named Otto Becker who had lived in Belgium for years before the war and who enjoyed a good reputation among the prisoners. From Germany, in late 1919, he sent a letter sharing his memories of Petit's prison time. Becker apparently struck up an immediate friendship with Petit. Having taken up his post in February, some time after her arrest, Becker first met her on his morning round; she asked him if he was "as much of a boche, as much of a brute" as his predecessor. Becker marveled at Petit's lack of deference: her words could have cost her three days' solitary confinement. She relished calling his superior a *Schwein*. In her cell, she sang satirical songs and shouted at the top of her voice, "always with the aim of taunting the wardens."[47] She talked to prisoners in adjoining cells via the radiator-pipe tunnels. The inmates called this "the telephone"—a joke that subverted their isolation and created an imaginary space of secrecy and of prestige. It was in this way that Petit, crouching near the baseboard where the pipe entered the wall, contacted a woman brought in the adjoining cell sometime in February: Marie-Léonie Van Houtte, Louise de Bettignies' associate, who had been in prison for months, awaiting trial. Suspicious at first, Van Houtte eventually entered into the conversation. She seems to have been a sounding-board for Petit's resolve and self-presentation; on one occasion, Petit told her that she had been "worked over" by her interrogators, but had told them to "forget about finding a coward in me"; on another occasion, she said she had taunted a guard with the words—in German—"*Pass mal auf, nicht nach Paris, nach Berlin.*" She told Van Houtte how she withstood the attempts made by Father Leyendecker to mollify her. (The chaplain had privileged access to the inmates who were not allowed to hear Mass in the chapel during the time of interrogation before their trials.[48]) In an apparent bid to make Petit see the futility of her resistance, Leyendecker called the Belgian king "a puppet," Petit told Van Houtte, adding that she had retorted that the king was worth more than "that goose-stepping Emperor of yours."[49] She also, "flushed with anger," told Becker about this exchange, adding that she had given Leyendecker a piece of her mind about "that dirty Kaiser of his" and that she had told him that henceforth she would only respect him as a priest.[50] (To her godmother, whom she saw again after her trial, Petit would embellish the story, ascribing the puppet taunt to one of the judges at her trial, and allotting herself a scathing retort which she may or may not have used in her conversation with Leyendecker: "At least my king is at the front with his soldiers."[51] Thus transposed, the vignette would become a centerpiece of her legend.) Leyendecker unwittingly corroborated the story, telling

Becker that in spite of Petit's recalcitrance he had at one point almost succeeded in getting her to confide in him—"but then, one day, she definitively refused, I do not know why." (To which Becker added, underlining: "We know why."[52]) She further strengthened her resolve by covering the walls of her cell with graffiti—a mode of expression common to political prisoners—that expressed her unshakable belief in ultimate Allied victory. "Her patriotism was boundless," Becker would recall; "she was absolutely convinced that the Entente would be victorious." Her mottoes, such as "Long Live Belgium, Long Live King Albert," were erased by the wardens every morning, only to be re-inscribed again.[53]

And so the weeks went by. "Time seems to pass more slowly," she wrote to Auguste Dickmans on February 22. "I am still waiting. I would certainly prefer a swift solution—I don't like things that drag on."[54] It seems typical of Petit's circumstances that she was in contact with her neighbor but not with her relatives. Ségard claimed—perhaps self-servingly, perhaps not—that Petit had told her not to make enquiries if she disappeared.[55] Her god-daughter only contacted her after the trial. Petit's reticence, or the weakness of her family, had far-reaching consequences. It meant that nobody interceded on her behalf once she came before the court. Other prisoners' families or friends contacted Belgian attorneys, who took on the defense of civilian arrestees before the German military courts. A Pro Bono Defense Committee, constituted to this end, never refused its help.[56] Then again, Petit must have known perfectly well that she was entitled to a Belgian lawyer, since she herself had, in 1915, interceded with a Brussels attorney to take on the defense of Jozef Baeckelmans (see Chapter Three). And even if neither she nor her friends called on a lawyer, the Defense Committee would have contacted her: its members checked in with the military police headquarters in Brussels and the larger provincial cities for arrestations, and then contacted the arrestees. Most of the major espionage and escape cases involved Belgian lawyers. They were forced to work within extremely narrow limits of action. They were never given the defendants' full dossier and so had to argue from imperfect information; nor were they allowed to confer with their clients. The prosecutors had all the information; the defense often had barely been told what the accusation was. Defense attorneys were usually left to invoke mitigating circumstances or to argue that the defendants had not fully realized what they were doing. This was the line that Sadi Kirschen, who defended Edith Cavell, had taken in October 1915. In the face of the court's determination to condemn her to death, there was little he could do. But other defenses were successful: death penalties were commuted, prison sentences reduced, and some defendants acquitted. And, for all the restrictions on their action, the fact remains that Belgian lawyers were usually admitted before the German military courts.[57]

But not always. There were instances when defendants did not receive a Belgian lawyer, presumably to keep details of the cases from leaking to the wider public.[58] There were at least three such instances in the first trimester of 1916. No Belgian lawyer was allowed at the trial of Louis Bril, the killer of the informer Neels.[59] Second, in February 1916, Police Bureau A had investigated yet another French GHQ sabotage scheme (this one involving blowing up Zeppelins as well as railways); at the subsequent trial, which ended in one execution, no Belgian lawyers were admitted.[60] And, an example even closer to that of Petit, Louise de Bettignies, who was condemned to death for espionage in a closed-doors trial on March 13–14, was not allowed a Belgian lawyer.[61] The Brussels attorney Victor Bonnevie, who headed the Defense Committee, wrote that such instances were extremely rare, especially in Brussels, but that they did concern some major cases. He blamed the German police: "it was almighty; it would answer all our protestations by invoking reason of state, before which the prosecutors and the [Military] Governor invariably bowed. We owe it to the police to have been excluded from some important espionage and escape cases, and would have been excluded from many more if it had been up to them."[62] Whether or not Bonnevie was correct in pointing to the police as the instigators, the main point here is that, by mid-January 1916, the rights of Belgian defense had already been curtailed to such a point that the Defense Committee sent a long letter of protestation to Governor-General Von Bissing. The letter pointed out that the messages sent by the Committee to recent arrestees to inform them that they were entitled to a Belgian lawyer were routinely sent back from prison unopened. Arrestees were interrogated "in complete isolation, left to their own devices, without support, without counsel." There was worse: on two recent occasions, military prosecutors had refused to inform lawyers of the court date, only to notify them, days later, that their client had already been condemned and shot. All in all, military necessity was being interpreted above and beyond what existing German laws on military courts, on the legal treatment of foreigners, or on military occupation had intended.[63] Von Bissing, in his answer on January 28, interpreted the existing legislation more narrowly and military necessity more broadly than the Belgian defenders did. He declared the existing German penal military legislation—which would have given Belgians appearing before German military courts the same defense rights that Germans would have—irrelevant. And he wrote that the right to choose a defender was limited by "the necessities of war, which, especially in espionage cases, would tend to exclude non-German defenders." (At least Von Bissing took the trouble to respond. An earlier protest had been brushed off more brutally: in June 1915, the chief legal counsel of the Government-General, Willeke, had told Belgian lawyers that their remonstrations were "unworthy of an answer," indeed "unseemly" vis-à-vis a victorious power.[64])

The Germans' invocation of military necessity struck many observers at the time as excessive. As the historian Isabel Hull has argued, imperial Germany had developed a more robust notion of the paramountcy of military necessity than had other states; and this notion had been exacerbated by the overly ambitious conduct of the war, which stretched German manpower to the limit even early on, and left the occupation regime short of administrators and policemen, a power lacuna filled with exemplary punishments.[65]

And so Petit spent the time of interrogation quite isolated. On February 20, she turned twenty-three. The investigation ended—inconclusively. Goldschmidt handed in his final report, which was eventually transmitted to the man in charge of the trial, the military prosecutor (*Kriegsgerichtsrat*), who was to lead the court proceedings, interrogate the accused and witnesses before the judges, and formulate the request for punishment.[66] Since October 1915, this crucial role had been fulfilled by a man widely held to epitomize belief in military necessity. Eduard Stoeber (1871–1960), a career military prosecutor from Bavaria in his mid-forties, took office in Brussels in October 1915, coming from the front in France, from where he brought an aura of impatient ruthlessness towards all impediments to the German army's safety and authority. He immediately acquired a reputation of "particular harshness," as Fritz Ball wrote. Stoeber's first trial, that of Edith Cavell and associates, had shown him at his most implacable: "his wish to make his mark with a spectacular coup led to a frenzy of authoritarianism," observed Kirschen (who was otherwise impressed by the prosecutor's command of military law). The tall, handsome, very *soigné* Stoeber thoroughly enjoyed the showcase for his prosecutorial dash that was the military courtroom. This was an all the more gratifying stage now that he had changed the venue for trials for "war treason" to the silenced Belgian Parliament. The stateliness of the Senate and Chamber halls underscored the Germans' victor status and cowed many of the accused brought in by prison-vans from Saint-Gilles. Here, Stoeber relished calling the defense attorneys to order, once ordering one of them to take his hands out of his pockets like a schoolboy, and taunting the accused, sometimes quite cruelly. (In May 1916, he would tell the insurance agent Prosper Krické, a widowed father, that he should have taken out life insurance since he would be shot; the judges greeted the joke with disapproving silence.) At the Cavell trial, in a telling gesture, he had deposited his helmet next to his case file. Stoeber's enactment of military superiority even influenced his living arrangements: residing in the Chilean consul's requisitioned house on the fashionable Avenue Louise, he had, in a gesture of taking possession, ordered the sealed cabinets in the house to be opened, a breach of law deemed scandalous on the part of a magistrate.[67] The historian Christoph Roolf has distinguished between those occupation officials in wartime Brussels who disliked and those who savored owing their status in the city to military conquest; clearly, Stoeber belonged to the latter type.[68] He liked to tell his entourage that he might not leave Brussels alive, and relished passing around the death threats he received—one of them swearing he would be shot in the street "like that traitor Neels." (At the end of the war, he took those with him to Bavaria.)[69] At the Cavell trial, Stoeber had required death penalties for nine accused, including a young Irish widow and mother of two, Ada Bodart née Doherty (whom Petit had contacted the year before in her quest to find an escape for her fiancé). For a case involving no espionage, such harshness was a shock, and even though the judges subsequently reduced the capital punishments to five, and three of those were commuted, the fact that two people were shot over this case at all caused "stupor" among the defense, which had expected at the most a five-year prison sentence for Cavell. From that trial onwards, Stoeber would continue to request the death penalty with terrifying frequency.[70] A chilling incident about Stoeber was recounted in 1917 by a witness to Cavell and Baucq's execution: Gottfried Benn, the poet, who was present in his capacity as army doctor. Benn told the writer Thea Sternheim that Baucq, standing a few paces before the execution squad, had said farewell to the men with the words "in the face of death we are all comrades," and that Stoeber had shouted at him to shut up before the shots rang out. Benn was no critic of the occupation regime and he considered the executions a matter of duty to the German Empire and army; but the *Kriegsgerichtsrat*'s brutality apparently stuck in his mind.[71] That Stoeber thought fit to silence Baucq's last message to the German ranks betrays a preoccupation with maintaining the imperial army's authority not just over Belgian civilians but also over its own soldiers. At the start of the occupation, trials had been public. But by early 1916, military court trials in Brussels generally proceeded in camera on orders of Stoeber—and the reason, openly stated, was to avoid German soldiers' exposure to justifications of "war treason." De Bettignies' trial, in mid-March, was held behind closed doors.[72]

Two weeks earlier, so did that of Petit. No documents on the preparations for her trial survive. In all likelihood, Stoeber, following procedure, read Petit's case file, then requested the military governor of Brussels to assemble five officers to serve as judges.[73] Like him, the military governor quite embodied the dogma of military necessity. General Traugott Martin von Sauberzweig (1863–1920), holder of the empire's highest military order, the *Pour le Mérite*, had made a name for himself as an occupier determined to rely on military might to the exclusion of other forms of authority. Having participated in the taking of the Russian fortress of Novo-Georgievsk in August 1915, he had been called to the military governorship of Brussels in September 1915, replacing a predecessor considered too lenient; as mentioned in Chapter Three, this was a time of greatly intensified suspicion of the occupied citizenry.[74] With a *modus occupandi* all about the imposition of obedience, Von Sauberzweig was variously called "a complete brute" (by the Brussels underground chronicler Charles Tytgat), "a prize brute" (by the Brussels municipal councilman André Brassinne), "a sinister brute" (by the United States envoy Brand Whitlock), "the foolishness of 'Wallenstein's Camp'" personified (by the German historian Gustav Mayer, a functionary in the civilian administration's Political Department), and, more diplomatically, an administrator whose "actions can hardly be called helpful on awkward political terrain like this" (by the head of the Political Department, the nimble diplomat Oscar von der Lancken).[75] The new military governor stood out even among German military administrators for the "crass insolence and brutality" with which he treated the municipal authorities.[76] Von Sauberzweig's deep suspicion of the metropolis and his insistence on unflagging shows of military superiority also made him attempt to rein in the scenes of debauch—including "undignified behavior with females in public"—that resulted from the city's status as a rest and recreation area for German troops. In an October 1915 secret order, Von Sauberzweig impressed upon his subordinates that while a certain amount of relaxation in the big city was permissible after the strains of battle or the boredom of small garrison towns, wearing an officer's uniform implied certain standards of conduct: "A German officer must never forget what he owes his honor and his German name. He must never incur the contempt of the enemy population. ... One is honor-bound to respect the uniform!"[77] Protecting the back of the fighting army, in other words, meant upholding victor status in the day-to-day dealings with the citizenry. (One observes in passing the contrast between Von

Sauberzweig's fixation on the uniform and the swank mufti of Goldschmidt et al.—the latter expressing a belief that domination need not entail incorruptible stiff-upper-lip distance but was, on the contrary, best buttressed by burrowing into the occupied city *via* its greedy, seedy side.) Von Sauberzweig insisted on enacting victor status in several other ways. The Brussels municipal police had to go out of its way to demonstrate obedience to the German authorities, such as saluting the Governor-General's car even when it drove by empty. The Military Police, ordered to aggressively repress signs of defiance, on one occasion shot at a group of school-boys humming the Belgian national anthem, and arrested ten of them.[78] Such displays of military might dismayed civilian administrators in the Government-General. In December 1915, Von der Lancken complained in a long secret message to Under-Secretary of State Zimmermann that Von Sauberzweig's "battlefield perspective," if left unfettered by civilian control, repeatedly threatened to bring "the whole vast apparatus of peacetime authority [by which he meant German civilian authority in the occupied country, SdS]" to a standstill.[79]

Von Sauberzweig expressed his view of occupation most spectacularly in the October 1915 Cavell case. Not only had he upheld the death sentence; he had refused to stay the execution, so that neutral diplomatic appeals could not run their course. Cavell and Baucq were shot early in the morning following the confirmation of the verdict. The ensuing uproar did not result in Von Sauberzweig's dismissal; he stayed in office until June 1916.[80] (He then joined German Supreme Headquarters as Quartermaster-General; in that capacity he was instrumental in urging on the deportations and forced labor of Belgian workers.[81] His reputation over Cavell—which he defended as an act of military honor—stayed with him through his subsequent postings in the East.[82] His last action was of a piece with his stated beliefs: in the spring of 1919, as commander of an artillery division, he set up a *Freikorps* in Erfurt, Thuringia, tasked with "self-defense" against organized labor.[83]) Von Sauberzweig was, then, still in function when Petit came before the military court.

After the Cavell fracas, Gustav Mayer had written in his diary that he did not expect women to be executed anymore.[84] In fact no such formal decision had been made, but it had been agreed that henceforth Von Bissing should weigh in on death sentences, and that those imposed on women should always be brought before the Emperor's attention.[85] The two other condemned women at Cavell's trial, Louise Thuliez and Jeanne De Belleville, had been pardoned at Von Bissing's intervention.[86] And, as it happened, since Edith Cavell no woman had been executed at all.

But other than that these had been months of harsh repression. Von Bissing, though he had reined in some of Von Sauberzweig's excesses, was, ultimately, being "an old soldier," always receptive to arguments of military necessity, as Von der Lancken had written in December. Moreover, the Governor-General suffered from being widely gossiped about in German ruling circles as lacking pluck (*Schneid*)—the joke was that "wild Moritz" had become "mild Moritz"—and was unwilling to appear lax by going against Von Sauberzweig's "stiff measures."[87]

Petit and Collet were to appear before the military court on March 2. As in all major cases, the trial was held in the Belgian Parliament. The two women were assigned a German defense laywer.[88] Stoeber once more was going to require the death penalty.

The Trial

And so the two women were briefly reunited. Early in the morning of March 2, a horse-drawn cab came from Saint-Gilles to pick up Collet at the military hospital (Petit had interceded with the prison doctor to have her friend treated for leg ulcers; Goldschmidt had allowed it).[89] Four years later, Collet still remembered the scene vividly. "She [Gabrielle] was in a little cab with two horses, with little gray curtains that were drawn; two Germans were with her. She lifted one of those curtains, I saw her and called out: 'Look, there's Gaby!' I climbed in next to her and we cried. I asked her where we were going. She said, 'Mother, we are going to our condemnation.'" Petit, then, was not sanguine about her chances of being acquitted. But she clearly had decided on a defiant stance. She called the guards taking them from the cab into the *Kommandantur* "our footmen," and taunted the soldiers in the vestibule. At nine in the morning, the two women were escorted to the Senate on foot. As they waited to be summoned inside the hall, Petit took off her hat and shook her hair loose to pin it up again. Goldschmidt came in and remarked on it. "Why yes, I am getting all dolled up for you," she retorted.[90]

In the Senate hall, where the trial was held behind closed doors, the two women appeared quite alone before the bench of uniformed judges and prosecutor; their court-appointed attorney, an officer, sat to the right; an interpreter to the left. The judges' dais was draped with veiled flags and surmounted by a large banner representing the Hohenzollern eagle. The set-up terrified Collet: "I can't deny it—I was piteous." She recalled feeling "like a little mouse let out of a trap into a big room where there's a cat." Petit tried to give her courage: "'It's <u>our</u> Senate, Mother,' she said."[91]

That the two women faced the *Kriegsgericht* alone, was exceptional. The usual pattern in espionage cases was that of a trial with at least half a dozen defendants, and sometimes far more than that, as one indiscretion or confession led to another.[92] This again testifies to Petit's silence under interrogation. How little the prosecution had to go on, appeared in the questioning; the dearth of evidence, as in Louise de Bettignies' case, would have been an additional reason to hold the trial in camera. The two women were interrogated by Stoeber, in German. There was an interpreter (possibly a gunner by the name of Bruck, whom Ball described as "extraordinarily brutal with the accused"). Their lawyer could take notes, but was forbidden to intervene.[93]

How to reconstruct what happened at the trial? Petit's stand before her judges would be much more central to her memory than the trials of Cavell and De Bettignies were to theirs. One is reminded of Joan of Arc—except that in *her* case, the official records exist. But no transcript of Petit's trial has survived.[94] Fritz Ball served as interpreter for some major espionage trials in 1916, but, unfortunately for the historian—for he was a good observer, as his report indicates—not in Petit's case. The Belgian defense lawyers of the Defense Committee left observations about the trials in which they served, most elaborately Sadi Kirschen, who in 1919 published a 500-page report (most of it written during the war) about "his" trials, with astute descriptions of court dynamics and vivid portraits of the protagonists. But Petit was not defended by one of the members of the Committee. The only eyewitness account of the trial is that of Marie Collet.[95] In addition, there is an account by Petit's godmother Hélène Ségard, based on what Petit told her in prison.[96] It is little to go on, especially as the importance of the trial for Petit's postwar legend, with attendant embellishments, predisposes one to extra caution; but it is not nothing. Collet's testimony, given in a blunt, unadorned style that gives it added credibility, corresponds to Ségard's recollection of what her niece told her. The latter source is more grandiloquent, an accent most probably due to Petit herself. But both accounts indicate that Petit's defiant attitude at her trial, which was to become the centerpoint of her postwar renown, was no legend. (Some defendants, blinking into the light on coming out of isolation at Saint-Gilles, were greatly intimidated by the court and they quite crumpled.) Both accounts express Petit's style of desperate, defiant mockery, occasionally descending into rudeness, at other times laced with pathos; and always coming back to her main point, that of the unacceptability of the invasion and the occupation. (She herself told her godmother that "I have been very frank before the judges, *Marraine*, I replied well."[97])

Stoeber started by asking Petit why she had entered the intelligence service. She answered: "because of the cruelties you commit." Asked which ones she referred to, she grew indignant: "You have the gall to ask me which ones. The ones you have committed in Charleroi, where you have burned people alive." This was a provocative statement and she knew it. All of the occupied knew that references to the massacres of 1914 (Petit was referring to the one in Tamines near Charleroi, a mauling of a small town so terrible that the German justification campaign had not mentioned it) made the occupants exceedingly testy. Stoeber banged his fist on the table and told Petit she was lying. "If you want to come with me," she responded, "I'll show you where it happened."[98] Next, she was asked about her intelligence work. Accused of spying on aircraft, she taunted the court by saying that "my men were better informed than yours." She answered a question about what she observed on the railways at night—a question most likely meant to find out what she knew about railway-sabotage schemes—with a quip: "What I see at night? Well it's dark isn't it?" ... To the accusation that she was "continuously" spying, Petit replied that the adverb "continuously" was surely superfluous. When asked what she would do if she were freed, she replied she would take up her work where she had left off. When asked to name her associates, she answered, "never." (To her godmother, Petit blew up the question: "You were in command of hundreds of men, give us their names.")[99] Feigning ignorance might or might not have been the more cautious course. (Sadi Kirschen and Fritz Ball both reported that affected obtuseness infuriated judges.) At any rate, defiantly withholding information was by now part and parcel of the ritual of confrontation at court: Baeckelmans, whom Petit so admired, had at his trial in September 1915, it was well known, refused to name names with the repeated refusal "That, I won't say *[Ça, je ne dis pas].*"[100] At Petit's refusal to name her associates, Stoeber claimed that three of them had already been arrested and she might as well name them. She did not take the bait: "you've looked for my name, now go look for theirs." Changing tack, Stoeber asked why Petit did not live with her parents. She answered that her private life had nothing to do with her espionage work.[101] As to Marie Collet, she was asked the same questions she had been asked in prison about Petit's actions; she once more pretended not to know anything, aided by Petit's insistence that this was so.

After the questioning, Stoeber may or may not have called in Goldschmidt to give his deposition and ask further questions of the accused. Then it was time for the prosecutor's speech. In most trials this meant that the prosecutor detailed the intelligence organization (up to and including the network heads in the Netherlands, if he had that information), and listed the charges against every one of the accused, including mitigating circumstances if any. He then required the different sentences according to specific articles of the German military penal code.[102] Exactly what Stoeber could have said about Petit's network, about which both he and the *Polizei* were still in the dark, is not retained. She and Collet would have sat through his speech without understanding it, since it was pronounced in German; only its conclusion was translated to them— namely, the charge.

Stoeber required the death sentence for Petit on grounds of war treason.[103] He asked for fifteen years' imprisonment for her accomplice. Marie Collet, in tears, said to Petit that she would never see her children again. "Wait, Mother," Petit answered, then stood and gave the prosecutor a piece of her mind. As Collet clung to her arm, trying to make her sit down and be quiet, "Gabrielle shouted abuse at him, telling him it was shameful to condemn an old woman, calling him a *Schweinhund*, calling down all manner of curses upon his head; telling him that she was happy to be condemned to death but that 'Mother Collet' was innocent." The interpreter would not have had to translate the insult. Their German lawyer beseeched Petit not to be so hostile, suggesting that things would be different in the morning. To Collet, he said she had reasons to be hopeful.[104]

After this, he pleaded their cause, only the gist of which would have been translated to them. To the extent that the shaken Collet remembered anything, she made out that he disputed the proofs brought against herself, and, as to Petit, that everyone had the right to defend their country.[105] Although there is no record of what he said—we do not even have his name—that he used this argument is plausible. German lawyers were documented to have used it in other cases, and commentators among the occupied citizenry praised them for it.[106]

Would this brave appeal to respect the patriotic feelings of the occupied have mitigated the impression left by Petit's brazen defiance? A week before, in Brussels, another woman had openly defied the court. On February 24, the typist Marguerite Blanckaert appeared before the *Kriegsgericht* for having helped an estimated two hundred Belgian volunteers leave the country to join the army. She transformed the proceedings into a passionate indictment of the "invaders," a word she repeated over and over again. Stoeber had required the death penalty; she declared to wish for it, regardless of what her lawyer might plead, and underscored her defiance by breaking into the anthem *De Vlaamsche Leeuw* (The Lion of Flanders). Kirschen, knowing her ardent patriotism would not help her case, dismissed it in his plea as the vanity of a woman bent on becoming the Belgian Cavell; he was helped in this by the police report which portrayed Blanckaert as an exalted old maid with nothing to live for. Blanckaert was given a life sentence. From prison, she wrote to Stoeber to protest the slighting of her motives as a citizen; but it had saved her life.[107]

The German translator at Saint-Gilles prison, Otto Becker, who became friendly with Petit, would write after the war that she had "categorically refused the assistance of an attorney." This was not strictly true: she had a defender. But openly defying the court and referring to the civilian massacres did amount to a refusal to be defended. She argued the cause, rather than the case, and so did herself in, knowing full well what she was doing.[108]

And, for the moment, she reveled in it. After the plea, the accused and the lawyer were led out of the courtroom to leave the judges to confer with Stoeber. The final verdict was scheduled for the next morning. Under guard, Petit and Collet were walked back to the *Kommandantur*, arms once more linked. Passers-by stared at them suspiciously. Much annoyed, Petit loudly repeated to everyone she saw gawking: "Gabrielle Petit, spy, condemned to death!" Collet asked her to stop. Petit answered there was no shame in it.[109] They arrived at the *Kommandantur* at noon. Collet, quite crushed, asked Petit for her rosary to pray. It was only then that Petit took steps to contact her godmother. She asked a woman who had been sentenced to two days' arrest to inform Hélène Ségard of her death sentence. The woman, later identified as one Madame Vekens, the mother of a well-known Dominican missionary in the Congo, asked Petit if she was to alert anyone else. Petit answered that she had no family, no-one else but Ségard, and that her fiancé was at the front—adding, with a shrug, "and he's a man." (Did she mean that Maurice Gobert would have scant sympathy for the fact that she had gotten herself in trouble, and that, like women prisoners everywhere, she could only rely on her women relatives? The meaning of her disillusioned little remark must remain forever unclear. She left a lasting impression on Vekens, who described her in that moment as "unbowed, stoic, and sweet" all at once.[110]) And so the two women, boarding a prison-van together with some German deserters and other prisoners, were taken back to Saint-Gilles. On arrival, Petit proclaimed to the guards that she had been condemned to death. They thought she was joking.[111]

Meanwhile, the judges deliberated with Stoeber. Then the votes were counted and the verdict was written up. The verdict then went to the military governor to be signed.

At eight o'clock on the morning of the next day, Friday, March 3, Petit and Collet were taken back to the *Kommandantur* to hear the final verdict. Petit remained defiant, as one eyewitness mentioned: the 39-year-old priest Auguste Mussche, in the prison-van on his way to his trial for having launched a clandestine periodical named *L'Âme Belge* [The

Belgian Soul].[112] His unknown fellow arrestee struck him as "an exuberant young woman." During the ride from Saint-Gilles to the center of town, she told him, laughingly, that she had been condemned to death, and said she would ask for her sentence to be upheld and for Madame Collet's to be stricken.[113] Petit's rhetorical flourish of turning a verdict into a chosen action on her part was yet another bit of defiance. Or perhaps of fatalism. In any event, she was right. Marie Collet was acquitted for lack of proof. Petit's death sentence was upheld.[114]

This was not a foregone conclusion. Even in these days of intensified repression on Von Sauberzweig's watch, quite a few of the death sentences required by Stoeber were not upheld by the courts. The October 1915 Cavell trial had yielded nine death sentences, with five upheld, and three of those then stricken. At the Parenté trial in May—another example of a "pyramid" trial with a small number of death sentences at the top and, for the "ranks," a range of prison sentences, fines, and even acquittals—there would be thirty-seven defendants (all men). Stoeber called for thirteen death sentences. The court upheld nine; Von Bissing commuted six of those; three people were executed. (Kirschen in asking for clemency had astutely appealed to Von Bissing's sense of legacy, pointing out that there were statues to Charles of Lorraine in Belgium, but none to the Duke of Alva.)[115] A week before Petit's trial, Marguerite Blanckaert was given a life sentence, against Stoeber's wishes. And one day before Petit's trial, another woman came very close to execution. On March 1 and 2 there was a major trial in Mons (in the Government-General, but outside of Stoeber's and Von Sauberzweig's remit). Death sentences were required against seventeen people; one of them was a young seamstress from Hainaut living in Brussels. Hermine Waneukem, twenty, had played a major role centralizing the different threads of a railway-observation network that had operated for British GHQ (Cameron's bureau) between July and December 1915 over a wide region from Ghent in the northeast to Saint-Ghislain, close to the French border, in the southeast.[116] Her role was confirmed. The prosecutor had required a double death penalty for her, with ten years' imprisonment thrown in for good measure. Like Blanckaert, Waneukem may have been saved by the intervention of a Belgian attorney, Thomas Braun; it may also have helped that several members of the Defense Committee were present, and that the trial was open to members of the German military. Braun, playing to his audience, alluded approvingly to Von Bissing's recent decree banning the blinding of songbirds, and compared the young woman—who was known to have sung in her prison-cell as she awaited trial, and now faced the court with charm and courage—to a songbird. ("How very French!" exclaimed one of the officers who had come to listen.) Braun then appealed to the judges' paternal sense: he painted them talking to their daughters after the war and mentioning the great Mons trial. "And when your daughter, General, will ask . . ., 'Father, you who held the fate of this young girl in your hands, what did you do?'—then, tell me, what would you rather answer: 'I had her shot', or 'I pardoned her'?" The plea proved effective. (So did, possibly, the fact that the young defendant would have been shot while her father, who was involved but not to the same extent, would have received a prison sentence.) Seven men were shot on the next day, but the young woman was saved. The court had pronounced a single death sentence for her, then introduced its own request for pardon, and immediately commuted it to life in prison.[117] "German justice," wrote a clandestine chronicler, "manifestly fears the repercussions of another Cavell case."[118]

Yes—to a point. Certainly there was the necessity of avoiding another international scandal. But there was also, among military commanders, an exasperated sense of being surrounded by stealthy enemies even as *"der letzte Schlag"*—Verdun—was stalling and German authority over the occupied was felt to remain relative.[119] Whether or not this led to an actual decision to lift the de facto moratorium on executing women, two possible checks on a fatal verdict for Petit had been eliminated: she did not have a Belgian lawyer, and her trial was held behind closed doors. Two weeks later, Louise de Bettignies would be condemned to death under the same circumstances.

But even with those two checks removed, given her gender and compared to the proven importance of other services, Petit's sentence seems particularly severe. To what can this be ascribed? In all probability not to the *Polizei*. Goldschmidt had a small role to play in sentencing: he would, as usual in these cases, have met with Stoeber a few days before the trial to hear Stoeber's intended required sentence, and he may well have intervened on Petit's behalf—word at Bureau A was that Goldschmidt "thought rather well of the little one." Stoeber would have put Goldschmidt's arguments before the judges during the deliberation.[120] Police arguments in favor of defendants sometimes swayed the judges. But not in Petit's case. The officer judges would not have appreciated the references to the 1914 atrocities, nor the other insults to the uniform hurled at them by this marginal young woman.

What had changed since Cavell—for men as well as women—was that the time of immediate execution was over. After the verdict, time was allotted for appeals to run their course. (Louis Bril was an exception.) Petit did not realize this; she expected to be shot the next day. The verdict shook her. After the confirmation hearing, which was over at half past eleven in the morning, she and Collet returned under armed guard to the courtyard of the *Kommandantur* to wait for their carriage back to Saint-Gilles prison. Finding *abbé* Mussche sitting in the janitor's room, she told him that her sentence was confirmed and Madame Collet was acquitted. She was, the priest recalled, "nervous—she laughed and cried." He and Collet recalled that she was singing the song "Paris-Berlin" to annoy the guards (containing the verse "We may be Germans / but not for long" and "They have Ferrer [a reference to the statue of Francesc Ferrer (see Introduction) which had been taken down, SdS] / but not the Yser"), telling them "that on the next day she would be 'boom', and she mimed the act of shooting." Then, calming down, she itemized her belongings for Marie Collet's benefit, to give to her family after her death.[121]

Though shaken, she remained practical for her friends' benefit. By noon, she ordered in coffee and smoked-meat *pistolets* for Marie Collet, Father Mussche, and a fellow arrestee, a man from Saint-Gilles condemned to ten days in prison for insult to the Germans. A lunch like that was a Belgian favorite, and a luxury even in peacetime. "It was the last meal she could offer me, she said," Marie Collet recalled. The meal created a little island of conviviality in the janitor's room at the *Kommandantur*; it was also a way to reclaim space in what had been a Belgian public building. (As Petit set the table, using the janitor's crockery, she told an apprehensive Collet that she was at home there whereas "they" were intruders.) Over lunch, Petit heard that Mussche was a priest. He offered to take her confession. She accepted, thinking it was her last day. With Marie Collet and the other arrestee on the lookout by the window, Mussche took Petit's confession. He urged her to take communion in prison. The little scene attests to the strong thread of catholicity that ran through Belgian wartime patriotism.[122]

At half past one, Mussche was called away. At four, he was reunited with Collet and Petit; they rode the carriage back to Saint-Gilles prison together. Both Mussche and Collet, after the war, left an account of this ride. "She talked—was quite nervous," Mussche recalled. Collet remembered Petit telling the priest "that she would show them how a Belgian woman knows how to die; that if they were to try to blindfold her she would spit in their faces."[123] (There is no reason to suspect that these words, which would become so much part of her story, were apocryphal; other condemned women used similar words, not in imitation of Petit—whose fate remained largely unknown during the war—but, like her, speaking in those tones of defiant pathos which Sadi Kirschen, with a hint of condescension, identified as coming straight out of the heroic novels so beloved by the lower middle class, such as Jules Verne's *Michael Strogoff*.[124])

En route back to prison, the question of pardon came up. (Most capital defendants had a request for pardon drawn up even before the confirmation of their sentence; if their verdict was upheld, they would then hand their request to the prosecutor.) Mussche asked Petit if she had appealed. She said she had not. He vehemently advised her to do so. As the priest persevered, Petit cut him short with the statement "I don't want to owe them anything"—spoken in such a tone, Mussche later said, that he thought it best not to insist. And so the conversation turned on "all kinds of things" during the rest of the hour-long ride. (In Collet's telling, her statement was more dramatic: "I will never lower myself before a German," she said.") Alighting from the van, thinking she would be executed shortly, Petit gave Marie Collet her prayer-book and rosary. It was Mussche's last view of her. Inside, at the doorstep of her cell, Petit handed Collet her other belongings of value: a fur muff, a pair of gloves, and a watch, to give to her sister Hélène after her execution. After this, Collet was taken to her own cell. She never saw her friend again. Although Collet had been acquitted, she was returned to the *Kommandantur* on the next day, March 4, and kept in custody for another month and a half—presumably to keep her from spreading news about Petit.[125]

CHAPTER 5
"UTTERLY ALONE," MARCH 3, 1916–
NOVEMBER 11, 1918

In 1922, Arthur Deloge would call *abbé* Mussche's farewell to Petit as she was led to her cell "Belgium's adieu to its child." From that moment onwards, Petit was still in the city—trams rode by the prison walls, the life of Brussels went on all around—but no longer of it. Isolated and confined, she was, Deloge wrote, to all intents and purposes already gone; "it remained for the casket to close to take her from us forever."[1] She was not that isolated, as the following paragraphs will show. Her relatives visited; she spoke to Otto Becker. But it was true that once Petit, condemned behind closed doors without an attorney who could have made her verdict known, was taken back to prison, her fate played out unnoticed by the public at large. Nor did she become a cause célèbre in the second half of the war. In contrast to Cavell's, hers was a forgotten fate by the time of the Armistice. This would make the discovery of her story all the more of an event: a speaker exhorted his audience in December 1918 to bear in mind that she met her end "utterly alone. She must have thought that her compatriots would never know her."[2]

Appeal

Yet that no-one would take Petit's fate to heart was not a foregone conclusion. The day after the verdict, Madame Vekens was released and immediately went to inform Hélène Ségard, much shaken, fearing the sentence had already been carried out. Ségard, by her own telling, refused to believe the worst—"Madame, . . . that child is so young, they cannot have taken her from me like this"—and the two women went out to find help, scanning the city walls for the dark pink execution poster.[3] Ségard might have come down in the world but still had some connections. She went to call on an acquaintance, a female German jurist (Ségard referred to her as a "lady lawyer," *dame avocate*) who had studied in Romania and had arrived in Brussels years earlier as a protégée of King Albert's mother Marie of Hohenzollern-Sigmaringen. (I have not been able to identify her.[4]) The jurist was skeptical that anything could be done, given Petit's trespasses against the German army, but promised to write to Stoeber forthwith to find out particulars and to draft an appeal. It was 10.30 in the evening. At seven in the morning on the next day, Ségard was back (after having inquired at the prison if her god-daughter was still alive). Nothing had yet been decided, the "*dame avocate*" told her, but, Ségard later said, "I could tell from her distressed look that the cause was lost." Ségard fetched Petit's sister Hélène and together they went to Saint-Gilles prison, where they found the Belgian administrator, Xavier Marin, unaware of imminent danger.[5] He was not typically informed of capital condemnations, and he thought Petit had been joking when she said that she had been condemned to death. When Ségard confirmed the condemnation, Marin reassured her that women would no longer be executed (like many others, he thought the Cavell fracas had seen to that) and that, at any rate, he had not seen the usual agitation that preceded executions. He told her to come back on the next day to enter a request for pardon.[6] The women then went to see the German prison chaplain, Father Leyendecker, at his residence at the German workers' confraternity (*Gesellenhaus*) in central Brussels. He laughingly dismissed their informant's credibility: "A lady! Go home and do not worry, I will inquire [but] it cannot be a serious matter. I know those ladies."[7]

On the next day, Monday, March 6 the German "lady lawyer" dictated Ségard the text of an appeal to Von Bissing. She remained pessimistic, telling Ségard to expect any visit she was granted with Petit in prison to be the last one. She had heard that Petit had "helped to annihilate entire regiments" and that the documents seized in her room were damning. She had been told of Petit's attitude at her trial and expressed her admiration. "What a woman! You can be proud of such a god-daughter." An upset Ségard announced she would lay the case before the Emperor himself, "tell him how young that child is and that she is my whole life." The "lady lawyer" dismissed her plan as naïve, but remained sympathetic; she promised to travel to Berlin herself if need be, and entreated Ségard to make sure her niece asked for pardon.

At the prison, Ségard presented her request for pardon, signed by herself and Hélène Petit, to Marin. Leyendecker was there; no longer mocking, he told her sternly that Petit was guiltier than Cavell and had made her case even worse by taunting her judges. He also told Ségard that Petit had refused to see him and to submit a request for pardon. Ségard gave him a statuette of Saint Joseph that had belonged to her dead sister to entice Petit to see him. Meanwhile, Xavier Marin handed the request to Wilhelm Behrens, the German commander of Saint-Gilles prison. He then alerted the Spanish legation, which phoned the Political Department of the Government-General. This was the moment when Petit's case, a complete secret up until then, became somewhat public; the Political Department, which had had to deal with the fallout from the Cavell case, now knew there was scrutiny from neutrals. After this, Marin went to alert the nuncio. It is unclear why he did not contact the United States legation as well.[8]

On March 8, Petit's godmother and sister were finally able to visit her. Gabrielle was led into the little *parloir*; she looked much the same and put the same brave face on things, saying that life was good at the prison: "we laugh, we sing, especially the Brabançonne [the forbidden Belgian national anthem]." She would keep up this image in later visits, joking how very chic it was to have a "telephone," refusing to complain about the prison food or the bedding. ("It is a bit hard, but I wrap myself in my coat, don't I?") Ever stoic, she made a point of paying her godmother's tram fare. She praised Becker as "nice." They clearly had a rapport: in front of her relatives, Becker gently reminded her that Chaplain Leyendecker's visit had made her cry. She admitted this. "He spoke about mother and about you; he said, 'your godmother was desperate, running along the prison corridors', and, yes, that made me cry."[9]

But not enough to make her want to sign a request for pardon. Petit's refusal took on a life of its own during the weeks that followed, as the specter of her execution waxed and waned. Meanwhile, the request signed by her godmother and sister made its way up the imperial hierarchy, unbeknownst to Petit and to all around her. Such requests typically went to the tribunal of the Government-General. This body was reputed to endorse pardon whenever feasible, but the Governor-General had the last word. If he rejected the appeal, the execution followed the next day. Between the confirmation of the sentence and the Governor-General's final decision, the interval could stretch to two or even three weeks. "One imagines," Ball wrote, "the agony of the poor prisoner."[10] In Petit's case, the interval was even longer. Otto Becker suggested in 1919, without knowing for certain, that Von Bissing had referred the matter to Berlin since he did not want sole responsibility for a woman's execution after the Cavell scandal.[11] Deloge, in 1922, suggested instead that Petit was kept alive so she would talk. In fact, the long wait was not deliberate, but the result of the appeals process, as I will show; but the interval may have been used for further questioning.[12]

As days followed upon days, Petit persisted in her refusal. Chaplain Leyendecker was instructed to advise her to appeal, and Otto Becker pleaded with her daily. "It was all in vain," he later wrote. "She would not bend; she was hard as steel. I tried to appeal to her pride by saying that with her superior intelligence, she could be useful to her fatherland after her return to Belgium if her sentence were commuted—but it was no good. She was adamant that requesting a pardon was a base thing to do. On the wall of her cell, behind the crucifix, she had written: 'I refuse to sign my request for pardon in order to show the enemy that I don't give a damn!'"[13] She was one of the rare capital defenders not to ask for pardon. Most of them had a request ready by the time of their final verdict; others drafted one shortly after. Some, like Baeckelmans, demurred but gave in out of consideration for their family. But a few defendants steadfastly refused to ask for pardon, Petit among them.

"I Can Do Anything If I Put My Mind To It"

She buttressed this terrible and lonely stance in loudly proclaimed defiance, just as she had done before her trial to strengthen her resolve not to name names. Indeed, for Petit, both seem to have been connected; requesting a pardon from the occupier was as shameful as giving away associates. Both were a sign of softening; both indicated a preference for life over resistance.[14] And so she continued to "make an infernal ruckus in her cell and in the exercise-yard," as Becker wrote, using all means possible to subvert the limits on expression that she was under. The day after the verdict, fellow prisoners heard her shout from the exercise-yard: "I have just been condemned to death. I will be shot tomorrow. Long live the King! Long live Belgium!" She even sang the aria "*Salut, ô mon dernier matin*" (from Gounod's *Faust*), Marie-Léonie Van Houtte reported.[15] Marie Collet, who was still held at the *Kommandantur*, at one point asked a woman guard and interpreter how Petit was doing. The guard took Collet's question as insolence and ordered her to shut up; Petit, she said, had harangued officers so rudely that she had been "too embarrassed" to translate her words.[16] In prison, Petit did not relinquish the claim to space that had been implicit in her war work. She who had "woven her way" across barriers, had refused to be intimidated by the stage-setting of military justice ("it's <u>our</u> Senate, Mother"), who had stared down gawkers on the way back from her trial, and had set the table at the *Kommandantur* to regale her fellow arrestees, would not now be crushed by the panoptic maze, designed to make prisoners feel very small indeed, that was Saint-Gilles prison. She would, wrote Becker, traverse the prison corridors on her way to and from the exercise-yard with "a proud, swift step," chin up, casting contemptuous glances at the wardens.[17] She continued to scribble graffiti on the walls of her cell, and managed to write little messages on the wall of the exercise-yard. (This was actually rather a grand term for the facility. In true panoptic fashion, the prisoners were led down a corridor to a little round vestibule, circled with doors that opened up into individual, steel-surrounded outdoor cages.[18]) Her graffiti were noticed by a fellow prisoner, a telegraph clerk named Chrétien Flippen who was awaiting sentencing in the Parenté trial, and was taken to the same "yard" at a different time. They struck up a conversation of sorts. As Flippen related it after the war, Petit had written down her name and cell number; he responded with some words of encouragement. Some of her notes were serene, others anguished: "No-one will ever know how much I have suffered," and "The days are centuries here, and I am so alone." One day, in response to his assurance that the German army would never execute a young woman, she answered: "No hope; I can be freed if I denounce my helpers. Never; I prefer to die."[19]

Her godmother recalled her looking deliberately disheveled, when she had always (according to Ségard) been so well put together. "You don't enjoy being elegant then, Gabrielle, at the Boches'?—Oh, that would do them too much honor."[20] Other prisoners made a point of sprucing up, as best the conditions of prison allowed, so as to demonstrate unbroken spirit. One of the defendants in the Cavell case, for instance, deplored that some of his fellow prisoners had showed up for the reading of the final verdict without ties or collars, their dishevelment expressing abject despondency.[21] De Bettignies and Van Houtte, before their trial, had managed to add a note of elegance to their drab clothes with little lace collars, carefully set aside for that purpose, which they had pressed by placing them under their mattresses. Petit, by contrast, with her hair undone and her long blue overcoat over her dressing-gown, exhibited a defiant dishevelment in prison— just as she had done, years ago, as an angry, bewildered teenager in Brussels. "I am at home here, no-one should disturb me," she told her godmother; which perhaps indicates that she considered her cell the place where she held on to her resolve, in the process turning almost feral.[22]

But she had a visitor in her cell: Otto Becker, who came to see her several times a day on the pretense of lending or borrowing books. He usually found her with an embroidery-work or with a book—always annotating her readings. Relishing their brief conversations, she talked so volubly that he had difficulty following her at times. Revealingly, Becker described her as "more man than woman," with "the free bearing of an American woman." He claimed that she exhibited a great hostility to all things German. "She would reject even the most perfect thing for being German. . . . Her hatred was implacable; I found something incomprehensible in it. It was, in my opinion, somewhat obsessive."[23]

It may have been. But no such reflexive xenophobia appears in a letter Petit wrote to Becker during those weeks (probably in late March). In December 1919, Becker would send it to Xavier Marin. Marin transcribed the parts he deemed suitable for public knowledge—that is, the parts that did not refer to her family. Unfortunately, this shortened transcript is the only form in which the letter survives; no archive possesses the original. Even so, it is a revealing document, expressing feelings about citizenship rather more sophisticated than the ones Becker ascribed to her—and showing keen insight in other matters besides.[24] She started by commenting on the "great liberty" she was taking in writing to him, but she wanted to communicate at some more length than was possible during "our furtive little visits," when the sound of steps in the corridor would shut them up. She told Becker what she thought of him: "I think you are a good person, ready to help within limits, that is, when you don't consider that your nation is being threatened." There followed a description of her life and of her fiancé which Marin, by his own admission, had cut, then allowed to resume mid-sentence: "and yet he [Gobert] loved me with all his soul; I tried everything I could to distance him from me, but to no avail. I tried to love him; I couldn't; I have a great deal of respect for him; but that's all. I did accept the engagement ring and I formally promised to be his wife, because I saw him so desperate. So if he returns and holds me to the engagement, I will marry him, because I respect formal engagements—and perhaps that man's devotion and the home will change me. He knows full well I don't love him, besides I have never been able to love anybody, I admitted as much to him." It is impossible to say whether Petit really believed Gobert was still hers for the taking, or used Becker as a sounding-board for a fantasy—or whether her portrayal of the dynamics between herself and Gobert might not perhaps have been closer to the truth than her onetime fiancé would acknowledge after the war. At any rate, there is no denying Petit's matter-of-fact appraisal of herself to Becker. "I do believe," she wrote, "that I will leave this life without ever having felt deeply. I only appear animated; when my nerves falter, I am quite worthless." Having said this, "underneath my nerves, I possess a very strong will; because I am high-strung, I appear to be something of a hothead and tend to be misunderstood; yet I am quite different from what people think of me." (She was not as misunderstood as all that. Abbé Mussche's assessment of her was strikingly similar. He described her after the war as "a valiant [woman] who knew what she was doing—[she had] a bit of an exalted temperament, but reasoned lucidly—a very determined character ... [who possessed a] sound understanding of things."[25])

Petit's letter then assumed a brisk enough-about-me tone. "Let's change the subject, because I am trying your patience." Why had she written about herself so confidentially? Because it was the only way to open up to someone with whom, things being as they were, she could not be friends: "[W]e will not be able to meet later on ...: you will be in an army that I execrate ... and I am a spy." She declared that she "loathed" the term spy. (In this, she shared the feelings of many intelligence agents; "spy" sounded louche.) Yet she would "enthusiastically" do it all over again, "for I like danger to begin with, and hatred does the rest." She then addressed Becker on his national loyalty. "The voice of blood talks in you; if you were asked to, you would fight us, and yet your country has not

been able to keep you" [because Becker had lived for years in Brussels]. She apologiz
for talking about Becker's national feelings, admitting it was a sensitive issue that w
none of her business—but in the same breath expressed confidence of being able
change his mind, telling him, in a tone both intimate and imperious, that "if I were to li
with you for a long time, I would ... try to convince you, and you know that you can
strong-willed but when I have something in mind I will achieve it come what may. Do
laugh; you don't know me. I can do anything if I put my mind to it."

In the final paragraph, she went back to talking about Gobert. "One more thing—st
pitying the man who will be my husband." Becker apparently had berated her on her la
of womanly meekness.

> I will do my duty; I will do everything in my power to thank him for the kindness
> he has shown me. I will ask him beforehand to be understanding. I will not let
> myself be dominated. Yet I will not be so silly as to try to dominate <u>him</u>, and if I
> should end up doing so anyway, it will never be in public. Even if I do not love him,
> I will respect him.

Sensing that Becker might contrast this with her present behavior, she added: "My rule
behavior in prison is different. Here I am facing the enemy. It is my right and even n
duty to despise him, to resist him and ... to give him a hard time, regardless of t
consequences." And with that, she announced that she was going to bed, expressing t
hope that Becker would not take her "litany" amiss and cease to visit her.

This remarkably level-headed letter shows that if Petit resented the Germans, it was
occupiers; and that she had a well-developed sense of what she considered her duty a
civilian under occupation. Her behavior in prison was a careful enactment rather th
mere unruliness. She accepted that her breaking of the rules entailed consequences, ar
bore no grudge. In a post-scriptum to her letter, she mentioned having been caught usi
the "telephone" that afternoon, and said she knew it had been Becker who had told t
guard. "I found this quite natural [on your part]. You don't want me to incite my priso
mates to rebel against an authority that you respect."[26]

Perhaps in an effort to bolster her resolve, she copied song lyrics from memory.[27]
transcribing such verse, she expressed pathos to a far greater extent than she did in h
own written words. For Petit, as for so many of her contemporaries, popular songs-
melodramatic narratives of misunderstood heroism, murdered innocence, or unrequit
love; protest chants, laments, satires, and so on, their lyrics sold on loose-leaf sheets c
the street, and sung to known tunes at home, in family gatherings, at work, in public-
offered a way to think through what she was facing.[28] In London, just parted fro
Gobert, she had transcribed love lyrics. The songs she turned to in prison offered mo
of a mix of public and private concerns. Two of them lamented France's loss of Alsac
In other words, she turned to French national pathos, much more developed befo
the war than its Belgian equivalent, though one notes that both songs were written b
Belgian immigrants in France.[29] Two more songs staged the brave death of milita
volunteers; both, tellingly, centered on parting from a beloved mother. At one poir

Petit's transcription features a telling lapsus: the hero becomes a woman ("Then, expiring, she [*sic*] said very softly: 'adieu, maman aimée' . . .").[30] The last two songs depart from these soldierly and patriotic themes. *Les Misères de l'Ouvrier* (The Sorrows of the Working-Man) is a startlingly bitter diatribe against the "accursed rich" who exploit the workers who work or fight for them and reduce working-class women to prostitution, then leave the poor, spent, to die in charity wards. And yet, as the song's bitter envoi has it, they inherit the earth: "Sons of Cain, you are the elected." A different, ambiguous note is struck by the last *chanson* in Petit's little anthology. *Qui M'aurait Dit* (Who'd Have Told Me) was a lilting romance about lost love, typical music-hall fare. After the war, Marguerite Blanckaert claimed that Petit in prison only sang Belgian patriotic anthems and Walloon folk-songs, not silly modern romances.[31] Yet this transcript—like the transcripts and sheet music of earlier periods in her life—hints that Petit was receptive enough to pop sentimentality. *Qui M'aurait Dit* tells the story of a lover who falls for a beguiling sprite of a girl and embarks on a steamy romance, only to have his heart broken. The story is told after the fact, when the lover, stumbling upon a stash of stale love-letters, suddenly discovers he is over the affair: "One suffers, one weeps, and then one day / The heart is tired of the pain / Who'd have told me that so much love / Would leave so little trace?"[32] Was Petit implicitly commenting on her relationship with Maurice Gobert? Did she cast herself as the seductress wary of commitment? It was not the first time she transcribed a romance about a cruel temptress.[33] Or was she the spurned one? At any rate this choice of song shows that she was familiar with the formidable dynamics of attraction.

"Never Mind, We'll See"

It shows her very much alive and hints that she veered between defiant acceptance of death and hoping for life. Meanwhile, she suffered greatly from isolation, as she wrote to Becker: "isolation saps me, silence weighs on me."[34] Apart from his furtive calls, she was visited regularly by Goldschmidt. It is unclear whether the detective superintendent still hoped for information, urged her to appeal, or both. He presented her with a satchel of chocolates on her name-day, Saint Gabriel, March 18. Postwar Petit lore had her trample those *pralines* to demonstrate resolve, but nothing indicates that such an indignant scene took place. She seems to have relied on Goldschmidt for practical matters: she asked him, for one thing, to settle the rest of her debt with her landlady.[35]

After the complete isolation of February, she was now allowed family visits. Her godmother was allowed a visit once a week, as was her sister. Both women would subsequently begrudge the other her memories of Petit, and claim to have been the one closest to her. For Petit, family brought solace, but also a resurgence of worries. Hélène Petit, especially, as seems to have been her habit, introduced an element of discord. She told her sister that her landlady Auguste Dickmans was badmouthing her and demanded rent; Hélène asked Gabrielle to itemize her possessions to make sure they were not taken. Hurt, Petit drew up a list. She also wrote a letter to Dickmans that expressed her sentiments eloquently—a mixture of dignity (with some pathos), practicality, and sadness at the estrangement of someone she thought of as an ally:

Madame,

I have been extremely surprised to hear that you have spoken so very ill of me, that is not very nice of you. What do you have to reproach me for? We got along so well . . . I know it is not very pleasant to come to grief with the German authorities or to see one's place upended, which is my fault . . . [After] I went on trial and was condemned to death [,] I had a hundred francs left [and] spent it all [because] I thought I would be shot on March 4 . . . I am still here, I still don't know what is going to happen, I have refused to ask for pardon up until now and will continue to do so. I feel that the decision is up to the judges and their conscience. . . . I am ready whatever comes. I have never been so calm in my life. I went to see the commissar [Goldschmidt] on the 18th, he gave me a satchel of pralines for my name-day. I mentioned you. I expect to have my money any day . . . and will then send you what you are owed, even though people tell me here that I don't really owe you any rent since I left your house under duress. But, you see, I don't care one way or another. So I will give you 19 francs' rent, 9 francs' sundry expenses, 75 centimes for the key and 2.50 francs for your travel costs and my laundry. But I will deduct 2 kilos of green coffee beans at 3.60 a kilo, and 1 kilo of sugar . . . Oh well! It's all past now but you should have understood that I could hardly tell you that I was a spy, and anyway there is no dishonor in that, these are services for the fatherland that I will soon pay for with my life. I believe that, as a lodger, I gave you no reason to complain . . . Now then, Madame, it's farewell probably, to you and all acquaintances.

Mademoiselle Petit.[36]

The letter never reached Dickmans; Hélène Petit held on to it, together with the list of personal effects that her sister drew up. The inventory itemizes the humblest object in her rented room ("2 large tin boxes, 1 small red one, 1 pretty carton with a faded ribbon") which shows that her things mattered to her. It also shows refinement—Petit listed soap and eau de Cologne, priceless commodities in wartime—and suggests elegance: "1 blue blouse with braids, 1 brown velvet one, 1 green, 1 white shirtwaist, 1 white blouse."[37] Petit came to regret her harsh tone to Dickmans, suspecting her sister had made up the story in order to get a list of her things; her godmother thought so too.[38] (Edith Cavell, in one of her last letters, had had a point in saying that, much as she liked the Belgians, malicious gossip was a national flaw and a drag on personal and professional relations.[39]) Up until the end, Petit was not allowed to forget that her relatives would never reconcile and that money was a source of unending bitterness.

Meanwhile, the question of pardon still hung. As the immediate threat of execution receded, Petit's hopes went up. Her wardens did not think she would be executed. On March 3, after Petit had handed Collet her belongings, "a German officer" came to instruct Collet "not to give away any of the little one's things ... because she would come back after the war, since they did not shoot women any more."[40] By the end of Petit's first week in prison, Wilhelm Behrens told Xavier Marin that he thought the execution was off.[41] She started to entertain hope. On March 10, she sent a card to Marie Collet's home (not knowing her friend was still incarcerated):

> My dear Mother,
> I am still here, waiting. I have received no news. I still believe the death sentence has been commuted to life in prison, otherwise it seems to me I would have been executed already. But never mind, we'll see. As for me, I am ready, I am not troubled at all. Do hold on to all my things, because if I do not get capital punishment, I would like to find everything when I return—and if I have to go, when you will be sure of it, then hand all the things I mentioned to Marraine. She and my sister have come to visit. I hope you are all doing as well as I do. Take heart. Kisses to all. [Signed] Gaby Petit, Cell 37, Saint-Gilles prison.[42]

She wrote a card to her godmother on the same day:

> 10.3.16. My dear Marraine, I was happy to see you and cousin [Ségard's cousin Alice Guilbau, who lived with her, SdS], it had been a while.... I still don't know anything. Will the death penalty be commuted to life in prison? I don't know, but I think so. I'm only 23, I am a bit young, that is probably the reason why I am still alive. Do me a favor and spare me some silk and an embroidery-pattern so I have something to do. I hope to see you next week. You can come pick up my laundry on Wednesdays and Saturdays. Kisses and courage to all three. Gabrielle Petit. Cell 37—Saint-Gilles Prison.[43]

Though she refused to sign an appeal, it could be that, with time, Petit came to expect her sentence to be commuted without having to ask for it herself. In mid-March, she told her godmother to say farewell to the family in Tournai, but she also said she might be sent to Germany, so did not need to enter a request for pardon.[44] Becker gave up trying to convince Petit to appeal, "because we Germans were persuaded that women would no longer be executed, after the commotion that the execution of Miss Cavell had made; and the delay in Gabrielle's execution only strengthened our belief, which was also shared by the political police."[45] The *Polizei*, the wardens at Saint-Gilles, and Becker all reassured Petit she was safe, and, Becker wrote, "as her imprisonment dragged on, she eventually became convinced of this herself." As was clear from Petit's letter to Becker, written in late March, she made plans for her future life. When Marie-Léonie Van Houtte, pardoned, was taken to Germany, Petit told her over the "telephone" to "keep a spot for me," but added that if she had to die, she would be strong. Van Houtte left on March 24.[46] A week later, Petit had still not been taken to Germany and started to expect the worst.[47] She was refused her heart medication for fear she would commit suicide (an overdose of digitalis was lethal), as well as scissors for her needlework. She told her godmother on March 30 that these precautions were unnecessary since she fully intended to "die with the honor guard," as she called the execution squad. At the same time, Ségard recalled, "she was in a laughing and confident mood," and joked: "can you imagine me going off to eat potato peels at the Boches'?" (Even in these circumstances, Petit partook of the occupied population's Schadenfreude over the effects of the blockade on Germany.) Yet there were notes of farewell too: she asked for a Belgian priest and talked about her feelings for her Tournai family in the past tense. At the same time, Ségard recalled, "She was smiling. I considered we were gaining time. I felt hopeful again. It seemed to me they could not wipe out such a young child." In the courtyard, Marin shared her optimism. And so she went home, determined to continue her appeals.[48]

Rejection

On the next day, March 31, at ten in the morning, an MP knocked on Hélène Ségard's door with a yellow envelope bearing a *Kommandantur* stamp. "I had a flash of hope. I looked at [my cousin] and saw her turn pale. The soldier was speaking German. I understood the words 'Gabrielle Bedide'. I took the envelope and opened it, saying to [my cousin] that it was the reply to my request for pardon. Seeing that I did not understand, the soldier cruelly mimed the act of shooting, saying: tomorrow . . . He was very harsh in front of two poor women." When the two women tried to get the soldier indoors to explain the matter to their neighbors to make sure they had not misunderstood, he fled, fearing a trap. (Fear of francs-tireurs had not completely abated among the troops stationed in Belgium.) Ségard and Guilbau rushed to the *Kommandantur* to "try to obtain a stay of execution, get a Belgian priest, and above all say farewell." They were made to wait, in vain, until the offices closed for lunch. They then walked a mile across central Brussels to Leyendecker, whom they saw at one o'clock. The chaplain confirmed that he was to read the rejection of the pardon to Petit in her cell that afternoon. He refused to intercede to obtain a Belgian priest, invoking "orders from my Emperor." Hélène Ségard shouted abuse at him; he shushed her. The women insisted they had to see their niece one last time: "we will not falter, we want to prepare her to die, as a priest you cannot refuse this," said Guilbau, who had known Petit as a little girl. Leyendecker gave in and handed them a permit to take to the *Kommandantur*. They walked back as fast as they could. The officer in charge claimed it was not in his power to grant such a permission, but, sympathetically, offered to go and talk to Stoeber. From behind closed doors, the women heard a vivid altercation. Re-emerging, the officer wanted to know who had told them the day and hour of execution, adding that "just because the pardon has been rejected does not mean that young girl has to die tomorrow."[49] (Actually, it did: in Brussels, executions always took place on the morning following the rejection of the pardon.[50]) Ségard and Guilbau mentioned Leyendecker and the messenger soldier. Both men, it turned out, had been out of line. The *Kommandantur* had wanted to keep the execution secret: "no-one, not even the relatives, was supposed to know, in order to avoid disturbance in town," wrote Otto Becker.

While Ségard and her cousin were kept waiting at the *Kommandantur*, observing the usual dismal cortège of arrestees and their desperate relatives, a phone call was placed to prison. Petit was to be executed on the next morning, but must not be told just yet, and neither should her sister, who would be visiting her shortly. Otto Becker was shocked. He could not resist going to Petit in her cell, where his devastated expression gave him away. ("She calmly said: 'I will be shot tomorrow.'") A quarter of an hour later, Hélène Petit arrived; Gabrielle, Becker wrote, was "very cheerful." After the visit, Becker broke orders and told Hélène that her sister was scheduled to die on the next day; he advised her to plead with Von Bissing at his residence, Trois-Fontaines château outside of Brussels. An hour later, an envoy from the *Kommandantur*, bearing the rejection of the pardon, interrogated Becker and the guards to find out who had leaked the secret. "The whole town knew."[51] Becker denied that he had said anything to anyone. He was ordered to accompany the officer to Petit's cell to translate the final verdict. "I had to follow orders," he wrote in late 1919. "It was the worst moment of my life. I had to announce her death sentence, to this heroic woman whom I admired so unreservedly, whom I had come to respect . . . and for whom I had a keen liking; I, who was so to speak her only friend in prison, the only one who took her mind off her plight" . . . It was six o'clock. Petit had twelve hours to live. Becker recalled her flushing violently as she heard the verdict but recovering her composure almost immediately. The officer told her to make arrangements regarding her money, which was still held at the *Kommandantur*. She "very calmly" took pencil and paper and "in a firm and swift hand" wrote a note.[52]

Goodbyes

The note still exists: sixteen hastily but clearly written lines in blue pencil on a note-card. It reads:

> My dear Marraine,
>   your request for pardon has been rejected. I thank you for your kindness. Farewell, I have courage.- You will be given from me a sum of FIVE HUNDRED EIGHTY-ONE FRANCS. Would you please share ~~it~~ [*sic*] with my sister Hélène. My clothes etc. to the two of you. Give my thanks to cousin Bara.
>   Kisses and farewell.
>   [signed] Gabrielle Petit.
>   30-3-16. [*sic*][53]

This was a strikingly matter-of-fact little note. Her very last messages to her family, written at daybreak on the next morning, would be slightly more effusive (see below), but they too mainly showed a stoic practicality. She was behind by one day; the date matters, as I will show. After this, Becker was briefly left alone with Petit; she laughed at his distraught mien and said that some would be relieved, meaning her collaborators whose names she had not given away. Allowed once more to take exercise in the little outdoor cage, she wrote on its doorjamb: "They consent to shoot me tomorrow. Farewell to all, my unknown and much-tried friends. Gaby Petit."[54]

In the meantime, Hélène Ségard and Alice Guilbau had finally obtained their permit. The sympathetic commander at the *Kommandantur* (possibly Wilhelm Behrens) told them how he admired Petit. "I rather liked that proud young girl. Such a pity, such a valiant one. She would have made such a good wife and mother, that brave Gabrielle!" He advised Ségard that the last visit would upset her too much. Ségard asked him rhetorically why her niece was to be executed if everybody thought so highly of her, assured him that they would be strong, and left thanking him.[55]

At Saint-Gilles, where the women arrived at six, the time of the announcement, Marin burst into fury when he heard Petit was not pardoned. Otto Becker led them to the visiting-room, telling them that she was "in a serene and laughing mood, as ever." They thanked him for his kindness.[56] They found Petit calm and upbeat. "Self-possessed, she got up and went towards us, and embraced us, smiling." She thanked Alice Guilbau for having come along, and told her godmother: "My path [*carrière*] is at an end, Marraine, I knew it." But she would do it all over again "even if it has all been for nothing." She told her not to be sad: "I leave without regrets." She promised to write and to finish the embroidery she had started for her. "I will never forget her attitude," Ségard later said. Standing proudly before her godmother, as she used to do as a child, Petit stated: "I have been condemned alone, I could have sold my people, I have refused. I did well, didn't I, Marraine?" According to Ségard, Petit then—speaking very rapidly—told her she would leave her a sum of almost 600 francs, money owed her because Petit's father had sold the piano that had belonged to the two Ségard sisters, and Aline, in hospital, had made the little girl promise to pay back her godmother. "I was so touched I could not speak," Ségard later said. "Valiant child! To think of something like that at such a time!"[57]

It seems almost impossible that Hélène Ségard could have made this exchange up, and yet the note Petit had written earlier, and another note she wrote on the following morning (see below), suggest that Petit wanted the money to be divided between her godmother and her sister. There is no need to suspect bad faith on Ségard's part. It is possible that Petit, as children of bitterly divided families will, was even in extremis trying to keep everybody happy. She hoped to see Goldschmidt, who was in charge of her funds, and make sure her money would go to her relatives; but contrary to his habits, he did not show up that day.[58] Petit deplored her sister's estrangement from her godmother; "my sister is hopeless."[59] She then hastily wrote down the address of the Brussels attorney whom she had contacted the year before to represent Baeckelmans, telling Ségard to greet him from her. (Reminding a member of the bourgeoisie of her existence, just as she had done with "cousin Bara," may have been an attempt to leave her family with socially useful contacts.) She kissed and comforted her godmother: "It is not such a pity, I have never been strong. Don't be too sad." Otto Becker, who as usual was present during the visit, recalled her as even more cheerful than usual; "she laughed in pride over her own strength and wished me all possible happiness."[60] She repeated: "I have always been firm in the face of danger, do not fear, Marraine." She was then led away; from the end of the corridor, she shouted "No blindfold!"[61]

Ségard and Guilbau left the prison, "barely knowing where we were." Marin suggested asking for help at the Spanish legation and at the nunciatura. Outside, the women found Hélène Petit waiting; she joined them on the five-kilometer trek to the Spanish legation. Marin went on his own steam. The Spanish envoy, the Marquis de Villalobar, was not in; they left a message and went on to the nunciatura in central Brussels. The nuncio, Monsignor Tacci, heard them out, then, "lifting his eyes to Heaven, said 'another martyr.'" He promised to see what he could do. Shortly after, they saw his automobile leave. By then, it was ten o'clock in the evening. Whether Tacci had managed to contact the German authorities, and whether he had pleaded for pardon or just for the consolation of a Belgian priest, they never knew.[62]

Meanwhile, at the prison, there was still hope for a last-minute reprieve, as Otto Becker later told Alice Guilbau.[63] At least until midnight; then, Petit, exhausted, went to sleep. When Becker came into her cell at 4.00 a.m., he found her tidying her things before sitting down to write. To her sister, she wrote:

> My dear Hélène,
>
> I send you my farewell, don't regret anything, it is nature! Such is life, you see, you leave it the way you entered it, I regret nothing. Above all be good and brave. Please don't forget what I told you about my English grammar-book. Be sure to say that it has to be kept in memory of me and to thank the person for their kindness to me. By all means do not forget. And when you receive good advice, do listen to it, in memory of
>> Your little sister
>> Gabrielle Petit
>> Saturday morning
>> March 31, 1916.
>
> It's the last day of Saint Joseph's month and a Saturday, what a beautiful day to die. Kiss Marraine and cousine [Alice Guilbau]. My best to you all and adieu

The "kind person" was Otto Becker. Bequeathing an English grammar-book to a member of the wartime German military was a legacy of some wit.[64] The message shows that Petit was still one day behind: it was a Saturday, but April 1. Her note that March 31 was "the last day of the month of Saint Joseph" was more than a rote indication of time; saints' time offered a sense of protection and the consolation of cyclicality. Petit, in her cell, had a medallion and statuette of Saint Joseph, the patron-saint of education; and she marked the passing days on a tiny saints' calendar.[65] Her belief that March 31 was her last day was, as her letter shows, a source of solace. Otto Becker may have had the date confused himself.[66] Either that or he—and the rest of the prison administration—deliberately kept the date from Petit to spare her the humiliation of knowing she would die on April Fools' Day. There is no direct indication that was deliberately chosen. Yet the interval between Tuesday, March 28, when Berlin's final rejection of the appeal reached Brussels, and the execution on Saturday was exceptionally long. The choice of date, if it was intentional, may have been calculated to keep the execution under the radar, since April Fools' Day was a tradition in Belgium as in Germany.[67]

She wrote a final letter—a note, rather—to her sister, godmother, and cousin Alice Guilbau.

> Dear all three,
>
> My last message, I will keep it short, it is 5 a.m. (Belgian time), in one or two hours' time I will send you my farewell from far away. As I mentioned, a sum of 581 francs will be handed to Marraine, she is to use it to pay for the five Masses I have requested from the prison chaplain, and to pay my outstanding rent at the rue du Théâtre—the rest is to be divided between Marraine and Hélène. All of my clothes will go to Hélène as well as several other things.
>
> My fur muff, my ring with the little diamonds and my good gloves are at Mother Collet's. I embrace her a lot, the dear old one. My farewells at Butin's— Mother Collet can take care of that.
>
> Be brave, kisses, and to all three of you from the heart.
>
> Gabrielle Petit.[68]

This letter clearly stated that her money was to be divided between her godmother and sister; her clothes went to her sister alone. To the last, Petit walked a fine line between competing loyalties. One notes too that one of her last thoughts was for her former employer Laure Butin. The terse practicality of this last message contrasts with other prisoners' last letters—and with her ironic and fond message to Otto Becker.

Execution

At five o'clock, Leyendecker came to give Petit communion.[69] For the first time, she broke down; Becker saw her coming out of her cell, eyes red from weeping.[70] The wardens formed a guard of honor in the corridor. As she passed Becker, she made a gesture of farewell. She left the prison "with a firm step, like a soldier," the guard at the door reported later. From the carriage, she waved at Becker. Xavier Marin, who had been up all night, had wanted to see her one last time, but missed her by minutes. Hélène Ségard and Alice Guilbau stood outside the prison to watch the little blue carriage leave. Ségard, unable to stomach the sight of the prison, then left to sit in a nearby church. Guilbau went in, finding Marin and his wife devastated. Marin told her he had wanted to show Petit a Belgian uniform, possibly to keep her courage up. Becker, too, was in tears; "one felt sorry for him," reported Guilbau.[71]

The ride would have taken some twenty minutes. At the execution-grounds, the officials present were Stoeber and his secretary, an interpreter, the German army chaplain Paul Le Seur, and the army doctor (possibly Gottfried Benn).[72] Both Le Seur and Benn relayed their impressions of the executions of Cavell and Baucq, as did Leyendecker. But the only confirmed eyewitness account of Petit's death is that of

Leyendecker. One of the guards told Otto Becker of Petit's sangfroid: when she and the chaplain left the carriage, she went back to get his prayer-book and calmly handed it to him.[73] Leyendecker did not mention this. He was, he wrote in early 1921, the last person she spoke to after the departure from prison. In the carriage, they recited the rosary with her. She told him she wanted no blindfold, saying "I am not afraid of looking into the rifles, I have been expecting this for a long time." He advised her to accept.

At the *Tir National*, the execution was set for six o'clock. As Petit was placed at the stake, she once more tried to ward off the blindfold, but Leyendecker silenced her with the words "let nothing disturb you in your thoughts of Heaven." They pressed hands. "Gabrielle Petit did not say another word."[74]

Her body, in its long dark overcoat, was placed in a simple wooden coffin and buried in an unmarked grave on the execution-grounds.

"Let Justice Run Its Course"

If Petit had wanted her end to be one last confrontation with power, the chaplain, the only eyewitness to her death, portrayed it as a moment of acquiescence. Patriotic accounts had her politely tell a guard, who offered his arm, that she could walk by herself and would show him how she could die, but Leyendecker denied such an exchange had happened; she had ended up accepting the blindfold ("one word from me was enough"); and she had died in silence, not with the defiant last cry ascribed to her.[75] A few days after the execution, the chaplain told Ségard and Guilbau that Petit had shown no fear, "she was a valiant girl," and that she had died serenely. "She had rid herself of her bellicose attitude and pardoned her enemies. Console yourselves, it was a fine death."[76] Around that time, the chaplain met Petit's aunt Louise Pilatte-Petit in the street. He knew her because she had spent half a year in prison for her involvement in the underground press.[77] She asked him how her niece had died; he assured her it had been "a very fine death." In fact, he added, "our Lord God has been most merciful on her, for with her character she would never have been happy in this world."[78] Military justice ultimately wrought serenity.

And so the dark pink poster went up. The authorities announced that:

> By a judgment of the military tribunal of March 2, 1916, GABRIELLE PETIT, saleswoman, living in Molenbeek, has been condemned
> TO DEATH
> for treason in wartime on grounds of espionage.
> The accused has confessed to having organized, for a substantial fee, a railway spying service [*sic*], and to have, over several months, transmitted to enemy intelligence the reports drawn up by the agents she had engaged.
> The judgment has been executed.

One notes that the poster did not mention the date of Petit's execution. In the same breath, the authorities announced that Louise de Bettignies of Lille, "without profession," had been condemned to death on March 16 but was pardoned on the 23rd.[79]

As it happened, De Bettignies' fate would be terrible. She underwent the harsh prison regime of Siegburg in Germany and died in a hospital in Cologne in 1918 after an operation to remove a chest tumor. She was thirty-eight years old and suffered so badly that she wrote to a friend she would have preferred execution.[80] But she *had* been pardoned, even though her wartime work was more important than that of Petit. At Police Bureau A, "we all thought it an injustice crying out for revenge that the Countess [*sic*] de Bettignies [was pardoned] whereas little Petit, much less compromised than she, had to die. They should both have been pardoned," wrote Fritz Ball; he said as much to Otto Becker during the war.[81] The general feeling was that De Bettignies' status had saved her and that Petit's lack of status and respectability had done her in. Jean Burtard, the star spy at Bureau A, swore that Von Bissing had decided to lift the ban on executing women, but selectively. With several women condemned to death, the Governor-General "asked after the social status and the morals of each one of them and pardoned several ladies of the nobility and bourgeoisie. His choice fell on Gabrielle Petit because she was registered as a prostitute with the German vice squad and was addicted to cocaine."[82]

Did Von Bissing make such a decision? Or was this just a story bandied about at Bureau A? It was, at any rate, not true that Petit was listed as a prostitute. It is possible to investigate this because the German vice squad (*Sittenpolizei*) of Greater Brussels kept meticulous lists of prostitutes under medical control (a task considered crucial to army health). These lists still exist, though it requires considerable effort to locate them. They cover the occupation years from the spring of 1915 onwards. It turns out that Petit is nowhere on these lists.[83] Nor is there any document that indicates she used cocaine.[84]

But it is true that Von Bissing had decided not to pardon her. He had done so early on, at the latest by March 11—in other words, at the time when she was starting to express hope. The text of his decision has not survived, but there is revealing documentation on how it was wrapped up at the highest level.[85] By March 11, Von Bissing's decision, with an additional message from military governor Von Sauberzweig, reached the Imperial Military Court in Berlin. One week later, the Court's president, infantry general Count Günther von Kirchbach, reported to the Emperor that he agreed "on all essential points" with Von Bissing's reasoning: Petit had been "an energetic and, it would seem, effective spy," demonstrably appreciated by her principals (judging from intercepted messages from the Netherlands). Von Kirchbach stressed that the police report brought out Petit's "superior intelligence" in striking fashion. She had known perfectly well what she was doing and what risks she ran in joining the Belgian [*sic*] intelligence service. (Clearly, Petit had given away so little that the German police and judiciary did not even know she worked for the British.) Her decision, Von Kirchbach wrote, seemed motivated above all by "fanatical German-hatred," although, he added, she might have hoped for substantial earnings later on. (So the police knew she had not been making a great deal of money.)

As a final point, Von Kirchbach cited Von Sauberzweig's argument that the safety of the army required "unrelenting action" against spies regardless of gender. He concluded his report by entreating His Majesty to "let justice run its course" and sent it to the Emperor on March 18.[86]

It cannot have escaped Von Kirchbach, or anyone else, that Petit would be the first woman shot behind the Western Front since Cavell. Right around that time, there was major diplomatic pressure to pardon a Frenchwoman named Adrienne Beljean. She was condemned to death in Charleroi in December 1915 for spying on the fortress of Maubeuge. Von Bissing refused to pardon her, but the execution was stayed for months, allowing a clemency campaign on her behalf to gain speed. In late February 1916, the Foreign Office in Berlin had suggested an exchange: Beljean would be pardoned if the French government would release German nationals jailed in Morocco. The proposal was put to the French via the Spanish embassies on March 29. Beljean was ultimately pardoned and sent to prison in Germany.[87] Petit, too, benefited from some diplomatic effort: on March 13, the Spanish Embassy in Berlin let the Imperial Foreign Office know that the King of Spain asked for clemency.[88] On March 20, the legal department of the Foreign Office asked both Von Kirchbach and the Political Department in Brussels where the matter stood.[89]

One week later, on March 27, Von Kirchbach telegraphed back to say that "His Majesty has ordered the execution of Petit's sentence."[90] If this caused any consternation in the legal department, there is no trace of it. The only response was an urgent demand to Brussels for immediate briefing on what the Foreign Office should tell the King of Spain.[91] Count Hans Albrecht Von Harrach of the Political Department in Brussels sent a brief, vague description of Petit's work, quoted her as saying that she had wanted to harm the German army, and pointed out, as a clinching argument, that "her attitude before the court has been extremely insolent and defiant."[92] The Foreign Office used this précis to respond to the Spanish Embassy. The response expressed "great regret" that the order to proceed had to be given since there were no mitigating circumstances. It was drawn up on March 29, with instructions not to deliver it—verbally—until April 1. In other words, the Spanish appeal was not answered until after it was too late.[93]

What all of this means is that once Von Bissing had rejected the request for pardon by Petit's relatives, neither the Emperor, nor the Foreign Office, nor the Political Department—the three authorities most identified with dismay over the Cavell fracas—raised objections. (Strikingly, the Foreign Office kept scrutinizing the Cavell fallout even as it did nothing about Petit's execution.[94]) No-one seems to have questioned the diplomatic wisdom of executing a young woman who posed an unproven threat; the only point raised was not whether to stop the execution, but how to justify it. The weeks since the verdict had shown that no scandal need be feared. The Spanish requested pardon, as they had done often since Cavell's death.[95] But there was no diplomatic request from any other quarter. And in occupied Belgium, few people knew of her condemnation and no-one spoke up for her, although a campaign could have made all the difference.

From the German army's point of view, it was time to (judiciously) lift the ban on executing women. Jean Burtard of Bureau A thought Von Bissing was acting in reprisal for French executions of female agents working for German intelligence.[96] These women's names were disseminated by the Imperial Foreign Office so that their deaths could retrospectively justify Cavell's execution.[97] But the *reason* to execute another woman was not reprisal; it was alleged military necessity. Executing women sent the message that the army's safety came first. And it asserted the primacy of German authority over the hinterland. That authority, precisely, was facing some limits in the very week following Petit's trial. Once again, Von Bissing had to confront Cardinal Mercier's continued defiance of the occupation regime. Mercier had issued another pastoral letter urging the faithful not to despair of the Entente's final victory. Von Bissing could do nothing: Berlin wanted no conflict with the Vatican for fear of alienating Catholic opinion in the Americas or the Austrian episcopate. In other words, Germany's global interests mattered more than asserting of German authority in occupied Belgium. When it came to the Cardinal, then, Von Bissing was helpless, an exasperating position to be in for a man already vexed by taunts that he had become "mild."[98]

But he *could* wield authority on behalf of the army's safety. Petit's war work was only vaguely known, but her judges had concluded that it constituted a severe enough threat, as Stoeber would later assert.[99] And anyway even a potential threat to the German army justified extreme harshness.[100] And it is likely that the army's wrath would descend hardest on an "extremely insolent" defendant. Even the Political Department, home of the moderate, stressed this point. Von Harrach, the author of the Petit brief, was a sculptor and esthete and generally regarded as a moderate influence on the occupation regime, but he had his share of "prussianism," as the playwright Carl Sternheim (not unapprovingly) noted—and it so happened that one element of Wilhelmine military culture was the officer's prerogative to strike down insolent civilians with swift ruthlessness.[101] And few civilians were as insolent as Petit. There were other outspoken defendants.[102] But it was something else to call the prosecutor a *Schweinhund* or to break the ultimate taboo—the massacres of 1914. Petit's subsequent refusal to sign a request for pardon was further proof of insolence. Would doing so have saved her life? The prison officers at Saint-Gilles and the *Polizei* were convinced it would have. "She owed her execution to her own swagger and obstinacy," said Becker, and Chaplain Leyendecker claimed that he had been assured from on high that "a simple short request would have secured her pardon."[103] Yet neither Von Kirchbach's nor Von Harrach's reports mention her refusal to sign as grounds for rejecting the pardon.

Petit's insolence in court, and the threat to the army she represented, in these weeks of concentrated military effort, made her into the perfect candidate—so to speak—to be denied clemency. The *Polizei* story that Von Bissing selected Petit because of her disreputable status was probably untrue: he denied pardon to Adrienne Beljean, and she was an officer's wife.[104] Nor could he have chosen between Petit and De Bettignies, because he had refused Petit pardon even before De Bettignies went on trial. Still, the difference in treatment between the women stands. The Frenchwoman, arguably, was the more dangerous spy, but Von Bissing pardoned her on March 23. Whatever the reason for this decision, it is likely that status played a role: Von Bissing had long been adamant that the working classes had to know their place.[105] The possibility of scandal related to

De Bettignies' status mattered too. She had a patrician name, and a family with contacts in high circles. Petit had none of these things. Otto Becker had no idea that it was Von Bissing who had decided not to pardon Petit. But he got the gist of the matter right when he sadly concluded that "Gabrielle was quite right to write on the walls of her cell that 'It's the humble ones that make obscure heroes.' "[106]

To drive home the difference in status, the poster went out of its way to refer to the "substantial fee" Petit had received for her work. This was purely meant to discredit her with fellow citizens; it is clear from the pardon file that her earnings had nothing to do with the decision to deny clemency. The same poster, to drive home the point, stressed that "De Bettignies claims she received no fee." This was untrue: De Bettignies had even chosen to work for British, not French, intelligence, because of the salary.[107] But then, tarnishing Petit's reputation was another way to avert scandal.

Reactions

The German authorities trusted that Petit's execution would remain out of sight. And they were right: no diplomatic storm followed. (Monsignor Tacci, the nuncio, may have been dissuaded from endorsing Petit's pardon on March 31; German diplomacy was trying to get rid of him because he was close to Mercier. Nor could he protest in the aftermath of her execution, when pressure on him built up: in May 1916, Von der Lancken demanded Tacci stop endorsing appeals for pardon, and he was made to leave Belgium in July.[108]) The Imperial Foreign Office tracked the repercussions in the Entente press and only found one article in the *Daily Express*, which in spite of an incendiary title ("Huns Execute A Belgian Lady") was very brief, mentioned Petit in one breath with De Bettignies, Van Houtte, and other condemned, and did not editorialize.[109] The occupied citizenry took little notice. Even her fellow prisoners did not know; one of them, a young man named Désiré Dufrasne who would be executed in July, rose at five-thirty on April 1; his diary entry for that day observed nothing out of the ordinary—"no [April] fish," he joked—save that it was the first mild spring day of the year.[110] Though Becker reported that "the whole town knew" of the impending execution, and though the poster was put up all over the Government-General a few days later, there were few echoes—in contrast to the clamor over the death of Cavell and Baucq half a year earlier.

The clandestine press did publish, it is true, two reactions to Petit's execution. Remarkably, they did not express a sense that a line had been crossed. Neither made anything of the fact that Petit was the first woman executed since Cavell, or depicted her as a victim. Rather, she immediately became an emblem of defiance. On April 19, a clandestine chronicle wrote that "Gabrielle Petit, humble sales employee, was 22. She was executed for having helped several young men cross the border, among others her fiancé (who was killed at the front several months later)." Such inaccuracy was rare for this chronicle, which was written by three seasoned journalists. But Petit's war work mattered less than her "indomitable resolve." After her trial, "they tried to make her give in by promising her a commutation of her sentence, even freedom, if she spoke ... but her energy remained unwavering until the end." Indeed until the very end: "At the foot of the stake, she refused to be blindfolded, and blasted her executioners with the proud cry 'Watch how a Belgian woman dies!'"[111] The chroniclers were not particularly incensed by the fact that the German army had executed a woman, but they were indignant over the slur on her motives. Petit's godmother suffered greatly from seeing the "lying pink poster" placarded everywhere; and as the chronicle demonstrates, this was not just a feeling of private and family humiliation, but a public feeling too.[112] "The Germans," wrote the journalists, "not satisfied with having taken her life, now try to blemish her memory by painting [her] as a salaried spy, motivated by greed and not at all by patriotism."[113] The underground *Libre Belgique* ran an angry comment along the same lines. "A young woman of modest condition risks her life in the service of her country; she accepts the fee she is offered for this dangerous work. No-one has the right to suspect her dedication. And yet that seems to be what our masters are hinting at, for why else would they make a point of bringing this detail to the Belgians' attention?"[114] What all of this means is that Petit became an emblem of self-immolating patriotism within weeks of her death, and that she was not remembered as a victim but as a heroine. Her gender and youth, far from turning her death into an atrocity, underscored her heroism.

Those who commented on her story were, as yet, very few in number. Still, her memory was transcending, however modestly, the scattered handful of people who had known her. A first public ritual in her honor took place on May 1, 1916: a 10.00 a.m. Mass to her memory, sung at the baroque church of Our Lady of the Rich Clares (*Notre Dame des Riches-Claires*) in central Brussels. It was organized by a service workers' union at the instigation of Petit's sister Hélène.[115] The eulogy was pronounced by Father Joseph Cardijn (a priest who would garner global fame after the war as the founder of the international Young Christian Workers movement). He portrayed Petit as the embodiment of the nation: like Belgium, she was of those who "conquer the world through self-immolation" and had the force of justice on their side. Their very vulnerability showed up brute force: nothing was more heartening than watching "the awkwardness of the mighty when made to battle the powerless." That was the confrontation Petit had sought, as had Belgium: "Belgium, my beloved mother, you have said: 'strike me, but you will dishonor yourself and you will not vanquish me ...'" (Cardijn, then, was explicit about the gendered implications of his comparison between Petit and Belgium.) He went on to say that Petit's story expressed faith both in the victory of the soul over death and in eventual liberation, and ended on an exhortation: "let us pray, my Brethren, for those who do not believe, let us pray for those who slide toward doubt and suspicion, let us pray for ourselves who do not believe enough ... Let us pray for the Fatherland that it may soon, crowned with glory, reward all heroism and commemorate all sacrificial offerings. Amen."[116] (Though all of this could be said in public because churches were off-limits to the German police, Cardijn was not invulnerable: he would be imprisoned twice between 1916 and 1918.)[117]

Petit, then, was an emblem of ongoing confrontation rather than a victim. At the same time, confrontational rhetoric was waning. The emphasis had shifted in the half year since the October 1915 execution of Cavell and Baucq, which had unleashed urgent indignation: at Baucq's memorial Mass, a vast crowd seethed with anger over the killing of a young family man "who had taken the liberty of helping his country."[118] But by April 1916, the pink posters had succeeded one another for months, and hopes for a swift end to the war receded. As a result, the tone of the mourning over Petit was, if not exactly resigned, then certainly couched in another temporal horizon, and Petit was described in legendary terms, as a figure out of time, a kind of myth outside of the concrete reality of 1916 Brussels: "she went to her death in a white dress with pink ribbons in her hair . . ."[119]

What was also new was that Petit was remembered as a rebuke to many fellow citizens. She might be an emblem of *Belgium*, but she did not personify all *Belgians*. Earlier rhetoric had not made this distinction: the image of executed patriots like Baeckelmans and Baucq somehow merged with that of the occupied. Petit was more of a foil. Cardijn contrasted her with the "scruffy young women writhing in the arms of jeering soldiers" who shouted obscenities at him as he walked home shaken from the sight of Petit's execution poster.[120] The *Libre Belgique* for its part criticized those among the occupied population who liked to take the Germans' word for it and dismiss resisters as shady mercenaries. "Some even say, taking a superior air, that they themselves could not stand to live in an atmosphere of mystery and shadow . . . Needless to say, you will find such excessive delicacy of feeling only among those who do nothing but criticize . . . To be sure, not everyone must fulfil a patriotic mission, but the least that can be asked of all is to recognize merits when they see them, and not discourage those who want to serve."[121]

Abeyance, 1916–1918

None of this meant that the citizenry had come to embrace the occupation regime. But the fierce mood of collective defiance, at its height in 1915, was subsiding. Through the year 1915, the quest for legitimacy on the part of the occupation regime on the one hand, and the denial of legitimacy by the occupied on the other hand, had made for a series of high-profile stand-offs; but that sense of urgent confrontation diminished as the war wore on. The clandestine press, at its height in 1915, entered a period of decline through 1916 and would be at its lowest ebb in 1917.[122] The July 21 national holiday was celebrated in 1916, but not as intensely as in 1915. Volunteers for the Belgian army still tried to cross the electrified fence into the Netherlands, but there were fewer of them, and fewer people put up money to help them. Intelligence networks too became fewer in number, if more efficient; tight organization replaced defiant panache.[123] Much of this shift away from a culture of defiance was due to repression: the German police services' fierce chase after clandestine press and secret intelligence; the prison sentences; and the crippling fines imposed for even symbolic resistance, all against the backdrop of worsening material misery. But the retreat from defiance was also fueled by a realization that the war would be a long one. The stalling of the Verdun offensive encouraged hopes of eventual liberation, but also turned people's gaze toward the disheartening long term. Brand

Whitlock observed that from Verdun onwards the phrase "after the war" cropped up more often; "people turned their thoughts and their hopes into that future where, after this horrid interruption, they could resume life again."[124] Up until then, hopes of imminent liberation made the war into an opportunity for immediate public engagement. Now that war's end receded from sight, more and more people dismissed it as a parenthesis in their actual lives, and turned towards personal matters—family, social life, career, political interests, survival, or even just respite. This made for a sense of relative normalcy not unrewarding to the occupation authorities.

This sense of normalcy was not created by the display of repression. On the contrary, the pink executions posters tended to jolt civilians out of whatever normalcy they had been able to piece together. In one particularly telling vignette, the Brussels writer Paul Max noted, on April 20, 1916, that he had spent an evening out on the town valiantly trying to have a good time, but that his mood had been quite deflated by seeing an executions poster: "one's legs give way, one's heart beats faster, and gone in an instant is the little bit of enjoyment one might have had that evening watching some old movie." Executions were a disturbing regression to times of capital punishment (abolished since the 1860s): "and to say we are living in a century of progress and electricity . . . to have to see this!"[125] The occupation regime eventually realized the impact of the pink posters and stopped issuing them from the summer of 1916. This ended an era of street scenes of mute rage: crowds silently reading the names, the men taking off their hats.[126]

Another vanishing locus of confrontation was that between the regime and the church. Mercier's pastoral letter of March 1916 was the last of the great altercations between the Cardinal and the German authorities. After this, the occupation government desisted from threats. The Political Department expected Catholic opinion in Belgium to come round; and, in turn, the Vatican, trusting Mercier would be safe, instructed him to turn down his confrontational tone.[127]

The next era in the German occupation of Belgium did herald a new brutality. But unlike the violence of 1914, which had not spared local elites, and the high-profile executions of 1915, this was directed specifically against the Belgian working-class: the deportations and forced labor of workers. As the historian Jens Thiel has noted, the deportations proceeded with so much inefficient brutality that they seemed more of a punitive than a logistic measure.[128] Belgian elites vehemently protested, and, as Mercier observed in late 1917, forced labor brought back a sense of "patriotic intransigence"— though he added that this admirable feeling might not otherwise have been galvanized.[129] For all the protest, the deportations also introduced a rift within the citizenry between the 'deportable' and the others. A flurry of actions to save employed men from deportation channeled patriotic energies; but it also, as an unintended consequence, implicitly justified the taking of the unemployed.[130]

Petit's confrontation with power, then, stood at the intersection of several dynamics. She was an iteration of the defiant confrontations between the occupying power and the Belgian citizenry that had started with the deportation of Burgomaster Max of Brussels at the start of the war. At the same time, she was, like the deported *chômeurs* of the second half of the war, low-status, expendable—the recipient of the regime's exemplary violence directed at the undistinguished masses; and her fellow Belgians deplored her fate in a tone of elegiac helplessness and in a turn towards the vindicating future. Her end seemed to be of a piece with the misery and violence of the times. Saint-Gilles prison, as Otto Becker wrote in December 1919, had seen so many sad events during the war years following Petit's death that his memory of her had faded; "if I had known then that Gabrielle would have become the most famous woman in Belgium, I would have taken notes."[131] His memory of her, as it turned out, was sharp enough; but it had lain in abeyance for years.

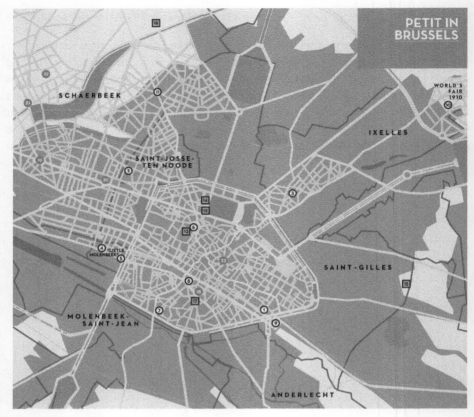

Map 2 Petit in Brussels

(1) **Petit's first job at Limage's,** rue Sallaert 10 (Central Brussels)
early February 1909 –?

(2) **Petit's second job at Carçan's,** rue Josaphat 34 (Schaerbeek/Saint-Josse)
late October 1909 –?

(3) **Petit's residence in early 1910,** rue de Longue-Vie 39 (Ixelles) January/February 1910—Spring or Summer 1910; she worked in her third job in a pastry shop around the corner.

(4) **Rue du Peuple,** no known number ("Little Molenbeek")
She lived here with her lover, Spring or Summer 1910—Summer 1911

(5) **Chaussée d'Anvers 61** ("Little Molenbeek")
She sublet at Marie Collet's from the Summer of 1911 to September 1913 and from the Spring of 1914 to December 1915.

(6) **Fur store job,** rue du Bois Sauvage 6 (Central Brussels)
She worked at Laure Butin's store "À L'Ours Noir" from late 1910 to late 1912.

(7) **Department store job,** rue de l'Éducation (Central Brussels)
She was registered here September 1913—December 1913.

(8) **Hotel laundry job,** rue Auguste Orts 1 (Central Brussels)
She was registered here December 1913—Spring 1914.

(9) **Waitressing near the Gare du Midi**
Early 1914. It was here that she met Gobert.

(10) **The World's Fair, 1910** (Ixelles)
Late April to mid-August 1910. It was here that she met Julia Lallemand.

(11) **Gobert's barracks, 1912–1914**
Gobert's unit, the First Carabineers, was housed in the new *Caserne Baudouin.* He lived here 1912–1914.

[12] **Kommandantur Brussels,** rue de la Loi 6 (Central Brussels)
Headquarters of the German military police.

[13] **Polizeistelle A,** rue Berlaimont (Central Brussels)
Headquarters of German counter-espionage.

[14] **Senate**
Petit's trial, March 2–3, 1916

[15] **Saint-Gilles prison**

[16] **Tir National**
Execution terrain; Petit's first grave, 1916–1919.

[17] **Leyendecker's Residence, Gesellenhaus,** rue Plétinckx (Central Brussels)

(18) **Petit's first funeral Mass, Notre Dame des Riches-Claires** (Central Brussels)
May 1, 1916.

(19) **Petit's funeral chapel, Schaerbeek City Hall, May 29, 1919**

(20) **Petit's funeral Mass, May 29, 1919**

(21) **Belvedere, May 29, 1919**
Outlook over the funeral cortège en route from the church to the cemetery.

(22) **Petit's grave in Schaerbeek Cemetery, 1919–1964**

(23) **Petit's monument, Place Saint-Jean** (Central Brussels), 1923–

Map copyright Helga Boeye. Base map: Louis Vollrath, ed., Plan-Pharus de Bruxelles et ses faubourgs. Brussels, 1910, copyright Brussels City Archives.

PART II
MEMORY

CHAPTER 6
MEMORY AGENTS, 1918–1919

Unearthing Civilian Heroism

On November 15, 1918, the German Soldiers' Council left Brussels; on November 22, King Albert I arrived at the head of Belgian and Allied troops. But during the week in between, applauding *civilian* heroism was the order of the day in the recovered public space of Brussels. On November 17, "Liberation Sunday," Burgomaster Max, back from four years in German prisons, returned to City Hall, where in an emotional meeting all agreed that the occupied population too had participated in the struggle between (as Max defined it) liberty and autocracy. Outside, the Grand'Place was heaving with people. Against the backdrop of terrible blasts (abandoned German munitions trains were exploding at the railway stations), a fervent dialogue of mutual congratulation unfolded: as Max congratulated the *bruxellois* on their resilience—"I don't deserve applause; you do"—the crowd interrupted him with cries of "no, you, *you!*"[1]

But Max could be hailed as a symbol of resistance because he had not lived through the occupation; the rancor it had sown was much in evidence at one City Hall reception, where guests shot each other nasty looks, questioning each other's behavior in the past four years.[2] Elsewhere, within hours of the Germans' departure, seething crowds went after the property—and occasionally the persons—of alleged hoarders, speculators, rapacious farmers, and Flemings and Walloons who had taken advantage of the occupying regime's ethnic policies (the "activists"). Women suspected of intimacy with enemy soldiers were publicly abused—more so, it seems, in liberated Belgium than in northern France; but then, unlike France, Belgium had been almost completely invaded and occupied, a disgrace taken out on women's bodies, as it would be all over occupied Europe after the Second World War.[3] This outburst of "popular violence" ended in mid-December 1918, when the judiciary took over punishment, and Parliament started debating taxes on war profits.[4] But public scrutiny of the state's actions against profiteers would continue for years afterwards; apparent signs of leniency came in for furious criticism in the press and in Parliament.

Stern state action against profiteers was a keen wish since the occupation. Secret memoranda to the government-in-exile had advocated it to forestall lynchings.[5] Echoing a widespread feeling, the Catholic journalist Charles Tytgat had written in November 1916 that punishing profiteers (nouveau riche middlemen, profitably cooperating journalists, career-obsessed civil servants, and others) would after the war be "a measure of public health," a way to lower the level of cynicism in society—to prevent "honest people" from feeling "duped." Tytgat wrote this in his clandestine chronicle of the occupation years. Like many journalists, he refused to work under German censorship, and with his family suffered severe deprivation as a result, plus harassment by the *Polizei* who suspected him (correctly) of working for the underground press, though they could never prove it.[6]

It was no coincidence that, in the weeks after liberation, Tytgat put his diminishing force (he died in the summer of 1919, aged forty-seven[7]) to the task of commemorating executed patriots, whose very existence, as he saw it, repudiated cynicism. They had died in the shadows, but their commitment was now "part and parcel of our common heritage of glory."[8] Again, Tytgat was echoing a widespread feeling, as early public ritual shows. On November 19, 1918, Burgomaster Max led a procession of mourners to the grand municipal cemetery, where a carefully tended plot held the graves of soldiers killed in the 1914 clashes around Brussels. From there, the cortège made its way to a much more obscure burial site: the former execution-grounds at the *Tir National*, a field at the edge of the city that had been off-limits for four years. It featured a cluster of burial-mounds with very recent wooden crosses (a last-minute concession by the departing occupation army) that bore serial-numbers but no names.[9] Listeners wept as Max declared the deaths of these unknown people "perhaps even more poignant" than those of soldiers on the battlefield.[10] Two days later, newspapers gave their names.[11] The *Tir* became a site of commemoration. Postcards showed its graves, now adorned with flowers. Thus emerged the image of the *fusillé* or *fusillée*, the man or woman executed under the occupation. As more of them emerged from the shadows, a small pantheon of civilian martyr-heroes took shape. The public quest for an emblem of unsullied valor during the occupation came to center on the executed patriots.

This spate of "heroizations" occurred, as heroizations will, in a climate of crisis. Many in the occupied population, though sincerely proud that the "home front" had been so resilient, lost heart because the peace had not immediately ended material misery. (During the war, Émile Francqui, the main organizer of relief in the occupied country, already predicted something like this would happen.[12]) It did not help that Belgians who had not lived through the occupation grew impatient with the complaints of those who had, and took to calling them JTS's, an acronym of their lament *J'ai Tant Souffert*—"I have suffered so much."[13] Public culture in penurious post-occupation Belgium, then, had an exasperated tinge to it. Rhetoric veered between execration and exaltation: execration of the "traitors" and "profiteers" of occupation times; exaltation of those who had taken the ultimate stand against the occupier. These were intensely emotional tropes, difficult to contain, and in no way initiated by the authorities. Vernacular memory harbored a fiercer take on the economy of sacrifice than did official discourse, which soothingly insisted that *all* had sacrificed. (Just as, in postwar Britain, official memory painted a picture of national bereavement, while private citizens—Rudyard Kipling, for one—called for special insignia for people who had *actually* lost a loved one on the battlefield.[14]) The reconstituted Belgian state was bid to throw its authority behind the punishment of the uncivic and the glorification of heroes, but the initiative came from civil society, as citizens were casting about for a way to make sense of the past occupation. Seeing "profiteers" everywhere was a way to elevate hardships into voluntary sacrifices, as the historian Laurence Van Ypersele has pointed out.[15] And unearthing hidden heroisms appealed to audiences steeped in the romantic notion of the humble, obscure hero.

In the days following the Armistice, only one name was really widely known: that of Edith Cavell. On November 15, the Brussels council planned a monument at the *Tir National* to "Miss Cavell and the others."[16] She personified civilian heroism during the ceremony that marked the grand entry of King Albert and his troops into Brussels on November 22. Among the elaborate ad-hoc monuments in stucco commissioned, at great cost, by the Brussels council to decorate the city (a tradition dating from early modern times) was a monument to Cavell, placed near the Grand'Place, the work of a prestigious sculptor.[17] It showed her at the foot of a high pedestal, atop which an allegorical Belgian nation proffered a wreath of gratitude to Britain. In chains, Cavell stood tall amidst her fellow nurses, shown bent with grief.[18] That winter, a steady stream of mourners deposited flowers on her grave at the *Tir*, and international film crews filmed "Cavell locations" all over Brussels.[19]

Meanwhile, other executed patriots came out of anonymity. Under the heading "Our Heroes," their names appeared in newspapers; associations formed to commemorate specific *fusillés*. Petit's memory too garnered its own renown—as yet, very modestly so. In December 1918, a street was named after her. It was not a grand event. A developer who owned large tracts of land on Hamburg and Frankfurt Streets in the industrial borough of Molenbeek had requested a change of names to spare inhabitants (and, one imagines, investors) reminders of "the loathsome [German] yoke." The developer regretted that the prestigious name of Clemenceau was already taken. (Indeed the broad street known until the Armistice as Rue d'Allemagne had just been rebaptized Avenue Clemenceau, following a brief, apparently unsatisfactory interval as Rue des Belges.[20]) He suggested names that were (then still) redolent of victory: Arras Street, Verdun Street. Three weeks later, the municipality obliged by erasing the "German" names (as did councils all over Belgium), but instead of battlefields chose local *fusillés*. Frankfurt Street became Frans Mus Street, after a secret intelligence agent executed in September 1916. Hamburg Street, a half-developed lane of warehouses next to the canal, became Gabrielle Petit Street.[21] The developer's reaction is not recorded. And so Petit's memory supplanted prestigious symbols of victory, if in a marginal corner of the city.

The day after, a short article in *Le Soir*, Belgium's largest evening newspaper in French, informed its readers that "among our executed at the *Tir National*, there is a little shop-girl, Gabrielle Petit," and she would be commemorated on December 22.[22] On that Sunday, there was a morning Mass in Petit's memory at Our Lady of the Rich Clares. After the service, a cortège of hundreds marched the five-and-a-half-kilometer route to the *Tir* behind an enlarged photograph of Petit, held aloft in the manner of an icon. At the *Tir*, a middle-aged jurist named Cyrille Van Overbergh compared Petit to Cavell—the first time the two women were publicly mentioned together. He praised both as having died "for Justice." But he also claimed that secret intelligence was a more important "military service" than helping men escape. With that, Van Overbergh challenged the bad reputation that clung to spying, and pulled Petit out, so to speak, from under Cavell's shadow. He could not resist hinting that Petit had faced death more unflinchingly than Cavell (who was reputed—incorrectly—to have fainted in front of the execution squad).

This small-scale but intense event placed Petit's memory into public view for the first time after war's end. Like her wartime memorial Mass in the same church on May 1, 1916, it was organized by a labor union: the *Syndicat National des Employés et Employées de Belgique* (National Union of Service Employees; Employees' Union for short). This Christian Democratic union defended the interests of commercial clerks, shop personnel and other members of the white- or pink-collar salaried masses. During the war, it had already claimed Petit as one of its own: union officials had exhorted members to attend her May 1916 memorial Mass to "*honor a colleague who has sacrificed herself for the Fatherland.*"[23] It was no coincidence that Father Cardijn, who had spoken the eulogy in 1916, started what would become his global social action by helping female service workers in Brussels unionize.[24] The initiative for the 1916 Mass had come from the Union's general secretary, Léon Christophe, as part of his effort to give the Union greater visibility.[25] What this means is that Petit's first *milieu de mémoire* was that of Christian Democratic social action—specifically, on behalf of workers in the service sector, who formed the vast majority of salaried workers in Brussels, and gave the city much of its profile. (Service workers still lived in town; the massive shift towards commuting from the provinces happened only after the Second World War.[26]) The same milieu that, under the occupation, had first broadcast her memory beyond the narrow circle of her immediate family, was the one that, after liberation, publicly gave her a name, a face, and a story. She became the patron saint of the Employees' Union: "God has wanted the service employees of Belgium to have their own martyr," declared a union official at her graveside. Her photo received pride of place at the Union's offices.[27] Speakers claimed that she had been a loyal Union member.

Was she? There is no way to tell, since there are no archives.[28] Her godmother at any rate said she was not. Already in May 1916, though still in shock over her god-daughter's brutal death and grateful for the Union's memorial service, Ségard had taken offense at hearing Father Cardijn call Petit "an obscure employee," when no-one, she insisted, would have mistaken Gabrielle for a working-class girl. (The Union's white-collar aspirations escaped Ségard; she referred to it as a "syndicate of *workers* and employees.") She was adamant that Petit had never been a member of the Union and had known no-one there, adding, tartly, that she felt it her duty to "point out the truth, which is the fundament of any institution." Ségard was to dispute Petit's public image tooth and nail on this as on other points.[29] On this point she was almost certainly right. Petit's service career had been chequered, to say the least, and she may not have been able to afford even the modest contributions needed for Union membership; she never identified with service work; and, after the war, her two closest women friends, Marie Collet and Julia Lallemand, never mentioned the Union. She was, then, probably chosen as a symbol.

But she was an apt symbol; she could be made to personify the Union's aspirations. Hers was a story that appealed to lower-middle-class, Christian Democratic *sensibilités*. Her modest condition had not stopped her making a name for herself in the service of a greater cause; this resonated with a yearning for both greater equality and opportunities for personal distinction. The lower middle class, apprehensive of being denied its own space in the newly-democratized public sphere of the postwar, found congenial accents in the Petit narrative.[30]

And no-one was better able to strike such congenial accents than Petit's eulogist on that December day, Cyrille Van Overbergh (1866–1959), who would become her most active "memory agent." This Flemish Catholic politician, union organizer, and high-ranking official at the Ministry of Education had by 1918 acquired a reputation as expert on a range of reform subjects such as labor accidents, physical education, and, importantly, women's suffrage, a cause he defended staunchly. We will never know how he came to devote his considerable energies to the commemoration of an unknown young woman, for in spite of Van Overbergh's long and distinguished career (he would end his political life as the *doyen* of the Belgian Parliament during the ouster of King Leopold II in the long wake of the Nazi occupation), his papers are presumed lost.[31] Van Overbergh himself wrote that he had heard of Petit shortly after her death from her sister Hélène (who may, as it happens, actually have belonged to the Union, since she worked in sales). She gave him a photo, which he had enlarged and placed in his drawing-room, surrounded by tricolor ribbons—one of many private patriotic shrines in occupied Belgium.[32] Van Overbergh was a champion of Christian lower-middle-class ambition, a defender of women's suffrage, and a critic of Marxism who couched social emancipation in terms of individual valor, middle-class resilience, and "great patriotic goals."[33] Petit's story must have struck him as particularly relevant. His eulogy stressed the moral value of resistance work and the glory of finding an example of it in "a girl of 22, of modest station in life, a simple employee, a very modest member of the Union"—who by her action and attitude had "placed herself in the first rank of the elite with one leap." This went to the heart of the Union's claim that virtue in its different forms—abnegation, courage, intelligence, deportment—would propel the lowly employee to elite status. Van Overbergh implicitly claimed that the past war's resistance had been in essence a manifestation of pluck, respectability, and decency, qualities to which the humble had every right to aspire. He highlighted Petit's graffito "it's the humble ones that make unknown heroes" to reinforce a sense that precisely in the Union's members' modest station in life lay the greatest potential for glory. That "the Society of Nations" was sure to venerate Petit would add to the "moral patrimony" of the white-collar salariat: "Ladies and Gentlemen, that this young girl comes out of your ranks is an incomparable honor for you. . . . Gabrielle Petit will henceforth be the pride of the Employees' Union."[34] His words struck a chord. Union members would remember the ceremony as an occasion of great fervor: "how simple it was, yet how beautiful! A flag—our flag—a wreath, flowers . . . but in that simplicity, what love! What admiration! What pride and patriotism!"[35]

Gabrielle Petit

Democratic Breakthrough—To A Point

Petit's emergence into public view coincided with the postwar democratic breakthrough. After four years of occupation and exile, the Belgian state and citizenry were reunited on the basis of a new compact: the ouster of the prewar plural-vote system that had offered wider representation to the propertied and educated. During the war, spokesmen in the occupied country had managed to let the King and government know that their credible return required getting rid of the plural vote.[36] The day after the Armistice, the Socialist Party placarded its resolve to establish simple universal suffrage from the age of twenty-one. At the highest level, the same conclusion had been reached within hours of the Armistice, in circumstances not lacking a certain swashbuckling glamor. King Albert, camping out in an underfurnished neogothic château in the village of Loppem near Bruges, held talks with a succession of spokesmen who had made their way by car from the still-occupied parts of the country, on roads congested by the German retreat. (Adolphe Max himself made for Loppem straight from his fortress-prison in Silesia.) All agreed that the time for simple universal suffrage was now. The government could ill afford the stately rhythm mandated by the Belgian constitution for electoral reform, for this would require a round of elections using the old system, an indefensible proposition in the shadow of the war: profiteers would have more of a voice than veterans and veterans younger than twenty-five would have no voice at all. On his triumphant entry into Brussels on November 22, Albert told Parliament that the "old barriers" to equal suffrage had to go—for "sufferings equally borne" had to bring equal public rights.[37]

Albeit not so equal as all that. Albert went on to advocate "equal suffrage for all men who have come of age." This was "a heartbreaking deception" to defenders of the women's vote.[38] But the post-Armistice political landscape of Belgium proved singularly inhospitable to this cause. Most Socialists and Liberals rejected women's suffrage because they feared that women would vote Catholic, a fear heightened by the fact that conservative Catholics (who saw their unassailable domination of Belgian politics come to an end after what they called the "Loppem coup") defended the women's vote as a counterweight to the coming onslaught of the "untempered" mass vote. Ever since the advent of mass politics in 1894, the women's vote had been discussed in terms of electoral arithmetic rather than principle,[39] and the post-Armistice climate was no different. The Federation for Women's Suffrage pleaded in vain not to couch the question in terms of "clericalism and anticlericalism." Albert himself, impatient to have done with clerical dominance, threw his immense prestige as "Soldier-King" into the fray, threatening to veto women's suffrage if need be.[40]

Albert's stature set aside, male martial prestige could not be harnessed against women's suffrage the way it could in France, where male voting privilege was strengthened by the fact that almost nine out of ten men of military age had served and 1.4 million had died. Only 20 percent of Belgian men had served, and most had lived the war under occupation—where not all had behaved exemplarily. The suffragists Louise Van den Plas and Jane Brigode quite devastatingly made this point in a December 1918 open letter to the government: "have we ... served our country less than the men who stayed in occupied Belgium? Those were, as you know, the overwhelming majority. Yet all men stand to benefit from what our valiant soldiers have conquered on the battlefield." Belgium's soldiers, a minority, had won the vote for other men, regardless of merit: "the cynical hoarder who starved us; the louche businessman who pursued his shady deals four years running . . . while the flower of our nation was mowed down in battle" would all be able to vote, whereas women who had seen their families through the war and done the heavy lifting in social work were excluded. Even female resisters "would not be citizens of the victorious Fatherland!"[41] In other words, the overwhelmingly civilian war experience of Belgian men and women made it difficult to repudiate women's suffrage by reference to wartime sacrifice. The December 1918 open letter started a five-month campaign for the women's vote. Gabrielle Petit's memory agent Cyrille Van Overbergh, a longtime suffragist, championed the cause with particular zeal.[42]

On March 26, when Parliament started discussing simple universal suffrage, suffragists handed in a petition with 180,000 signatures in favor of votes for women. It had little impact on most Liberal and Socialist delegates. Some mustered wartime prejudices: one Socialist delegate suggested that votes for women were a "Germanic" principle alien to "our women's spirit." A Catholic colleague retorted, to applause from his fraction, that if German women had had the vote in 1914, the German Empire would not have gone to war.[43] On April 9, the suffragist Federation offered a compromise: votes for mothers and for educated women. It was rejected. On April 10, the day slated for the final decision, the large audience that had gathered in the gallery expecting a vigorous debate was treated to the sight of groups of delegates scurrying in and out, conferring frantically. Behind the scenes, parliamentarians offered the suffragist leaders another compromise: the vote for mothers and widows of fallen soldiers and of civilians killed during the war and for female resisters who had spent time in prison. It was a paltry and symbolic gesture but better than nothing, and the suffragist leaders accepted because they did not want to be held responsible for a political crisis even as Belgium's foreign interests required especial vigilance in Paris. And so, at 6.00 p.m., the delegates came out of the corridors and the parliamentary session started. Once more, the theme of male sacrifice resounded. Prime Minister Delacroix declared that the vote given to wives and mothers of the fallen was a vote given to the dead; words greeted, as the parliamentary report noted, by a "storm of applause." Much moved, adversaries shook Delacroix' hand and declared their misgivings allayed. And with that, a little under 12,000 women—0.5 percent of the electorate in 1919—qualified to vote in national elections.[44] It was, of course, this relative modesty of numbers that had made the agreement possible, although nobody said so openly. In France, projects for a similar "vote of the dead" foundered—equally implicitly—on the fact that this would have enfranchised hundreds of thousands of women.[45] But Belgium counted "only" some 40,000 fallen and missing in action; 2,600 forced-labor deportees who had died in the camps (those who had died shortly after returning home did not qualify); and a group of *fusillés* and other occupation victims (such as men who had died trying to cross the electric fence) as yet untallied but known to number in the mere hundreds.[46] The thousands of men killed in the 1914 massacres did not qualify.[47]

For a breakthrough, it was a demeaning one. The "vote of the dead" concept, wrote Van den Plas, gutted "the feminist import" of the reform, especially as the dead heroes would lose their posthumous say in public matters if their widows remarried (and their mothers could vote only if they were widows). But at least female resisters with a proven prison record could now vote—a concession passed without any comment, as the parliamentary records indicate. These *électrices* were few—the exact number remains unknown—and never manifested themselves as a group, not even within associations of political prisoners.[48] Still, theirs was a straightforward enfranchisement, not a sleight of posthumous ventriloquy.[49] The moral legacy of the occupation had created a space—a small and symbolic one, but a space nevertheless.

At the same time, there was no broadening that space. Political rights granted to these exceptional women could not be leveraged into political rights for all: their valor did not reflect on all women. Nor could Catholic suffragism invoke them, because the Catholic argument for women's suffrage was a differential one: the woman's vote was the vote of the wife and mother, the vote of the home and family—an argument that did not mesh with that of women's individual achievements.

The Waning of "Brave Little Belgium"

Because the stature of exceptional women could not be leveraged into an argument for the women's vote, Petit's memory was not invoked as an argument for the woman's vote, not even by Van Overbergh.[50] Nor was she, as yet, nationally known. Because no record of her trial and no last letters had circulated, she remained, at first, a footnote; quite literally so.[51] On April 1, 1919, the third anniversary of her execution passed without ceremony.[52]

On that day, King Albert flew to Paris, the first head of state in history to take a plane: a theatrical gesture meant to bolster Belgium's case before the Supreme Council at the Peace Conference. It needed bolstering. Years of paeans to "Brave Little Belgium" had given way to comparisons of the number of fallen, in which Belgium fell short.[53] It was true that *civilian* Belgium had suffered badly. Four years of exploitation and imposed immobility had left businesses reeling and infrastructure in tatters; many people were malnourished, the damage in children's health especially hard to bear.[54] (Children were also prime victims of a new killer: the masses of unexploded ordnance left behind. Horrendous accidents happened all over Belgium, not just in the front regions: in one Brussels apartment, on the day of King Albert's solemn entry, a small boy was ripped apart and his mother badly mutilated by a grenade left in a cupboard by a German officer who had been billeted there.[55]) But such misery hardly counted as a contribution to the Entente war effort.

Belgium's diminishing prestige abroad added to the malaise of the spring of 1919. The public mood soured; recriminations over occupation-time behavior ran rampant. In reaction, the unearthing of civilian heroism further crystallized as a collective effort.[56] In March, the first *fusillés*' remains were exhumed from their temporary graves near execution-grounds, and returned to their native towns and villages.[57] These were small-scale ceremonies, but a first grand manifestation took place in Antwerp on March 17, 1919: the public funeral of Baeckelmans, Franck, and eighteen other executed citizens of the city. Vast crowds lined the sidewalks as the long cortège passed by; Cardinal Mercier pronounced the eulogy; newspapers framed their front pages in black mourning bands. Observers described the public mood in the great port city as solemn and somber. It was the first grand homage to civilian heroism of postwar Belgium. It was not quite a national ceremony: the dead were identified with Antwerp.[58] Also, it was a group homage; no single national hero had yet emerged. Perhaps no need for such a figure was felt as yet.

The Antwerp ceremony was organized by a new, energetic *milieu de mémoire*, the local chapter of the Association of Former Political Prisoners of the War, one of many voluntary societies formed to honor wartime heroism. Another was the Patriotic League (*Ligue des Patriotes*), a Brussels association created just days after the Armistice, during a patriotic banquet at the smart *Taverne Royale* "to reconstitute the moral unity of the nation" by fostering "the religion of the dead and the cult of the heroes," as the first issue of the *Ligue*'s periodical, *Le Drapeau* stated in early December 1918.[59]

This elite club would be Petit's second *milieu de mémoire* after the Employees' Union, and the one that first anointed her national heroine. It was presided by José Hennebicq, a magistrate in his late forties who had served as counselor with the Persian government before the war; during the war, he had organized charities and written for the underground press in Brussels.[60] The association's name was probably chosen in homage to the French *Ligue des Patriotes*, the old, now almost spent, revanchist organization of 1882 that had become ever more reactionary since the Dreyfus Affair. In 1921, Hennebicq would speak at the unveiling of a monument to the French *Ligue*'s founder, Paul Déroulède.[61] Yet the Belgian *Ligue*, if reactionary, was much more conventional than its French counterpart; *Le Drapeau*, of which Hennebicq was sole editor, would during its brief existence (it tailed off for lack of funds in 1920 and ceased to appear after April 1921), grumble against Belgian society's perceived disregard of its elites, but maintained a respectful enough tone towards the postwar Belgian state.[62] But, then, the *Ligue*'s main committee was a gathering of two dozen middle-aged men from solidly established strata of the Brussels bourgeoisie; lawyers and magistrates formed the largest single group.[63] None played a role in active politics, but they seem to have shared a sense of their own status as members of a patriotic elite, plus a particular *Weltanschauung*. Several knew each other from their days as young men of means in the *fin-de-siècle*. Some had spent their formative years under the influence of various cultural-pessimist creeds, which, it would seem, had predisposed them to welcome the war as a triumph of idealism over materialism. Self-appointed guardians of Belgium's wartime prestige, the members of the *Ligue* sought to safeguard it through the commemoration of the war dead. Their adopted motto was *"N'Oublions Jamais!"* [Let Us Never Forget!]

From an early emphasis on military heroes, the *Ligue* by April 1919 had come to specialize—so to speak—in the commemoration of civilian dead, presenting itself to municipal governments and to the families of the executed as the organization best able to give the exhumation ceremonies the required solemnity.[64] The reburial of Petit, too, caught the *Ligue's* attention. On April 22, her relatives requested permission to have the body exhumed and transported to Tournai.[65] Hennebicq wrote to Hélène Petit to ask if the *Ligue* could organize the burial of her "glorious sister." He urgently requested a meeting: "I have heard that we have to act fast ... I hope that you will not begrudge Tournai the honor of glorifying its heroic child."[66]

As it happened, begrudging Tournai the honor of burying her sister was exactly what Hélène Petit had in mind. Between the family's black sheep and her home town, there was no love lost; and she was prepared to take on the entire family to stake an exclusive claim to her sister's memory. In this she would soon gain a mighty weapon: her sister's sudden elevation to the status of national heroine. The first to bestow this title was, precisely, the *Ligue*. On May 1, *Le Drapeau* splashed the headline "GABRIELLE PETIT: NATIONAL HEROINE" across the full width of its front page in sixty-point boldface; the editorial proclaimed that it was time people recognized Petit as Belgium's very own Cavell. "If the English honor Miss Cavell's memory, and they are quite right to do so, then it is the Belgians' duty to render to Gabrielle Petit the homage due her. She is one of ours; she is our NATIONAL HEROINE." It was not true, as some thought, that Petit had been a subordinate of Cavell's: "she organized her *own* spy service." The article then gave details about Petit's bravery in prison (provided by her godmother) and printed the text of Petit's last letters. It was a compact but complete heroization profile in an issue clearly meant as a keepsake: it was the first *Drapeau* with an illustration (the photo of Petit in the white blouse); the layout was far more dramatic than usual; and it cost double the usual price.[67]

One National Figure

The conceit of one single national figure emerged at this point because of two elements that marked Belgian public culture between late April and mid-May. The first was disappointment over the Paris peace treaty. The second was the reburial of Edith Cavell.

The treaty's doggedly gained concessions to Belgian interests fell a great deal short of expectations; public opinion reacted with dismay. The Belgian press unanimously decried the treaty's disregard for the specific economic problems of an ally who had had to deal with a military occupation. As the historian Sally Marks has noted, the critics had a point: "the net effect of the war and the peace settlement was to leave Belgium permanently weaker economically."[68] More than a material setback, this disregard counted as a moral slight: *Het Laatste Nieuws* called the treaty "wounding, dishonorable and immoral."[69] On a symbolic but keenly felt level, the choice of Geneva over Brussels as the seat of the League of Nations was a blow, since it ended Belgium's status as an emblem of the international rule of law.[70] The *Ligue des Patriotes* sprang into action to channel public disappointment into demonstrations against the peace treaty. A march was held in Brussels on Sunday, May 11.[71]

But it turned out to be a dismal failure: no more than five hundred marchers showed up, gleefully described by the press as elderly out-of-touch dilettantes. For it was one thing to be disappointed with the treaty; it was another to take to the streets and scream ingratitude. What should have been a unifying moment of indignation, in fact exposed the *Ligue's* position as well out of the mainstream. "There is something disgusting, and we are putting it mildly," wrote the impeccably patriotic *Libre Belgique*, "to see marchers brandish placards saying 'Has England forgotten August 1914?' Those cranks seem to have forgotten that if they are free today to march in Brussels . . . it is partly thanks to the British army, which has left 700,000 corpses in the Ypres mud." The rest of the press was equally scathing.[72]

As if to underscore these feelings, two days later, vast crowds turned out as Edith Cavell's body was moved from the execution site to be transferred to England. The Brussels police had cordoned off the route of the funeral procession, closed café terraces and banned advertisements. As the cortège wound its way from the *Tir National* to the North Station, people thronged the sidewalks, although it was a working-day; flags hung at half-mast, tens of thousands of school-children waved Union Jacks and Belgian flags, and the lighted street lanterns were shrouded with black crêpe—a sight that particularly impressed the United States envoy Brand Whitlock, who back in October 1915 had been part of the desperate effort to stay Cavell's execution. As the procession reached the North Station, the dense crowds that had been there for an hour broke loose from the sidewalks to surround the hearse "with such impetuosity that it took a while to restrain them," the police reported. During the brief funeral service in the station-hall, the people thronged on the vast square outside stood silent and "very moved," with many in tears. The newspapers gave extensive accounts. The *Libre Belgique* represented her not as a victimized angel of mercy in sedate nurse's uniform—as she would come to be remembered—but as an "antique hero" (not a heroine), a "lesson in far-reaching duty."[73] (*Le Drapeau*, unsurprisingly, dispatched the ceremony in a few words.[74])

The newspaper reports show that Petit's status as Belgium's pendant to Cavell was now firmly established. The *Libre Belgique* assured its readers that "the little shop-girl who is certain to become a legend" would soon receive similar honors.[75] *Het Laatste Nieuws* called Petit "a worthy and noble collaborator of Miss Edith Cavell" and announced a "national funeral" of grandiose proportions."[76] *Le Soir* struck a more churlish note: "As we contemplate the imposing funeral that Brussels gave to Miss Cavell, we cannot but think of that other valiant woman, a Belgian, whose remains are still in the little cemetery at the *Tir National*. . . . One was left to wonder, a little anxiously, if the services rendered by our admirable compatriot were to be paid with ingratitude." But those doubts were dissipated and Petit's funeral promised to be "no less grandiose."[77]

To sum up: if Petit had come out of the shadows, in late 1918, in an atmosphere of social emancipation, her anointment as national heroine, in May 1919, happened against the backdrop of waning national prestige. Yet her story resonated both in circles of resentment over loss of prestige *and* in circles that considered such resentment unseemly.[78] Likewise, Petit was elevated as a pendant to Edith Cavell both in the eyes of those who couched this elevation in either–or terms and in the eyes of those who did not. What this means is that, once Petit was brought to public attention, her appeal as a symbol was wide and immediate. The only Belgian woman executed in the national capital, she could personify the entire nation; as a young and pretty woman, she could serve as a national allegory; as a "valiant virgin" (Father Cardijn's words), she reminded people of Joan of Arc. Moreover, her gender resolved the vexed question of Belgium's military sacrifice deficit: making a national hero out of a male civilian, even if he had been shot as a resister, might raise eyebrows. A national heroine faced no such scrutiny.

There was a vast difference between Petit's two *milieux de mémoire*. The Christian Democratic Employees' Union represented the growing and striving service salariat; the *Ligue des Patriotes* claimed enduring relevance for the *grande bourgeoisie* of magistrates, bank managers and high-ranking officials. The small world of Petit's memory agents, then, replicated the tension between established and striving social groups that existed across post-Armistice Europe.[79] The *Ligue* had been first to declare Petit national heroine, but the Union followed suit: in mid-May, Cyrille Van Overbergh published his December 1918 speech at Petit's grave, complemented with a short, stirring biography, in a twenty-seven page booklet titled *Gabrielle Petit: Héroïne Nationale*. It became the *Ur*-text of the Petit myth into the 1960s. I have summarized it in the Prologue, but it is worth dwelling a little longer on this extraordinarily influential little book.

Narrating a Legend[80]

Van Overbergh's homily underscores Jay Winter's point that the First World War did not comprehensively usher in a time of irony: older, pathos-laden forms of expression offered the consolation that high modernity withheld.[81] *Gabrielle Petit: National Heroine* was a "drama of the triumph of good over evil" that provided much-needed purchase on past events to the lower middle class, the striving, the baffled.[82] In making the Petit myth, Van Overbergh did not so much distort his evidence as arrange it into a moral tale—he himself called it "a fable"—that divested Petit's death of randomness and made her life into a destiny.[83] Its high points were Petit's decision to engage in resistance, her defiant attitude at her trial, and her resolve in the face of death. That her life before the war did not figure and her intelligence work remained sketchy, befitted the genre. Hagiography did not highlight action so much as motivation and its consequences—the choice made, the faith maintained under interrogation, the defiant appearance before the judges, the bravely borne suffering and death.[84] At the same time, Petit's import went beyond martyrdom: Van Overbergh portrayed her as a paragon of energy. Urging on her fiancé, she provided the patriotic impetus and chose the more autonomous war service; her resilience in prison was further proof of vigor.

The narrative invoked the occupation through many concrete details. People's houses were regularly searched for copper utensils, wool mattresses, and other valuables. So was Van Overbergh's. During one search, a German asked him about the proud-looking young woman in his living-room shrine. Van Overbergh told him of Petit's heroism and called her "one of our Joans of Arc." To his surprise, the *Landsturmmann* then bowed before the photo and revealed that he was from Lorraine, like Joan. Whether or not this vignette was invented, audiences who remembered having their houses searched and their possessions carted off while they stood by in mute rage would have liked the idea that a shrine to a heroine could mitigate such defenselessness—or at least reveal the *lorrain* in the German. The booklet offered further striking details: Petit was arrested as she was enjoying "a cup of *torréaline* after her frugal lunch." In reality, Petit could afford real coffee and regale her friends; but this would not have sat well with audiences who remembered the vile coffee substitute that went by the name of *torréaline*. (Ads in the papers played on that distaste: "How about a nice cup of *torréaline*? No thanks! No more of *that* for me! Three cheers for proper coffee . . ."[85]) The unequal access to food was still a prime moral issue and a spy's wages were as yet an unmentionable subject. More mentionable was the possibility of reconciliation with Germans: the booklet did not wallow in Germanophobia. Rather, as befitted a drama of redemption, it hinted at mutual understanding: Petit's bravery in prison, Van Overbergh wrote, impressed even her jailors.

The trial, a stage-ready dialogue between Petit and her judges, was a high point of the narrative. It deftly emplotted things Petit really had said, if not necessarily on that occasion. That her defiance was only now uncovered, added to the drama: "do not forget that she was alone, all alone . . . facing the entire German military apparatus." She brazenly threw an atrocity story in her judges' faces, telling them that she had seen a man shot by invading troops as he was hiding under his wife's skirts. This curious vignette—the source was Petit herself, who had told her godmother, who had told *Le Drapeau*— highlighted the defenselessness of Belgian men during the invasion. Entente propaganda had portrayed the massacred as women, children, or elderly men. But in reality, the invading troops had mainly targeted Belgian men of military age. Not all Belgians liked to hear this; it is remarkable that Van Overbergh's booklet, a mass-market publication, placed it front and center.

In presenting Petit as a heroine, Van Overbergh regularly had her burst into high-flown rhetoric: "If I must die, it will be because Providence will have judged me worthy of the most beautiful death there is: death for the Fatherland and for Justice." Her actual take on death, as her godmother reported it, had been rather more laconic: "all I risk is a few bullets." Ségard insisted that her god-daughter never expressed her resolve in exalted terms. "She spoke simply, like a soldier. . . . People falsely attribute many empty, hollow phrases to her. Gabrielle was not a talker."[86] But these "phrases" were central to the framing of Petit as a heroine; they spoke to audiences that were not, in the main, as receptive to the understated as they would become by the 1930s. (Not coincidentally, Petit's graffito'd statement that she refused to appeal "to show my enemy that I don't give a damn" would give the Prime Minister pause at her funeral; instead of quoting it, he discreetly alluded to the heroine's "unpolished language," hastening to add that circumstances gave it "a grandeur worthy of Corneille.") In the same noble register, Van Overbergh gave Petit a sublime scene on her last night: guarded by an atheist warden, serenely working on her embroidery—even if the parallel to Mary Queen of Scots seems too felicitous to be true, Petit really did needlework that night—she got the better of the man's nihilism by her ardent exposition of Christian doctrine. There was some basis for this story. Petit's sister Hélène claimed to have heard from a German warden (possibly Otto Becker) that Gabrielle, on her last night, sat sewing and told him of her wretched childhood; and that her faith had impressed him.[87] Chaplain Leyendecker, on the other hand, dismissed the scene as "legend."[88] Either way, the conversion vignette—a staple of hagiography[89]—burnished Petit's status as Christian heroine. Van Overbergh also had her greet her end with joy, when, in reality, she took death into account but hardly saw it as the crowning glory of her striving. Among the last letters of the *fusillé(e)s* of the First World War, Petit's fatalistic messages—"Such is life, you see, you leave it the way you entered it"—were far removed from those that expressed a "joyful acceptance" of death, such as the ecstatic *adieux* of the very young and very pious brothers Collard, *Dame Blanche* agents executed in 1918.[90] But *National Heroine* needed to have Petit greet death as glorious, just as it needed to present her end as an apotheosis—without blindfold, on a last cry that expressed the ultimate patriotic credo: she might die, but the nation would live.

A Fight Over a Grave[91]

It says much about Van Overbergh's stature as memory agent that he was invited to the exhumation of Petit's body on May 27, when most of her own relatives were not.[92] But, then, that sad little ceremony came at the end of a bitter dispute in the family. On April 22, relatives had requested permission from the borough of Schaarbeek (where the *Tir National* was located) to have her body exhumed for reburial in Tournai. This was not unusual; all of the executed were eventually buried in their home towns. But Schaarbeek council claimed the prestige of burying the national heroine and denied the family's request. It had an ally in Hélène Petit, who wanted her sister buried in the Brussels area. By mid-May, the matter seemed decided: newspapers announced that Petit would be buried in the capital on Sunday, May 25.[93] The Ségards sprang into action and persuaded Petit's brother Jules to lodge a formal protest. (Jules Petit junior, twenty-one, had grown up partly in foster families, partly at his father's; he had no contact with his sisters. He was not doing well. After his father's death during the war—three months before his sister's execution—he landed himself in some trouble and spent time in jail for theft. An electrician by trade, he signed up to join the regular army as a career private in February 1919. Since April 6, he had been stationed with the Belgian occupation army in the Rhineland. He suffered from rheumatoid arthritis and did not have long to live.[94]) In response to the Ségards' protest, Hélène Petit, backed by Schaarbeek, called her brother to court. On May 23, matters came to a head at the Brussels Palace of Justice. The papers spoke of an "embarrassing incident."[95] This extraordinary litigiousness testified both to Petit's public stature—the fact that it mattered enormously where she was buried—and to the family's lack of cohesion. In other words, present public fervor and past private indifference converged.

Three points were discussed at court: first, determining Petit's last wish; second, if this were impossible, determining which of the relatives could decide; and, third, if this too were impossible, determining which city would prevail—Tournai or Schaarbeek (that is, Greater Brussels).

Hélène Petit claimed that her sister had told her she wanted to be buried in Brussels, but she had to retract this. No-one at court believed that Gabrielle had let her sister in on her dangerous work. By contrast, the Ségards' claim that *they* had known Petit was a spy, was not in dispute; no-one therefore thought it unlikely that she had told them she wanted to be buried in her home town if worst came to worst. But Petit had left no will. And so the discussion shifted to the question of family precedence. The Ségards were not Petit's legal heirs; her siblings were. This raised the question which of them had been closest to her. While Hélène Petit's assertion that she had "always" lived with Gabrielle was in some doubt, everybody knew that Jules and Gabrielle had had no contact whatever. Jules Petit had to admit as much, to the great fury of his aunt Hélène Ségard, who championed the claim of Tournai. (Although she lived in Brussels, her choice made sense socially: in Tournai at least the family name still counted for something, which meant a lot to the impoverished Ségard.) She lashed out at her cousin Jules and his sister: "worthless, both of them; worse, a pair of retards."[96] The neglected children of Aline Ségard and Jules Petit senior had not come to much in life and continued to count for little in the extended family.

Since Petit had left no will and there was no deciding between her relatives, the third element took effect—the public question of what city could claim her. "One does not conceive," Jules Petit's lawyer pleaded, "that Gabrielle Petit should be buried in Schaarbeek to which she had no ties whatever." Tournai, her "*petite patrie*," had been at the center of her intelligence work and was now "ardently clamoring for the remains of its glorious child;" nowhere else would her cult be more fervent. This, as Petit's memory over the long run would prove, was quite true. But she was now anointed national heroine and the claims on her memory by her *petite patrie* had to take a back seat to those of the *Patrie*. As decisions were made, the Tournai press, municipality, and *milieux de mémoire* were not in the loop.[97] By contrast, all of the Schaarbeek municipal government was at court. Hélène Ségard darkly hinted that Jules Petit was pressed to drop his claim. (He did receive a desk job at the Ministry of Defense in June, as his military file shows.)[98]

The final decision was couched as a temporary measure, but in effect enshrined Petit's status as an emblem. The presiding judge, Maurice Benoidt, declared that a final decision was not within his rights, since there was no will and no way to decide between the relatives, but that the matter was urgent enough to warrant an interim solution. Fond of patriotic rhetoric, Benoidt stated that Petit, ultimately, belonged "to the Nation," and ruled that she would *temporarily* be buried at Schaarbeek cemetery because it was closest to where she had "fallen under the German bullets."[99] In other words, the invoked urgency of the matter prompted a solution that confirmed Petit's status as a heroine of war. Like a soldier, she would be buried close to where she died. As national heroine, she had to be buried in the capital. The verdict fell in the morning of May 27. That afternoon, Petit's coffin was dug up.

The Funeral as Performance

Schaarbeek's original plan was to bury Petit alone, in a grand ceremony on Sunday, May 25. Because of the court case, the burial was postponed to May 29, a weekday; and the plan was altered to include two other executed patriots, Mathieu Bodson and Aimé Smekens. This did not diminish the prestige of the ceremony. The 29th was Ascension Day; and in this triple funeral, Petit could represent the entire nation, the two men its constituent elements, Flanders and Wallonia. Another bid for prestige by Schaarbeek which had required some maneuvering, for Bodson, like Petit, had had no ties to the borough, and Smekens' body had to be brought in from Antwerp, where he had been executed.[100]

The carefully organized funeral mustered great names, large crowds, and considerable pomp.[101] The long cortège featured an array of associations old and new: a two-thousand-strong delegation of former political prisoners as well as delegations from the Employees' Union, the *Ligue des Patriotes*, the Association of French Combatants, the Belgian Red Cross, and many others, marching with flags, banners, and music. The daily press covered the ceremony assiduously; illustrated weeklies ran photos (in a kind of echo chamber of interest, photographers took pictures of photographers taking pictures of the cortège); documentary footage recorded the event.[102] Journalists lauded the "compassionate and at the same time justly proud" expression on people's faces and stressed that while some might have come out of mere curiosity, most were "clearly or dimly conscious of a pious duty to fulfil."[103]

The grandeur of the event mattered: the pageantry of post-Armistice Belgium resembled the public ceremonial of the French Revolution in that it enacted citizenship in an imagined community of fate. In public ceremonial, "the individual is rebaptized as a citizen," as Mona Ozouf has written in her classic study.[104] In another parallel with the French Revolution, the type of public ceremonial most filled with significance was the *funeral* ceremonial—the public honors paid to those who had sacrificed their lives to the greater good. The first people so honored were civilian resisters, not fallen soldiers, because exhumations and repatriations from the front zone were forbidden until April 1920. (At that point, the United States authorities decided to repatriate the dead; Belgium, then France, followed suit.[105]) Remembrance of the fallen of course loomed as large in 1919 Belgium as elsewhere; but the actual funerals that marked the year were those of civilians, most intensely in May–June, a time culminating in the so-called "Manifestation of National Piety" of June 15, 1919, when twenty patriots (Baucq, Bril, and Mus among them) were buried in Brussels in the presence of the figureheads of Belgian war glory: King Albert, Cardinal Mercier, and Burgomaster Max.[106]

These ceremonies certainly expressed a widely shared desire to honor civilian heroism. They were not imposed by the state; the initiative came from civil society.[107] But they were also a deliberate effort undertaken against a host of countervailing forces—indifference, exhaustion, unspoken skepticism about the notion of *civilian* heroism, hostility to resisters as troublemakers in occupation times, and, lastly, a growing refusal

Figure 4 Petit's funeral, May 29, 1919.
Brussels, Royal Army Museum, Prints Cabinet

to consecrate the war's suffering. (The extreme left stated its refusal clearly: "all those glories being exhumed with great pomp are nothing but stagecraft," wrote the radical *L'Exploité* a few weeks before Petit's funeral. "It's the continuation of wartime propaganda."[108]) In addition, the calls to commemorate civilian heroes were full of anxiety. One editorial called on the government to organize more grandiose funerals for the *fusillé(e)s* to shake the postwar malaise: "do [the authorities] realize how disillusioned most of us are today, after the high hopes of victory? . . . A worthy celebration of our martyrs would allow us to shake off a little of that torpor that dispirits us . . ."[109] Another paper hoped that the funeral of Petit, Smekens and Bodson would bring back some of "that Belgium of 1914 and 1915" that had grown "strangely lethargic and corrupt" from overlong exposure to the occupation.[110] In other words: the stepping-up of commemorative effort betrayed the anxieties it was designed to quell. The disillusionment was not exclusive to Belgium: even in "victorious" societies, no postwar restoration could possibly satisfy the exacerbated, exasperated hopes of wartime; and, everywhere, ceremonial provided some solace.[111] Petit's funeral exemplifies this. Flanking the nation (Petit) with valiant Antwerp (Smekens) and valiant Liège (Bodson) provided a much-needed reprieve from a bitter controversy that raged that spring over allegations that Antwerp had surrendered ignominiously in 1914, in contrast to heroic Liège.[112] In fact, Aimé

Smekens, the token *anversois*, was posthumously pressed into the service of national discourse, for he had no ties to Antwerp other than having been shot there.

Still, his grand funeral was not an empty rite. His widow took out an ad to thank "the municipalities, associations, schools and friends" for their homages.[113] That the executed were out of the shadows and enveloped in the collective story had genuine emotional significance.

The Funeral as Lesson[114]

On the day of the funeral, every school-child in Schaarbeek received a memento: a beautifully printed card with a photograph of Petit and the solemn injunction "NEVER FORGET, CHILD."[115] Many such notes rang that day. Petit served as a lesson in patriotism. Her cult was didactic: it rendered the national community thinkable because she was commemorated as having chosen death on behalf of it. Her death in and of itself contributed to the nation's war effort; whether her war work had been useful was irrelevant. What mattered were bravery and sacrifice. (For instance, Petit's choice of the pseudonym Legrand was, as one journalist wrote, "not exactly hermetic," but then "extreme caution is a value that the valiant disdain."[116]) Much of the rhetoric surrounding executed resisters in 1919 Belgium partook of this perspective. There were contrasting views, of course. One example is the May 1919 memoir of the celebrated lawyer Sadi Kirschen, who had defended civilian resisters before German military courts. Kirschen praised the accused, but he also painted many of them as hapless victims, in over their heads, thrown before the inexorably turning wheels of German military justice by vainglorious intelligence chiefs abroad—all in the service of an endeavor that really should have been left to military experts.[117] This was a significant departure from reigning *fusillé* rhetoric. Yet Kirschen's discordant note was barely picked up on; the press imperturbably folded his book into heroizing discourse. An ad in *Le Soir* praised it as "a book of justice—that justice which gives to the martyrs of that most noble of causes the place that they deserve in our memory and in our admiration . . ."[118] Kirschen's skepticism fell on deaf ears, because resistance did not count as practical action but as moral protest. Sacrifice was national action by definition, because self-immolation for the nation validated the nation as a principle.

Petit discourse circled around this notion of conscious sacrifice entirely; not only had she offered up her young life "on the altar of the Fatherland" (*Le Drapeau*), she had sustained her resolve over weeks. This touched upon the major trope of scheduled death. Books bore titles such as *How They Saw Death Coming* and *The March to The Stake*, and the last letters of the executed circulated widely. Two generations of Belgians had grown up unaccustomed to the death penalty, let alone to death meted out to members of the "respectable" classes; this made for an awed fascination. Moreover, scheduled death highlighted civilian bravery. The fallen on the "battlefield" had died in the heat of battle, in a blaze of glory, and surrounded by comrades, or so speakers in 1919 still liked to imagine; the *fusillé(e)s*, by contrast, had faced a long-announced death alone, in the shadowy ignominy of prison. Such long-drawn-out defiance of the instinct for survival counted as the ultimate act of faith in the nation. Petit's refusal even to apply for clemency inspired awe. So did her alleged rejection of the blindfold and defiant last cry. Such death-defying faith in the nation created an imagined national community uniting the living and the dead. The living pledged never to forget the dead, and in turn, the dead would intercede for the living. "Dear heroes," exclaimed Mercier at Petit's funeral, "go and prepare a place for us!" The fervent communion of their compatriots brought the executed to life: "There are graves that are alive," declared the president of the National League of Remembrance at Petit's grave. He was an ardent Catholic, but orators from the anticlerical end of the political spectrum voiced similar conceits: "Gabrielle . . . you are not dead!" declared a Liberal alderman of Schaarbeek. Petit now lived "in that beautiful kingdom of memory, from where the dead address the living with such authority," wrote a journalist.[119] The *fusillé(e)s'* death-defying faith in the nation conferred immortality, because the national community would never cease to exist—thanks, precisely, to those that died for it—and would never cease to commune with the dead. Sacrifice, then, created a common city of the living and the dead.

But how common was this common city? Was Petit's sacrifice representative of virtues widely shared? Here, the discourse of remembrance bifurcated. Official rhetoric painted a flattering picture of Belgium-at-war. Prime Minister Delacroix considered Belgium's attitude during the war proof that the easy life of the *belle époque* had not softened the nation's moral fiber. Even though Petit and her fellow heroes represented the ultimate sacrifice, they still personified the sacrifices that Belgium—all of Belgium—had made for the just cause. By contrast, unofficial speakers brandished Petit's example as an admonishment. The Brussels attorney Albert Van de Kerckhove (also known as "Fidelis," his wartime alias as a pillar of the clandestine *Libre Belgique*) contrasted Petit to those young Belgians who were "without ideals" and wanted nothing more than an "empty and easy existence." He admonished audiences that the nation-in-arms presupposed a moral base of stern duty: "it is not by enjoying oneself that one honors and expands the Fatherland, it is not by enjoying oneself that one saves the Fatherland! It is certainly not by enjoying oneself that one raises it from its ruins!"[120] Fidelis' shrill tone well expressed many Belgians' sense of bewilderment after the war. It was in this atmosphere of crisis that an unknown like Petit could rise to the status of national heroine.

At the same time, there was more to it than crisis. Petit's elevation to the status of national heroine was borne by a groundswell of egalitarian imagining, as all "national heroizations" are: democratic-egalitarian political cultures are more likely to generate heroes than political cultures that take stratification and hierarchy for granted, as the French cultural anthropologist Jean-Pierre Albert points out.[121] Even before 1914, as the historian Christophe Charle writes, a latent mobilization for war across Europe hinged on the defense of a set of social references which ordinary people had started to master through a mass culture that held out the promise of distinction to all. Ordinary people had become used to reading that they, too, "could become heroes or heroines in extraordinary circumstances." Not coincidentally, the prewar cult of Joan of Arc was first and foremost that of a "girl of the people."[122] After the war, Joan of Arc's cult reached an apex in May 1919 (she was canonized a year later); and in that same month, Petit, so insistently held up as Belgium's pendant to the Maid of Orleans, became the first contemporary woman of modest status in Belgian (or, indeed, in European) history to be so fervently heroized.

That Petit was a civilian, strengthened her status as heroine: a leap of faith on behalf of the community made by someone not called upon to do so, was all the more providential. The hero, Albert writes, is one who does not *have* to risk life and limb; that is why partisan warfare, which presupposes voluntary engagement, generates more individual heroes than wars waged by regular armies. In the latter, duty is routine—or, to be more precise, the mantle of heroism and sacrifice covers all, so that to be singled out as an *individual* hero requires actions beyond the call of duty. And, of course, Petit was not only a civilian; she was a young woman of low status. National hero standing requires another discrepancy: that between someone's heroism and his/her social circumstances. Albert has called this the "double discrepancy" (*double décalage*). That is to say, there is, first, a gap between expected and exceptional merit, and, second, a disproportion between exceptional merit and station in life. Joan of Arc was not merely a civilian who took command of the army, ousted the invader, defended herself bravely before her judges, and died a horrible death; she was an illiterate teenage girl from a farm. Likewise, the nineteenth-century Bulgarian national hero Vasil Levsky was not just someone who took action to defend faith and nation when aristocrats and princes of the church did not; he was a penniless, nameless young man from the sticks.[123] All commemorations of *fusillé(e)s* emphasized this "double discrepancy." Not only did these men and women take on a risk they did not *have* to take on and for which they were not prepared—the lack of preparation deepened the heroism, effacing questions of efficiency—but they were cast against type: family men like Baucq and Smekens; adolescents, peasant sons, women. Nowhere was the "double discrepancy" theme stressed more than in the case of Petit. That a young woman of little education and modest circumstances was capable of such bravery seemed to prove the organic nature of national feeling. "When such an example is given by a woman, by a young girl from the people that nothing, it seems, had prepared for such a role, it commands our admiration with singular force," declared the Prime Minister. Petit's now-very-famous graffito "It is the humble ones that make hidden heroes," epitomized her import: it was as a humble heroine that she had saved the fatherland—and would continue to save it, wrote Fidelis.

She had saved it not only as a humble but also as a hidden heroine. The discourse on civilian heroes stressed both their humble status and their obscure deaths. The thrill of unearthing sacrifices made in the shadows deepened the drama of commemoration. Benedict Anderson, in examining the place of the dead in nationalist imagining, has quoted the French historian Jules Michelet's invocation of "those *miserabilis personae* who in Roman law have to be taken care of by the magistrate," because they have no clan to do so. For Michelet, the obscure dead throughout national history were like those *miserabilis personae*, and the historian—that is, the national narrative—was in the position of the Roman magistrate. The glorious dead (princes, generals) do not need commemoration; it is the obscure ones, the orphans of attention, that are the true wards of the nation's memory.[124] In post-occupation Belgium, the quest for an intensified national narrative made for the fervent exhumation of heroes whose stories combined the motifs of humbleness and of unknown sacrifice. This mood galvanized the nineteenth-century trope of the "humble hero," giving his or her all voluntarily and in secret. The aria *"Pauvre martyr obscur,"* a eulogy for a working-class hero from an 1886 opera about Flemish patriots under the Spanish regime, became a staple at events commemorating civilian heroism ("Poor obscure martyr, an hour's humble hero / I salute you and weep for you / Legend will teach our children your name").[125] That same pathos of anonymity suffused the discourse at Petit's funeral. One of the speakers was Chrétien Flippen, who had communicated with Petit in prison through graffiti. Flippen, a former telegraph operator now working at the Ministry of the Interior, had joined the *Ligue des Patriotes* and was becoming a memory agent of Petit's: he had attended the court hearing that decided on her place of burial. At the cemetery, he highlighted the sorrow of Petit's messages—"the days are centuries here, and I am so alone"—furtively scribbled on the doorjamb of the prison yard, to be read by people she would never see. His speech was soon reprinted in a mass format.[126] Lifting the veil of anonymity made for a literary thrill that paralleled national imagining. As Benedict Anderson has famously observed, national imagining weaves simultaneous events into one narrative, in the same way that the novel is "a complex gloss upon the word 'meanwhile,'" that weaves simultaneous occurrences into one "firm and stable reality" apprehended by the omniscient reader.[127] This very thrill of the "meanwhile" characterized the Petit narrative. In prison, she had been entombed alive amidst the ongoing life of the city; now, the national narrative uncovered this poignant simultaneity and enveloped the "meanwhiles" in one and the same radiant light. The commemorative effort aimed at making the very "humility" and "obscurity" that formed the heart of heroism into self-denying prophecies. As a Senator exclaimed in July 1919, looking back on Petit's funeral, "the little shop-girl . . . would never have thought that her poor bullet-torn body would be . . . carried in triumph through the mourning streets of Brussels . . . [and] that she would enter posterity with a title of nobility surpassing all others, that of national heroine!"[128]

Deepening Fervor

This lengthy Senate speech, pronounced by Eugeen Jan Keesen, a seventy-eight-year-old priest from the Flemish province of Limburg—known for his interest in the plight of the poor, his fierce anti-Masonic crusade, and his championing of the women's vote—was the next step in Petit's symbolic rise.[129] Keesen interpellated the government on what it planned to do to "perpetuate the memory of Gabrielle Petit, the national heroine." His interpellation took place in the usual atmosphere of heated debate over the moral economy of the past occupation; he took the floor after a debate over punishments for war profiteers.[130] His high-flown speech ended in a set of demands. He asked for a plaque in the Senate to commemorate Petit's condemnation, as well as that of Cavell; he recommended distributing Van Overbergh's booklet to all Belgian households and school libraries; and he suggested the state buy the house where she was born to make it into a memorial. He also suggested commemorating "all Belgians who immolated themselves during the world war" on the anniversary of Petit's death, and called on Brussels to create a Gabrielle Petit Avenue. These were surprisingly modest demands. Keesen did not suggest a monument; in these still-laissez-faire times, such expenditures were left to civil society. Still, he *was* requesting a permanent place in public space for Gabrielle Petit. No such request had ever before been formulated on behalf of the memory of an ordinary citizen, let alone a woman. The government refused to commit itself: Delacroix declared Petit's story fine enough, but too short to stand on its own. What was needed was a general history of civilian resistance—and that, the Prime Minister assured the Senate, was being worked on.

That Petit's story was too short, did not deter vernacular fervor. "Hers is a short enough story," Father Cardijn had said at her funeral Mass in 1916.[131] This would become a Petit trope: the very simplicity of her story made her into "a legend, swift and pure," as Michelet had written about Joan of Arc.[132] At the same time, her story gained some biographical depth. In July, another mass-produced booklet, the forty-three-page *Childhood, Youth, and Martyrdom of Gabrielle Petit*, appeared on the market next to *National Heroine*. Both booklets were sold together, almost as companion volumes.[133] Their view of Petit differs. *National Heroine* paints an icon, serene and triumphant; *Childhood, Youth, and Martyrdom* stresses poignant suffering. In *Heroine*, Petit enters fully formed upon the scene in 1914; *Childhood* paints Petit's early years as "sad, even very sad." The prison narrative depicts Petit as brave but shaken, mustering defiance with great effort, and harboring hope of being pardoned because of her youth. In this telling, it was Petit's sister who told her on March 31 that she would be executed in the morning. The scene of the sisters' farewell would be replicated in many a Petit narrative. As Hélène sobbed uncontrollably, Gabrielle, finding the strength to joke, told the interpreter to fetch her bed-sheet to stanch her sister's tears. After a last embrace, Hélène Petit found herself, dazed, in front of the prison. She saw a car arrive: German officials come to read the death warrant. "I could barely stand; I imagined them entering my poor sister Gaby's cell, and I pictured her, pale and proud."[134]

Childhood was published anonymously. It was almost certainly written by the Countess d'Oultremont, née Renée de Mérode (1859–1941), who, like Van Overbergh, had come by the story through Petit's sister Hélène.[135] D'Oultremont was a diligent observer of life under occupation, as her four-thousand-page diary shows.[136] She worked on behalf of invalided soldiers, malnourished children, and resisters on death row. Her son was at the front; her husband was deported to Holzminden camp as a hostage and died soon after returning home in 1917. D'Oultremont's ardent patriotism, her own penchant for military observation (evident in her diary), interest in endangered childhood, and possibly an inclination (which she shared with Van Overbergh) to combat the "lure" of Socialism among the working class through uplifting stories, all explain her receptivity to Petit's story. Though she stayed behind the scenes, she was closely involved with the effort to commemorate Petit. She attended the trial hearing about Petit's place of burial.[137] Her booklet was first serialized in *Le Drapeau*.[138] And, like Van Overbergh, d'Oultremont attended Petit's exhumation.[139]

Meanwhile, the rift in the family showed no signs of healing, and it was now quite public. Hélène Ségard had not attended her god-daughter's funeral; *Le Drapeau* accused Hélène Petit of deliberately excluding her elderly aunt. The Tournai press jibed at "the sister of the heroine—a status she only remembered after her death." Hélène Petit furiously contested that she had excluded her aunt and that she and her sister had been estranged.[140] *Childhood* was based on *her* recollections. Her aunt in turn vehemently disputed them: Hélène Ségard scoffed at the depiction of the sisters' childhood ("two abandoned girls, she says; why sure, two orphans!") and claimed that *she*, Ségard, had said farewell to Gabrielle in prison, not her niece Hélène, who had not known that her March 31 visit would be the last.[141] Ségard disputed her god-daughter's public image on many counts: the oratory Van Overbergh ascribed to her; her humble status; and the now very widely distributed picture in the white blouse which, Ségard said, did not resemble her at all, for she was petite and blonde and looked younger than her age. "She did not look anything like those pictures that want to make her look taller, with those hard features and that dark hair."[142] Again, Ségard had a point. It was true that some postcards offered a crudely elongated image.[143] And the lock of Petit's hair preserved at the Army Museum in Brussels is blonde.[144]

Hélène Ségard meanwhile took steps of her own to be Petit's memory agent. In mid-April, she wrote to the Mother Superior at Brugelette to ask for "some information about her character, etc., during the years she spent in your establishment" in view of a short memoir.[145] She gave an interview to *Le Drapeau* on May 1. And on the first anniversary of the Armistice, she sat in the front row at Brugelette to attend a lecture in honor of Petit. The speaker, Father Émile Paquet, drew heavily on her reminiscences, including the self-serving ones: in this telling, Marie Collet appeared as an elderly neighbor whom Petit generously helped out before the war.[146] In early 1920, Paquet published the text of his speech as a booklet. Like d'Oultremont's narrative, it stressed Petit's childhood, but unlike d'Oultremont, Paquet portrayed her as the beneficiary of a careful education—there is no mention that it was truncated—that had formed her character as a Christian heroine. This allowed Paquet to present Petit in conformist terms: he compared her to Antigone—portrayed more as a heroine defending divine law than as one defying power—and to a saintly young French aristocrat executed during the Terror. And he portrayed Petit in prison on the eve of her death, dreaming of being reunited with her former employers and her fiancé, in other words, taking her allotted place. Hélène Petit owned a copy of Paquet's booklet; she wrote on its cover, in a furious scrawl, "this book contains false information." She referred to a facsimile of a last letter by Petit to Ségard, printed in the booklet. In this letter, Petit promised her godmother some mementoes and took a tone of shared concern ("I have made an embroidery for you last night and I cut the hair you loved so. Give my farewell to Hélène and to Maurice, I hope my sister will follow your good advice, I wish her a happy life . . ."). Hélène Petit dismissed it as false:

Gabrielle Petit

"this letter is a fake, it was made by Miss Hélène Ségard, a scheming woman who put that ghastly death to profit."[147] The letter probably *was* a fake. Though it has been cited often, there is no original. A comparison with Petit's authenticated last letters reveals a far less confident hand; some characters seem crudely traced off of Petit's actual writing. A sad little fabrication to cover up past unconcern.

CHAPTER 7
NATIONAL HEROINE, 1919–1923

Elevated to the status of national heroine in May 1919, Petit was now a theme—and the next two years saw an explosion of variations on that theme. At the same time, in a parallel and unrelated effort, former resistance agents undertook to collect actual documentation about her. In 1922–1923, both endeavors came to an end: the discursive fervor around Petit and the effort to research her life and work. Two works, each in their own way, claimed the final word on Petit: her 1922 biography, by Arthur Deloge, and her 1923 monument in Brussels. This chapter addresses these four elements of the postwar Petit cult in turn.

Variations on a Theme, 1919–1921

The celebration of Petit spanned many media: commemorative plaques, postcards, pilgrimages to her cell, plays, poems, public lectures, illustrated books and booklets, paragraphs in school manuals, songs, and instrumental music. In late 1920, a first Petit film, featuring known actors from the Brussels stage, opened in four major movie theaters in the capital. "*The* national film," as *Le Soir* called it, was a crude affair, but it touched a chord: a movie magazine reported that "the scenes from the life of Gabrielle Petit moved audiences to tears."[1] Petit fare in general was straightforward stuff. In Belgium, functional illiteracy was still prevalent in those years; and this made for a very small elite of extremely sophisticated readers, fewer middle-brow readers than elsewhere in Western Europe, and a large audience for rough and ready fare. Petit discourse was no exception. One also notes that it was written, composed and staged by people situated far from the sources of academic or literary prestige. (Even if some were popular authors.) Neither learned historiography nor famous *littérateurs* took up her story. Heroes of the war did attract major authors and official works: leaders of men such as King Albert and General Leman, eloquent symbols of civic values such as Burgomaster Max or Cardinal Mercier. The memory of two of the executed, Edith Cavell and Philippe Baucq, two solidly middle-class people, garnered some official status. But the story of Petit, a young woman with a sketchy background who had left so little in writing, stayed in the minor genres.

But those minor genres took it up with fervor. The Petit theme had great didactic and emotional appeal: here was someone who had come from nowhere to take up the defense of the community against overwhelming odds, had gloriously perished, and whose story was now coming into the light. The Employees' Union suggested founding a "Gabrielle Petit Society" that would provide patriotic education to young people.[2] In August 1919, a

Flemish school-teacher composed a long "Patriotic Poem" for grade-schoolers: "may Gabrielle Petit remain an example to you! She was poor . . . but she remained loyal to her given word."[3] The Petit film, *La Libre Belgique et l'Héroïque Gabrielle Petit*, produced and subsidized by two well-known crusaders for edifying cinema,[4] interwove the story of Petit with the equally uplifting one of the clandestine paper *La Libre Belgique*.

In December 1919, "pilgrimages" started to Petit's cell at Saint-Gilles prison, which was maintained as a kind of shrine, as was Cavell's. (None of the other cells were, since Saint-Gilles was—and still is—a working prison.) Every week, a small number of visitors was admitted; visiting associations—mutual-aid groups, music societies—left small plaques as a kind of ex-votos.[5] Postcards depicted Petit's cell. Petit literature reprinted these pictures with reverent captions: "This new sanctuary, where one can see the *folded bed*, now supporting the large, beautiful portrait of the heroine set amidst flower wreaths and sprays, the *prayer-book* and *rosary*, the little kitchen-*cabinet*, the *sink*, etc., will forever remind us of she who suffered and died so valiantly for the Fatherland."[6]

Commemorative plaques appeared at the house in the rue du Théâtre in Molenbeek where she had rented a room and where she was arrested,[7] and at the house in Tournai where she was born (a major ceremony featuring Mass in the cathedral and celebrations throughout Petit's neighborhood; a cinema newsreel showed a solemn all-male audience in front of the little house, undaunted by the rain, while the minister of war declared— not altogether correctly—that Petit's execution had "shaken the entire country with indignation").[8] At the orphanage in Brugelette, a bas-relief showed Petit facing the execution-squad, torn-off blindfold in hand; the caption stressed that she had been raised in the orphanage and quoted her motto "It is the humble ones that make obscure heroes."[9]

Petit's story was so edifying because it was all about will. Several narratives dwelled on her action, such as the Flemish booklet that portrayed Petit as the axis of all intelligence work in occupied Belgium and illustrated this with striking color drawings. (One shows her at the border, the very image of panache in her smart traveling-garb, directing an escape operation across the electric fence.[10]) Another, very lengthy tale of her war work had her realize from the very first days of the war "that she had a role to play in the terrible drama"; in subsequent scenes, she witnessed atrocities, met with Edith Cavell, spirited army volunteers out, liaised at The Hague, foiled the secret police, assisted fellow resisters, reflected on her choices, and interacted with a large cast of secondary characters in ways that demonstrated her unwavering sense of purpose.[11] But the theme of Petit's will also marked those narratives that concentrated on her martyrdom and merely indicated her war work. The passion-of-the-Christ theme certainly loomed large in Petit texts, as it did in all *fusillé* narratives.[12] But it did so with an emphasis on volition. Even the most pious authors emphasized will rather than faith; at no point did they show Petit propelled by mysticism. She did not hear voices or submit to a higher command. Even her profession of faith was couched in this-worldly, voluntarist terms. In one play written by a parish priest, an eve-of-execution scene showed Petit's warden disparaging the idea of eternal life: "tomorrow, Miss, your body will slowly start disintegrating, all of

Figure 5 Petit's cell, 1919.
Brussels, Royal Army Museum, Prints Cabinet

your elements will rejoin the great vortex of atoms—and that will be that." She replied that her soul would continue to "judge your crimes and aspire to victory"—in other words, would continue to seek secular outcomes.[13] It all shows that the theme of energy was a leitmotiv. This theme fully squared with the era's high praise for will in the face of will-sapping times. Petit appeared as a paragon of purpose who chose her course, enunciated it in ringing tones, and followed it, cutting a path through confusion and oppression. In one Flemish play Petit told her godmother of her joy in having found her path: "Godmother, I have never been happier than I am now.... I never would have thought that a life fully lived in the service of a good cause would bring so much initiative and force."[14] Petit, as a symbol, meant not just the ultimate sacrifice but also the career freely chosen, the expanded horizon of action, the satisfaction of a difficult and dangerous, but also mobile and adventurous, task well done—by a woman. An Antwerp publisher used her name and part of her story for the mass-market adventure booklet *Gaby the Little Flying Ace*.[15] A play by a popular Tournai author, which premiered in September 1920, showed Petit waving away her sister's fears by saying that her "intense life of adventure" made her happier than ever. "And if they catch me, they put me up against the wall, so what?"[16]

The theme of the voluntary nature of Petit's engagement allowed ambivalence over military service to creep in. One tale used the joint enlistment of Petit and her fiancé to highlight the contrast between military and civilian engagement. The fiancé found no warm welcome at the Belgian recruitment bureau in England: NCOs called him an "idiot" for enlisting—"the front isn't all you think, mate." By contrast, Petit encountered nothing but praise at the intelligence bureau. On the next day, Petit, now Mademoiselle Legrand, on board ship, prayed for protection for the young soldier, "alone, lost, drowned in that army . . . in which all individuality vanished once one put on the uniform."[17]

Throughout the corpus, Petit is seen charting her path independent of male authority figures. Her father is absent, her intelligence chiefs give her a free hand, fellow resisters are comrades, she recruits helpers, and the fiancé's role is passive. She gains masculine glory through her own actions. The Order of Leopold citation lauded her "manly courage." Women, Petit exclaimed in one play, should not be spared "the glory of dying for the Fatherland"; in another play, she stated that "everyone must be a soldier now, so that, in peacetime, Belgian women will be able to claim their rights as Belgians."[18] As the historian Venita Datta has observed, French heroizing discourse of the *fin-de-siècle* broadened the definition of female self-sacrifice beyond the traditional association with motherhood; Petit discourse shows a similar shift.[19] This, in Petit tales, awarded her masculine freedoms: her steely sense of purpose rendered her as above reproach in public as a man would be. In one narrative, she met a young man in a Dutch hotel in private; her no-nonsense professionalism nullified the ambiguousness of this situation. (The scene was imagined, but the image of a young woman claiming masculine freedoms because of the authority of her mission corresponded to Petit's own awareness that her new status brought her freedom from innuendo: "it remains to be seen, Marraine, whether [Grandfather] would not have been proud.") The question of whether this theme meant a rethinking of women's rights to public space or whether its impact remained limited because Petit was confined to a status as "honorary man," must remain open. One ad for the film certainly expresses ambivalence, describing Petit as having "died for a cause surpassing her destiny as a woman, and with an energy and splendor worthy of that cause."[20] But Petit's image certainly presents a contrast to that of other spies of the First World War, who, as Tammy Proctor has argued, tended to be commemorated in highly genderized terms—as seductresses or as saintly victims.[21] By contrast, the Petit figure that appeared on stage, in film, and in fictionalized narration in 1919–1921 was a pure embodiment of resistance. Her import resided in the *res publica* and nowhere else. The actress playing Petit in the 1921 film was a dark-haired, middle-aged *tragédienne* with severe features; although there is no documentation on the film's casting, this choice does not seem coincidental. She was the national heroine: iconic, unwavering. Others—the fiancé, the sister, the godmother—might represent vacillation before sacrifice; she remained steadfast.

Around this unbending core, Petit discourse—crude as it was—offered ways to think through postwar issues: women's public role, paternal authority, the social order. The theme of postwar reconciliation with Germany—or, at least, with Germans—appeared too, in the guise of the German warden or translator—in short, the Otto Becker figure. One vehemently Catholic and Germanophobe booklet from early 1920 painted Petit's atheist guardian as a "monster," but such accents were rare.[22] Most staged a kindly German, misguided but well-meaning. (One notes in passing that none of the variations on the Petit theme bore anti-Semitic accents. Her interrogator Goldschmidt appeared as a member of the secret police and as a German; only his fellow countryman Fritz Ball had thought it fit to disparage his former boss by referring to his Jewishness.) Similar contrasts between the vengeful and the conciliatory had marked the discourse at Petit's funeral. Official speakers had not mentioned Germany at all, but others had struck vengeful tones, one speaker calling for nothing less than everlasting anathema—"through the centuries, this soil drenched with the martyrs' blood must call forth censure."[23] But there were other accents too. In his speech at the cemetery, Chrétien Flippen, Petit's fellow prisoner, went out of his way to praise Otto Becker's humanity. What was more, Flippen pointed out that German soldiers too had been executed because they had refused to shoot Belgian patriots. This was an extraordinary statement to make on such an occasion; I will return to it.[24] In short, even at Petit's funeral some speakers made a difference between individual Germans and Germany-at-war. In subsequent Petit discourse, this theme intensified. One play featured several praiseworthy Germans, among them Petit's defense counsel, who pleaded her "pure patriotism, shared by an entire nation whose liberties were violated flagrantly," and bravely added that "the General [the presiding judge] is entitled not to have any scruples, but I have my conscience as a lawyer to think about."[25] The Petit literature, then, for all that it was crude, did not exclude nuance.

Another point to be made is that the Petit discourse spanned both languages of Belgium. This was exceptional; even in these years of fervently professed national unity, most books on the war never made it from one language to the other.[26] This gap mattered all the more given the enormous broadening of Flemish reading audiences in those years. The wartime proliferation of lending libraries organized by charities both in the occupied country and at the front had helped create a vast reading public among Flemings without secondary education—that is, the majority—and who therefore did not read French routinely.[27] Petit discourse by no means closed the gap between war writings in French and in Dutch, but her story was one of the few common themes. The Antwerp publisher Opdebeek (who specialized in children's books and in popular didactic melodrama) published five Petit titles, among others two massive fictionalized biographies of Petit, one in Dutch, one in French. The Dutch author's name was given as Jan Verbeke; the French book was signed A. Du Jardin. In fact, as I was able to establish, both were pseudonyms for the popular Flemish writer Abraham Hans (1882–1939).[28] This matters a great deal, for Hans loomed very large in the cultural landscape of interwar Flanders. He was a writer capable of not just broadening, but of actually creating readerships; well into the 1960s, his work was avidly read by people who did not usually read. Hans wrote over nine hundred novels, all in his trademark mix of didacticism, adventure, and melodrama, savvily marketed in cheap, attractively illustrated instalments. That a writer of Hans' popularity and commercial clout contributed, albeit under pseudonym, to the Petit literature at such length and in both languages indicates the enormous vernacular appeal of her story. Moreover, the two versions of Hans' book suggest the emergence of two diverging discourses on the war. There was no straightforward translation; the Petit yarn in Dutch and the one in French each seem to cater to two audiences assumed to have distinct *sensibilités* towards the war. Both versions were, to be sure, written in an earnest, emphatic tone; both presented Petit all of a piece as a heroine; and both shared the exact same moral outlook on "Prussian militarism" and on the scandal of the invasion and occupation. Yet the Flemish version was a little lighter on oratory; there were fewer rolling phrases on "the altar of the Fatherland," "the valiant army," and "civilization." Also, it did not stress resistance as much. The French version noted (not incorrectly) that most civilians were reluctant to work for the Germans; the Flemish one did not. By contrast, the Flemish version stated (again, correctly) that the occupied citizenry disliked the German-controlled newspapers but read them anyway—a comment that is not in the French version. Through these small touches, the Flemish version implied that the occupied had resigned themselves to the state of things somewhat more readily than would appear from the French one, and that this was nothing to wax indignant about.

But the most striking difference is the account of an episode of the invasion, the massacre of civilians of August 22, 1914 in the industrial town of Tamines. The Flemish version spends barely two pages on this event; the French version runs to over six pages. In the French version, the German troops, portrayed as one "demoniac band," killed people in Tamines by rifle and machine-gun fire, and finished off survivors with rifle butts and bayonets. In the Flemish version, the German soldiers "fired too high, disgusted with the barbaric command," forcing "the officer" to man the machine-gun himself. As it turns out, both versions of Hans' narrative offered a part of the truth. A total of 383 people were killed in the small town, 269 of them in a mass shooting. The historians John Horne and Alan Kramer have used survivors' accounts (some published by 1920, and available to Hans) to describe the events: the civilians herded together on the square "were executed by rifle and machine-gun fire in a chaotic manner.... Many German soldiers fired too high or too low, and an officer had to complete the execution by machine-gun. Other soldiers, by contrast, were only too willing to finish off the killing with bayonet and rifle butt."[29] What this means is that the two versions of Hans' text each pulled only one strand, so to speak, out of the complexity of the event. The vengeful French-language version painted the invading troops as an undifferentiated mass that mowed down a defenseless crowd and then delected in face-to-face killing; the conciliatory Flemish version staged one single perpetrator against an unwilling majority of troops, and did not mention that survivors were killed off. The French version fit in with war culture; the Flemish version foreshadowed what Horne and Kramer have called the "pacifist turn" of the mid-1920s. That both perspectives were grafted onto Petit's story shows how her narrative served as a conduit for thinking through postwar issues.

Even as Petit discourse allowed contemporaries to think through public matters, it transformed the events of her life into one taut arc. Hers was not a life cut short, but a calling fulfilled: that is why several narratives—plays, poems, prose, illustrations, and the movie—ended on an apotheosis made to stress that, although Petit had died in the shadows, she would henceforth be enveloped in her compatriots' gaze. That hers remained a thin story, as Prime Minister Delacroix had told Senator Keesen in July 1919, did not stop fervent vernacular commemoration. For the point of this commemoration was to edify and to move, not to present further documentation about Petit, which from the point of view of popular heroization would have added nothing to her relevance anyway. That is why, although Petit was a contemporary and a compatriot, who had lived and worked around the corner, as it were, in Brussels and Hainaut, and who had died just three-and-a-half years earlier, the purveyors of Petit discourse left her story in its legendary haze and do not seem to have felt the impulse to seek out witnesses and documents.

Meanwhile, at some remove from public view, research for a general history of civilian resistance was underway: the very endeavor Prime Minister Delacroix had mentioned to Senator Keesen. It aimed not so much to stick to what was known and glorify it (as Keesen had advocated) but to demonstrate and prove; not to address the story of one individual but that of a collective endeavor. It was in this context that a start was made on actually documenting Petit.

The Archive, 1919–1921

Petit's fiancé was but a wan presence in the Petit literature. If he appeared at all, it was to highlight the heroine—a parallel in duty at best; at worst, a faintly silly minor character. And yet Maurice Gobert was around, limping from his war wound but alive and well and living in a small town south of Brussels with his wife, the young Frenchwoman he had met during the war. "It is most regrettable," he wrote in March 1921, "that I have never until now been officially asked for my assessment ... despite being, I should think, one of the parties most directly concerned and most able to provide serious testimony."[30] He wrote this in answer to a request for information by the Commission of Patriotic Archives (*Commission des Archives Patriotiques*, hereafter CAP), an agency that had been created in April 1919 to document resistance in occupied Belgium and France.[31]

As the historian Maria Todorova has pointed out, archives are never dispassionate repositories of "sources" that somehow well up naturally from historical events; they are constituted, in processes that involve struggles for power.[32] The archives of Belgium's civilian resistance in the First World War are a case in point. After the war, the impulse to document resistance did not come from the Belgian government but from the British War Office. Its emissary, the intelligence officer Henry Landau, crossed into Belgium within days of the Armistice. Keen on finally meeting the people on the other end, whose lives he had held in his hands during the war, Landau made straight for Liège, where he found himself finally facing the organizers of the formidable *Dame Blanche* network. He later remembered that first meeting with these middle-aged, austere-looking men—engineers, college professors, priests, their demeanors and their lives such a contrast to the swank night-life in post-Armistice Brussels—as one of the most important events of his life.[33] As the historian Emmanuel Debruyne has observed, the moment the door of that house in Liège was opened for Landau was the very moment that the secret intelligence agents of the occupied territories finally came out of the shadows. It was the start of a concerted effort to document resistance work and determine who deserved decorations. In April 1919, with subsidies from the Belgian government, the documentation commission started work; it was staffed by former resisters, with veterans of the *Dame Blanche* taking the lead. Two-and-a-half years running, until late 1921, the CAP charted the nebula of resistance efforts network by network, complete with occasional helpers, safe houses, "letter-boxes," providers of false papers, and legal defenders, but also informers, moles, *Polizei* agents: in short, all of the efforts that had kept networks going—or had done them in. Going beyond conventional materials, researchers assembled oral testimonies, press clippings, commemorative brochures, and photographs—of agents and informers, of secret reports and maps, and of prisons, execution-grounds, graves, and memorial plaques. This massive effort was an homage to civilian resistance, like the solemn funerals of 1919; but unlike those funerals, it honored surviving resisters too. The Belgian government was far less willing to do this. The idea—floated during the war by the British War Office—that intelligence agents could receive military status, met with derision.[34] Vernacular memory praised civilian resisters precisely because they had acted freely. ("*Godmother.*—You are the only one that senses [patriotic] duty, Gaby. *Gabrielle.*—There are many that sense this, Godmother. *Godmother.*—Really? Who? *Gabrielle.*—Well, our soldiers. *Godmother.*—Yes, because they are forced to."[35]) By contrast, official circles believed that resisters did not deserve military honors precisely because they had not been subject to military discipline. Moreover, the argument went, resistance had attracted shady folk, resisters had been "lavishly paid," and many had worked for what now (revealingly) counted as a "foreign" power. The minister of war, Fulgence Masson, was especially dismissive. (His exalted tone at the unveiling of the plaque at Petit's birth-house in Tournai, in September 1919, was no paradox: she was a woman, so could not be suspected of shirking, and she was dead, so would not voice pedestrian demands.) Harsh words were spoken during the parliamentary debate from February through August 1920.[36] Eventually, agents' time spent in action entitled them to half the equivalent military pension.[37] This half-recognition did not stop detractors from maintaining that able-bodied men should have joined the army and not civilian resistance.[38]

In short, resisters never quite received the recognition they claimed. Nor were they allowed to write the history of civilian resistance. In 1921, the CAP researchers were ordered to hand over their files, unprocessed, to an official archives commission, presumably to benefit academic historiography. Dismayed, the CAP team pointed out that the documentation so painstakingly assembled would become unintelligible if those who had gathered it and knew the subject could not process it for the public benefit. Events proved them right. During the interwar years, academic historians showed no interest. In 1940, the files were evacuated to England to shield former agents' identities from the invading army; stored in a country house, they suffered much water damage. Shipped back to Belgium after the war, the files were dumped in a warehouse for decades, before joining, in a further-depleted state, the Belgian State Archives, where they are today.[39]

In the course of ninety years, many documents have become difficult to identify and others have gone missing. The file on Petit, for one, has no order at all and contains some loose ends. Unlike some other networks' files, hers has no general report. An itemized list of its documents, drawn up by the CAP for internal use, no longer corresponds to the holdings: at least one piece, a list of agents, has gone missing; added documents are undated, unsigned, and hard to identify. Carbon copies stand in for vanished originals. There is one hand-drawn sketch of a German air field near Tournai, but it cannot be Petit's work, because it features details that do not predate 1917.

For all that, this raw set of materials contains much that is valuable; and a reconstruction of the CAP's work on Petit is instructive in its own right. The search for Petit material, it turns out, started in July 1919—exactly when the Prime Minister promised Senator Keesen it would. The first report was by Marie-Léonie Van Houtte, Louise de Bettignies' closest associate, who had known (or at least heard) Petit in Saint-Gilles prison, and sent in a pathos-laden account. Six months later, the next testimony came in, a terse spoken report by Marie Collet that gave valuable details about Petit's drifting years in Brussels, mentioned that Petit and Gobert had left occupied Belgium separately, and confirmed Petit's defiance at her arrest and trial. Collet's report in turn led the CAP to Father Mussche, who sent a calling-card to confirm that he had seen Petit at the *Kommandantur* after her death sentence was confirmed and to promise that "as soon as I have a moment, I will share some interesting details with you, specifically regarding her refusal to request a pardon. I can tell you that Gab. Petit really possessed the soul of a heroine and knew perfectly well what risk she was taking."[40] Elsewhere in the Petit file sits a five-page set of dashed-off notes, undated and unsigned; I have identified it as a transcript of a talk with Father Mussche, probably by the archivist Jules Germain, a CAP associate. Indecipherable in places, the hasty scrawl, a few words per line, has a certain poignancy:

All back in the van en route to St Gilles with guard
she talks—
was quite nervous—
The priest advises her to appeal
He asks her have you appealed
   no—
tells her you should—
I don't want to owe them anything
In sch [such] a tone he does not insist
small talk
[illegible] back to St Gilles—[41]

And with this, a key element in Petit's legend was corroborated.

In February–March 1920, the Jesuit priest Henri Philippart, a secret intelligence organizer during the war who now led the Tournai branch of the CAP, concluded from talks with Petit's Tournai relatives that her "network" had been small. At the same time, Philippart stressed her sense of noble defiance, the essence of her heroism as far as he was concerned: "The more one enters into the details of that brief and heroic existence, the more admiration one feels . . . Though hardship could have soured her, there was nothing base . . . in this child! . . . And she's a Belgian! . . . Ours to be proud of! . . ." For all this effusive praise, Philippart did not consider Petit a network organizer at all; he did not mention her journeys into France; and he thought her too "exuberant" to be an efficient spy—a trait stressed to the detriment of the "superior intelligence" highlighted in her German case file. Petit knew that she was often mistaken for a hothead: she had written as much to Otto Becker.

A stock figure in the Petit narrative, the real Otto Becker had left Brussels at the end of the war to return to his home town of Bochum, where he lived with his parents and had an administrative job in a steel mill. He was in contact with Hélène Petit; she let him know that her sister was buried in Schaarbeek. On October 15, 1919, Becker wrote back to say he was happy that "your admirable Gaby" had been laid to rest in the capital, so that "her grave is bound to remind all of that most valiant of the valiant Belgian women." He planned to bring flowers as soon as the Belgian authorities would allow him to return. (Most German nationals were expelled.[42]) "Believe me, I am homesick for Brussels, a city I love with all my heart! I am dying here!" This brief glimpse of a correspondence between these two young people, both starting out on their "settled" lives, hints at avenues of reconciliation. Both were looking for allies: Becker needed Belgians to vouch for his decency during the war, and Hélène Petit may have sought a sympathetic ear after the burial decision which had pitted her against the rest of her family. Becker consoled her for her loss by saying that her sister "was not victimized uselessly, since Belgium has emerged independent from this terrible war. If she could have foreseen the honors that would surround her, she would surely have died smiling. You valiant little Gaby! I will never forget you!" They touched on sublime and on practical matters: in response to

Hélène Petit's query about her sister's last moments, he told her of Gabrielle's self-possession; in response to her wish to buy furniture in Germany (she was getting married), he told her that "Germany has become the most expensive country in the world," and went on to lament that "things are not rosy at all here. Life is difficult. We will all be broke for having lost the war!" He himself was doing relatively well, "but I need Brussels!" He closed his letter on a reference to shared disillusionment: "and you, dear Miss, what are you doing? Has Belgium shown you some gratitude, at least?"[43] Hélène Petit never shared the letter with the CAP, which was not interested in her point of view either. Her papers contain no further correspondence with Becker.

On December 1, 1919, Becker, in his quest for a character reference, wrote to Xavier Marin, the associate director at Saint-Gilles prison. Marin was coming forward as a memory agent: he had attended the exhumation of Petit's body and given an emotional interview to a Brussels newspaper, recalling his last view of Petit as she was led away to be shot; reports noted that he could not speak of her without bursting into tears.[44] His grief may have been compounded by his awkward wartime situation; Marin was not directly involved in the German repression apparatus, since the occupying authorities had taken over part of Saint-Gilles prison, but he still oversaw the facility's routine functioning. A counterpart of his, the French director of Loos prison, faced some questioning after the war.[45] Marin suffered no such upset: he was awarded the honors and distinctions that came with his position (though it is remarkable that he never progressed beyond the rank of deputy director).[46] But his statements suggest an enduring sense of unease: to Deloge, he expressed regret not to have helped political prisoners escape, and he made much of his acquaintance with Petit, although he probably no more than glimpsed her in prison, if that. (That he described her as dark-haired and wearing a large hat cocked sideways hints that he only ever saw her photo.) He even felt the need to assert that Cavell—whom he also claimed to have known in prison—had had nothing on Petit.[47]

Becker's very long letter to Marin established, like his letter to Hélène Petit, a mood of shared grief: he reminded the director that they had wept together on the day of the execution. In his letter to Hélène, Becker wrote that he would never forget her dead sister. Vis-à-vis Marin, he admitted that his memory of her had faded somewhat. "If I had known then that she would become the most famous woman of Belgium," he wrote with some candor, "I would have been sure to note her actions so as to share them with the Belgian public later." But he did apparently retain some fairly sharp memories of Petit, which he proceeded to share with Marin; and he bolstered their rapport further by sending Marin an extremely valuable document: the letter Petit had written to him in late March 1916. He had taken it with him to Germany. It is unclear why he was now giving it away, and why he sent it to Marin and not to Hélène Petit. It might have been a strategic choice: the deputy director of Saint-Gilles prison would have been in a better position to vouch for his, Becker's, uprightness during the war than an unknown shop assistant in a working-class borough, for all that she was the national heroine's sister. At any rate, Becker's decision to send the text to Marin had the result that this extraordinary text, the single most important egodocument by Petit, is now available only in transcript and in a censored version. At some point in early 1920, Marin decided to share Petit's letter with the CAP researchers—but he only handed them a transcript, from which he had cut, by his own admission, passages about her life before the war, about her family and about her fiancé. Marin kept the original. What happened to it is a mystery.[48] His transcript was hedged about with an explanation—"it is to be noted that Gabrielle Petit was confined to strict solitary detention and could not communicate with anyone"— meant to justify such an affectionate letter to a member of the German military. Still, the letter *was* put in the public domain; and even in its cut version remained extraordinarily frank. It showed, after all, a young woman, the "national heroine" no less, discussing her less-than-passionate feelings for her fiancé, a Belgian soldier, with a German—with whom, but for his temporary status as occupier, she would be friends and maybe more. That such a letter could be included in the official files on resisters, suggests that the CAP was not in the business of perpetuating wartime bigotry; it once more indicates how Petit's memory opened up space to think through the issues of the postwar.

Through 1920, a steady trickle of documents brought her war work into somewhat sharper focus: it was now clear that when Petit left occupied Belgium in 1915, she was not yet involved in secret intelligence, which qualified the straight course of invasion-propelled purpose advanced by Van Overbergh *et al.* At the end of the year, the single largest document in the Petit file reached the CAP: a transcript of a spoken testimony by Hélène Ségard, Petit's godmother, weighing in at forty-one typewritten pages. Hélène Ségard had made her declaration a year earlier, probably to her brother Eugène, the Antwerp doctor who the Ségard family claimed was working on a myth-busting biography of his niece.[49] In the following months, the CAP tried to contact Eugène Ségard directly, with no apparent result. He never published the announced study of his sometime ward. His only contribution to the Petit documentation is, then, this very lengthy statement by his sister. The CAP never seems to have attempted to contact Hélène Ségard to verify her statements; no elucidation of the document is offered, and so the testimony comes to us raw. Ségard gave much detail about Petit's early childhood, waxed vague about her god-daughter's years at the orphanage, painted a cheerful picture of Petit's prewar years in Brussels that suggests they were barely in contact, and gave a credible account of the days of terrible anxiety after Petit's return to occupied Brussels and of Petit's terse appraisal of her war work and the risks she ran. In relating the fight over Petit's memory, the oral testimony becomes expressive in its very disjointedness: recalling her god-daughter's reburial case, Hélène Ségard seems to have waxed incoherent with indignation, and the transcript becomes hard to follow, with non sequiturs, sudden exclamations, and opaque charges.

In January 1921, another important document reached the CAP: a long letter by Leonard Leyendecker, the "death row chaplain" at Saint-Gilles prison, who at the Armistice had left Brussels, where he had lived for thirty years, and was now stationed near Fulda in Hesse.[50] Leyendecker wrote in answer to a request by a Belgian-Dutch *confrère*, Father Jan Nysten, who had sent him a book he had written on the last days of the executed, entitled *Comment ils meurent* [How They Die], and had long pleaded with him to share his reminiscences.[51] Leyendecker started his letter on a note of disapproval of the *fusillé* mystique. "Spying," he wrote, "has always seemed to me a less honorable enterprise than soldiering; why then all this talk about spies, almost at the detriment of the many soldiers about whom we know so little?" He chose to remember the executions as instances of justice, meted out with honor. On one occasion, the chaplain wrote, a prisoner had offered to name names to save his life, but prosecutioner Stoeber had declined to take such an ignoble confession. He stressed that all of the executed had reconciled with religion and had died in a spirit of acceptance. Nysten's book, the chaplain scolded, was still steeped in "the mind-set of the war" and did nothing to advance the cause of Christian reconciliation.[52] This was not altogether fair on *How They Die*: Nysten went out of his way to praise German Catholics.[53] In fact Nysten wanted to establish what John Horne and Alan Kramer have called a "community of truth" between Catholics over violence against civilians. But Leyendecker denied that the invasion and the occupation were issues; striking tones of cultural demobilization, he posited a serene synthesis brought about by German military justice.[54] (Van Overbergh, in *National Heroine*, railed at the chaplain's "air of smug serenity."[55]) Because Leyendecker refused to see the encounter between civilian resister and military regime as a confrontation, he contested the Petit chapter in Nysten's book. As far as he was concerned, Petit had been mainly a troublemaker. Leyendecker would think so all his life. In a 1955 memoir of his years in Brussels, he still felt compelled to dismiss her as "a fanatic, not a Christian."[56]

In March 1920, Maurice Gobert told the CAP that he would be delighted to help. He asked for a month's time, because "I want to say all that I know in this matter, for I want nothing but the truth and the whole truth." In the event, Gobert never shared his memories of Petit with the CAP. "We have obtained a formal promise," the archivist and CAP researcher Jules Germain said later that year, "but we have not received anything yet."

Germain said this in a lecture to a professional audience, in all likelihood the Belgian Academy of Arts and Sciences, possibly in the spring or early summer of 1921. The Petit file contains the undated and unsigned lecture notes, or at least a fragment.[57] This modest occasion, so deeply sunken as to be almost irretrievable, was the only time Petit registered with professional historiography; it was an occasion for the CAP to present a *status quaestionis* of what could be known with certainty about Petit.

In sticking to the sources, did Germain diminish her import? Heroines, as the historian Anne Eriksen has pointed out, have tended to lose out in the nineteenth-century transition from folk legend to scholarly historiography—which elevated historic women to the status of national heroines while diminishing them as agents. Their range of action withered under the glare of source criticism, which privileged the kind of report more likely to document men's actions. Some of their achievements were doubted and dismissed because they were considered unfeminine. As a result, their tales became singularly thin; and their agency took second place behind their status as symbols.[58] Petit's case is not dissimilar. Her "folk" cult—if a body of vernacular discourse in post-Armistice Western Europe, consisting of pink-collar-union literature, small-town Catholic confraternity drama and mass-market melodrama can be so described, which I believe it may—ascribed to her a wide and almost magical realm of action, which shrunk when tested against documentary evidence; *abbé* Philippart's report (see above) shows this. Germain, at any rate, stressed that he did not intend to diminish Petit's stature when he pointed out that she had become a legend: "her bold defiance in word and deed was bound to speak to the imagination of the masses." He then proceeded to reconstitute Petit's life before 1914 from the descriptions by Hélène Ségard and Marie Collet. Given that Petit's sister and father had no contact with her, he dismissed what they might have to say. (The CAP apparently did not know that Petit's father had died during the war.) He praised Marie Collet's testimony as "excellent from a historical point of view," clearly appreciating her matter-of-fact tone, in contrast to, for instance, Marie-Léonie Van Houtte's bravado-inflected account, which he did not cite. Quoting Collet meant acknowledging Petit's not exactly virginal past, which was a first in Petit discourse, even if Germain couched it in veiled terms. He narrated Petit's war work with the precision his sources allowed, which rather diminished the import of her work. He noted her eventual betrayal by Keurvers, by then well known as a major informer. (Nikolaas Keurvers was, at the time, living in the Netherlands, out of reach of Belgian justice, but not above turning a profit off it: he had written to offer proof against other informers, "for a fee, of course."[59]) Talking about Petit's time in prison, Germain read out in full Becker's assessment of Petit and Petit's letter to Becker, which was quite a revelation to make. The notes end on a few sentences, scribbled in pencil, on Petit's refusal to appeal. The lecture as eventually delivered, probably followed her story to the end. Germain made one further contribution to Petit scholarship in the form of a two-page article published in mid-1922. In it, he presented her fourth intelligence report, ending on an all-too-brief assessment of her: pluck [he used the term *énergie*], he wrote, was her determining but not her sole trait, and Petit lore had not done justice to her complex, anguished individuality.[60]

These fragments are the only scholarly writing about Petit in existence. Meanwhile, the missing pieces of the puzzle were collected elsewhere. Germain had mentioned awaiting Maurice Gobert's testimony with bated breath. But Gobert seems to have changed his mind about working with the CAP. Instead of sharing his memories with an archivist of civilian resistance, he chose to share them with a fellow veteran.

The Biography, 1922[61]

The documenters of civilian resistance had to relinquish their files before they could write them up. But the file on Petit was processed; not by a member of the CAP, but by a forty-year-old war veteran named Arthur Deloge (1881–1951). During the war, as an NCO in the Belgian corps of engineers, Deloge had made his name with a short handbook of subaltern command entitled *How to Lead Men*.[62] In 1921, he published a well-received biography of Léon Trésignies, a Belgian soldier killed in a bravura action in 1914.[63] For all that, not much is known about Deloge; he was the kind of in-between author—nonprofessional historian, occasional military expert, sometime poet and dramatist—who escapes the reach of biographic dictionaries, or receives only truncated entries. The *Encyclopedia of the Walloon Movement* only mentions his activity from the 1930s, when he became a Walloon militant of sorts, not his earlier, "Belgian" oeuvre. No archive holds his papers.[64] Still, his oeuvre explains his interest. His prewar elegy "Our Little Ones" (*Nos P'tits*) commemorated the tragic 1906 sinking of a Belgian Navy training ship with its pupils as a tale of valiant young lives offered up.[65] He was, like Van Overbergh and Cardijn, a militant Christian Democrat who focused on the plight of service personnel: a few months before war's outbreak, he published a unionizing novella titled *La Demoiselle de Magasin* [The Shop-Girl].[66] His wartime command manual warned against drowning individual worth in mass organizations; and, finally, Léon Trésignies, subject of his 1921 book, was a classic emblem of the heroism of the humble.

He wanted his Petit biography to be a warts-and-all account that would enlarge her import, by making her "far more interesting than she has been represented until now: deeply human, truly great."[67] The book, *Gabrielle Petit: Sa Vie et son Oeuvre*, was published in 1922 (by Larcier, a well-known Brussels publisher who was secretary general of *Ligue des Patriotes*)—a handsome, illustrated little tome of a little over 200 pages, costing a not unsizeable six francs. The advertising leaflet promised readers that it was scrupulously documented but also read like "the most thrilling of novels."[68]

It was indeed scrupulously documented. He enjoyed direct access to the CAP file— some documents bear his annotations—and other material, some of it now lost and only available through his book. And he spoke to several people who had known Petit. His main coup was getting Maurice Gobert to share his memories and the letters from his onetime fiancée (which he reproduced, but with some parts taken out). Other witnesses included her friend Julia, whom the CAP in spite of repeated internal reminders had not had time to contact. That Deloge did not speak with Petit's godmother (though he quoted her testimony), or to her sister, whom he dismissed as a reliable witness, underscored the gist of his narrative: Petit essentially had no family and relied on the kindness of working-class strangers. He considered Marie Collet the most reliable witness to her life in 1911–1916 and spoke to her at length. To bolster his portrayal of Collet as Petit's new-found mother, Deloge inflected the sources a little. Though Petit's letters refer to "Mère Collet," he had her use the more intimate "*maman* Collet." In her last letter to her godmother, sister, and cousin, Petit had added a greeting for Collet— "I embrace her a lot, the dear old one." Deloge's transcript skips this—possibly because it sounds too much like a nice thought for an old family servant.

Still, Deloge presented his audience with a great deal of new and spectacular information. He revealed Petit's bourgeois but reduced background and the wretchedness of her life in prewar Brussels. (Jules Germain, in his 1921 lecture, had still downplayed her 1912 suicide attempt as "not very serious.") He exploded the myth of the fiancés' joint departure and patriotic leave-taking. He devoted one-fifth of his book to Petit's war work—though the writing here is very confusing, going back and forth in time and space, as befitted a part of her life that even in spite of Deloge's best efforts could not be completely charted. His account of her time in prison avoided hagiographic flourishes such as the "conversion" of the atheist warden, though he did try to impose an unproven sequence on Petit's last letters in order to establish that she knew she would die on April 1. Throughout, he was quite present as an authorial voice. He ended his narrative of Petit's return to prison after her condemnation on a mournful note: "Father Mussche's tearful farewell was, in a sense, Belgium's adieu to its child." Defining March 3, 1916 as the date when Petit forever entered an alternate universe, in the heart of Belgium but separated from her fellow Belgians, was Deloge's way of dismissing her closest relatives as relevant compatriots, and of making her a ward of the nation.

Three questions might serve as a lens through which to view this book. How did Deloge, as a war veteran, assess civilian resistance? Did he question Petit's right, as a young woman, to her choices and actions? And how did his concrete portrayal of Petit influence his sense of her as a heroine?

To answer the first question: civilian and military experiences of the First World War were not separated by an abyss, as recent scholarship had shown, and Deloge's take on Petit was no exception. At no point did he posit a uniqueness to the trench experience that would diminish civilian resistance. As far as he was concerned, the national heroine and the war hero Léon Trésignies were two of a kind. Both were of the urban working poor. "Gabrielle was a servant; Trésignies was a factory worker, part of the anonymous throng that presses against the doors of the workshops at the end of the working day." Both had faced a superior power voluntarily: Petit chose to be a spy; Trésignies had volunteered for his suicide mission. (To cover his unit's retreat, he had jumped into a canal to turn a bridge-lifting lever.) Their action was not propelled by mass emotion—by "the intoxication of battle." Their sober choice of self-annihilation underscored their individuality. And, just as Trésignies was also a civilian (that is, an individual acting autonomously), Petit was also "a soldier in the full meaning of the word" (that is, someone who accepts duty unflinchingly). Nor was she the only one. During the war, Marie Collet's cozy kitchen became a kind of front; Deloge painted the two women seated at table, worrying about the disappearance of their courier, knowing themselves tracked. "Unrecognized soldiers who waged war in the dark for a sacred cause, the two women continued their work, comforting each other to calm their anxious hearts."

Did Deloge diminish Petit's import because she was a woman? A "documentary" gaze on Petit's work was bound to diminish its range. Deloge was a veteran in a time when veterans' rights as men were fervently affirmed. His take on the social order was patriarchal: his command manual claimed that good NCOs made good soldiers just as good husbands made good wives. And his book was presented in a manner that spelled the end of Petit as a Joan of Arc-like icon. The publisher's leaflet placed her romantic misfortune front and center: "One's eyes well up before the tragic misunderstanding that separates these two beings who were made for one another, that perfect couple, the most beautiful couple of Belgium. Haunted by the terrible question 'Did my beloved betray me?' the fiancé escapes, crosses the border, rejoins his regiment. Then the abandoned one pursues him, before returning to the occupied country, no longer towards *him*, but towards *it*, the Fatherland . . ."[69]

Deloge certainly sought to impose a gender order. He portrayed Petit as lacking softness: her wretched childhood had erased "the young girl's usual attitude" in her. He called her stoicism at age nine an "American" trait, meaning she was indifferent to the hierarchies of age and gender. (One recalls that Otto Becker too had called her "American.") While disapproving of the brutal parenting of Petit *père*, Deloge thought Gabrielle's refusal to submit to constraint excessive. He was the first to state that Gobert left Petit, when earlier Petit discourse had her shaking off her fiancé in the higher interests of her service. In Deloge's telling, this split, the second time a man broke up with her, put the final touch on her already overly virile personality: "she was already swayed by the power of the 'head' to the detriment of the other sentiments of her gender; now, more than ever she wanted to be a 'man-woman,' as she liked to call herself." In fact there is no indication that she liked to call herself anything of the kind. It is true that Deloge painstakingly cleared Petit of all suspicions over Gobert's escape. But he couched his conclusion in terms of masculine approval: the great *fusillée* had been "worthy of a veteran's esteem," if not perhaps "of the love of a fiancé"—in other words, she was not marriage material. At the same time, he had Petit look forward to being married, though her letter to Becker stated otherwise, and her godmother remembered her as wary of marriage. (He could not know that at some point Petit had aspired to become a teacher: the relevant sources were not known at the time.) Deloge's assessment of Petit, then, like that of Otto Becker, wavered between two rigidly gendered images: now "more man than woman," then an excellent future wife and mother. He had Petit tell Becker that she would die thinking of Gobert, when her letter said no such thing and her authenticated last messages to her relatives do not mention her fiancé at all. He also concluded that Petit had been "under the spell of [Becker's] charm," though her affectionate and ironic letter to him does not suggest such a helpless infatuation.

But Deloge did not take away from her public stature: he called her letter to Becker her "patriotic testament" and repeatedly stressed that her sense of duty did not come from a male authority figure. He did not saddle her with a definition of virtue centered on sexual irreproachability. His portrayal aimed at making her a more fully rounded character, complete with private aims and deceptions; a young woman of uncommon intelligence—he kept stressing this—who wanted to make something of herself in the world, including the founding of a household on her own strength. His take on her as a private person was not so much about gender per se as about connection—the unraveling of family; the kindness of strangers; the hoped-for reconstitution of a home; pride vis-à-vis family.

Social class, not gender, is what marked Deloge's view of Petit. He emphasized class as constitutive of people's lives, including their lives in the war. He was the first author to address head-on the fact that Petit had been paid for her intelligence work. He approached it militantly, as a champion of the rights of lower-class patriots: not having the independent means to set up a network did not preclude disinterested sacrifice. Moreover, he thought Petit fully justified in taking on a well-paid task that would allow her, in the most honorable way possible, to finally escape "terrible poverty" and dependence, and provide for others: "a noble ambition!" In other words, that she had been paid did not diminish her agency, but placed it in its full context as a praiseworthy public and private striving.

Likewise, Deloge took an ample view of her war work: he thought it more wide-ranging than did Philippart et al., reporting on her *Libre Belgique* and escape work. Stern fellow resisters might consider these multifarious efforts inefficient; Deloge applauded them. The occupied country was a theater of multiple confrontations: "everywhere, there were hand-to-hand combats in which audacity and ruse prevailed. Hundreds of German spies ... seconded triumphant tyranny; thousands of Belgians ... foiled the German plans ... None of these ten thousand braves ... showed more panache than Gabrielle Petit." Her attitude in prison was part of her war work: "to refuse to submit to prison rules, to refuse to request a pardon, to refuse to betray to save her life, that is how Gabrielle served her country until the end ...!"

To address the third question: Deloge's book, unlike the Petit lore of 1919–1921, placed her life in concrete circumstances. This did not, as far as he was concerned, diminish her stature as a heroine—rather the opposite: her wretched childhood, truncated education and drifting years threw her wartime bravery into sharper relief. His book espoused the "double discrepancy" notion of national heroism that marked Petit lore—heroism meant both going beyond the call of duty, *and* beyond what is expected of the humble—and gave it nuance, precision, and depth. It eliminated the legendary parts of Petit's story, but ultimately sketched a similar arc to her life as a destiny, divested of the random. And, like the Petit hagiographies, it ended on an apotheosis: Petit's induction into the national pantheon.

Deloge's definitive account of Petit's life—after this, "nothing new will ever be said" on the subject of the national heroine, the publisher's leaflet stated—had a 1923 pendant that was never published: the account of Petit's childhood written by one teacher at the orphanage, Berthe Depaquier, in religion Sister Marie-Walthère, in response to Deloge's somewhat condescending portrayal of the school. "Mr. Deloge," she wrote, "seems to me to take a slightly denigrating tone towards the institute ... But every cloud has a silver lining: these little barbs, veiled with an air of bonhomie ..., allow us to respond [as] we would not otherwise have done, as it is not in our habit to divulge ... family secrets. So I thank Mr. Deloge for the freedom he grants us." These notes, written in pencil on the back of used exam copies held together by a pin, were never published or disseminated, and have only survived in photocopy version. They date, in all likelihood, from the second half of 1923.[70] As I have noted, this extremely precious source offers a great deal of striking detail about Petit's childhood. But there is more to it than the factual. Though only a rough draft, the nun's text possesses biographical depth and a sense of a life's arc, unlike the mythical perspective of Petit lore, and similar to Deloge's take on Petit. But, unlike Deloge, Sister Marie-Walthère stressed Petit's background not to show how even ordinary people could accede to the highest honors, but to portray Petit as one of the elect. She prefaced her account by quoting a lecture that the French right-wing nationalist celebrity Maurice Barrès, known for his disquisitions on "national energy," had recently given on Pascal: "What near-religious enigma makes for the apparition of genius? Why does the spark spring from one child, and not from another of the same blood and born under the same sky? How did this point of perfection emerge . . .?"[71] Petit, the nun wrote, was elected to her destiny; her—Sister Marie-Walthère's—notes were meant to "take stock of the emergence of this extraordinary character." Petit had inherited intelligence and aristocratic refinement from her father's family's side (if not from her father), and generosity and virtue from her mother's. Her bitter early years had made her resilient. And her education at Brugelette—the Reverend Sister glossed over the fact that it had been cut short—had rounded off her development: "we may proudly consider her achievement the result of our work." In other words, by the time Petit left school, she possessed all that she needed to fulfil her glorious destiny—a destiny that in turn made up for (or, as Sister Marie-Walthère expressed it, "absorbed") the sad, even sordid details of her childhood.

Neither Deloge nor Sister Marie-Walthère, then, considered detail to detract from iconic status, on the contrary. Petit was both "sculpted in high relief" *and* a "symbol of total bravery," as the ad for Deloge's book had it. In other words, she could be fleshed out even as she was set in stone. Meanwhile, preparations to literally set her in stone—or, to be precise, cast her in bronze—were afoot.

The Monument, 1923

Just as Deloge's biography was meant to be definitive, the monument in central Brussels aimed to give Petit's memory a definitive place in the heart of the nation's capital. The monument was unveiled on July 21, 1923, Belgium's fifth national holiday since liberation. The city was aswarm with visitors from the province; in a traditional ceremony known as the *fête du dévouement*, the king handed out medals to meritorious citizens; and the entire royal family with entourage, as well as the government, Parliament, and top army brass attended the Te Deum Mass that ended at 2.30 in the afternoon.[72] The unveiling of Petit's monument was scheduled at 4.30. A thick file in the Brussels municipal archives attests to the ceremony's meticulous preparation.[73] The Place Saint-Jean, a pretty little square on the winding slope of streets that descended from the government district to the baroque Grand'Place and the populous quarters beyond, was transformed into a stage. (The square implicitly referred to the war: a cluster of apothecaries' shops specialized in prostheses, the manufacturing of which had become a sad Belgian specialty; and one of the shops belonged to the pharmacist Louis Séverin, who had been condemned to death for his participation in the Cavell network.) As the hour approached, a chorus of nine hundred school-children took their places behind the monument, which was veiled with a large Belgian flag. Off to the side, hundreds more children stood to attention, bearing their school standards. Facing them from the other side of the square, some five hundred worn-looking, dignified people, flags and banners aloft, took their place: Allied and Belgian veterans, former political prisoners, and family members of the executed, wearing their relatives' posthumous medals. Facing the monument was a large tribune for special guests—cabinet ministers, members of Parliament, army commanders, Allied ambassadors, municipal dignitaries, and other invitees, 450 people in all. It was built with an eye to social hierarchies. The "Royal Salon" in the middle sheltered the highest-ranking guests; it featured two gilded *fauteuils* to seat Queen Elisabeth and her daughter, princess Marie-Josée. (The Queen's acceptance of the invitation, a carry-over of her homage to Petit at the funeral, had delighted the organizers; the princess, known for her gamine flapper style, could represent contemporary youth's awareness of past sacrifice.) On each side of the "Royal Salon" were standing-room-only compartments. The left-hand one, set aside for the least distinguished guests, crammed some 320 people into a 45-square-meter space. To avoid cross-status confusion, differently-colored invitations and passes gave access to prearranged places on the tribune. A flurry of internal notes had specified the finer points of the ceremony. The school-children's procession past the monument was to be scrapped in case of rain, but not that of the veterans and political prisoners, who, as city officials warned each other in internal notes, would insist on marching in all weather. There was a *défilé* of boy scouts too. An official inquired if this included Socialist scouts; Max replied that he had never heard of such. A quick investigation confirmed that there was indeed no such thing as a Socialist boy-scout troop, so this potentially delicate matter could safely be shelved. (The first Socialist boy-scout troops in Belgium appeared in 1929.)

In the event, the sun shone, and the ceremony went ahead as planned. The neighborhood overflowed with people, standing behind crowd-control barriers. The inhabitants of the square had hung out national flags, provided by the municipality. The children burst into the national anthem as the royal car entered the square. Speeches extolled Petit's heroism. Minister of Defense Albert Devèze, for one, held her up as an example to "our young soldiers," hoping that "the cult of the heroine will inspire us with some of her sublime ardor, amidst this treacherous peace that still holds so many dangers."[74] The monument was unveiled with a flourish. The Queen and princess deposited a wreath in solemn silence. To cheers from the crowd, the French ambassador conferred the Cross of the Legion of Honor on Petit, an expression of French-Belgian concord much appreciated now that both states were jointly occupying the Ruhr following Germany's default on reparations payments.[75] In answer, the children's chorus sang the Victor Hugo hymn "Those Who Have Piously Fallen For the Fatherland," by now a staple of *monuments aux morts* ceremonies in France.[76] To the sounds of the municipal marching-band, two thousand pupils then marched past, each school with its own wreath—Max had insisted on this expense—followed by a procession of veterans' associations, invalids (cheered with especial fervor), former political prisoners, nurses, and other societies, all bearing garlands. The barriers were then removed and the crowds thronged into the square, depositing yet more flowers, leaving the pedestal entirely covered, while guests left in a carefully-planned exit choreography of automobiles, horse-drawn coaches, and banner-bearing pedestrians.[77]

On the face of it, seeing the dignitaries, hearing the speeches, and taking in the national symbolism, one would think that this commemorative effort came from the authorities. In fact, the Belgian state had had nothing to do with it. It was not even an initiative by local government: although the city of Brussels hosted and organized the unveiling ceremony with great care and a significant outlay of public funds, it was the recipient of the Petit statue; it had neither taken the initiative, nor paid for it. Burgomaster Max had been entreated to give a speech, but declined, declaring that he had spoken quite enough since the war and felt he was starting to get in the way.

The monument project had come from civil society; specifically, from the *Ligue des Patriotes*, the *milieu de mémoire* that had first declared Petit the national heroine. The *League* had started collecting funds in late May 1919. One *Ligue* member, the famous occultist painter Jean Delville (1867–1953), proved particularly active: by 1923, he had collected the staggering sum of 150,000 Belgian francs.[78] From mid-1919 through mid-1923, the *Ligue*'s periodical, *Le Drapeau*, published lists of donors; the majority, as far as they can be identified, belonged to the Brussels bourgeoisie.[79]

The *Ligue* aimed high: the distinguished architect Adrien Blomme (1878–1940), soon to revolutionize the Brussels cityscape with striking Art Déco buildings, was commissioned for the pedestal. The statue's sculptor was an even bigger name. Égide Rombaux (1865–1942), one of Belgium's best-known *statuaires*, had been riding a wave of commemorative commissions since the end of the war. For the Petit monument, he chose his favorite model.[80] The Petit commission took him considerable time to finish, to the chagrin of the *Ligue*. (Work on the pedestal's foundations, too, had lagged to the point that city officials had given up on the due date; but last-minute agitation by the *Ligue*'s secretary-general Larcier, who browbeat architect Blomme into offering to advance the money for the foundations, had ensured the unveiling on the national holiday.) The result, however, was more than satisfactory. Though sculpture critics would soon dismiss the statue as dated and emphatic, as they did all war monuments, the press was jubilant, calling it "one of Rombaux' best works" (*Le Soir*) and "an impressive work" (*La Nation belge*); *Le Drapeau* praised its "clarity of line, as pure and fair as the life of the young heroine itself."[81] Rombaux, rejoiced *Le Droit de l'Employé* (the periodical of the Employees' Union), instead of producing "a massive pile of bronze and stone," had simply depicted a girl who had died for her country.[82] The bronze shows Petit standing in defiant posture, in a draped dress *à l'antique* that has fallen off one shoulder. She is turned slightly sideways, fine-featured head flung back, one arm slightly raised with discreetly clenched fist, the other gathering the folds of her garment.

It represented, of course, Petit facing her executioners. The pedestal quoted her as saying "I will be shot tomorrow. Long live Belgium! Long live the King!" The entire drama of her existence was crystallized in this moment. This was exactly what the *Ligue des Patriotes* had had in mind. As José Hennebicq stated in the ceremony's opening speech before the still-veiled monument, Petit's existence started the moment she dedicated herself to the fatherland; and her *essential* existence started at death's door. "The existence of our heroine is *entirely* comprised in this supreme moment ... which we wanted to see eternalized in bronze." Petit's essence was her facing of death—and "the Fatherland is made above all by its dead."[83]

Hennebicq's speech well expressed the tone of the occasion, which was marked by the complete absence of any reference to Petit as a concrete being. Petit's relatives were there, except for her uncle Eugène Ségard, too sick to attend (he died a few days later). One can only guess at the feelings between them. At any rate they were not supposed to speak. "Having only rudimentary instruction," Larcier had told city officials three days earlier, Petit's brother and sister "would hardly be able to pronounce even a few words of thanks," and so none of the relatives were given the floor. Nor did they receive much space. Hennebicq and Larcier sat in the Royal Loge, but Petit's relatives were on the least distinguished tribune, standing all the way, including her crippled brother Jules (who would die less than a year later), and Marie Collet, who suffered from leg ulcers. Collet was there because a city official had added her to the list at the last moment: none of the relatives had thought to invite her. None of Petit's other friends and wartime associates were at the tribune—Theodoor Broeckx, Frans Laukens, Julia Lallemand, or Marie Collet's sons. Dignitaries and guests of the *Ligue*—including the Countess d'Oultremont and prison director Xavier Marin—far outnumbered actual resisters. The CAP was not involved at all. (A desultory effort to invite women who had been condemned to death came to nothing because the relevant commemorative organization had never bothered to update addresses; its *présidente*, one Baroness Van der Bruggen, did not even know that Louise de Bettignies had died during the war. Marguerite Blanckaert, Petit's fellow prisoner, attended, but she was not invited to speak, perhaps so as not to mar the occasion with what her erstwhile defender Sadi Kirschen had gently mocked as her wrong-side-of-the-tracks style.) Finally, the Place Saint-Jean, though charming and central, was an abstract location, unconnected to Petit's life or to her death.

That the *monument* condensed Petit's life into a freeze-frame of sublimity was inevitable; but the *ceremony*'s silence on who Petit had been, was striking. It was also political. Hennebicq, for one, engaged in a rhetorical shortcut on the matter of Petit's social class that showed all of the postwar effort to recast bourgeois Europe. Because the nation was a spiritual principle, he declared, "the poor can love the Fatherland as much as the rich: they defend more than just territory, they defend the soul of the Fatherland." This less-than-emancipatory take on the working classes saw them as a vessel of patriotic mystique, static, silent, and humble in essence. (The same front page of *Le Soir* that announced the unveiling of Petit's monument also featured an op-ed essay lamenting the "deplorable mentality" that turned young women away from domestic service—precisely the fate that Petit had tried to escape.[84] Nor is it a coincidence that José Hennebicq would eventually opt for an openly aristocratic take on merit: his 1936 novella *Une lignée* [A Lineage] linked noble birth and honor in—tellingly—a colonial setting.) This emphasis stood at a great remove from the Christian Democratic accents of Cyrille Van Overbergh, Petit's first memory agent, and Arthur Deloge, her biographer. Neither had been invited to the ceremony.

Petit's first *milieu de mémoire*, the Employees' Union, was not represented on the tribune, though it too had raised funds for the monument; over 6,000 francs by September 1920. "Belgium's employees," the fund-raising appeal went, "must help build this monument, which will remind future generations that the employees knew how to do their duty during the great war and that one of us has taken heroism to the level of the sublime!"[85] In contrast to the *Ligue*, donations came in by subscription lists circulated within local union chapters, not individually; the lists show donations from all parts of the country.[86] Petit was an emotional trope for the Union: in 1922, the execution scene of a three-act drama performed on the yearly commemoration of her death, at the filled-to-the-rafters Employees' Club (*Foyer des Employés*) on the Brussels Grand'Place, had "made many tears flow."[87] Though the Union was not represented at the tribune during the unveiling, a banner-bearing delegation had marched in the procession; and, on 5 August, the employees organized a little homage of their own at the monument.[88] In other words, whatever peremptory readings might be imposed on the monument, no-one owned it. Its pedestal, wrote the *Droit de l'Employé*, was low enough that it "blends in with life itself,"[89] and indeed before long it was written into the urban landscape, a fond *lieu de mémoire* represented on dozens of postcards—often garlanded, always surrounded—and a halting-place of homage for civic associations and distinguished foreign visitors, on a par with the monument to the Unknown Soldier.[90] Even though the municipal authorities refused to rename the square, by the Fall of 1923 the *bruxellois* referred to it as the "Place Gabrielle-Petit."[91] Petit came to be identified with the monument: school textbooks illustrated their Petit paragraphs with a picture of Rombaux' statue.

Counterheroes, 1919–1923

The 1923 monument in Brussels burnished Petit's status as an emblem of sacrifice, as did its 1924 pendant in Tournai. The monuments ended a chapter in Petit memory: she was now a marker in the commemorative landscape more than a focus of urgent fervor. More generally, it was the end of an era in Belgium's First World War memory. Around 1924–1925, as Laurence Van Ypersele has pointed out, the years of fervent memory gave way to a more pacified perspective.[92]

But even the years of fervent national heroization had seen strong countercurrents. A cryptic reference in Deloge's 1922 biography to "the jeers of the skeptics and the internationalists who strive to diminish her whom we love so" indicates that Petit's apotheosis was heckled in some corners.[93] From the start, some Belgians openly derided efforts to muster civic pride over the occupation. In 1919, the Belgian government chose August 4, the day of the invasion, as national memorial day: at 9.30 in the morning, sirens wailed and activity ceased for half an hour to commemorate the start of Belgium's heroic era. The young avant-garde art critic Paul Colin scoffed in the radical weekly *Haro!* that if this was the price of glory, "the Belgians would have preferred to remain inglorious."[94] His remark was not unrepresentative: much of the criticism of postwar patriotic culture came from young men who had spent the war years marooned in the occupied country, at the mercy of cruel barbs from elders whose sons were at the front. After the war, patriotic commentators disparaged as hedonistic fops the sons of the bourgeoisie who had not served, and they did not spare young working men either: Deloge, for one, dismissed forced laborers' claims to recognition with the startlingly callous argument that they would not have been deported if they had bothered to join the army. In short, the culture of postwar commemoration had little to offer the large group of men who were of military age but had not served, and so some rejected this culture altogether.[95] Before long, a small pantheon of new heroes challenged patriotic discourse. In early 1920, the front page of *Clarté*, the French pacifist periodical, ran a statement entitled, simply, "Des Hommes" [*Men*]. It called attention to German soldiers executed by their own army for refusing to shoot Belgian civilians. Their story had emerged when they were exhumed from the *Tir National*. "Des Hommes" declared that their sacrifice was vastly more relevant than that of the executed Belgians. These had enrolled in a national cause: they were "real Belgians." But the executed Germans had fought war itself and that made them "real Men!"[96] The manifesto stood *fusillé* discourse on its head. It was written by Georges Eekhoud, the Brussels novelist who had observed the fervent national mood at the start of the war. In 1919, Eekhoud came in for some criticism and lost one of his teaching jobs because during the war he had published his work under German censorship; in response, the embattled younger generation lionized him as a champion of anti-chauvinist thinking.[97]

Given its fierce symbolic stakes, it seems almost incidental to mention that the story was probably untrue: the three German soldiers exhumed from the *Tir* were shot for espionage or murder.[98] Moreover, men who did not want to serve in an execution squad faced no punishment. But the story was widely believed. Importantly, critics of postwar chauvinism were not the only ones to underwrite it. Eekhoud's biographer erroneously presents "Des Hommes" as the sensational unearthing of a secret: in fact, by the time his manifesto appeared, the Brussels papers had long disseminated the story.[99] (In the process inflating the numbers of executed German soldiers to as many as three hundred.) At Petit's funeral, one of the speakers stressed how German soldiers had refused to shoot Belgian patriots. Patriotic opinion openly confessed its bafflement: "We are at a loss," wrote the *Libre Belgique* in mid-July 1919, "to find a position that blends our patriotism with our gratitude towards these men."[100] The story spread through other media: grisly postcards showed an exhumed body with the caption "the remains of the German soldier Rammler, executed for having refused to shoot Miss Cavell." (In reality, a German private by that name was shot a few days before Cavell and Baucq for having sold military intelligence.[101]) A similar story did the rounds about Petit.[102] Finally, in late 1920, official rhetoric enshrined the memory of the executed Germans side by side with that of Belgium's *fusillé(e)s*.[103] In other words, these men, transformed into counterheroes, were first made to challenge national heroization in the name of international understanding, and then made to merge (awkwardly) with the commemoration of patriots. The salient fact is that their memory was not suppressed.

This points to a conciliatory strand in *fusillé* discourse that predated the pacifist turn of the mid-1920s.

Other counterheroes challenged the national narrative not in the name of international reconciliation, but in the name of a nation regarded as more authentic. On July 17, 1920, angry crowds in Antwerp, the city that had hosted the first major funeral of *fusillés* in March 1919, attended the burial of a teenager. The nineteen-year-old student Herman Van den Reeck had been fatally shot by a policeman during a demonstration. Instantly, he became a martyr. Van den Reeck had made a name for himself during the last year of the occupation as editor-in-chief of a student periodical that, in agreement with German censorship, championed an end to Belgium and called for "a more authoritarian state." After the war, not altogether paradoxically, he became an anti-establishment militant.[104] Much of Flemish public culture, from fringe to mainstream, took to outraged mourning over Van den Reeck, commemorated as yet another young life cut short by the war; in the process, pacifism and Flemish militantism merged. The indignation played out against the backdrop of Flemish disappointment over the slow pace of change in linguistic rights. In May 1919, discontent deepened. Even as commemoration of civilian heroism was at its height, bitter parliamentary discussions of language reforms revealed many French-speakers' contempt for Flemish culture; in a significant recycling of a wartime trope, even *Het Laatste Nieuws*, hardly the most militant of Flemish papers, referred to government promises as "scraps of paper."[105]

In this disgruntled atmosphere, the first Flemish activists stood trial. The most spectacular case was that of August Borms, a Germanic philologist in his early forties, who during the war had aligned himself closely with the occupying regime.[106] At his trial, his defenders argued that he could not be a traitor, since his real fatherland was Flanders. This heroization of a man who had condoned the deportation of forced laborers from Belgium, including from Flanders, was by no means general, not even in Flemish militant opinion, let alone among the Flemish public in general. But it was vehement, and it points to a rethinking that would by and by make its mark on popular literature. One example of such rethinking is the 1923 novella *De vulgaire geschiedenis van Charelke Dop* [*The Unedifying Tale of Charley Dop*] by the popular novelist Ernest Claes (1885–1968), a writer who, like Abraham Hans, appealed enormously to the expanding Flemish readership. *Charley Dop* is a satire of the occupation; the protagonist is a war profiteer. After the war, he escapes retribution craftily and even manages to get himself decorated for patriotism. He scoffs at activists: "not one of them made any profit from the war, and it was a good thing they put those chaps in jail." This was a roundabout homage to activists, of course: Claes' way of saying that they were the only ones to come out of the occupation unsullied. Conversely, *Charley Dop* portrays secret intelligence agents as shady folk who spy for pay—anything but paragons of sacrifice.[107] This little satire, then, like the Borms cult, points to a redrawing of the moral map of the occupation. How general was this redrawing? And did it necessarily run along linguistic lines? Certainly, local memories of resistance were lively enough in Flanders.[108] But at the same time *fusillé* discourse—like the narrative of Belgian national sacrifice generally—became more and more exclusively couched in French.[109]

Having said this, the narrative of national sacrifice faded overall, and this even before the "pacifist turn" of the mid-1920s. In 1919, radical critics had derided the choice of invasion day, August 4, as national memorial day. Two years on, it had ceased to command much zeal even among the general public, as the *Libre Belgique* noted.[110] In July 1922, national memorial day was shifted to November 11. As with all shifts in Belgium's war memory, this was no top-down decision: the state had to follow the wishes of the electorate.[111] And, clearly, most Belgians preferred to commemorate the end of the catastrophe rather than the start of an allegedly heroic time. The fervor over Belgium's specific "sacrifice" had levelled off.

What about Petit? She was invoked as a warning against slackening alertness. Deloge, in 1922, linked her memory to the need for continued vigilance. Her monuments, built in the midst of the Ruhr crisis, with their theatrical pose and vehement national message—"How A Belgian Woman Dies"—did not accommodate conciliatory reinterpretation in the manner of Edith Cavell's serene statue near Trafalgar Square. In 1924, Cavell's famous last statement "Patriotism is not enough. I must have no hatred or bitterness for anyone" was added to the plinth.[112] No such re-inscription layered Petit's monuments; and, through the 1920s, her memory would serve to repudiate domestic reconciliation—specifically, amnesty for former activists.[113] And yet Petit's memory also accommodated conciliatory messages (if in a less articulate way than Cavell's), as the next chapter will show. This was because, in spite of Deloge's biography, which seems to have had little impact, she never became a historical figure but remained a folk heroine, a protean emblem of sacrifice who could be invoked by surprisingly varied constituencies.

CHAPTER 8
PALIMPSEST, 1924–2007

No longer commemorated as intensely, Petit was now a constant emblem of sacrifice, so invoked by varied groups through the interwar years. She symbolized resistance during the Nazi occupation and after. The mid-1960s saw a flare-up of her memory, but the rhetoric of national sacrifice was on its way out; from then on onwards, her memory retreated into the local, the gendered, or the ironic.

Interwar Emblem, 1924–1940

By and by, as the memory of the war became a part of Belgians' routine life, so did Petit's. In Brussels, the "Gabrielle Petit Home" (*Maison Gabrielle Petit*), near the gothic church of Saints Michael and Gudula, not far from the fur store where she had once worked, offered single working women on a budget modest meals and cups of tea, a place to sit down and read a magazine, the occasional educational lecture. Educators took school-children to see "films on the glorious fate of Edith Cavell and Gabrielle Petit" as a customary outing in the same way that people used upside-down helmets as flower-pots: the war was now part of the décor.[1] Its memory no longer commanded the same vehemence. Internationally, it was a time of thaw. It was therefore no coincidence that a new Petit film struck conciliatory tones vis-à-vis the Germans. In 1928, the year of the Kellogg-Briand agreement that condemned recourse to war, *Femme belge* [Belgian Woman] reached cinemas. This renewed take on Petit, by the young director Francis Martin, differed from the 1921 film in significant ways.[2] Her judges were no longer grimacing clowns. She now had a German attorney, played, in a telling choice of casting, by a distinguished-looking, very handsome young man. In prison, close-ups of the warden's face showed his grief. And at the end of the film, the single word "PAX" flashed in large letters upon the screen, soaring above a radiant horizon. Petit's story, then, could be folded, however inarticulately, into a narrative of reconciliation. It was perhaps no coincidence that the film painted her in a more conventionally feminine manner than its predecessor. Unlike the 1921 film, it featured a fiancé; and the Petit role went to a striking brunette, the well-known actress Renée Liégeois. The film showed her in several fetching if modest disguises. A 1929 German book by the former war correspondent Heinrich Binder took the disguise theme further: it portrayed Petit as a sexy *garçonne* with cropped hair, now cross-dressing as a young German officer, now flitting about as a coquettish salesgirl. (In 1930, sexual reformer Magnus Hirschfeld in his "Sexual History of the World War" took over the cross-dressing theme, while stressing that Petit, an agent of "peerless daring," had been exceptional among woman spies for never having engaged in sex in order to gain information.[3]) Binder too, significantly, struck notes of international reconciliation: he praised Belgian spies as heroes. Even a "small and culturally insignificant" people was invincible, he wrote (somewhat condescendingly), if it fought superior power with patriotic sacrifice.[4] Likewise, a massive 1931 German tome on wartime espionage stressed that the executed spies in the occupied territories had been patriotic heroes; Stoeber himself chimed in with words of praise for Petit and others. (That the volume was illustrated with grisly pictures of mass hangings in wartime Eastern Europe suggests, however, that the new gentlemanly rapport applied to the West only.)[5]

Still, the above examples suggest that "sacrifice" remained the ultimate touchstone of valor even in these years of relative cultural demobilization. It is true that some perspectives on the war deliberately stepped away from heroization. In 1928, the most articulate interpretation of Belgium's occupation experience, the Carnegie Foundation monograph *La Belgique et la Guerre Mondiale* by the medievalist Henri Pirenne, had no place for the rhetoric of sacrifice (even if he personally was no stranger to its drama: his underage son had volunteered and was killed in 1914). Pirenne's interpretation of occupied Belgium as a theater in a war against autocracy did not need the justification of heroism. This confidently Liberal interpretation by a professional historian was in tune with the cooling-down of passions in the later 1920s. But it also underestimated the enduring appeal of the rhetoric of sacrifice, which made for fierce vernacular heroizations.[6]

Unresolved war issues tended to galvanize this rhetoric. And no issue was more unresolved than that of activism—to recall, the wartime collaboration, on the part of Flemish and Walloon militants, with the German occupation regime's policy of dividing the Belgian state along linguistic lines. Defined as "crimes against the security of the State," their actions had been punished after the war with fines, prison sentences, and loss of official positions. (No-one was executed.) As the issue continued to fester into the later 1920s, moderates advocated amnesty for all of the condemned so as to put an end to it. Granting amnesty, they claimed, did not condone what these people had done under the occupation; it expressed a decision on the part of victorious Belgium to deliberately forget what they had done.[7] It so happened that, by 1928, there was only one activist still in jail.[8] But he proved the single largest obstacle to closure. For this prisoner was the very controversial August Borms, who had been sentenced to death in 1919 for his extreme complicity with the occupation regime; his sentence had been commuted. He was still in prison because he refused to be freed if it meant giving up his political rights. Through the 1920s, a Borms cult had grown especially in rural and small-town Catholic Flanders. Just as the Petit cult had helped many in the general public make sense of the occupation in the immediate postwar years, the Borms cult throughout the 1920s provided purchase on reality to those groups who felt increasingly alienated by reconstituted Belgian society with its extended electorate, its union rights, and its refusal to acknowledge the specific sacrifice of Flemish soldiers at the front—a sacrifice which now obscurely embraced that of activists as well. As to the most radical of Flemish nationalists, they invoked Borms as a figurehead for the campaign for amnesty—amnesty sought, or, rather, demanded, not as a measure of forgetting and renewal, but as a long-overdue righting of wrongs committed by the loathed Belgian state. Conversely, Borms was the *bête noire* of Belgian patriots. They considered him the ultimate traitor. To oppose his possible rehabilitation, some made the strongest point they could muster: they invoked Gabrielle Petit. During a 1928 discussion, a speaker in Parliament declared—to enthusiastic cries from many benches—that amnesty ought never be voted in that very Senate where Petit had been condemned to death.[9] It was not the only time Petit served as a rebuke to Borms. And yet, remarkably, though not surprisingly, Petit and Borms were glorified in exactly the same terms. Both were painted as pure souls who followed their conscience to the end, defiant at their trial, unflinching in prison. Both personified the possibility of sacrifice even in "materialist" modern times. In other words, "sacrifice" could equally consecrate completely opposite wartime choices.[10]

Petit's "sacrifice" could even consecrate activism—a conceptual leap made, spectacularly, in 1937. By then, Borms was out of prison. His 1928 win in a local by-election had revealed the depth of Flemish discontent, and the linguistic equality of French and Dutch in Belgium made new strides. Yet radical Flemish militants were becoming ever more anti-Belgian. From exile, a former activist inveighed against the Belgian state as "the Beast of the Apocalypse."[11] The question of amnesty for activists was still unresolved. Though by now largely symbolic, it vehemently divided war veterans. The National Federation of Combatants heatedly protested amnesty; the League of Flemish Veterans (*Verbond van Vlaamse Oudstrijders*, hereafter VOS) demanded it as acknowledgement of Flemish blood shed at the Yser. (One of the more peculiar developments in interwar Belgium was the merger between, on the one hand, some of the Flemish veterans who had contributed to rolling back the German conquest of 1914, and, on the other hand, the self-appointed Flemish community spokesmen who had assisted the German occupying regime of 1914–1918.[12])

On May 23, 1937, provincial VOS delegations converged on Brussels for a vast demonstration in favor of amnesty. Adolphe Max, still Burgomaster and still iconic, had restricted the route of the demonstrators: they had to march through the closed-off central boulevards. Still, the march riled patriotic opinion, especially since Borms was a featured speaker. One association had seen fit to place a funerary wreath at Petit's statue. It bore a ribbon with the single word "Pardon" ("Please forgive").—In other words, Petit was asked to "forgive" Brussels for the intrusion of "traitors" and their apologists. The sneer did not miss its target, even if the mainstream Flemish press dismissed it as a "silly incident." Radical circles, in reaction, appropriated Petit as their ally. A cartoon appeared on the front page of a vehemently anti-Belgian Flemish periodical. It showed Petit, in the guise of her statue, holding out the "Pardon" wreath to the triumphant demonstrators with the words "BRAVE Flemish veterans, we know each other." The image inverted the meaning of the word "Pardon": Petit asked the demonstrators to forgive Brussels for its unworthy behavior towards her "Flemish Brethren." She was a fellow emblem of disinterested sacrifice: "We belong together!"[13] What this means is that Petit personified sacrifice so widely that even radical Flemish nationalism could invoke her. This capacious and hazy appeal demonstrates, once more, that she was not an official symbol but a folk heroine.

By now, the rise of Nazi Germany had lent the notion of national sacrifice renewed urgency.[14] In 1936, the twentieth anniversary of Petit's execution had come in for special attention. Militant as ever, wearing her medals, in front of an audience of banner-bearing patriotic organizations, Petit's fellow prisoner Marguerite Blanckaert held a radio speech in front of her statue. Blanckaert quoted her as saying that "a Belgian woman dies, but does not betray."[15] It was the first time a woman spoke in public about Petit. Through her memory, women, it seems, gained more of a place in public space. It was fitting that the *Maison Gabrielle Petit*, for all its relative drabness, offered something that *belle époque* Brussels had lacked: an affordable yet respectable public place that women could visit on their own. Female resisters, who had not manifested themselves as a group at all after the war, by and by acquired some visibility. Several of them wrote memoirs. Occasionally, they came together over the memory of their executed *consoeur*: in 1931, five women who had escaped execution—Blanckaert and Marie-Léonie Van Houtte among them—paid a visit to Petit's cell. A photo shows the group posing pensively in front of the cell door. Blanckaert sent it, with a fervent dedication, to the Royal Army Museum in Brussels, where Petit mementoes—her embroidery tools, a picture of her former grave at the *Tir National*, her war medals, a lock of hair—were displayed prominently.[16]

In 1939–1940, as anxieties over a new German invasion rose to a pitch, Petit discourse revived, though not all projects came to fruition. In April 1939, as the film historian Leen Engelen has discovered, Francis Martin announced another film about Petit ("that woman of the people who died for Justice"), but nothing came of that.[17] In 1940, a female author of edifying books published a short biography of Petit in a Catholic series of adventure tales for children. Clearly writing with national defense in mind, she reminded young readers of the shock of the invasion of 1914 and stated that centuries of history had predisposed Belgians to resistance; even women, who wisely kept to their domestic role in peacetime, exchanged "devotion for heroism." Her booklet came out on March 10, 1940.[18] Around that same time, the Parisian writer Jane Catulle-Mendès expressed an interest in Petit. Her project was, it seems, cut off by the war, and only one trace of it remains. The encounter between Petit as a subject and this particular *femme de lettres* would not have been a banal one. Catulle-Mendès had enacted female sacrifice as an actress before 1914, and championed the French cause in lecture tours in the first half of the war. The death of her youngest son at the front in 1917 had plunged her into an abyss of mourning which she documented in the long memoir *La prière sur l'enfant mort* (Prayer over a Dead Child), written in 1918–1920—a bleak, highly original text that bitterly rejected the idea of sacrifice, instead embracing a kind of grim absolute of loss. But subsequently, as Stéphane Audoin-Rouzeau has shown in a luminous analysis, Catulle-Mendès re-embraced the idea of dying for the national cause. By 1940, she was a well-known purveyor of elevated thoughts on the past war. That this high priestess of sacrifice considered bringing her literary prestige to the subject of Petit is significant, even if nothing came of the project and we do not know how she planned to go about it.[19]

But this avenue of enquiry broke ground for another one. Catulle-Mendès, through an intermediary, collected information about Petit in Brugelette.[20] This little investigation

Figure 6 Marguerite Blanckaert's speech in front of Petit's monument, 1936.
Brussels, Royal Army Museum, Prints Cabinet

prompted Sister Marie-Walthère to add to her 1923 notes. She now, for the first time, mentioned Petit's thwarted wish to become a teacher. But she also painted Petit's life as a destiny fulfilled: the war lifted her to "the level for which she was made." This was not a life cut short: "the apex of her existence" was that of "sacrifice at the age of 23." A perfect fit of temperament and circumstances: "how complete, how finished this exceptional creature was." This ended Sister Marie-Walthère's second set of notes. They were dated April 8, 1940.

On May 10, 1940, the Wehrmacht invaded Belgium. On May 16 and 17, the Luftwaffe bombed Tournai. On May 19, Wehrmacht troops occupied the hamlet of Bauffe, home of the Bara family (now residing abroad). Within days, locals were enrolled to work on a vast airfield, from which bomber planes soon took off in the direction of Britain. The airfield administration took over the Baras' manor. Soldiers cleared family papers from cabinets to make space. Some of those private papers were salvaged by neighbors. Among them were two letters from the teenage Petit to her "benefactor," Charles Bara, beseeching him to lend her money to study. After Liberation, they landed in a Tournai museum.[21] That they reached the public domain so circuitously testifies to the fiercely private habits of bourgeois families: the Baras apparently never thought of going public with their memories of the national heroine. More importantly, it underscores Petit's status as a mythical rather than a historical figure: although her mementoes were piously displayed all through the interwar years, efforts to document her life made little impact on her image.

Face of the Resistance, 1940–1949

That mythical impact remained through the next war. In Brussels, the new occupation regime placed an armed guard near Petit's monument to stop the locals bringing flowers.[22] Several First World War memorials were blown up, such as the Schaarbeek monument to Philippe Baucq.[23] "People are sure," a private diary asserted, "that Petit's monument will suffer the same fate."[24] But the occupation regime left it alone, and did not even touch the inscription on the pedestal—"what compunctions keep them from it, we do not know," as a clandestine chronicler remarked.[25] The National Socialist regime may well have spared Petit's monument because her name resonated in "folk" memory, whereas Baucq was more of an educated people's hero. It was not because of her gender: in Paris, the German army destroyed the memorial to Edith Cavell within hours of taking the city. Meanwhile, in Catholic milieux Petit was the most potent national symbol among First World War heroes, in spite of or precisely because of the hazy, idealized quality of her image.[26]

The specific patriotic culture—Catholic, relatively a-political, lower middle class and middle class—in which Petit as a symbol loomed so large also permeated her own family, as the tragic fate of her cousin Hélène Pilatte shows. Six years younger than Petit, Pilatte was the daughter of Petit's paternal aunt Louise Pilatte-Petit, who, during the first occupation, was imprisoned twice for her clandestine work. Hélène Pilatte joined holy orders, then left and became a nurse in 1938. Known as a "patriotically minded" woman, she was contacted in March 1943 by members of the famous "Comet Line" (*Réseau Comète*), a vast escape service for British pilots. (It was launched by Andrée de Jongh, a headmaster's daughter from Schaarbeek raised on the examples of Cavell and Petit.) Hélène Pilatte managed to spirit trapped pilots into France, from where they could make their way to Spain. She was arrested and interrogated by the Gestapo in June, then held at Saint-Gilles prison. On November 12, 1943, the military tribunal of the Luftwaffe condemned her to death. She was not executed because of memories of the First World War: in March 1942, a German military administrator championed commuting the death sentence of a female spy so she would not become "a national martyr, a second Gabrielle Petit."[27] Instead, Pilatte was taken to Germany, head shaven, in chains, and shunted from prison to prison, before landing in Ravensbrück concentration camp in November 1944, while her family was kept in the dark on her fate. In Ravensbrück, she was made to work in the Siemens factory, before being sent, "very sick," to the extermination camp at Uckermark, where she died in January or February 1945—her family never knew exactly when. In June 1945, her brother Léon backed up his frantic request for information with the argument that "we are cousins of Gabrielle Petit, killed by the Germans of [sic] 1914–1918."[28]

Léon Pilatte was, at that moment, serving with a Belgian army group that seized smuggled coal to distribute it to the Allied forces; one of his fellow NCOs was Maurice Gobert, Petit's onetime fiancé, who had volunteered for this service. Gobert had worked as a bookkeeper between the wars and had, in 1942, aged fifty, joined the resistance *Mouvement National Belge*.[29] Gobert, like the Pilattes, belonged to that lower-middle-class Catholic milieu, steeped in a sense of patriotic engagement as a form of respectability, that provided, if with twists and shifts, a continuity between the two occupations—a milieu where, perhaps ironically, his ex was the symbol of symbols.

Petit figured in Belgians' retaking of public space at the liberation. As Brussels was liberated in September 1944, the downtown *Théâtre de la Gaîté* put on a variety show titled "Les Germanos filent" ("The Germans Scamper," a play on words on "Germanophiles"). It staged a *tableau vivant* of Gabrielle Petit—that is, of her statue. Sixty years on, a witness, who had seen the show as a child, still remembered it. "The stage scenery showed the Place Saint-Jean. On a pedestal, an actress stood in the same pose as the statue, in the same dress and hairdo. Men in Belgian soldiers' uniforms . . . stood to her left and right. They sang a song against the occupation—of '14–'18. . . . Applause, tears, emotion, handkerchiefs. . ."[30] That Petit endured as a folk emblem was evident one year later in a parade in the village of Warchin near Tournai. One float depicted "Sabotage by the Resistance" with a maquette of a stretch of railway and a bereted resister lurking. The other showed Petit in defiant pose, blindfold flung off, before a pin-helmeted execution squad. In other words, Petit was so iconic that she could personify both iterations of resistance: that of the First and that of the Second World War. Patriotic commemoration gathered around her as a *lieu de mémoire* that had no Second World War pendant: after 1945, no single resister was glorified in the same way. Heroines of the second resistance were praised as followers of Petit: on the thirtieth anniversary of her execution, speakers mentioned the "glorious death" of her cousin Hélène Pilatte in Ravensbrück as proof of her impact.[31] In 1949, footage of the yearly commemoration of Petit's death was shown in cinemas. The voice-over on the newsreel sonorously honored the memory of "she who showed the invader how a Belgian woman knows how to die," over images of veterans of the resistance and dignitaries solemnly bowing.[32] By now, the Cold War had frozen—the NATO agreements were signed that week—and the relative chaos of the postwar had ended. Petit might have served as a symbol to the now-triumphant Christian Democrats in the reconstituted Belgian state.[33] (Cyrille Van Overbergh was still around, the eldest member of Parliament.) But the mass of grave-looking people on the sidewalks in the newsreel indicates that her memory carried genuine emotional overtones. As the rock journalist and movie director Marc Didden recently recalled, "when I was a child in the early 'fifties [1950s], Gabrielle Petit was still a folk heroine in Brussels. Everybody knew who she was ... and knew that she had told the executioners: 'I will show you how a Belgian woman dies.' "[34]

Last Efforts, 1964–1966

A decade and a half later, in September 1964, Brussels saw a major manifestation around Petit's memory and even a new monument. The occasion was the transferal of her grave to an outer suburb as Schaarbeek dismantled its old cemetery to make space for apartments. The move to the new cemetery generated some anxiety. Petit's old grave in the middle of the urban fabric had never lacked for attention. There were always flowers, and school-children were taken to pay homage every year. Schaarbeek City Hall launched an appeal to schools to make sure her memory would still be honored in the exurbs. In heartening response, high-school students organized a fund-raising drive to build a grave monument, and even contributed its original design themselves. The resulting and quite prestigious monument, dedicated to "the national heroine" by "the youth of Schaarbeek," as the now faded text on the granite stone in front declares, does not look like a grave at all. A white marble statue on a low pedestal, it depicts a woman on one bended knee, one arm across her chest, the other lifted in salute. Part heroine, part torch singer, the image is much more sensuous than the monuments from the 1920s: the hair is stylishly bobbed; a clinging garment showcases a full woman's figure.[35] Petit's new grave was unveiled on 20 September 1964. The papers announced the event in tones that posited an unbroken continuity of commemorative fervor, forty-five years after her 1919 funeral: "readers will remember," wrote Le Soir, "that national funeral of such grandiose and poignant beauty."[36] The new ceremony was organized carefully and attended by "a great mass of people." A tribune held the guests of honor, including representatives of the royal court. This time, unlike in 1923, Petit's family sat on the VIP tribune: her sister Hélène, now seventy-four, as well as her half-siblings Émile, Alfred, and Marthe, a nun. Many hundreds of school pupils gathered in front. They were both the ceremony's main actors and its focus of attention. For the first time on such an occasion, young people were invited to speak. Elders hailed the new generation's embrace of Petit as proof of "the permanence of moral values across generations," just as she had been an example to those who had "faced the tortures of the Gestapo."[37] The positive emphasis on youth contrasted with the ceremonies of 1919–1924, when an earlier baby boom generation[38] had not been invited to speak, but had been spoken to—indeed had been scolded for its frivolousness. Now, it was taken as given that the young wanted to be worthy of Petit and were "perfectly aware of the fatherland's new challenges in these times."[39]

What was not being said was that these "new challenges" no longer came from the outside. The Korean War had caused genuine fears for a third worldwide conflict. But after that, the process of demobilization which the historian James Sheehan has observed for all of Europe had set in; by 1972, a survey would find that no more than one out of fifty Belgians considered national defense a top priority.[40] The 1960 declaration of Congolese independence had provoked no mobilizing impulse. (Admittedly, a smoothly enforced transition to a neocolonialist order gave Belgian companies privileged access to mineral resources; still, it is telling that the "loss" of a vast region that had been constitutive of the national self-image since the 1920s caused little or no clamor over lost national grandeur.) The United States' embroilment in Vietnam, just when France had extricated itself, humiliated, from the region, met with bemusement, whereas many had still applauded the American stand in Korea. The building of the Berlin Wall had, if anything, strengthened a sense of a new postwar order, perhaps unlovely but making war a less probable prospect. Germany no longer appeared as a threat; war-mongering did. (The inscription "shot by the Germans" on Petit's old grave, effaced in 1941 and carefully restored in 1946, did not appear on the new grave.) In sum, in 1964, Belgian public culture was well on the way to demobilization. The citizenry, in Belgium as elsewhere in Western Europe, had started to make quite different demands on the state—demands for education, health, social services. Though Petit's sacrifice was invoked, death was no longer part of the social compact that bound citizens to the state. Thus ended a cycle of political imagining that had started—fitfully—in the *belle époque*.

It is more likely that the patriotism so insistently invoked by school-age and official speakers in 1964 referred to developments *within* Belgium. A much more intractable problem was present as the elephant in the room. All of the speeches were held in French. This had been the case at the Petit ceremonies of 1918–1924 too—but language now carried a different connotation. French had long been the common language of Belgium's educated elites: eminent Flemish politicians like Petit's memory agents Cyrille Van Overbergh and Jan Keesen expressed themselves in French in public life routinely. But by the 1960s, expectations of equality had risen to the point of excluding such automatic acceptance of French as the *lingua franca* in public matters; and the fact that Brussels was now overwhelmingly a city of French-speakers ignorant of Dutch rendered it less credible as the capital city of all of Belgium.

Meanwhile, the economic boom leeched the meaning out of the tangible space of Brussels as capital. The removal of Schaarbeek's cemetery to the exurbs was one instance among many of changes made for logistical or speculative reasons that had profound symbolic consequences. The Brussels cityscape lost the theatrical dimension that had so shaped the first—or, for that matter, the second—postwar era and its ceremonies. In the 1950s, expressways were cut through the very center of town and residents left in droves. Place Saint-Jean, where Petit's statue stood, remained more or less intact, yet the little square was enlarged to accommodate an office complex, which made it a less intimate forum and constituted a slide away from the walking and theatrical city. Elsewhere, too, the move towards a purely functional use of space rendered the loci of commemoration less legible. The open-air grand staircase that had provided a belvedere at Petit's 1919 funeral became part of an expressway. The Beaux-Arts *Tir National* buildings were replaced by the vast, blank office complex of the national broadcast corporation (soon to be split along linguistic lines). Squeezed behind it, the little cemetery at the former execution-grounds—where resisters from the second occupation now lay buried, with a plaque listing the names of those of 1914–1918—escaped destruction, but the layout of the area, with its parking lots and its flyovers channeling commuters out of the city, made very distant memories of the kind of procession that had taken place in December 1918, when a delegation of employees had marched all the way from the city center to pay homage to Petit's very first grave, or, for that matter, the celebrations of 1944, when the *Tir*, where the first British tanks arriving in Brussels had halted for the night, had briefly been a hotspot of liberation merriment where all the town converged.

Given that Brussels no longer carried as much national meaning, it was no coincidence that the fiftieth anniversary of Petit's execution, in April 1966, was celebrated in Tournai—as if to signal a regionalizing of her memory. (Though even in Tournai, a Petit locus had disappeared. Her house of birth, a museum since 1924, was badly damaged during the 1940 bombing. There was no money to restore it; the entire area was demolished in 1962 to broaden the Scheldt river.[41]) Not that the overtones of the ceremony in Tournai were in any way regional.[42] The commemoration was organized on a grand scale and couched in national terms. A representative of the royal court attended, as well as an army delegation and a roster of patriotic societies. Petit's fellow detainees—the surviving members of the *Amicale de Siegburg*, the association of women who had been imprisoned at the Fortress of Siegburg in 1914–1918—received special honors. To a large extent, Petit was remembered exactly as she had been after the Armistice. She was hailed as the "national heroine, who will not need the distance of legend to gain the veneration of the masses"— Van Overbergh's words in December 1918, though quoted without attribution, as if to signify they were as relevant as ever. Speaker after speaker stressed the sublime nature of a young person's self-immolation for the greater good. The acme of the event was a speaking-chorus, written by city archivist Lucien Jardez, that expressed the high points of the Petit narrative—her trial, condemnation, and execution—in hammering cadences:

GABRIELLE PETIT.– It is the humble ones that make the heroes of Liberty!
MALE NARRATOR.– It is the humble ones that make the heroes of Liberty!
FEMALE NARRATOR.– It is the humble ones that make the heroes of Liberty!
MALE NARRATOR.– Arrested, manhandled,
        Here she stands before her judges!
        ...
        Alone, all alone!
CHORUS. –   ...
        Before the negation of Right ...
MALE NARRATOR.– Alone, all alone!

But there were new elements too. Several speakers expressed a keen fear that Petit's memory was no longer relevant. None insisted more that this was not so than the aged Marthe Doutreligne. At the start of the First World War, she and her sisters had felt their father's lament that he had no son to give the fatherland "like a smack in the face," and they had sworn to serve.[43] Doutreligne had coordinated a network for British intelligence after the execution of her fiancé Jozef Baeckelmans. She herself was condemned to death in December 1916; she was pardoned and had spent the rest of the war in Siegburg fortress. She had never married.

In her speech, Doutreligne insisted that the experience of the war of 1914–1918 was not, fifty years on, irrelevant. This was a new sound: earlier speakers might have scolded the next generation for its obliviousness, but they did not feel the need to point out that the First World War was important. Nor had they felt the need to claim that Belgium was a national community. Doutreligne was adamant that it was. Like the fiancé she had lost a lifetime ago, she was from Flanders; and her words implicitly invoked the ongoing split in national imagining. She urged young people to "take over the torch," because "our dear and beautiful little Belgium, for which we, survivors of a tragic epoch, have sacrificed our youth and the best years of our lives without hesitation ... possesses qualities that ought not to be squandered." The entire history of Belgium had been one of struggle, and "that nation of 1914 and 1940" was still the same nation. It would live if the next generation embraced Petit's values; for "it was so that Belgium would live one and indivisible that that slip of a girl looked the enemy in the face." Doutreligne, then, stressed continued collective identity, to be sustained by the memory of Petit's ultimate leap of faith. Petit's national faith in the face of death was not a new theme. But never before had anyone felt the need to insist that there was such a thing as Belgium. By 1966, such an insistence was defying what would soon emerge as the dominant rhetoric: that of a redefinition of the nation along linguistic lines.

Doutreligne's speech also defied another current: that of the refusal to see the past wars in national terms at all. The conceit of national heroism, with its dimension of sacrifice, was in full recession. Other speeches that day expressed this shift. But the waning of sacrifice as the ultimate value is perhaps expressed even more eloquently in a photo taken later that day, at the luncheon offered to the ladies of the Siegburg association. It shows a cheerful group of elderly women, some tenderly arm in arm. Doutreligne, standing in the second row, seems more preoccupied—though that may be reading too much into the image. She was offered flowers to commemorate the fiftieth anniversary of her death sentence. So was Hermine Waneukem, who as a young woman of twenty had been condemned to death one day before Petit, her sentence commuted because of her youth. "And everyone present," wrote a journalist, "told the two women how happy they were that they could give them those flowers instead of having to place them on a monument."[44]

Meanwhile, private memory offered itself a last hurrah. Hélène Petit, long-widowed and still lamenting her life's hardships to the considerable irritation of her son and his wife, was now the sole direct heir to her sister's memory, and she kept everything—press clippings, invitations, and memorabilia. Days before the unveiling of Petit's new grave in September 1964, she gave a lengthy interview to the *Libre Belgique*. She used the opportunity to put her own stamp on things. She emphasized her family's social distinction, claimed to have met Petit's "Dutch traitor" after the war in dramatic circumstances, and "revealed" the name of her sister's fiancé on the interviewer's urging—"none of the books about Gabrielle Petit give the name of her fiancé; surely, fifty years on, you can tell us"—which once more showed what little impact Deloge's book had made.[45]

In 1966, Hélène Petit appeared on television. She was interviewed for the series *14–18*, a remarkable 118-episode documentary on the First World War that ran from 1964 to 1968, produced by the French-speaking section of the national broadcasting corporation, the Radio Télévision Belge. The interview was a static and low-tech affair. Interspersed only with a shot of a picture of Gabrielle Petit and a shot of a picture of her cell door, it featured only Hélène Petit, by now an aged, surprisingly rustic-looking woman in a buttoned-up cardigan and headscarf, a front tooth missing, but still showing traces of past prettiness. She spoke fast and clearly and sounded as if she had appropriated her sister's story thoroughly. Lips primly pursed, she accused the Collets—without naming them—of having betrayed her sister. ("Those people went to alert the Germans that she was at the rue du Théâtre.") There was a note of poignancy when the interviewer asked her if she had expected her sister to be executed. Sighing and speaking more softly, she answered that she had not. "No sir, no, that, I never thought, I always thought she would be saved." A silence followed. Regaining composure, she recited Petit's last letter to her from memory, ending on her sister's wish that she have a happy life. Then, blinking, she fell silent. With that, the interview ended and the report shifted to Verdun.[46]

The interview was, in many ways, transitional. Its emphasis on Petit's last days—"she spent them at Saint-Gilles prison as a patriot and as a fervent Catholic," the interviewer intoned—and its reverent tone were those of earlier commemorations. At the same time, its insertion in the succession of the war's and of global events—Verdun, the Chantilly accords, Pershing's Mexican campaign—hinted that Petit now belonged to history rather than memory. The shot of the picture of the cell door—its contents described by Hélène Petit—showed residual reverence, yet no footage was shot in the actual cell, which still existed.

Retreat, 1986–2007

Twenty years on, Saint-Gilles prison, needing the space, recuperated cell 37 for use and got rid of its once-hallowed contents—"the *folded bed*, the little kitchen-*cabinet*, the *sink*, etc."[47] (By then, Hélène Petit had died, leaving her treasured archive to her son, Gabriel Célis, who did not set great store by it; he and his wife thought Petit had received altogether too much attention compared to other war victims. After Célis' own death in 1983, the papers went to the Royal Army Museum in Brussels, where they were promptly misfiled.[48]) None of the contents of Petit's cell ended up in a museum; they went without transition from relics to encumbrances, and were last seen in the late 1980s in a government surplus warehouse.

One author insistently deplored the "lack of interest that has befallen that sacred place and its onetime occupant."[49] This was a new memory agent, a writer in his early fifties named Pierre Ronvaux, a local historian, and, importantly, the principal of the former orphanage at Brugelette, now a school for at-risk children. He considered Petit an alumna; Brugelette had been, he wrote, "her nurturing ground."[50] His biography of Petit appeared in 1994 under the title *Gabrielle Petit: La Mort en Face*, an illustrated hardcover of almost 500 pages.[51] The book presents a remarkable continuity with earlier Petit discourse. Very much in the vein of Deloge and of Sister Marie-Walthère (whose notes he discovered), Ronvaux both gave a deeply researched warts-and-all account of Petit *and* posited her as a national heroine, "made for immortality!"[52] His perspective on her circled around the notion of sacrifice, in seamless continuity with all of Petit discourse since Cardijn's 1916 eulogy: "she personifies the sacrifice of all of those civilians who consciously gave their life for the Country [*le Pays*] when nothing obliged them to."[53] This continuity in take on Petit was the continuity of an entire assumptive world: Ronvaux' own stoutly Catholic and patriotic world-view was that of those milieux that had formed the backbone of First World War engagement and of its memory. No professional historian would have taken on the task of resuscitating Petit's memory, let alone in such confidently patriotic tones. For all of the wide research, it was not a scholarly biography. Edifying and colloquial in turns, evincing a confident authorial presence—with astute insights especially into Petit's bereft childhood—through sometimes confusing narration, indulging in instructive asides tangential to the narrative (such as snippets on the founding of the cloister at Brugelette), and without referencing its rich material, the book was meant for the general reader. It was a book of popular history in the vein of earlier ones, complete with ringing moral judgments contrasting Petit's sense of duty with contemporary frivolity. The book's place in a long line of self-evidently patriotic narratives, in the middle of an era of cultural demobilization and of the evanescence of the national, is striking.

Perhaps tellingly, the book was not widely distributed and received mainly local attention, whereas the national press did not pick up on its heroizing message at all, instead highlighting its alleged deconstructionist approach.[54] What this means is that the massive imagining effort that had painted Petit's life as a destiny all of one piece and culminating in the patriotic leap of faith that placed her forever in the national pantheon, was losing its cultural underpinnings. Petit was still a name—she still, if barely, made the top one hundred in a 2005 media survey of "Greatest Belgians"—but few could remember what she stood for: "can someone with the name Petit claim the title of Greatest Belgian?" joked one newspaper.[55] What appearances she still made, were highly gendered. In August 2003, the Brussels collective *Féministes toujours* (Feminists Forever) convened at her statue to protest violence against women on the occasion of the murder of the French actress Marie Trintignant. It was the first time Petit's death was ever imagined as an instance of gendered victimization.[56] She was now firmly gendered: a 2006 radio broadcast commemorating the ninetieth anniversary of Petit's execution featured a novelist's reading that imagined her war work along lines of the sexy spy trope. In a gracelessly worded if not necessarily implausible scene, Petit lets German soldiers ogle her breasts.[57]

As if to cap the disappearance of a particular memory of Petit, the next major evocation of her was, precisely, wrapped in a reflection on the evanescence of memory. The 2007 novel *Slagschaduw*—an untranslatable play on words, meaning both "cast shadow" while referring to the war with the word "slag," battle—by the writer and historian David Van Reybrouck was an ironic, knowing look at Petit's memory, light-years removed from Pierre Ronvaux' perfectly straight, passionately earnest take on the "national heroine." It was a reflection on the conceit of national heroism itself. *Slagschaduw* tells the story of a contemporary journalist's vain query for the young woman who was Égide Rombaux' model for the 1923 statue of Petit, and who, while posing, contracted an incurable illness. (The novel offers meticulous documentation, unearthing, among other things, the sculptor's stupendous nastiness.) In his quest for the model, the journalist meets several elderly, charming *bruxellois*, who represent living memory of the 1920s, the heyday of Belgium's Great War memory, a time when "memory solidified into the past."[58] His informants represent, in other words, living memory of a time of living memory. Meanwhile, Brussels is a locus of lucid alienation, and the now-orphaned statue symbolizes the absence of coherent narratives. The novel stands at the end-point of a cycle of cultural effort. The monument has become just another statue; the model has vanished.

CONCLUSION

In some ways, Petit's story came full circle. The conceit of national sacrifice—indeed, the conceit of the national itself—started to cohere at the turn of the century. It reached an apex in 1914–1918 and the fervent postwar years. The next war offered an iteration of sorts. The idea of "national sacrifice" inflected sharply towards the obsolete in the 1960s, and by the early twenty-first century had exhausted even its afterlife. Petit's memory was tightly linked to the history of this conceit. Her life was too: it offers an example of the way in which aspirations to excellence reached the "masses" in the early-twentieth century via national imaginings.

This book traces this arc, while dwelling on the specifics of Petit's life and commemoration because they are instructive. Her childhood and youth, described in Chapter One, show that she was not a "child of the people" (as her legend had it) but a disinherited child of the downwardly mobile provincial bourgeoisie; bereft, unhappy, and fiercely determined to make something of herself, but defenseless in the face of crushing structural obstacles. As Chapter Two demonstrates, the war was her chance and she took it, aware of the risk but resolved to show her worth, especially since her fiancé and his family rejected her as shady. In the face of this renewed rebuke to her aspirations, she swore she would be "done being worthless." The extant correspondence suggests that British intelligence went after her enthusiastically. Belgians willing to return to the occupied country, which as the hinterland of an enemy army was a prime observation post for the blinded Entente armies on the Western Front, were in high demand overall. And Petit was a particularly valuable recruit because of her keen intelligence, her determination to prove herself, her gender—women could roam more freely than men—and, possibly, the fact that she was from Tournai, which was relatively close to the German Sixth Army's front line. Chapter Three charts her brief career as an intelligence agent against the backdrop of the formidable German defense effort that ran occupied Belgium through with barriers and closed it off from the outside world. Petit, so hemmed in before the war, now claimed a range of movement greater than that of most.

But this episode was bound to be brief: as Chapter Four shows, it was a matter of time before German counter-espionage tracked her down. Counter-espionage burrowed deep into the occupied country through its weaknesses and corruptions. (It is not coincidental that counter-espionage agents, who mainly saw this face of Belgian society, had no difficulty believing the false rumor that Petit was a prostitute.) By contrast, wartime resistance efforts reached for respectability. These efforts—running a clandestine press, spying on the German army, helping war volunteers leave the occupied country—created a civilian "front" that aimed to keep the patriotic spirit alive and aid the Belgian and Allied armies. This entailed a division of labor between military and civilian efforts.[1] Civilian resistance behind the Western Front defined itself first and foremost as civilian:

the very unarmed nature of its effort was part of its impact, and patriots condemned armed resistance as giving in to normlessness. The task of civilian resistance was also demonstrative: the idea was to demonstrate absence of fear in the face of armed force, and so deny legitimacy to a regime based on that force. Such defiance was precisely what Petit's behavior was all about once she was caught: she named no names and, at her trial, turned her judges' accusations around.

Chapter Five describes how defiance remained her modus operandi once she was condemned to death. She refused to ask for pardon, holding on to her resolve in prison as best she could, in the process finding a friend in one of her wardens: Petit, like many in the occupied country, was perfectly capable of friendship with individual Germans while rejecting the occupation regime absolutely. Her execution is a mystery: the only eyewitness account is by someone who was resolved to disregard what combative touches the young woman might have brought to her final moments. Petit's death came at a turning-point in the occupation. In the spring of 1916, the occupied realized just to what extent this was a war of attrition. As a result, visions of time changed: from urgent engagement (if not practical, then at least emotional) to a view of the war as a parenthesis before real life could resume. While the execution of Edith Cavell in October 1915 had caused a storm, six months later, Petit's death made no ripples, and those few who commented on it, did so in almost legendary terms, as an event outside of time. The view of the occupied community had changed as well. In 1915, executed patriots were held to personify the entire country; in 1916, by contrast, Petit was seen as a foil to weak fellow Belgians. On the part of the regime, too, the decision to execute Petit signifies a shift. The demonstrative stand-offs of the first half of the war, where the occupation authorities had clashed with well-known adversaries belonging to the elite, were at an end. Before the year was over, the occupation regime, in a Ludendorffian turn towards all-out instrumentalization, gave up on seeking legitimacy and started deporting working-class men en masse towards forced labor; at the same time, and this is no coincidence, the regime stopped placarding the executions of resisters. Petit stands at the intersection between these two logics of occupation. At her trial, she had demonstrated lack of fear just as her famous compatriots Burgomaster Max and Cardinal Mercier had done; and it was precisely this defiant behavior that condemned her, as the German sources show. But she was liquidated as an expendable member of the "masses" whose death was calculated to pass unnoticed. And indeed her fate remained largely unknown until shortly after the Armistice.

Chapter Six describes the weeks following the retreat of the German army as a time of praise for civilian heroism. A small pantheon of civilian heroes emerged. By and by, it featured Petit. At first, modestly so: she became the patron saint of a Christian Democratic service workers' union. Through her, the white-collar and pink-collar drudges of Belgium claimed their place in society against the backdrop of the postwar democratic breakthrough. This breakthrough excluded women, but female resisters, significantly, received the right to vote, which shows once more how the occupation generated *its* heroes. This drive to stress that occupied civilians had done their bit deepened as Belgium's heroic aura abroad waned. Pathos replaced prestige: it is no coincidence that Petit became the "national heroine" in May 1919, in a context of bitter public disappointment over the peace treaty. Her solemn funeral was an occasion to affirm community.

Chapter Seven describes Petit's apex as a folk heroine in 1919–1923 both in Flanders and in French-speaking Belgium. Because her cult was not orchestrated from above, it channeled themes that ran counter to official memory: it emphasized engagement outside of existing structures, it marginalized male authority and even questioned military discipline. In the process, the image of Petit that emerged was surprisingly ungendered. Whereas Edith Cavell had been made to personify murdered virtue so as to appeal to the sense of chivalry of a crusading army, Gabrielle Petit was painted as charting her own course, like all inhabitants of the invaded country, their army heroic but far away. Her image therefore, unlike that of Cavell, was that of a fiercely independent embodiment of the *res publica* in the manner of Joan of Arc. As a folk heroine, it was irrelevant that so little was known about her. But other commemorative efforts aimed to flesh out her story. An association of former resisters documented her war work; this resulted in her first actual biography, published in 1922. It extended the range of her heroism to her entire life, stressing her sense of aspiration in the face of inauspicious beginnings. But the book's concrete portrayal seems to have had little impact on Petit's memory: her contours remained hazy, her impact magically wide. Meanwhile, her cult, which had served to make sense of the past occupation in the immediate postwar years, was now past its peak of intensity. The unveiling of her Brussels monument in 1923 both signified the end of this urgent fervor and consecrated her status. The unveiling ceremony also showcased Belgian elites' attempt to recast bourgeois dominance by portraying her not as an agent but as a vessel of patriotism, so forcing her engagement back into existing structures; fittingly, the ceremony gave voice only to a select few. No woman, no resister, no member of the salaried classes, and no relative of Petit's were allowed to speak.

But the monument could be read in multiple ways, like her memory. She remained a folk heroine to widely varying constituencies, as Chapter Eight shows. Through the interwar years, she personified a wide range of causes. She could channel both continued vigilance against Germany and pacifist conciliation. Petit's monument was not layered with a conciliatory message like of that of Edith Cavell ("patriotism is not enough"). But then, Belgium harbored still-raw memories of invasion and vulnerability, unlike 1920s Britain. (As if to underscore this point, the protagonist of Kate Atkinson's latest novel is moved by the London Blitz to question the motto on Cavell's monument. "'*Patriotism is not enough.*' Do you think that really? . . . Personally, I think it's more than enough."[2])

Still in the interwar years, Petit as an emblem spoke to both Belgian patriotism and radical Flemish challenges, which once more shows the range of her image. She remained the embodiment of resistance through the Nazi occupation, which did not generate a national icon of the same stature. Her memory flared up in the mid-1960s with two major commemorations. But, after that, as both the conceit of national sacrifice and the idea of Belgium waned, Petit's memory retreated into the local, the genderized, and the ironic.

This book does not aim to contrast "life" and "myth." Of course Petit became a myth. As political myths will, hers served to render contemporary events legible, especially in the immediate post-Armistice years. In the process, her messy, stunted life became one taut destiny; she became an emblem of public service with nary a private goal; and her improvised, out-on-a-limb war work morphed into a vast organization. Her entrapment and her end, which she met stoically, turned into a blaze of glorious self-immolation; and she was given an emphatic register at odds with her own, ironic one. But dwelling on the myth-making yields only so much. It is more rewarding to see "life" and "myth" as being of a piece. It is fitting that she came to personify voluntary engagement outside of existing structures, because she did indeed chart her own path as she went along; and she really did exhibit all of the defiance for which people liked to remember her. Both her life and her myth, taken together, shed light on ambition and allegiance in a particular corner of the twentieth century.

It is not a prestigious story. Petit did not change the course of history. Her life has to be pieced together with snippets of sometimes contradictory, always insufficient evidence. The dramatis personae in her story are unknown women: a middle-aged provincial bourgeoise fallen on hard times, a generous neighbor, a sister who claimed her memory to make sense of her own bleak life. The story of Petit's posthumous life as a folk heroine is equally minor: the cult she inspired was vehement and protean but crude. She was a national heroine for a nation that had been central to European, indeed global imaginings of the First World War, but lost most of its prestige shortly after the war, and where, from the 1960s onward, the balance tipped towards a regionalization of imagined communities. And her death occurred in the margin of a hecatomb that would become— correctly so—*the* salient element to take away from the First World War and that would— perhaps less correctly so—make it impossible to imagine dying for a national cause in 1914–1918 as relevant.

Yet both Petit's life and her memory are episodes in the history of private ambition, public engagement, and common imaginings as they intersect with the First World War and its long memory. Episodes that are illuminating precisely because they are obscure. They repay close attention, for they reveal "that roar which lies on the other side of silence," to quote George Eliot's *Middlemarch*—not coincidentally, a book about "a certain spiritual grandeur ill-matched with the meanness of opportunity."[3]

NOTES

All translations, unless otherwise stated, are the author's. For abbreviations, see the Bibliography below.

Introduction

1. Todorova, *Bones of Contention*; Pickles, *Transnational Outrage*.
2. Berenson, *Heroes of Empire*; Maza, *Violette Nozière*; Baumel-Schwartz, *Perfect Heroes*.
3. Corbin, *Le monde retrouvé*.
4. Winter and Sivan, "Setting the framework," p. 10.
5. Laqueur, "Memory and Naming," p. 154; Julien, *Paris, Berlin*, p. 87.
6. Mosse, *Fallen Soldiers*; Becker, *Les monuments aux morts*; Becker, "Le culte des morts"; Julien, *Paris, Berlin*, p. 97.
7. There were individual memorials in city cemeteries. Also, affluent families commemorated their own in statues placed near mansions or factories (such as the monument to the brothers Mathieu in Armentières). But monuments in public space to the individual fallen are rare. Those few that exist, are placed not in town centers but near battlefields or military cemeteries. Also, most of them refrain from figuration: they consist of a terse stele, cross, or memorial tablet; e.g., the monument to the French MP and officer Émile Driant at Verdun, to the French poet Charles Péguy at Villeroy (Marne), or to the Belgian corporal Léon Trésignies at Grimbergen (Brabant). One exception is the *gisant* monument to the French MP André Thomé, representing "The Soldier of Right," right outside Douaumont military cemetery. Another is the 1923 Belgian monument to the lancer Antoine Fonck, the first Belgian soldier killed in the war, near where he fell in Thimister (Liège). It shows him on horseback, hand shading his eyes, gazing at the frontier. This monument, however, is an allegory of the invasion rather than a monument to an individual.
8. Laqueur, "Memory and Naming," p. 160; Julien, *Paris, Berlin*, p. 92.
9. Hargrove, *Les Statues de Paris*, p. 263.
10. Vergara, *Le culte Francisco Ferrer*; Tyssens, "Le monument Ferrer."
11. Debruyne and Van Ypersele, "Le monument à Omer Lefèvre"; cf. Becker, *Les monuments aux morts*, p. 78.
12. Volunteers, to be sure, counted for more than draftees: hence the monuments to, for instance, Péguy and Trésignies, mentioned in note 7 above. Still, there are no monuments to individual volunteers in city centers either: the main difference remains that between heroism in uniform and heroism out of uniform.
13. Nabulsi, *Traditions of War*.
14. Beernaert speech in Scott, *Proceedings*, pp. 502–504; "Gumz, Norms of War."

15. From the vernacular Latin "volus", "who flies/flaps in the wind." The word "veule" existed before the nineteenth century, but as a concept—and as an obsession—it was more recent: the term "veulerie" only appears in 1862. *Le Petit Robert (Dictionnaire alphabétique et analogique de la langue française)*, Paris, Littré, 1970.

16. Rabinbach, *The Human Motor*; for Belgium, Tollebeek et al., *Degeneratie in België*.

17. Becker, *Les cicatrices rouges*; De Schaepdrijver, *La Belgique*; "Belgium"; "Military Occupations"; Proctor, *Civilians in a World At War*, Chapter 4.

18. Hoover Institution Archives, Stanford (CA), Eugène Poncelet, *In years gone by . . .*, typescript memoir, n.d. [c1970], pp. 33–34.

19. Émile Desprechins, "Pour Miss Cavell," *La Libre Belgique*, May 14, 1919, p. 1.

20. Hargrove, *Les statues*, pp. 263–264, 343; "To Charge Nothing for Cavell Statue," *New York Times*, November 2, 1915, p. 3; Snider, "Propagande."

21. Darrow, *French Women and the First World War*, p. 283.

22. Brown, *Courage*; cf. McCain and Salter, *Character Is Destiny*.

23. Audoin-Rouzeau and Prochasson, *Sortir*; Cabanes and Piketty, *Sorties*; Claisse and Lemoine, *Comment (se) sortir*; Tallier and Nefors, *When the Guns Fall Silent*.

24. Horne and Kramer, *German Atrocities 1914*; Horne, *Démobilisations culturelles*.

25. Sheehan, *Where have all the soldiers gone?*

Prologue: Exhumation

1. *Le Soir*, May 29, 1919, p. 1; Anonymous, *Enfance, jeunesse*, pp. 27–28.

2. *Het Laatste Nieuws*, May 29, 1919, p. 2.

3. *Le Vingtième Siècle*, May 29, 1919, p. 1.

4. *Le Drapeau*, 1:11 (May 1, 1919).

5. "Gabrielle Petit: de grootste der gefusiljeerden," *Het Laatste Nieuws*, 15 May 1919, p. 3; *La Libre Belgique*, May 14, 1919; *Le Soir*, May 15, 1919.

6. *La Libre Belgique*, May 30, 1919, p. 1; *Le Soir*, May 30, 1919, p. 1.

7. *Translation des restes de Gabrielle Petit, de Bodson & de Smekens (fusillés par les Allemands)*. Pathé newsreel, June 1, 1919.

8. *Libre Belgique* and *National Bruxellois*, May 30, 1919.

9. *Le Soir*, May 28, 1919, p. 3.

10. *Libre Belgique* and *National Bruxellois*, May 30, 1919; *Le Vingtième Siècle*, May 29, 1919, p. 1.

11. Van Overbergh, *Gabrielle Petit*.

12. *Le Peuple*, May 31, 1919, p. 1; May 29, 1919, p. 1.

13. BRAM, PC, GP, DE (a) 2000 / 77: Knighthood of the Order of Leopold, July 18, 1919.

14. Speeches in *Le Soir*, *La Libre Belgique*, and *Le National Bruxellois*, May 30 and 31, 1919; *Enfance, jeunesse et martyre*, pp. 29–36; Schaarbeek, *Bulletin Communal*, June 12, 1919; M.S., *La vie et la mort d'une jeune héroïne*.

15. PA: S, July 2, 1919, pp. 416–418.

Chapter 1

1. Detournay, *La Grande Guerre*, pp. 53–57.
2. Ronvaux, *Petit*, pp. 30, 41–42.
3. Entry on Bara by Robert Demoulin in Belgium, *Biographie Nationale*, Vol. 30 (1958).
4. *Liste des électeurs . . . 1877; Arrondissement de Tournai*, 1883; Rousset, *Annuaire*, p. 358; Ronvaux, *Petit*, p. 42.
5. So did some in the Ségard extended family: Antwerp, OCMW, Eugène Ségard file; Deloge, *Petit*, pp. 167–168.
6. BSA, SPA, 173, HS, pp. 2, 7–8.
7. BSA, SPA, 173, HS, pp. 1–4.
8. Deloge, *Petit*, p. 19.
9. MW 1923.
10. BSA, SPA, 173, HS, pp. 4–5.
11. BSA, SPA, 173, HS, p. 2; Ronvaux, *Petit*, pp. 27, 40; MW 23.
12. BSA, SPA, 173, HS, p. 4; Paquet, *Petit*, p. 12 (information given by Hélène Ségard); Ronvaux, *Petit*, pp. 40–41, 47.
13. Ronvaux, *Petit*, p. 40.
14. Deloge, *Petit*, p. 39; Ronvaux, *Petit*, pp. 44, 46.
15. BSA, SPA, 173, HS, p. 5; Paquet, *Petit*; MW 1923.
16. MW 1923; Deloge, *Petit*, p. 6; Ronvaux, *Petit*, pp. 47–67.
17. BSA, SPA, 173, HS, p. 5; Ronvaux, *Petit*, p. 46.
18. BSA, SPA, 173, HS, pp. 5–6; Ronvaux, *Petit*, pp. 54–67.
19. Paquet, *Petit*; Ronvaux, *Petit*, pp. 53–54.
20. Paquet, *Petit*; Ronvaux, *Petit*, pp. 60, 64; Deloge, *Petit*, p. 7; BSA, SPA, 173, HS, p. 7.
21. Deloge, *Petit*, p. 11.
22. Ronvaux, *Petit*, pp. 60–67.
23. MW 1923, four last pages of the 41–*ff.* manuscript; Deloge, *Petit*, p. 10, via Hélène Petit (see his footnote on p. 11).
24. *Enfance, jeunesse et martyre*, 1919, p. 4; Hélène Petit interview, *La Libre Belgique*, September 19–20, 1964, p. 1.
25. MW 1923: the orphanage housed 290 girls; she listed 11 from "excellent families."
26. Ronvaux, *Petit*, p. 63.
27. Dumoulin, "L'entrée dans le XXe siècle," p. 61.
28. Next to the orphanage, the institute ran a regular girls' boarding school with a home economics section and a teachers' college (Ronvaux, *Petit*). In Petit's time, it had 150 pupils; the orphanage's middle-class girls transferred there (MW 1923).
29. Ronvaux, *Petit*, pp. 60–63, 80, 98–99; MW 1923; MW 1940.
30. TMF, GP, Hélène Ségard to the Mother Superior at Brugelette, April 14, 1919.
31. BSA, SPA, 173, HS, p. 8.
32. Ronvaux, *Petit*, 1994, pp. 113–114 and 118 (on Jules Petit senior, pp. 65–72); MW 1923.

33. MW 1923; Ronvaux, *Petit*, p. 114.

34. *Enfance, jeunesse et martyre*, pp. 3–5.

35. MW 1923; Ronvaux, *Petit*, p. 118; BSA, SPA, 173, HS, p. 6.

36. MW 1923.

37. Ronvaux, *Petit*, p. 69.

38. BSA, SPA, 173, HS, pp. 6–7; Deloge, *Petit*, p. 14.

39. MW 1923; on "maisons de préservation" (literally, "safeguarding homes"), report by Louis Albanel in Ernst Rosenfeld ed., *Mitteilungen der internationalen kriminalistischen Vereinigung*, Vol. 11 (Berlin, Guttentag, 1904), pp. 147–150.

40. d'Ursel, *La Belgique Charitable*, p. 57. Examples elsewhere, Dubesset, "Le couvent-ouvroir"; Finnegan, *Do Penance*; Smith, *Ireland's Magdalen Laundries*.

41. Piette, *Domestiques et servantes*, p. 445.

42. François, *Guerres et délinquance juvénile*, vol. I, pp. 221–223.

43. Aurore François, e-mail to the author, December 1, 2009; Christiaens, "Stoute kinderen."

44. Piette, *Domestiques et servantes*, pp. 445–446.

45. MW 1923.

46. Ronvaux, *Petit*, pp. 118–119. This was probably the "Asile Roland" in Mons; Aurore François, e-mail to the author, December 1, 2009.

47. Deloge, *Petit*, p. 14.

48. *Enfance, jeunesse et martyre*, p. 6.

49. MW 1923; BSA, SPA, 173, HS, p. 7.

50. BSA, SPA, 173, HS, pp. 3–4.

51. MW 1923.

52. MW 1923.

53. Paquet, *Petit*.

54. Deloge, *Petit*, p. 12.

55. MW 1923.

56. BSA, SPA, 173, HS pp. 5–7; MW 1923; Paquet, *Petit*.

57. Paquet, *Petit*; MW 1923.

58. MW 1923.

59. Paquet, *Petit*.

60. MW 1940.

61. *Enfance, jeunesse et martyre*, pp. 5–6; Deloge, *Petit*, p. 20.

62. Deloge, *Petit*, pp. 19–22, original presumed lost.

63. MW 1923.

64. MW 1923.

65. Hélène Petit kept one of her father's handsomely printed business envelopes all her life: BRAM, CP, folder 2.

66. Ronvaux, *Petit*, pp. 65–66; Deloge, *Petit*, p. 28; MW 1923.

67. Paquet, *Petit*; BSA, SPA, 173, HS, p. 7.

68. MW 1923.

69. MW 1923; BSA, SPA, 173, HS, p. 5.

70. MW 1923.

71. Paquet, *Petit*.

72. *Enfance, jeunesse et martyre*, p. 5.

73. MW 1923, 1940.

74. Paquet, *Petit*.

75. MW 1923. (She later crossed out the "smack in the face" and replaced it with "chastisement.")

76. TMF, GP, Gabrielle Petit to Jules Petit, undated; cf. Ronvaux, *Petit*, pp. 124–126.

77. MW 1923; Paquet, *Petit;* Deloge, *Petit*, pp. 11, 78.

78. MW 1940.

79. Viaene, "Reprise-remise"; Dumoulin, "L'entrée dans le XXe siècle," pp. 33–34.

80. Van Reybrouck, *Congo*, p. 77.

81. MW 1940.

82. MW 1940.

83. MW 1940.

84. BSA, SPA, 173, HS, pp. 8–8bis.

85. Ronvaux, *Petit*, p. 199.

86. BSA, SPA, 173, HS, pp. 8–8bis.

87. BSA, SPA, 173, HS, pp. 7, 9; she collected love-song lyrics, example in BRAM, CP, Folder 3. On Louise De Bettignies: Redier, *La Guerre des Femmes*, p. 17; Deruyk, *Louise de Bettignies*, p. 18 and passim.

88. Deloge, *Petit*, pp. 22, 64.

89. Deloge, *Petit*, pp. 22–23; Ronvaux, *Petit*, pp. 138–142.

90. TMF, GP, Gabrielle Petit to Charles Bara, n.d. (presumably mid-1909).

91. Leblicq and De Metsenaere, "De groei," pp. 174–175.

92. De Belder, "Socio-professionele structuren," pp. 228, 233–234; Gubin, "La grande ville"; Piette, *Domestiques et servantes*, pp. 161, 163.

93. BRAM, CP, folder 2, Gabrielle Petit to Hélène Petit, n.d. (early 1909).

94. BRAM, CP, folder 2, Gabrielle Petit to Jules Petit, February 4, 1909.

95. BRAM, CP, folder 2, Jules Petit to Hélène Petit, n.d. (early February 1909), underlining in original.

96. BRAM, CP, folder 2, Gabrielle Petit to Jules Petit, Brussels, February 16, 1909. Advice to work in a shop also mentioned in BRAM, CP, folder 2, Gabrielle Petit to Hélène Petit, n.d. (early 1909).

97. TMF, GP, Gabrielle Petit to Charles Bara, n.d. (1909), underlining in original.

98. Van den Plas, "Les rapports des enfants avec les domestiques."

99. Piette, *Domestiques et servantes*, pp. 166–168, 174–175, 183–185.

100. She must have earned between 20 and 30 francs a month; cf. Piette, *Domestiques et servantes*, pp. 161–162.

101. TMF, GP, Gabrielle Petit to Charles Bara, January 8, 1910.

102. Deloge, Petit, pp. 22–24.

103. Piette, *Domestiques et servantes*, pp. 191–193, 206.

104. MW 1923; BSA, SPA, 173, HS, p. 22.

105. Deloge, *Petit*, 1922, p. 24.

106. *Enfance, jeunesse et martyre*, p. 6; Deloge, *Petit*, p. 31.

107. In 1910, aged fifty, Hélène Ségard was living in the Rue des Hirondelles with her 49-year-old cousin Alice Guilbau, who was registered as a massage therapist; Ségard was listed as having no profession. BCA, Population Registers 1910, Vol. O folio 1816. This was an unprepossessing street with "modest houses and small shops": d'Osta, *Dictionnaire*, pp. 147–148.

108. BSA, SPA, 173, HS, p. 8bis.

109. *Enfance, jeunesse et martyre*, p. 9; Deloge, *Petit*, p. 31.

110. *Enfance, jeunesse et martyre*, pp. 4, 9.

111. Ronvaux, *Petit*, p. 174.

112. BSA, SPA, 173, MC (a); Ronvaux, *Petit*, p. 168; Deloge, *Petit*, p. 24.

113. Piette, *Domestiques et servantes*; Gubin and Piette, "Les Employées à Bruxelles."

114. Piette, *Domestiques et servantes*, pp. 451; also 38–39, 113, 205, 346, 351; Gubin, "La grande ville."

115. BRAM, CP, folder 2, Gabrielle Petit to Jules Petit, February 13, 1910.

116. Deloge, *Petit*, pp. 26–30.

117. De Schaepdrijver, "Regulated Prostitution."

118. Deloge, *Petit*, pp. 32, 34.

119. BSA, SPA, 173, MC (a).

120. Deloge, *Petit*, pp. 33–34; BSA, SPA, 173, MC (a); MMA, Population Census 1910, card catalog, box 45; Population Registers 1910, *Registres par folio*, Volume 34, folio 6660.

121. Toelen, *De grote en kleine geschiedenis van de kassei*; Vanden Eede and Martens, *De Noordwijk;* see also http://www.quartiernord.be

122. De Belder, "Socio-professionele structuren," p. 233.

123. MMA, Population Registers 1910, *Registres par rue*, Vol. 18, folio 8042.

124. Hélène Ségard, still living with her cousin Alice Guilbau, moved into the Rue du Marché 103, in rooms above a druggist's shop, on March 3, 1914. Guilbau left some time before 1920. Ségard lived there until 1926, when, now enjoying an old-age pension, she moved to the much tonier Chaussée de Waterloo in Brussels *intra muros*. StJMA, Population Registers 1910, Vol. 81 folio 71; 1920, Vol. 85 folio 73.

125. Michel Collet was born in Brussels in 1864; in 1899, he had married Marie Adèle Sauvage. She was born in Brussels in 1854 according to the population registers; in Tournai in 1854 according to BSA, SPA, 173, MC (a). She was registered as "without profession." The next generation may have moved up somewhat: one of Marie Collet's sons, Henri Anneet, born in 1892, worked as a technical draughtsman. MMA, Population registers 1910, *Registres par folio*, vol. 23 fol. 4535; Deloge, *Petit*, p. 33.

126. Deloge, *Petit*, pp. 35–36.

127. Deloge, *Petit*, pp. 30–32, 38–40; BSA, SPA, 173, MC (a).

128. BSA, SPA, 173, MC (a); Deloge, *Petit*, p. 24.

129. BSA, SPA, 173, Laure Butin report, March 8, 1920.

130. Deloge, *Petit*, p. 32.

131. Deloge, *Petit*, pp. 25–26; Paquet, *Petit*.

132. Deruyk, *Louise de Bettignies*, p. 27.

133. BSA, SPA, 173, MC (a); compare to BSA, SPA, 173, HS, p. 8.

134. BSA, SPA, 173, MC (a); Deloge, *Petit*, p. 24.

135. BRAM, CP, folder 3, excerpt from Brussels Population Register 1910, M 1667.

136. BSA, SPA, 173, MC (a). Yet the population registers listed the move to the department store, in rue de l'Education, in September 1913 (MMA, Population Registers 1910 (*Registres par folio*), vol. 34, folio 6660; BRAM, CP, Folder 3, excerpt from Brussels Population Register 1910). The period of unemployment and destitution mentioned by Marie Collet may also have occurred between the Butin years and the department-store job.

137. BRAM, CP, Folder 3, excerpt from Brussels Population Register 1910, N 2272.

138. BRAM, CP, Folder 2, François Broudéhoux to Gabrielle Petit, October 30, 1913.

139. BSA, SPA, 173, letter from Oscar Lepage, March 1921.

140. BRAM, CP, Folder 3, migraine remedy; Deloge, *Petit*, pp. 27, 48; BSA, SPA, 173, HS, p. 29.

141. BRAM, CP, Folder 2, Broudéhoux to Petit, November 2, 1913 (part of the letter was torn off, either by Gabrielle or by her sister Hélène who inherited it); BRAM, CP, Folder 2, Broudéhoux to Petit, January 9, 1914; Deloge, *Petit*, 1922, pp. 27, 48.

142. BSA, SPA, 173, MC (a).

143. Gobert was born in 1892; he signed up for the army in October 1911 and joined the year after, making corporal grade in November 1912 and sergeant in December 1913. BAAE, Gobert file.

144. Deloge, *Petit*, pp. 38–39.

145. BSA, SPA, 173, HS, pp. 8–9.

146. Deloge, *Petit*, pp. 38–39; Ronvaux, *Petit*, p. 182; BSA, SPA, 173, MC (a).

147. Bernard, *L'An 14*, pp. 16–21.

148. Deloge, *Petit*, p. 40.

149. Bernard, *L'an 14*, p. 17.

150. Deloge, *Petit*, pp. 40–41.

151. Bernard, *L'an 14*, p. 18.

152. Deloge, *Petit*, pp. 40–41; BSA, SPA, 173, MC (a); BSA, SPA, 173, HS p. 10.

153. BSA, SPA, 173, MC (a); the Molenbeek population registers show her re-registered in Little Molenbeek in June 1914.

154. Deloge, *Petit*, p. 39.

155. BSA, SPA, 173, MC (a).

156. BRAM, PC, GP, Portfolio 2, Gabrielle Petit to Marie Fourmois, 27 June 1914.

157. BSA, SPA, 173, HS, p. 7; MW 1923; Picardie, *Coco Chanel*.

Chapter 2

1. Bitsch, *La Belgique*, pp. 487, 494–503; Devleeshouwer, *Les Belges*, pp. 248–259; Stengers, "L'entrée."

2. Deloge, *Petit*, pp. 41–43.

3. Gobert was posted to Maxim's machine-gun company 19 with the Sixth Division. BAAE, Gobert file; Deloge, *Petit*, p. 43.

4. Text of both documents, with English translation, *Belgian Grey Book*, online at the World War I Document Archive: http://www.gwpda.org/papers/belgrey.html, accessed February 27, 2013.

5. Claes, *Ik was student*, p. 464.

6. Bernard, *L'An 14*; Bitsch, *La Belgique*; Claes, *Ik was student*; De Lichtervelde, *Avant l'orage*; De Muêlenaere, "An Uphill Battle"; Devleeshouwer, *Les Belges* (p. 72 note 2 for conscription rates); Haag, *Broqueville*, vol. 1, pp. 123–138, 154–229; Vanschoenbeek, "Leger en socialisme."

7. Horne, "Public Opinion," p. 280.

8. Pirenne, *La Belgique et la guerre mondiale*, p. 208.

9. Majerus and Vrints chapters in Jaumain, *Une guerre totale ?*; De Cloet, Part I, August 1–9, 1914.

10. Audoin-Rouzeau and Prochasson, *Sortir*, p. 13.

11. Audoin-Rouzeau and Prochasson, *Sortir*, p. 416.

12. BAML, Eekhoud, notebook 11, August 3, 1914.

13. Whitlock, *Belgium*, Chapters XVII–XXI; Nevins, *Brand Whitlock*, Vol. II, pp. 7–37.

14. BAML, Eekhoud, 5–7 August 1914; Bertrand, *Souvenirs d'un meneur socialiste*, Vol. II p. 232; Piette and Jaumain, *Bruxelles en '14–'18*, pp. 6–10.

15. BSA, SPA, 173, HS, p. 10; BRAM, CP, folder 3 (a September 1915 letter about Petit's fund-raising); MMA, Population Registers 1910, *Registres par folio*, Vol. 23, ff. 4534–4535; Deloge, *Petit*, pp. 44–45.

16. BAAE, Gobert file; Bernard, *L'An 14*, p. 83; Deloge, *Petit*, pp. 43–45; Tasnier and Van Overstraeten, *Les opérations militaires*, pp. 33, 133–136; "Les opérations: première sortie d'Anvers"; Commission d'enquête, *Rapports sur les attentats*, vol. 2, pp. 132–141; Horne and Kramer, *German Atrocities*, p. 234.

17. Deloge, *Petit*, p. 46; Gille et al., *Cinquante mois*, vol. I, p. 43 (September 2, 1914).

18. Deloge, *Petit*, pp. 46–47; underlinings in text.

19. BSA, SPA, 173, HS, p. 10; BRAM, CP, folder 4, undated note (late 1914 or 1915) with an illegible signature from a Brussels physician; BRAM, CP, folder 2, 8-pp. list of Petit's possessions, a.o. a white nurse's apron and a Red Cross pin; BRAM, CP, folder 3, "Ordre de laisser-passer (éventuellement avec automobile)," delivered in Brussels (no date), stamped at Fontaine l'Évêque on October 5, giving her residence as Antwerp.

20. BAAE, Gobert file, 1921 documents, pp. 2 and 4; BSA, SPA, 173, HS, p. 11; Deloge, *Petit*, pp. 49–50, 73.

21. BSA, SPA, 173, HS, p. 10. Gobert's military file counted these months as time served: BAAE, Gobert file, Dossier d'Immatriculation, p. 3.

22. Deloge, *Petit*, pp. 49–50; by contrast, BRAM, PC, GP, Folder 1, VIII 2987, Petit IOUs to Marie Collet (who had returned to Brussels) for room, board, and laundry, late September to mid-December 1914, suggesting that Petit lived mainly in Brussels in these months.

23. BSA, SPA, 173, HS, p. 10.

24. Deloge, *Petit*, pp. 50–54.

25. Souhami, *Cavell*, pp. 190–252; Lombard, *Zone de mort*.

26. Gille et al., *Cinquante mois*, I, p. 240 (January 27, 1915).

27. Souhami, *Cavell*, pp. 230, 232, 245.

28. Gille et al., *Cinquante mois*, I, p. 240 (January 27, 1915); Lombard, *Zone de mort*, pp. 25–26; Vanneste, "Le premier 'Rideau de fer'?."

29. Lombard, *Zone de mort*, p. 27.

30. Gille et al., *Cinquante mois*, I, p. 347 (June 3, 1915).

31. Gille et al., *Cinquante mois*, I, p. 362 (June 28, 1915).

32. Souhami, *Cavell*, pp. 252–271.

33. Gille et al., *Cinquante mois*, III, pp. 187–189 (April 14, 1917), 451–452 (October 2, 1917), IV, 135 (March 7, 1918); Druart, *Franz Merjay*.

34. BSA, SPA, 173, MC (a); Deloge, *Petit*, p. 53.

35. Deloge, *Petit*, pp. 53–59; BAAE, Gobert file.

36. Deloge, *Petit*, pp. 55–59.

37. Majerus, *Occupation et logiques policières* 2005, vol. 1 p. 40.

38. Sent to the Government-General in Brussels. BSA, SPA, 195, Wartel, p. 71.

39. BSA, SPA, 248, *Haftzettel* "Gabriela Petit," July 11, 1915.

40. BSA, SPA, 173, MC (a).

41. BAML, Eekhoud, September 3, 1915.

42. Deloge, *Petit*, pp. 78–80; BSA, SPA, 173, HS, p. 12.

43. Benn, "Wie Miss Cavell erschossen wurde", p. 197; cf. De Schaepdrijver and Debruyne, "Sursum Corda."

44. BRAM, CP, folder 3.

45. Amara, *Les Belges à l'épreuve*; De Roodt, *Oorlogsgasten*.

46. BSA, SPA, 173, Petit to Delmouzée-Gobert family, Harderwijk, stamped July 20, 1915 at The Hague, certified copy.

47. Deloge, *Petit*, p. 61, original presumably lost.

48. BRAM, CP, folder 3 (embarcation permit); recruitment by Ide: BSA, SPA, 173, Germain; Deloge, *Petit*, p. 60, footnote 1.

49. Van Ypersele and Debruyne, *De la guerre de l'ombre*; Jeffery, *MI6*, Chapter 3.

50. Beach, *British Intelligence*, Chapter 2; Beach, *Haig's Intelligence*.

51. Andrew, *Her Majesty's*, pp. 139–140; Occleshaw, *Armour,* p. 149.

52. Andrew, *Her Majesty's*, 140–141; Occleshaw, *Armour*, 150; on Wallinger's Dutch bureau, BSA, SPA, 39, Wallinger.

53. Beach, "Intelligent Civilians", pp. 6, 12, 21; ICM, Payne Best, p. 13.

54. BSA, SPA, 39, Doutreligne; BAAE, Ide file. Ide's military file is hazy on the Fall of 1914. He was officially enlisted as interpreter in the British Intelligence Corps in March 1915. Cf. Deloge, *Petit*, p. 62.

55. Andrew, *Her Majesty's*, 141.

56. BSA, SPA, file 39, Doutreligne; "fiche organique"; statement Marie-Jeanne Willockx April 6, 1920; ICM, Payne Best, p. 16.

57. BSA, SPA, 173, Petit to the Delmouzée-Goberts, Folkestone, July 24, 1915 (certified copy).

58. BRAM, CP, folder 2, "Emile" to Petit, July 24, 1915. "Emile" was Ide's alias: ICM, Payne Best, p. 15.

59. IWM, Kirke, December 3, 1915, see also November 29, 1915.

60. IWM, Kirke, January 23, 1916.

61. Deloge, *Petit*, p. 62.

62. TMF, GP, "Notes de cours prises par Gabrielle Petit lors de son instruction, pendant une douzaine de jours, à Londres (fin juillet et début août 1915)."

63. BSA, SPA, 173, HS, pp. 11–12.

64. Andrew, *Her Majesty's*, 140.

65. BSA, SPA, file 173, BSA, SPA, 173, D-M, p. 2.

66. Deloge, *Petit*, pp. 63–64.

67. Deloge, *Petit*, p. 65.

68. BRAM, CP, folder 3, English copy-book, n.d., presumably from her days of instruction since it contains a telegraph code.

69. BRAM, CP, folder 2, Gabrielle Petit to Hélène Petit, n.d., underlining in original. Hélène Petit dated the note July 30, 1915, but it must date from after Petit's return on August 17.

70. Deloge, *Petit*, pp. 58–60; BSA, SPA, 173, MC (a).

71. BAAE, Gobert file.

72. ICM, Payne Best, pp. 15, 23.

73. Van Tuyl van Serooskerken, *The Netherlands and World War I*; Abbenhuis, *The Art of Staying Neutral*.

74. BSA, SPA, 173, Petit to the Delmouzée-Goberts; BSA, SPA, 173, HS, p. 12.

75. Deloge, *Petit*, pp. 69–70. As with all Gobert's documents, the only source is Deloge.

Chapter 3

1. Binder, *Spionagezentrale Brüssel*.

2. Deloge, *Petit*, p. 32.

3. BSA, SPA, 173, HS, p. 18.

4. BSA, SPA, 173, Otto Becker to Xavier Marin, December 1, 1919.

5. Deloge, *Petit*, pp. 78–79, cf. p. 128.

6. BSA, SPA, 173, Mons 1921.

7. Keegan, *The First World War*, pp. 179–201.

8. Occleshaw, *Armour*, pp. 37–39, 70–72.

9. Debruyne and Paternostre, *La résistance au quotidien 1914–1918*; Van Ypersele and Debruyne, *De la guerre de l'ombre*.

10. IWM, Kirke, 11, 14, and 25 June 1915.

11. Gille et al., *Cinquante mois*, I, pp. 352–353 (June 8, 1915); Gille et al., *Cinquante mois*, I p. 361 (June 20, 1915).

12. BSA, SPA, 39, "Résumé historique du service Backelmans [*sic*]" and "Service Backelmans [*sic*], fiche organique," n.d.

13. BSA, SPA, 39, "Résumé historique du service Backelmans [*sic*]"; cf. BSA, SPA, 196, Ball. GHQ never knew how Baeckelmans had been trapped: ICM, Payne Best, p. 16.

14. BSA, SPA, 173, HS, p. 14; BSA, SPA, 173, Leyendecker. Yet nothing in Baeckelmans' file (BSA, SPA, file 39) indicates any overlap between the services.

15. BSA, SPA, 125, "Schéma général de l'organisation des services de renseignements officiels en Hollande"; Deloge, *Petit*, p. 69.

16. Van Ypersele and Debruyne, *De la guerre de l'ombre*, pp. 35–36.

17. Redier, *La guerre des femmes*, p. 58.

18. IWM, Kirke, September 27, 1915; see also June 11, September 11, September 13.

19. BSA, SPA, 173, D-M.

20. BSA, SPA, 173, Germain.

21. TMF, GP, "Notes de cours"; BRAM, CP, folder 3, copy-book with a telegraph code written by Petit.

22. BSA, SPA, 173, MC (a); Deloge, *Petit*, p. 69.

23. Deloge, *Petit*, p. 80.

24. Gille et al., *Cinquante mois*, I, p. 335 (May 8, 1915); also p. 361 (June 25, 1915); p. 358 (June 14, 1915); p. 416 (August 18, 1915).

25. Deloge, *Petit*, p. 79.

26. Deloge, *Petit*, p. 90.

27. BSA, SPA, 173, HS, p. 12.

28. BSA, SPA, 173, D-M.

29. BSA, SPA, 173, D-M; Deloge, *Petit*, p. 96.

30. BSA, SPA, 173, D-M.

31. Redier, *La guerre des femmes*, Chapter IV.

32. Detournay, *La Grande Guerre*, pp. 70–72, 117, 121–122; Redier, *La guerre des femmes*, p. 26; Van Ypersele and Debruyne, *De la guerre de l'ombre*, p. 31; Preud'homme, *Un jésuite résistant*; Debruyne and Paternostre, *La résistance au quotidien*, pp. 101–108.

33. BSA, SPA, 173, D-M; BSA, SPA, 173, HS, pp. 12, 14.

34. BSA, SPA, 173, Philippart (a); BSA, SPA, 173, D-M.

35. Debruyne and Paternostre, *La résistance au quotidien*, pp. 92–93.

36. BSA, SPA, 173, D-M; BSA, SPA, 173, Philippart (a).

37. BSA, SPA, 173, D-M; BSA, SPA, 173, Philippart (c).

38. BSA, SPA, 173, HS, pp. 11–13.

39. BSA, SPA, 173, HS, pp. 13–14, 33–34; Kirschen, *Devant les conseils*, p. 144; Deloge, *Petit*, p. 68.

40. Gille et al., *Cinquante mois*, I, pp. 436–440 (September 30, 1915).

41. BSA, SPA, 173, HS, p. 14.

42. Note from "Cereal Company" (illegible signature), September 23, 1915; transcript in Deloge, *Petit*, pp. 96–97. This message, and two others from "Cereal Company", plus a report by Petit, were in Marie Collet's possession. After the war, she gave them to an attorney only identified as "*Maître Duval*" (BSA, SPA, file 173, MC (b)). He in turn gave Deloge permission to consult these documents (Deloge, *Petit*, p. 96). One message is now at BRAM (see following note); the report is in BSA, SPA. The whereabouts of the other originals are unknown.

43. BRAM, PC, GP, folder 1, VIII 802986, note from "Cereal Company" (illegible signature), September 24, 1915.

44. BSA, SPA, 173, fourth report Petit, September 30–October 4, 1915. Cf. Germain, "Autographe de Gabrielle Petit."

45. Weber, *Hitler's First War*, p. 106.

46. Preud'homme, *Un jésuite résistant*, pp. 391–393.

47. Keegan, *First World War*, pp. 202, 275–276; Strachan and Herwig chapters in Horne, *A Companion*, pp. 35–48 and 49–65.

48. Even if Loos did strengthen the Germans' resolve to thicken their zone of defense: Duménil, "De la guerre," p. 74.

49. Majerus, *Occupations et logiques policières* 2005, vol. 1, p. 38; Gille et al., *Cinquante Mois*, I, p. 460 (October 20, 1915).

50. BSA, SPA, 173, Philippart (b).

51. BSA, SPA, 173, transcript of postcard to "my dear cousins," Petit, October 5, 1915.

52. BRAM, PC, GP, folder 1, VIII 2988; transcript, Deloge, *Petit*, pp. 103–105.

53. BSA, SPA, 173, HS p. 20.

54. BRAM, PC, GP, file 1, VIII 2988. The transcript in Deloge, *Petit*, pp. 105–107, is incomplete and spells some place-names wrongly (e.g., Taintignies in Hainaut becomes Tintignies, the site of a massacre in Belgian Luxembourg).

55. BSA, SPA, 195, GQG Français, Béliard to Derny, August 28, 1915; prices in September 1915, Gille et al., II, p. 423.

56. BSA, SPA, 173, D-M; Deloge, *Petit*, pp. 84, 118, 193–194.

57. Deloge, *Petit*, p. 98.

58. Deloge, *Petit*, p. 99.

59. IWM, Kirke, June 4, 1915.

60. Van Ypersele and Debruyne, *De la guerre de l'ombre*, pp. 46–47.

61. BSA, SPA, 40 (Daubechies), Eugeen Van Assche testimony, August 15, 1920.

62. BSA, SPA, 173, Doutreligne; Van Tichelen.

63. BSA, SPA, 173, Laure Butin, March 8, 1920 and February 24, 1920; MC (b); Doutreligne; Van Tichelen. Butin received a British decoration for her intelligence work: National Archives (UK), British Army Medal Index Cards 1914–1920, WO 372/23/6022, accessed online March 12, 2013.

64. BSA, SPA, 173, excerpt from report by V. Moreau, July 28, 1920; Landau, *All's Fair*, pp. 48–51; BSA, SPA, 35, Loos; BSA, SPA, 35, Joseph Peeters, 50-pp. notebook. Cf. Vanneste, *Kroniek*, vol. 1, pp. 319, 339, 341–369; vol. 2, 386–452. A commemorative brochure about an executed local *passeur* offers some detail: Ballings, *Ter herinnering*.

65. BSA, SPA, 35, Loos; Deloge, *Petit*, pp. 84–87.

66. BSA, SPA, HS, 16; Deloge, *Petit*, p. 92.

67. BRAM, CP, folder 3.

68. It is reproduced on the cover of Paquet, *Petit*, but the dates are not legible. In 1920 it was owned by the Gabrielle Petit Committee of Tournai, which kept it in a bank safe (BSA, SPA, 173, Philippart (a)); the present whereabouts are unknown.

69. BRAM, PC, GP, file 1, VIII 2982.

70. Deloge, *Petit*, pp. 107–108; original presumed lost.

71. BSA, SPA, MC (a); BSA, SPA, HS, p. 13.

72. BSA, SPA, 173, transcripts of postcards by Petit, December 16 and 23, 1915.

73. BSA, SPA, 173, MC (b).

74. BSA, SPA, 35, Loos.

75. BSA, SPA, 35, Joseph Peeters report.

76. Van Ypersele and Debruyne, *De la guerre de l'ombre*, pp. 39–41.

77. Deloge, *Petit*, pp. 91–92, 116. Petit's participation in the *Mot du Soldat* left no paper trace (BSA, SPA, files 83, 84, 85, box 84bis). This in itself does not prove she was not involved: she is not mentioned either in the files of the clandestine periodical *La Libre Belgique*, with which she was definitely involved (see note below).

78. BSA, SPA, 173 MC (a); BSA, SPA, 173, HS, pp. 16, 19; Deloge, *Petit*, pp. 108, 118.

79. BSA, SPA, HS 15–16.

80. Goemaere, *Histoire de la Libre Belgique*, second edition, 1919. This edition listed 667 collaborators; Petit did not yet figure in the first edition (also 1919), which listed 539. Cf. BSA, SPA, 173, D-M. Petit does not figure in the files of the *Libre*'s clandestine network: BSA, SPA, files 81, 193, 194, but neither do several other collaborators whose participation is proven. On the *Libre*, De Schaepdrijver and Debruyne, "Sursum Corda."

81. Deloge, *Petit*, pp. 92–93.

82. BSA, SPA, 173, MC (a), though a later declaration, MC (b), places it on January 17 or 18; Deloge, *Petit*, pp. 88, 110–111.

83. Deloge, *Petit*, pp. 88–90, 111–112; BSA, SPA, 173, HS, p. 21; Hélène Ségard in *Le Drapeau*, May 1, 1919.

84. BSA, SPA, 173, Philippart (a); Deloge, *Petit*, pp. 81–83.

85. Ségard mentioned that after Baeckelmans' execution her niece had worked with the notary Léonce Roels (who worked for Cameron's bureau at British GHQ and was executed in March 1916) and the railway inspector Adelin Colon (executed in July 1916): BSA, SPA, 173, HS, pp. 14–15, 37–38. The resistance files do not link Petit or her small band of associates to any of these three networks, which may or may not be conclusive. On Baeckelmans file, BSA, SPA, 39; On Roels, BSA, SPA, 92, folder 602(b), report Fernand de Looze; on Colon, BSA, SPA, 46. Cf. Deloge, *Petit*, pp. 62, 68.

86. BSA, SPA, 173, transcript of a postcard to the Delmeules stamped at Antwerp, January 15, 1916.

87. BSA, SPA, 173, transcript of a postcard to the Delmeules, January 20, 1916; Philippart (c).

88. TMF, GP, Report January 26 or 27–February 1 1916; Deloge, *Petit*, p. 113; Ronvaux, *Petit*, pp. 220–221.

89. BSA, SPA, 173, transcript of postcard to the Delmeules, February 1, 1916 (a Tuesday). This message was dated "Tuesday evening," which corresponds to what Petit wrote her godmother from prison ("*I returned Tuesday evening and was arrested at 1 o'clock on the Wednesday*"), TMF, GP, Gabrielle Petit to Hélène Ségard, March 10, 1916. Cf. BSA, SPA, 173, Philippart (c); Deloge, *Petit*, pp. 110–113.

90. BSA, SPA, 173, Doutreligne; MC (a); MC (b); Germain; Van Tichelen; BRAM, Belgian GHQ, Box 10, file 7, list of "suspect couriers," September 7, 1916. Cf. Decock, *La Dame Blanche*, 1981, p. 14; Landau, *Secrets of the White Lady*, pp. 18, 23; BSA, SPA, 40 (Daubechies).

91. Decock, *La Dame Blanche*, 1981, pp. 12–18, 62; Landau, *Secrets of the White Lady*, p. 18; Van der Fraenen, *Voor den kop geschoten*, p. 164.

92. The most complete work is Decock, *La Dame Blanche*, 1981, long unpublished but recently available as *La Dame Blanche. Un réseau de renseignements de la Grande Guerre*, Raleigh, NC, Lulu, 2011. See also Landau, *Secrets of the White Lady*, and the relevant chapters in Proctor, *Female intelligence*.

93. BSA, SPA, 173, HS, p. 21.

94. The following paragraph gives a general overview of the German police apparatus in occupied Belgium. Chapter Four below offers specific detail on the counter-intelligence services (Police Bureau A). References for this paragraph: Majerus, *Occupations et logiques policières* 2005, which offers more information than the 2007 published version. See also Van der Fraenen, *Voor den kop geschoten*, and Pöhlmann, "German Intelligence at War." Also CEGESOMA, War Office, *The German police system;* BSA, SPA, 196, Ball; BSA, SPA, 195, Wartel. Of some use is BBL, RI, Polizeiwesen. Of less value is Nicolai, *Geheime Mächte*. Binder, *Spionagezentrale Brüssel*, is of no use at all.

95. Vierset, *Mes souvenirs*, p. 362 (October 12, 1915); "M. Von Bissing se plaint officiellement de l'hostilité des Bruxellois," *La Libre Belgique* 55 (December 1915), pp. 2–3; Gheude, *Nos années terribles*, vol. 2, p. 187; Majerus, *Occupations et logiques policières* 2005, vol. 1 pp. 37–38, 165–182.

96. BSA, SPA, 196, Ball; BSA, SPA, 195, Wartel; Majerus, *Occupations et logiques policières* 2005, vol. 1 p. 39.

97. BSA, SPA, 196, Ball, report 1, p. 16.

98. De Moffarts, *Un enfant belge fusillé à Lille*. Execution totals, Van Ypersele and Debruyne, *De la guerre de l'ombre*, pp. 79–81; Majerus, *Occupations et logiques policières* 2005, vol. 1 p. 40 and vol. 3 p. 543; and the database in Van der Fraenen, *Voor het Duitse vuurpeloton*.

99. BSA, SPA, 195, GQG Français, Wallner (Folkestone) to Derny (Flushing), September 13, 1915, underlining in original. Derny had by then unsuspectingly revealed the plan to a star agent of German counter-espionage: BSA, SPA, 196, Ball, Report 3, pp. 18–19bis.

100. BSA, SPA, 141, Lauwers; BSA, SPA, 173, Leyendecker.

101. Kirschen, *Devant les conseils*, pp. 294–296.

102. BSA, SPA, 39, Wallinger.

103. Emmanuel Debruyne, personal communication, March 2011.

104. Felger, "Das Netz über Belgien."

105. BSA, SPA, 173, Doutreligne. On Doutreligne, ICM, Payne Best, p. 17; Landau, *Secrets of the White Lady*, p. 294; BSA, SPA, 196, Ball, report 3 p. 3; Redier, *La guerre des femmes*, pp. 53, 164, 165; De Weerdt, *De vrouwen*, p. 273.

106. BBL, AA, R 901/26415, President of the Military Court (Kirchbach) to Emperor, March 18, 1916; Transcript (deciphered telegram), Count Harrach to Foreign Office Berlin, n.d. (March 28 or 29, 1916).

107. Stoeber, "Vier Jahre Feldjustizbeamter," p. 393.

108. "Falcon," "En patrouille chez l'ennemi: l'activité de Gabrielle Petit," *La Dernière Heure*, May 29, 1919. The article mentions Petit's fourth, fifth, and sixth reports.

109. Gheude, *Nos années terribles*, vol. 1, pp. 167–168 (October 1, 1914).

110. BSA, SPA, 173, Philippart (a).

111. BSA, SPA, 173, HS, p. 19, 22; D-M. Deloge, *Petit*, pp. 32, 89–92, 152.

112. BSA, SPA, 173, HS, p. 16.

113. BSA, SPA, 173, Philippart (b).

114. BSA, SPA, 173, HS, p. 14.

115. BSA, SPA, 173, HS, p. 19.

116. The intelligence agent Aimé Smekens (who would be buried together with Petit in 1919) allegedly warned the agent Alphonse Stroobants, with whom Petit worked to help war volunteers escape Belgium, that she was too voluble: Deloge, *Petit*, pp. 83, 150. Stroobants was arrested together with his wife, who was so terrorized she committed suicide in prison: Frick, *Saint-Josse*, p. 157.

117. BSA, SPA, 173, Philippart (a).

118. Deloge, *Petit*, p. 83.

119. BSA, SPA, 173, Philippart (a); Doutreligne.

120. A very summary overview of the holdings mentions a list of agents: BSA, SPA, 40, "Service Petit—Nomenclature générale des pièces," n.d., but there is no such list.

121. From her godmother's statement, it seems that she worked with at least three other networks (BSA, SPA, 173, HS pp. 14–15, 37–38), but there are no other traces of this, see note above.

122. BSA, SPA, 173, MC (b), with covering note, unsigned, n.d.

123. BSA, SPA, 173, D-M; Philippart (a), (b), and (c); MC (a); HS; Deloge, *Petit*, pp. 83, 108, 150.

124. BRAM, CP, Folder 3, Petit notes on a saints' calendar.

125. Deloge, *Petit*, pp. 168, 194.

126. BRAM, CP, folder 2, Gabrielle Petit to Hélène Petit, n.d.

127. BSA, SPA, 173, MC (a).

Chapter 4

1. Gille et al., *Cinquante Mois*, II, pp. 42–43 (January 19, 1916); pp. 62–63 (February 12, 1916); pp. 66–72 (February 26 1916); Kirschen, *Devant les conseils*, pp. 409–435; Tytgat, *Nos Fusillés*, pp. 140–172; "Justicier Criminel," by "Belga" (the Jesuit Peeters), *La Libre Belgique*, 61 (January 1916), p. 1; "À propos d'un drame," *L'Âme Belge*, 1st series number 5 (January 1916).

2. Gille et al., *Cinquante Mois*, II, pp. 42–43; Kirschen, *Devant les conseils*, pp. 409, 434; Frick, *Saint-Josse*, pp. 194–195.

3. BSA, SPA, 195, Wartel, p. 60.

4. Moriaud, *Bettignies*, pp. 178–184, 187, 197.

5. Kirschen, *Devant les conseils*, pp. 150–238; BSA, SPA, 196, Ball, report 2 p. 1; report 3, pp. 4–12.

6. Kirschen, *Devant les conseils*, pp. 150–298; BSA, SPA, 196, Ball, report 3, pp. 4–12, 19–37.

7. Decock, *La Dame Blanche*, 1981, p. 22.

8. References for this paragraph: BSA, SPA, 196, Ball; BSA, SPA, 195, Wartel; CEGESOMA, War Office, German Police System; BBL, RI, Polizeiwesen; Majerus, *Occupations et logiques policières* 2005, pp. 37–40, 540–541.

9. CEGESOMA, War Office, German Police System, pp. 214, 216, 466; BBL, RI, Polizeiwesen, vol. 1, pp. 16–17; BSA, SPA, 90, (Police allemande); BSA, SPA, 196, Ball, report 1 p. 28; report 2, p. 31.

10. BSA, SPA, 196, Ball, report 1, p. 17; BBL, RI, Polizeiwesen, vol. 1, p. 16.

11. BBL, RI, Polizeiwesen, vol. 1, p. 16; BSA, SPA, 196, Ball, report 1 p. 18. (Wartel, perhaps erroneously, wrote that Goldschmidt was a former police commissar: BSA, SPA, 195, Wartel p. 66.)

12. BSA, SPA, 196, Ball.

13. BSA, SPA, 196, Wartel.

14. BSA, SPA, 195, Wartel, pp. 57–77 and passim; BSA, SPA, 196, Ball, report 1, pp. 18–28 and passim. None of these undercover agents are included among the twenty-one Police Bureau A detectives listed in CEGESOMA, War Office *German Police System*, nor do they appear in BBL, RI, *Polizeiwesen*.

15. BSA, SPA, 195, Wartel, pp. 66–72.

16. Landau, *Secrets of the White Lady*, p. 28.

17. Pöhlmann, "German Intelligence at War", p. 49.

18. Letter to Judge Fromès, March 10, 1919, BSAA, *Cour militaire. Dossiers des arrêts 1915-1954*, Box 157, nrs. 728–729.

19. BSA, SPA, 195, Wartel, pp. 59–61.

20. BSA, SPA, 196, Ball, report 3, pp. 18–19.

21. Brassinne, "Nos maîtres."

22. Rumold and Werckmeister, *The ideological crisis*, p. 115; Van De Woestijne, *Verzameld journalistiek werk*, vol. IX, p. 420; *Libre Belgique* quoted in BSA, SPA, 195, Wartel, p. 57.

23. BSA, SPA, 196, Wartel, pp. 56–57.

24. BSA, SPA, 196, Wartel, p. 82.

25. BSA, SPA, 195, Ball, report 1, p. 18, report 2, pp. 53–54; BSA, SPA, 196, Wartel, pp. 55–56.

26. Pasquier, *L'occupation allemande*; De Schaepdrijver, *La Belgique*, p. 218.

27. BSA, SPA, 40 (Daubechies), Joséphine Genin, December 9, 1918; Landau, *Secrets of the White Lady*, p. 18.

28. Cyrille Van Overbergh, *Gabrielle Petit*, p. 10; "Gabrielle Petit: Héroïne Nationale," *Le Drapeau*, May 1, 1919.

29. A fatal example in BSA, SPA, Port. 40 (Daubechies), excerpt from statement by Joseph Duez, n.d. Daubechies was executed in October 1916.

30. Decock, *La Dame Blanche*, 1981, pp. 35, 45, 52–53; cf. Van Ypersele and Debruyne, *De la guerre de l'ombre*, pp. 68, 81.

31. De Schaepdrijver, "Vile Times."

32. BSA, SPA, 195, Wartel, pp. 58, 105.

33. BSA, SPA, 196, Ball, report 1 pp. 28–29, 36; Ballings, *Ter herinnering*, pp. 5 and 10.

34. Deloge, *Petit*, pp. 114–118; BSA, SPA, 173, MC (a); HS, p. 38; *Le Drapeau*, May 1, 1919, p. 1.

35. Kirschen, *Devant les conseils*, p. 12; Tallier, *Service des prisons*; Pousset, *La geôle*; BSA, SPA, 46 (Adelin Colon), Dufrasne; BSA, SPA, 141, Lauwers.

36. Gille et al., *Cinquante Mois*, I, p. 469 (30 October 1915).

37. BSA, SPA, 173, MC (a); BSA, SPA, 143 (Prison de Saint Gilles); Bonnevie, *La défense*.

38. BSA, SPA, 173, HS pp. 38–39; Deloge, *Petit*, pp. 139–140.

39. BSA, SPA, 173, MC (a); BSA, SPA, 196, Ball, report 1, pp. 36.

40. *Enfance, jeunesse et martyre*, pp. 18–19.

41. Examples: BSA, SPA, 40 (Daubechies), Eugeen Van Assche, August 15, 1920; BSA, SPA, 141, Lauwers, p. 2; BSA, SPA, 169, Jacques Wauthy, February 24, 1917; Kirschen, *Devant les conseils*, pp. 8, 417; Landau, *Secrets of the White Lady*, 1935, p. 21; Lombard, *Le drame*; Debruyne and Van Ypersele, *Je serai fusillé demain*; Van der Fraenen and Lachaert, *Spioneren*; and *La Libre Belgique*, 1915–1918. By contrast, the Spanish arrestee Jaime Mir, of bourgeois background, reported physical abuse—he was stripped and deprived of food—but no beatings: Mir, *Mémoires d'un condamné*.

42. "A Woman 'Spy' to Tell her Story: Alleged Libel in Book," *Evening Post* (New Zealand), December 20, 1937, p. 5. (The article originally appeared in the *Daily Telegraph and Morning Post*.)

43. Deloge, *Petit*, p. 140.

44. BSA, SPA, 173, Leyendecker.

45. Bonnevie, *La défense*, pp. 6–7, 13; Kirschen, *Devant les conseils*, pp. 6, 8; articles in *La Libre Belgique*, 1916, 1917; Redier, *La Guerre des Femmes*; Mir, *Mémoires d'un condamné*.

46. BSA, SPA, 173, HS, pp. 18–19.

47. BSA, SPA, 173, Otto Becker to Xavier Marin, December 1, 1919. I have not identified Becker's file at the Brussels Foreigners' Registers: there are several German men by that name, all, like him, from the Rhineland. Cf. BSA, SPA, 173, HS, p. 27; Deloge, *Petit*, p. 158.

48. BSA, SPA, 46, Dufrasne, p. 4.

49. BSA, SPA, 173, Van Houtte.

50. BSA, SPA, 173, BM.

51. *Le Drapeau*, May 1, 1919, p. 1.

52. BSA, SPA, 173, BM.

53. BSA, SPA, 173, BM. Cf. Tytgat, *Bruxelles sous la botte*, p. 479.

54. Deloge, *Petit*, p. 140.

55. BSA, SPA, 173, HS pp. 18–19.

56. Kirschen, *Devant les conseils*, pp. 3–50; Bonnevie, *La défense*; Tytgat, *Acta Martyrum*, pp. 8–29; Moriaud, *Bettignies*, pp. 208–209; Gille et al., *Cinquante mois*, II, p. 481; Garnir, *Pourquoi Pas?*

57. Bonnevie, *La défense*, pp. 2, 5–11; Kirschen, *Devant les conseils*, Chapter 1; also pp. 52, 85–87, 95, 100–106 and annex; BSA, SPA, 196, Ball, report 1 p. 37; Tytgat, *Acta Martyrum*, pp. 66–69; Gibson, *A journal*; Souhami, *Cavell*.

58. Bonnevie, *La défense*; Tytgat, *Bruxelles sous la botte*, p. 213; Gille et al., *Cinquante mois*, IV, pp. 134–138.

59. Gille et al., *Cinquante mois*, II p. 71 (February 26, 1916); Kirschen, *Devant les conseils*.

60. BSA, SPA, 196, Ball, report 3, pp. 14–17.

61. Redier, *La guerre des femmes*, pp. 145–146.

62. Bonnevie, *La défense*, pp. 2, 13. Neither Bonnevie nor Kirschen mentioned Petit or De Bettignies.

63. Bonnevie, *La défense*, pp. 13–23.

64. Bonnevie, *La défense*, pp. 11–12, 24.

65. Hull, *Absolute Destruction*, p. 231.

66. BSA, SPA, 196, Ball, report 1 p. 36; Van Ypersele and Debruyne, *De la guerre de l'ombre*, p. 80.

67. Kirschen, *Devant les conseils*, pp. 56–59, 88, 399–400, and passim; Redier, *La guerre des femmes*; De Cröamy *Souvenirs*; BSA, SPA, 196, Ball, report 1 pp. 37–38; Commission d'enquête, *Rapports sur les attentats*, vol. 2, p. 121. Eduard Stoeber (1871–1960) received his doctorate in law at the University of Erlangen in 1896 and was named, in 1904, military prosecutor with the Fifth Division of the Bavarian Army (Von Frobel, ed., *Militär-Wochenblatt*, p. 52). In 1906, he married the daughter of a developer in Rosenheim, Bavaria (Mair, *Der Traum*). The couple had three daughters. Stoeber transferred from the Fifth to the First Division in March 1914. In the field since August 6, 1914, he obtained the Iron Cross on November 10, 1914. After the war, in 1921, he became army legal counsel (*Heeresanwalt*) in the *Reichswehr*. With the resumption of military justice in 1934, he was promoted to *Oberkriegsgerichtsrat* (member of an appellate military court) with the rank of general; he retired in 1937. (BHMK, Von Hurt papers, Personalakte Eduard Stoeber. This file contains no information on the First World War years.)

68. Roolf, "Besatzungsbeamte."

69. Kirschen, *Devant les conseils*, pp. 105–106; Stoeber, "Vier Jahre Feldjustizbeamter," p. 396.

70. BSA, SPA, 173, MC (a) and MC (b); Tytgat, *Acta Martyrum*, pp. 63–64; Kirschen, *Devant les conseils*, pp. 53, 100–102, 291.

71. Benn did not mention it in his short account "Wie Miss Cavell erschossen wurde," but he told Sternheim (Sternheim, *Tagebücher*, entry 553, February 3, 1917); he also told the Socialist historian Gustav Mayer, then serving in the occupation administration (Gustav Mayer, *Erinnerungen*, p. 245, diary entry of October 23, 1915).

72. Bonnevie, *La défense*, p. 20; Kirschen, *Devant les conseils*, p. 28; Redier, *La guerre des femmes*.

73. BSA, SPA, 196, Ball, report 1, p. 37.

74. Nevins, ed., Whitlock, *Diary*, October 19, 1915, p. 222.

75. Tytgat, *Acta Martyrum*, pp. 63–64; Brassinne, "Nos maîtres"; Nevins, ed., Whitlock, *Diary*, October 19, 1915, pp. 222–223; Mayer, *Erinnerungen*, p. 245; BSA, LKP, LZ. Also Vierset, *Mes souvenirs*, pp. 363–364; Gille et al., *Cinquante Mois*, I p. 474.

76. Nevins, ed., Whitlock, *Diary*, February 22, 1916, p. 240.

77. Secret Order of October 22, 1915, cited in Wandt, *Etappe Gent*, p. 164.

78. Vierset, *Mes souvenirs*, p. 362; Nevins, ed., Whitlock, *Diary*, p. 240; Gille et al., *Cinquante Mois*, I p. 459 (October 20, 1915).

79. BSA, LKP, LZ.

80. The claim that Von Sauberzweig was dismissed following the Cavell case (Souhami, *Cavell*, p. 348; Tytgat, *Acta Martyrum*, 1919, pp. 63–65) is incorrect. Nevins, ed., Whitlock, *Diary*, pp. 218–223, 232, 240, 284–285.

81. Thiel, *Menschenbassin Belgien*, pp. 107, 127.

82. Whitlock, *Belgium*, II pp. 378–379; Nevins, ed., Whitlock, *Diary*, pp. 284–285. On Von Sauberzweig's aura in the Baltic, Scheidemann, *Memoiren*, vol. 2 p. 80.

83. Spinney, *A Nation in Peril?*, pp. 129–130, 136.

84. Mayer, *Erinnerungen*, p. 245.

85. BSA, SPA, 196, Ball, report 1 p. 41; Kirschen, *Devant les conseils*, p. 102.

86. Nevins, ed., Whitlock, *Diary*, p. 222 (October 19, 1915); Kirschen, *Devant les conseils*, p. 102.

87. BSA, LKP, LZ. On martial *Schneidigkeit*, Ullrich, *Die Nervöse Grossmacht*, pp. 398–399.

88. BSA, SPA, 173, MC (a); Kirschen, *Devant les conseils*, p. 289; BSA, SPA, 196, Ball, report 1 p. 38.

89. BSA, SPA, 173, HS, p. 26; Deloge, *Petit*, pp. 124, 140.

90. BSA, SPA, 173, MC (a); Deloge, *Petit*, pp. 125–127.

91. Deloge, *Petit*, pp. 127–128. Judges: BSA, SPA, 196, Ball, report 1, p. 43.

92. CEGESOMA, War Office, *German Police System*, p. 215; Kirschen, *Devant les conseils*, passim.

93. BSA, SPA, 196, Ball, report 1.

94. The military justice files of the Prussian Army, housed in the Prussian Military Archive, were destroyed in an air raid during the Second World War. In the months following the Armistice, they may briefly have been in civilian hands: one unsigned, undated document in BSA, SPA, 128, presumably written by a member of the Council of the People's Deputies in Berlin, mentions that wagonloads of military justice files were brought to Germany from occupied Belgium. They were stored in the Prussian National Library to be examined (presumably by the newly-constituted *Kommission zur Prüfung der Geheimakten und Archive*) so as to discredit what the document's author called "the Ludendorff clique." But the documents were seized *manu militari*, in late January 1919, by a confiscation party of some thirty officers possibly led by General Walther Reinhardt, the last Prussian minister of war. I have not yet been able to trace this event with certainty. We know at any rate that the *Kommission zur Prüfung der Geheimakten und Archive* was ordered in January 1919 to hand over files concerning the Government-General: Conze, *Quellen*, part 2, pp. 308–309, footnote 7.

95. BSA, SPA, 173, MC (a); Deloge, *Petit*, pp. 127–133, 174.

96. BSA, SPA, 173, HS, pp. 26–29; *Le Drapeau*, May 1, 1919, p. 1.

97. *Le Drapeau*, May 1, 1919, p. 1.

98. BSA, SPA, 173, MC (a); *Le Drapeau*, May 1, 1919, p. 1.

99. BSA, SPA, 173, MC (a); HS, p. 26; Deloge, *Petit*, pp. 128–133; *Le Drapeau*, May 1, 1919, p. 1.

100. Gille et al., *Cinquante mois*, I p. 438.

101. BSA, SPA, 173, MC (a). It is true that the police had had to search for Petit's name: her arrest warrant bears the name Legrand. BSA, SPA, 248 (Police Allemande), *Vorläufiges Aufnahmeersuchen, Polizeistelle Brüssel*, for "Gaby Legrand, 19 rue du Théâtre," February 2, 1916.

102. BSA, SPA, 196, Ball, report 1, pp. 38–40; Kirschen, *Devant les conseils*, pp. 42–50.

103. Text of the poster announcing the verdict in *Le Quotidien*, April 4, 1916, front page. Paragraph 58 of the 1872 German military penal code stipulated the death penalty on grounds of war treason for spying. The All-Highest Imperial Order of 1899 gave military commanders the authority to have foreign civilians executed for aiding the enemy. Kirschen, *Devant les conseils*, pp. 42–44.

104. BSA, SPA, 173, MC (a); Deloge, *Petit*, pp. 131–132; *Le Drapeau*, May 1, 1919, p. 1.

105. BSA, SPA, 196, Ball, report 1, p. 40; Deloge, *Petit*, p. 132.

106. Gille et al., *Cinquante mois*, IV p. 134; Kirschen, *Devant les conseils*, p. 362; cf. Von Lettow-Vorbeck, *Die Weltkriegsspionage*, p. 680.

107. Kirschen, *Devant les conseils*, pp. 109–114. Blanckaert's defiance in Siegburg prison, De Croÿ, *Souvenirs*, p. 194.

108. BSA, SPA, 173, BM. Cf. Kirschen, *Devant les conseils*, p. 111.

109. BSA, SPA, 173, MC (a); Deloge, *Petit*, p. 133.

110. BSA, SPA, 173, HS, p. 27; Deloge, *Petit*, 1922, pp. 134–135, 168–169; BSA, SPA, 173, MC (a); *Le Drapeau*, May 1, 1919, p. 1.

111. BSA, SPA, 173, HS, p. 25; BSA, SPA, 173, Marin January 1921.

112. Gille et al., *Cinquante mois*, II, pp. 186–188; Deloge, *Petit*, p. 138; Kirschen, *Devant les conseils*, p. 350; BSA, SPA, 81 (Revue de la Presse), 505, *Histoire de La Revue de la Presse clandestine*, undated report [early 1921], p. 68; Perry, *Clandestine publications*, pp. 44–47.

113. BSA, SPA, 173, Mussche calling-card; Mussche/Germain.

114. BSA, SPA, 173, MC (a).

115. Kirschen, *Devant les conseils*, pp. 231–237.

116. Gille et al., *Cinquante mois*, II, pp. 83–88 (March 7, 1916); Tytgat, *Acta Martyrum*, pp. 119–139; Emmanuel Debruyne, "Patriotes désintéressés"; BSA, SPA, 92, folder 602(b), report Fernand de Looze.

117. Tytgat, *Acta Martyrum*, pp. 119–139; BSA, SPA, 92, folder 'Avocats belges', file 'Mons'; Kirschen, *Devant les conseils*, p. XIII; Frick, *Saint-Josse*, p. 157.

118. Gille et al., *Cinquante mois*, II, pp. 83–88.

119. Whitlock, *Belgium*, Vol. II, pp. 223, 227; Nevins ed., Whitlock, *Diary*, p. 240.

120. BSA, SPA, 195, Wartel, p. 77.

121. BSA, SPA, 173, Mussche/Germain; MC (a); Deloge, *Petit*, pp. 126, 135.

122. BSA, SPA, 173, Mussche/Germain; MC (a); Deloge, *Petit*, pp. 136–137.

123. BSA, SPA, 173, Mussche/Germain; MC (a); Van Houtte.

124. Kirschen, *Devant les conseils*, pp. 109–114. Another condemned woman, Marie-Thérèse De Cock (née Goffaux), made a similar statement in 1917: Gille et al., *Cinquante mois*, III p. 189; Akersen, *Geteisterd België*, p. 506. De Cock was not executed. Similar words were ascribed to Élise Grandprez, a young woman executed in July 1917: Hardy, "Une héroïne ardennaise."

125. BSA, SPA, 173, Mussche/Germain; MC (a); Deloge, *Petit*, pp. 138, 142.

Chapter 5

1. Deloge, *Petit*, pp. 141–142.

2. Van Overbergh, *Petit*, 1919.

3. BSA, SPA, 173, HS, pp. 23–24.

4. BSA, SPA, 173, HS, pp. 24–25. Neither the correspondence of Marie von Hohenzollern-Sigmaringen nor the Foreigners' Registers in Brussels offer any clue as to her identity.

5. BSA, SPA, 173, HS, p. 25.

6. BSA, SPA, 173, Marin January 1921; HS, p. 25.

7. BSA, SPA, 173, HS, p. 25.

8. BSA, SPA, 173, HS, pp. 25–27; Marin January 1921.

9. BSA, SPA, 173, HS, pp. 27–29; Marin January 1921; Paquet, *Petit*, p. 15.

10. BSA, SPA, 196, Ball, report 1 pp. 41–42; Kirschen, *Devant les conseils*, p. 30.

11. BSA, SPA, 173, BM.

12. Deloge, *Petit*, pp. 142–143, 152–153; *Enfance, jeunesse et martyre*, pp. 18–19; BSA, SPA, 173, HS, pp. 36–37, note.

13. BSA, SPA, 173, BM; Leyendecker.

14. Cf. Tytgat, *Acta Martyrum*, pp. 85–92.

15. BSA, SPA, 173, Van Houtte.

16. BSA, SPA, 173, MC (a); Deloge, *Petit*, p. 153.

17. BSA, SPA, 173, BM.

18. Deloge, *Petit*, pp. 141–142; *Le Drapeau*, May 1, 1919, p. 1; Redier, *La Guerre des femmes*, pp. 131–132; BSA, SPA, 46, Dufrasne, p. 8.

19. *Enfance, jeunesse et martyre*, pp. 30–31; Deloge, *Petit*, pp. 147–149; Kirschen, *Devant les conseils*, pp. 205–206, 236.

20. BSA, SPA, 173, BM; HS, p. 27.

21. Kirschen, *Devant les conseils*, p. 94; Hostelet, "Nurse Cavell."

22. *Enfance, jeunesse et martyre*, pp. 18–19; BSA, SPA, 173, HS, p. 27.

23. BSA, SPA, 173, BM; HS, pp. 27–28.

24. BSA, SPA, 173, Petit to Becker.

25. BSA, SPA, 173, Mussche/Germain.

26. BSA, SPA, 173, Petit to Becker.

27. BRAM, PC, GP, folder 1, VIII 2993.

28. Declercq and Vanden Borre, "Cultural integration"; cf. Francis, *La chanson des rues*.

29. *L'Oiseau [Qui Vient] de France* (1880) was written by a former *communard* who called himself Camille Soubise (a Belgian journalist living in Paris, his real name was Alphonse Vanden Camp). *Le Légionnaire* was made famous, a few years before the war, by the Parisian singer Paul Dalbret (1876–1927), a son of Flemish immigrants to Paris whose real name was Auguste Paul Van Trappe.

30. Last stanza of "*La Mort du Ga[r]s!!!*" (The Death of The Kid); the other song was *La Mort du Volontaire* (The Death of The Volunteer), to be sung to the tune of *Le Légionnaire* (see above).

31. Deloge, *Petit*, pp. 149–150.

32. *Qui M'aurait Dit* was a 1905 hit by the French singer Henri Dickson (pseudonym of Élias Cohen, born in French Algeria in 1872).

33. BRAM, CP, folder 3, the romance *Joujou* (Toy).

34. BSA, SPA, 173, Petit to Becker.

35. BRAM, CP, folder 2, Petit to Auguste Dickmans, n.d. [after March 18, before March 31, 1916]; BRAM, CP, folder 3, bill from Dickmans to Petit (n.d., probably mid-March 1916), with Petit's reply telling her to contact Goldschmidt; see also BSA, SPA, 173, HS, p. 35 and BSA, SPA, 195, Wartel, p. 77. By contrast, Deloge, *Petit*, p. 152; BSA, SPA, 173, Van Houtte; *Enfance, jeunesse et martyre*, p. 25.

36. BRAM, CP, folder 2, Petit to Dickmans, n.d.

37. BRAM, CP, folder 2, Petit, 4-pp. list of items, n.d. (March 1916).

38. BSA, SPA, 173, HS, p. 29; Deloge, *Petit*, p. 171.

39. Souhami, *Cavell*, p. 369.

40. BSA, SPA, 173, MC (a).

41. BSA, SPA, 173, Marin January 1921.

42. BSA, SPA, Port. 173, MC (a); Deloge, *Petit*, p. 160.

43. TMF, GP, Gabrielle Petit to Hélène Ségard, March 10, 1916.

44. BSA, SPA, 173, HS, p. 28.

45. BSA, SPA, 173, BM; BSA, SPA, 196, Ball, report 3 pp. 13–14; BSA, SPA, 195, Wartel, p. 77.

46. BSA, SPA, 173, Van Houtte; Redier, *La guerre des femmes*, p. 260.

47. *Enfance, jeunesse et martyre*, p. 21.

48. BSA, SPA, 173, HS, pp. 29–30.

49. BSA, SPA, 173, HS pp. 30–32.

50. BSA, SPA, 196, Ball, report 1 p. 42.

51. BSA, SPA, 173, BM; HS p. 32; *Enfance, jeunesse et martyre*, p. 21.

52. BSA, SPA, 173, BM.

53. BRAM, CP, folder 2, in an envelope bearing Hélène Petit's note "Authentic letters of Gabrielle Petit written on the eve of her death."

54. *Enfance, jeunesse et martyre*, pp. 30–31.

55. BSA, SPA, 173, HS, p. 32.

56. *Le Drapeau*, May 1, 1919; BSA, SPA, 173, HS, p. 33; compare to "À la mémoire de Gabrielle Petit," interview with Marin, *L'Indépendance Belge* 336 (December 2, 1919), p. 1.

57. BSA, SPA, 173, HS, pp. 33–34.

58. BSA, SPA, 173, HS, p. 35.

59. BSA, SPA, 173, HS, p. 33.

60. BSA, SPA, 173, BM.

61. BSA, SPA, 173, HS, pp. 13, 33–34. Among Petit's papers is an empty envelope addressed to the attorney Raymond Bôn, with a note, in her handwriting, "from Miss Petit who contacted you on behalf of Mr. Baeckelmans." BRAM, CP, folder 3.

62. BSA, SPA, 173, Marin, January 1921; HS p. 34.

63. BSA, SPA, 173, HS p. 34. Cf. Deloge, *Petit*, pp. 188–189.

64. BRAM, CP, folder 2; BSA, SPA, 173, HS, p. 28; BM.

65. BRAM, CP, folder 3; Deloge, *Petit*, pp. 140, 152.

66. As suggested in BSA, SPA, 173, BM; Marin January 1921.

67. Deloge, *Petit*, is confused about the dates: see pp. 174, 176, 188–189, and especially 185. He dated Petit's letter to her godmother, sister, and cousin Alice on April 1 (p. 189), but in fact the original carries no date: BRAM, CP, folder 2. He claimed she wrote to her sister on the afternoon of March 31, when the letter was written in the morning of April 1, which Petit thought was March 31: she dated it "Saturday morning." (BRAM, CP, folder 2) On April 1, 1916, Petit's fellow prisoner Désiré Dufrasne joked that there was "no [April] fish" (BSA, SPA, 146, Dufrasne); and, in town, people played pranks—some cruel ones—on each other: Jérôme Niset, *Le quotidien d'information*, p. 150.

68. BRAM, CP, folder 2.

69. BSA, SPA, BM. Postwar Petit lore had her refuse to confess to Leyendecker on the morning of her execution. She had certainly intended to refuse: BSA, SPA, 173, Mussche/Germain; HS, p. 30. Some prisoners could confess with a Belgian priest (Sorgeloos and Veirman, "La guerre du silence," p. 128), but Petit was not given that option, not even on the eve of her death: BSA, SPA, 173, HS, p. 31. Leyendecker did not dispute that she had refused to confess: BSA, SPA, 173, Leyendecker.

70. BSA, SPA, 173, BM.

71. BSA, SPA, 173, BM; HS, pp. 34–36; *Le Drapeau*, May 1, 1919.

72. BSA, SPA, 196, Ball, report 1 p. 42.

73. BRAM, CP, folder 4, Otto Becker to Hélène Petit, October 15, 1919; BSA, SPA, 173, BM. Deloge mentioned that a member of the execution squad had praised Petit's bravery, but, possibly mistrusting the source, put this in a footnote: *Petit*, p. 197.

74. BSA, SPA, 173, Leyendecker.

75. BSA, SPA, 173, Leyendecker.

76. BSA, SPA, HS, p. 36.

77. RvO, Louise Pilatte-Petit files; Goemaere, *Histoire*, p. 168; Anciaux, *Un martyr national*, pp. 53–54, 91, 119.

78. Deloge, *Petit*, pp. 196–197.

79. *Le Quotidien*, April 4, 1916, p. 1; *Les avis*, volume 10, p. 81. A copy of the poster is preserved at Saint-Gilles prison.

80. Redier, *La guerre des femmes*, p. 156; Proctor, *Female Intelligence*, pp. 119–121.

81. BSA, SPA, 196, Ball, report 3 pp. 13–15; BSA, SPA, 173, BM.

82. BSA, SPA, 195, Wartel, p. 77.

83. The *Sittenpolizei*, upon its creation in March 1915, drew up a list of 511 women under the title "*Liste der unter ärztlicher Aufsicht stehenden Personen*" (List of Persons Under Medical Control). A further 250 women were registered on the periodically updated lists drawn up from May 28, 1915. These lists were kept after the war and can now be consulted by special permission in BCA, Police 1914–1918. The very summary inventory places the first list (with 511 names) in box 420. I found it missing in 2011, looked for it (in vain) through the 113 boxes of the "Police 1914–1918" papers, and was finally able to consult a colleague's photocopy. (Sincere thanks to City Archivist Dr. Jean Houssiau for his help in the search and to Dr. Benoît Majerus for sharing his photocopy.) The periodical lists were in place. I have thus been able to consult all registrations from March 1915 to March 1916. None of the lists register a woman by the name of Petit, nor any of her possible aliases (Legrand, Ségard). The few women from Tournai have different dates of birth.

84. BCA, Police 1914–1918, Box 418, "Autorités allemandes—vente illicite de cocaïne et d'opium."

85. Petit's police file was sent to Berlin along with Von Bissing's decision not to grant pardon, and a message by Von Sauberzweig; none of these documents survive. The decision was then referred to the Emperor and the Imperial Military Court. The full file concerning their decision has not survived either, but their decisions were sent to the legal department of the Foreign Office (*Auswärtiges Amt*). Its archives contain a series of appeals for pardon and attendant correspondance. The few documents concerning Petit are in BBL, AA, R 901/26415.

86. BBL, AA, R 901/26415, President of the Military Court to Emperor, March 18, 1916. Von Kirchbach, a scion of a Prussian military family, had been president of the Court before the war. Though 64 years old in 1914, he had taken service and been wounded. He then became president of the Court again before returning to active duty in the Baltic and in Ukraine, where he replaced the murdered Von Eichhorn as head of Army Group Kiev.

87. BBL, AA, R 901/26415, documents concerning Adrienne Beljean, née Durand, from Maubeuge. She was condemned to death in Charleroi on December 28, 1915 for war treason. Von Bissing refused clemency. Von Kirchbach, on March 11, 1916, called her action "*a very grave offense.*" But Beljean was pardoned. She was in prison in Delitzsch, north of Leipzig: De Beir, *Eagle's Claws*.

88. BBL, AA, R 901/26415, Royal Spanish Embassy Berlin to Imperial Foreign Office, verbal note.

89. BBL, AA, R 901/26415, Foreign Office (on behalf of Secretary of State) to President of Imperial Military Court and to Political Department in Brussels, March 20, 1916. An annotation to the Foreign Office's transcript of the Spanish Embassy's March 13 phone message shows that the department had checked the foreign press for reactions to Petit's March 3 condemnation, but had not found any (BBL, AA, R 901/26415, Royal Spanish Embassy Berlin to Imperial Foreign Office, verbal note). This demonstrates how much the Foreign Office dreaded a scandal.

90. BBL, AA, R 901/26415, Telegram, President of the Military Court to Foreign Office Berlin, March 27, 1916.

91. BBL, AA, R 901/26415, transcript of a coded telegram (marked "Immediate !"), Foreign Office Berlin to Political Department Brussels, March 28, 1916.

92. BBL, AA, R 901/26415, transcript (deciphered telegram), Count Harrach to Foreign Office Berlin, n.d. (March 28 or 29).

93. BBL, AA, R 901/26415, Foreign Office, Legal Department, "Verbal note" to Royal Spanish Embassy, marked "from 1 April." Between March 29 and April 1, it was initialled by the principal jurists at the department, Wedding, Kriege, and Prittwitz; Under Secretary of State Arthur Zimmermann was the last to sign off on it on April 1. The note was vetted by an outside legal expert, one "Professor Schmitt"—which probably does not refer to the prominent jurist Carl Schmitt, who had not yet started his academic career. Sincere thanks to Isabel Hull.

94. A much-initialled press clipping in BBL, AA, R 901/26415 shows that on March 30, the entire legal department read a *Daily Mail* advertisement for a medallion in honor of Cavell, "murdered on orders of the Kaiser."

95. BBL, AA, R 901/26415 (pardon cases February through April, 1916) contains many requests by the Spanish Embassy; only two interventions each by the Vatican and by the Dutch; and only one by the United States.

96. BSA, SPA, 195, Wartel, p. 77.

97. Toppe, *Militär*, pp. 126–128; Stoeber, "Vier Jahre Feldjustizbeamter"; Tytgat, *Acta Martyrum*, p. 73.

98. Meseberg-Haubold, *Mercier*, pp. 120, note 10 p. 307; Jan De Volder, *Benoît XV*, pp. 108–109; LKP, LZ.

99. Stoeber, "Vier Jahre Feldjustizbeamter."

100. Hull, *Absolute Destruction*; Toppe, *Militär und Kriegsvölkerrecht*; BSA, SPA, 173, HS, pp. 24, 26.

101. Quoted in Roland, *La "colonie"*, pp. 128–130, 154; cf. McAleer, *Duelling*.

102. Gille et al., *Cinquante Mois*, IV, p. 134; Kirschen, *Devant les conseils*, p. 332; Tytgat, *Bruxelles sous la botte*, p. 452.

103. BSA, SPA, 173, BM; Leyendecker.

104. Beljean, Petit, and De Bettignies were, at that point, the only women prisoners who had been condemned to death. Blanckaert had received a prison sentence, and another condemned woman, Jeanne De Beir of Bruges, was pardoned in late February after a clemency campaign.

105. Ulrich et al., *Untertan in Uniform*, pp. 164–165.

106. BSA, SPA, 173, BM.

107. Proctor, *Female Intelligence*, p. 117.

108. BBL, AA, R 901/26415, pardon files February through April 1916, contains only two appeals by the nuncio, neither on behalf of Petit. Tacci, De Volder, *Benoît XV*, p. 115; cf. Tacci to Gasparri, May 17, 1916, VC, ASG, B, 1904–1922, item 118, pp. 5–6; listed in http://www.vaticana.be/regesten/4760.php, accessed July 11, 2011.

109. BBL, AA, R 901/26415, clipping from the April 8, 1916 *Daily Express* with the title "Huns Execute A Belgian Lady. More Fierce Sentences for 'Treason'." Information from the Belgian newspaper *L'Echo Belge*, published in exile in Britain. Clipping initialled by all heads of the legal department at the Foreign Office.

110. BSA, SPA, 46, Dufrasne, p. 10.

111. Gille et al., *Cinquante mois*, vol. II, pp. 117–119 (April 19, 1916).

112. BSA, SPA, 173, HS, pp. 29–30.

113. Gille et al., *Cinquante mois*, vol. II, pp. 117–119 (April 19, 1916).

114. "Victimes" by "X" [Victor Jourdain], *La Libre Belgique* 73, May 1916, p. 4. Emphasis in original.

115. BRAM, CP, folder 4, invitation to memorial Mass on May 1, 1916; BSA, SPA, 173, HS, p. 39. Hélène Petit also organized a Mass in her sister's memory the year after, in a parish church in the borough of Saint-Gilles: BRAM, CP, folder 4, invitation to memorial Mass on March 31, 1917.

116. Manuscript notes, BRAM, CP, folder 4, "Allocution (de mémoire) faite par Monsieur l'Abbé Cardijn." Full text of the eulogy, *Enfance, jeunesse et martyre*, pp. 39–41. Cf. Van Overbergh, *Petit*, p. 5.

117. Walckiers, *Joseph Cardyn*, pp. 204–250, 260, 262–316; Mayence, *La Correspondance*, pp. 128–134; Gille et al., *Cinquante Mois*, II, pp. 461–462, December 8, 1916; III, pp. 64–65, February 8, 1917; IV, pp. 317–318, September 28, 1918; Tytgat, *Bruxelles sous la botte*, p. 213; BSA, SPA, 196, Ball, report 3 pp. 64–72; BSA, SPA, 83 (Mot du Soldat), file Madeleine De Roo. Also *Het Laatste Nieuws*, December 10–11, 1918, p. 2.

118. Gille et al., *Cinquante mois*, I, pp. 458–459 (October 19, 1915).

119. Gille et al., *Cinquante mois*, II, pp. 117–119 (April 19, 1916). A similar elegiac tone one year later in Michel Jadin [pseudonym of the Brussels lawyer Henri Puttemans], "La couronne de myosotis" [The Circlet of Forget-me-nots], *L'Âme Belge*, 7, April 28, 1917, pp. 1–2.

120. *Enfance, jeunesse et martyre*, pp. 39–41.

113. "X" [Victor Jourdain], "Victimes," *La Libre Belgique* 73, May 1916, p. 4.

122. De Schaepdrijver and Debruyne, "Sursum Corda."

123. There were exceptions, such as the small railway-observation network "Alice," operated by three young women, which functioned from January to June 1918 in Antwerp province for British GHQ. BSA, SPA, file 40 (folder Alice).

124. Whitlock, *Belgium*, Vol II, p. 228.

125. Majerus and Soupart, *Journal de guerre de Paul Max*, p. 96; the execution in question, Gheude, *Nos années terribles*, Vol. II, pp. 287–293.

126. Gille et al., *Cinquante mois*, II, p. 245 (July 28, 1916); "Les crimes s'accumulent," *La Libre Belgique* 68 (March 1916), p. 2; De Thier and Gilbart, *Liège*, vol. III, p. 228 (cf. vol. IV p. 145); vol. IV, p. 113.

127. Meseberg-Haubold, *Mercier*, pp. 121–125; Amara and Roland, *Gouverner;* De Volder, *Benoît XV*, pp. 114–115.

128. Thiel, *Menschenbassin*.

129. Meseberg-Haubold, *Mercier*, pp. 139–140.

130. Implied, a.o., in Tytgat, *Bruxelles sous la botte*, pp. 202, 206–207.

131. BSA, SPA, 173, BM.

Chapter 6

1. Millard and Vierset, *Burgomaster Max*, pp. 235–238; *La Libre Belgique*, November 19, 1918; Jaumain et al., *Brussel 14-18*, pp. 53–57; BAML, Adrien Bayet diary, notebook 25, November 17, 1918.

2. BAML, Eekhoud diary, November 22, 1918.

3. Women *were* abused in northern France (Nivet, *La France occupée*, pp. 343–345), but, it seems, to a lesser extent than in Belgium (Connolly, *Encountering Germany*, and personal communication). Two contrasting interpretations of this difference: Le Naour, "Femmes tondues," p. 154; Van Ypersele, "Héros, martyrs et traîtres", p. 218.

4. Van Ypersele and Rousseaux, "Leaving the War."

5. BRPA, KC, A 14–18, 1918 survey, chapter "Maintien de l'ordre."

6. Tytgat, *Bruxelles sous la botte,* pp. 126–127.

7. Obituary in *Le XXième Siècle*, September 1, 1919, p. 1.

8. Tytgat, *Acta Martyrum*, pp. 74–81.

9. BAAE, C-R, Brassinne; André Brassinne in *Le Mercure de France*, January 15, 1930, p. 507; March 15, 1931, p. 533; Anciaux, *Un martyr national*, p. 135; *La Libre Belgique* and *Het Laatste Nieuws*, November 21, 1918.

10. *La Libre Belgique*, November 20, 1918.

11. 39 names, with another two as yet unidentified: *La Libre Belgique*, November 21, 1918. Similar lists were published for other execution sites, in Ghent, Antwerp, Liège, and elsewhere. In total, 274 people were executed for acts of resistance during the occupation: Debruyne and Van Ypersele, *Je serai fusillé*.

12. BRPA, KC, A 14-18, "Secours accordés, dons," file 429, Francqui to Belgian government in exile, April 17, 1917.

13. Davignon, *Souvenirs*, p. 304.

14. Gregory, *The Last Great War*, pp. 249–250.

15. Van Ypersele, "Héros, martyrs et traîtres", p. 223.

16. *Le Soir*, November 18, 1918, p. 2.

17. Claisse, *Ils ont bien mérité,* vol. I, pp. 69–79 (analysis), vol. III (images).

18. The historian Katie Pickles' claim that this monument depicted Cavell in action, welcoming escaped soldiers, rests on a hazy IWM photo (Pickles, *Transnational Outrage*, pp. 123–124). In reality it represented imminent death, not action: Claisse, *Ils ont bien mérité*, vol. III, p. 21; Engelen and Sterckx, "Herinneringen"; cf. a picture in *Bruxelles, Louvain*, pp. 7–8.

19. Pickles, *Transnational Outrage*, pp. 78–79.

20. Van Audenhove, *Les rues d'Anderlecht*, p. 41.

21. December 17, 1918; Francis, *La chanson des rues*, p. 98.

22. "Nos martyrs civils," *Le Soir*, December 18, 1918; earlier, *Het Laatste Nieuws*: "Ter eere van Pieter Poels. Ter nagedachtenis van Edith Cavell en Gabrielle Petit," December 16–17, 1918, p. 1.

23. BRAM, CP, folder 4, invitation to memorial Mass on May 1, 1916.

24. Walckiers, *Joseph Cardyn*; cf. Cardijn, "Employées," *La Femme belge*, 7 (November, 1919), pp. 319–335; cf. Conway, "Building the Christian City," pp. 123, 128.

25. In late May 1916, Christophe was arrested by the *Polizei*, possibly on suspicion of smuggling correspondence. *Le Droit de l'Employé*, January 1, 1919; cf. Lehouck, "De 'grote' vakbonden."

26. Gubin and Piette, "Les employées."

27. Van Overbergh, *Petit*, 1919, pp. 17–18.

28. Dresse, *La Centrale Nationale des Employés*; Florence Loriaux and Sven Steffens, personal communications.

29. BSA, SPA, 173, HS, pp. 39–40, cf. Van Overbergh, *Petit*, 1919, p. 16.

30. Apprehension, *Le Droit de l'Employé*, January 1, 1919.

31. On the absence of Van Overbergh's papers, Verhamme, *Van Overbergh*, p. 3; personal communications, Peter Heyrman and Emmanuel Gerard.

32. Van Overbergh, *Petit*, p. 7.

33. Van Overbergh, *La Classe Sociale*, pp. 229, 236.

34. Van Overbergh, *Petit*, pp. 5, 16, 17, 31–32.

35. Jeanne Rondoe, "Gabrielle Petit," *Le Droit de l'Employé*, January 1, 1919, p. 2; *Le Soir*, December 23, 1919, p. 1.

36. BRPA, KC, A 14–18, 1918 survey, chapter "Réforme électorale"; Haag, *Broqueville*; Meseberg-Haubold, *Mercier*.

37. PA, CP, 1918–1919, "Ouverture de la session législative de 1918–1919 (22 novembre 1918), séance royale, Discours du Roi."

38. Van den Plas, "Notre campagne suffragiste," pp. 9–10.

39. Gubin, *Choisir*, p. 100.

40. Gubin, *Choisir*, pp. 73–144; Gubin and Van Molle, *Femmes*, pp. 29–42. Quote, Van den Plas, "Notre campagne," p. 9.

41. Van den Plas and Brigode, "Lettre ouverte." Entries on Van den Plas and Brigode in Gubin et al., *Dictionnaire des femmes belges*.

42. Van den Plas, "Notre campagne"; Gubin, *Choisir*, pp. 98–99; Verhamme, *Van Overbergh*, pp. 48–50, 59–60; Keymolen et al., *De geschiedenis*, pp. 43–44, 51; Van Overbergh, *Le vote politique des femmes*, pp. 23–25. See also Van Overbergh's response in BRPA, KC, A 14-18, 1918 survey, chapter "Réforme électorale" and his front-page editorial in *La Libre Belgique*, March 28, 1919.

43. *La Libre Belgique*, April 4, 1919, p. 2.

44. Gubin, *Choisir*, p. 102.

45. Le Naour, "Le suffrage des morts."

46. Olbrechts, "La population."

47. PA: CR, 1918–1918, Part 1, pp. 634–648 (March 26); 665–676 (March 27); 691–711 (April 2); 726–730 (April 3); 733–739 (April 3, continued); 757–760 and 761–774 (April 9); 791–802 (April 10). Reporting in the column "À la Chambre," *La Libre Belgique*, March 27–28, April

3–4, 8–11, 1919, p. 3; "Ce qui s'est passé dans les coulisses de la Chambre," *La Libre Belgique*, April 12, 1919. Also Van Overbergh, *Le programme*, p. 3.

48. *Congrès National des ex-Prisonniers*, p. 127.

49. Van den Plas, "Victoire suffragiste"; "Notre campagne."

50. Except very implicitly: Van Overbergh, "Gabrielle Petit, Martyre."

51. Tytgat, *Acta Martyrum*, pp. 72–73, footnote.

52. *La Libre Belgique*, April 1, 1919.

53. Marks, *Innocent abroad*.

54. Scholliers and Daelemans, "Standards of living."

55. *Het Laatste Nieuws*, November 25, 1918, p. 2; cf. the extremely frequent reports on such accidents in the daily press throughout the post-Armistice year.

56. E.g., PA: CR, session of April 3, 1919, especially pp. 720–725. Cf. Masoin, *Après la Victoire*.

57. Claisse, *Ils ont bien mérité*, vol. I, p. 103.

58. Van Ypersele and Debruyne, *De la guerre de l'ombre*, pp. 124–126; Akersen, *Geteisterd België*.

59. *Le Drapeau*, 1:1, December 8, 1918, p. 1; cf. Foucart, "Les œuvres."

60. There is no scholarship either on the *Ligue* or on Hennebicq, cf. Claisse, *Ils ont bien mérité* (vol. 1, pp. 280–281). Some information in J.-M. Jadot's entry on Hennebicq in *Biographie Coloniale Belge*, 1955; Hanlet, *Les écrivains belges*, vol. II, pp. 790–791; *Le Drapeau*, 1918–1921; BSA, ASP, 81, *Histoire de La Revue de la Presse clandestine*, p. 77.

61. Barrès, *La Glorification*; "Pour l'érection d'un monument à Paul Déroulède," *Le Drapeau*, 1:11, May 1, 1919, p. 3; 1:6, February 15, 1919, p. 2.

62. *Le Drapeau*, 1:26, September 15, 1919, p. 2; August 1, 1919; December 15, 1919, p. 2; October 1, 1919, p. 1; but also "Serrons nos rangs!" 1:11, May 1, 1919, p. 3.

63. The first steering committee was composed of 24 men. Nine were lawyers and magistrates (including Hennebicq). Others were notaries, high-ranking civil servants, and men active in banking, insurance, and other business. *Le Drapeau*, 1:1, December 8, 1918.

64. *Le Soir*, January 14, April 12, April 15, May 25, May 28, May 31 (p. 2), and June 6, 1919 (all front page except when otherwise indicated).

65. BSAA, May 1919 injunction, deposition by Jules Petit's attorney Georges Max.

66. BRAM, CP, folder 4, José Hennebicq to Hélène Petit, n.d.

67. Le Drapeau, May 1, 1919; it cost 20 centimes instead of the usual 10.

68. Marks, *Innocent abroad*, pp. 197–199.

69. Jules Hoste Jr, editorial, *Het Laatste Nieuws*, May 13, 1919.

70. "Een belangrijke Senaatsvergadering," *Het Laatste Nieuws*, April 30, 1919, p. 2; Pirenne, "Le pangermanisme," pp. 339–340.

71. The march was co-organized by an ad-hoc association called the "groupement de la Politique Nationale," which rather unwisely advocated annexation of, among other things, a border strip with the Netherlands (*Le Courrier de l'Escaut*, May 15, 1919, p. 1). Cf. Claisse, *Ils ont bien mérité*, 280, note 524; *Le Soir*, May 5, 1919, p. 1.

72. Overview of French-speaking press in *Courrier de l'Escaut*, 90:114, May 15, 1919, p. 1; further, *Het Laatste Nieuws*, May 12, 1919, p. 2; "Na een mislukte betooging. Meer dan ooit: leve Wilson!" *Het Laatste Nieuws*, May 13, 1919, p. 1. *Le Drapeau* retorted with "La Manifestation de la Ligue des Patriotes" and "L'infamie de la *Libre Belgique*," 1:12 (May 15, 1919), pp. 1, 2.

73. Emile Desprechins, "Pour Miss Cavell," *La Libre Belgique*, May 14, 1919, p. 1; on Cavell's gendered, victimized image, Proctor, *Female Intelligence*. See also "Les restes de l'héroïne en route pour l'Angleterre," *La Libre Belgique*, May 14, 1919, p. 1; Henri Davignon, "Les claires funérailles," *La Libre Belgique*, May 15, 1919; BCA, Police Papers, Box 431, file "Translation des restes de Miss Edith Cavell le 13 mai 1919"; Nevins, ed., Whitlock, *Journal*, p. 562. Photo in *Bruxelles, Louvain*, pp. 7–8.

74. *Le Drapeau*, 1:12, May 15, 1919, p. 4.

75. *La Libre Belgique*, May 14, 1919.

76. "Gabrielle Petit: de grootste der gefusiljeerden," *Het Laatste Nieuws*, May 15, 1919, p. 3.

77. *Le Soir*, May 15, 1919.

78. The May 15 front page of the *Courrier de l'Escaut* that disparaged the *Ligue* demonstration also ran *Le Drapeau*'s May 1 heroic profile of Petit verbatim.

79. Charle, *La crise*, pp. 29–30.

80. All references to the booklet in this paragraph: Van Overbergh, *Petit*, 1919.

81. Winter, *Sites of Memory*.

82. White, *Metahistory*, pp. 8–9.

83. Cf. Anderson, *Imagined Communities*, pp. 10–12, 206, and passim.

84. Cf. Van Ypersele and Debruyne, *De la guerre de l'ombre*, pp. 116–119.

85. *Le Soir*, 25 May, 1919, p. 2.

86. BSA, SPA, 173, HS, pp. 12, 14, 39.

87. *Enfance, jeunesse et martyre*.

88. BSA, SPA, 173, Leyendecker.

89. Delehaye, *Les légendes*, pp. 87–89 and preface.

90. Debruyne and Van Ypersele, *Je serai fusillé demain*, Chapter II.

91. All references for this paragraph, unless otherwise indicated, from the judicial file on the burial dispute: BSAA, May 1919 injunction.

92. "Au Campo-Santo," *Le XXième Siècle*, May 29, 1919; BSA, SPA, 173, HS, p. 37.

93. *Le Soir* and *Het Laatste Nieuws*, May 15, 1919.

94. Jules Petit junior (1897–1924) was condemned to three months' prison by the Brussels correctional tribunal on May 28, 1917. At the time of his sister's exhumation, he was stationed with the Belgian Sixth Army Division in Dülken near Düsseldorf. He returned to Belgium in June 1919, left the army in July 1921, married, and died in Anderlecht (Brussels) in June 1924, 26 years old. BAAE, Jules Petit file. Death of Jules Petit senior, Ronvaux, *Petit*, pp. 320–321.

95. "Nouvelles judiciaires: pénible incident," *Le Soir*, May 21, 1919, p. 2, also p. 1.

96. BSA, SPA, 173, HS, p. 40.

97. *Le Courrier de l'Escaut*, May 16, 21, 22, 26, 27, 28, 1919.

98. BSA, SPA, 173, HS, p. 40; BAAE, Jules Petit file.

99. *Le Soir,* May 28, 1919. On Benoidt, *Het Laatste Nieuws*, November 23, 1918, p. 2; November 26, 1918, p. 2; Niset, *La Belgique*, pp. 153, 173, 175, 180.

100. *Le Soir*, May 29, 1919, p. 1.

101. SMA, *Communiqué*.

102. *Vingième Siècle*, May 29, 1919; *Le Soir, La Libre Belgique, Het Laatste Nieuws, Le National Bruxellois, L'indépendance belge, L'Étoile Belge, La Gazette*, May 30, 1919. *Le Soir* and *De Standaard*, May 31, 1919. Illustrated weeklies, a.o. *De Zweep*, 24 (the first week of June 1919). Footage, *Translation des restes de Gabrielle Petit, de Bodson & de Smekens (fusillés par les Allemands)*. Pathé newsreel, June 1, 1919.

103. *La Libre Belgique* and *Le National Bruxellois*, May 30, 1919; *La Gazette*, May 31, 1919.

104. Ozouf, *La fête révolutionnaire*, p. 16.

105. Claisse, *Ils ont bien mérité*, vol. I, pp. 118, 124–126; Prost, "Les cimetières."

106. BCA, Police Papers, Box 431, file "Manifestation de piété nationale."

107. Van Ypersele and Debruyne, *De la guerre de l'ombre*, p. 133.

108. Théo Connet, "Auréoles de gloire," *L'Exploité*, May 5, 1919.

109. *Le Soir*, May 19, 1919.

110. *La Gazette*, May 31, 1919.

111. Charle, *La crise*, pp. 29–30 and passim; Audoin-Rouzeau and Prochasson, eds, *Sortir*.

112. "Antwerpen en Luik—de eer der Scheldestad," *Het Laatste Nieuws*, May 1, 1919, p. 1, and articles in preceding weeks.

113. *Het Laatste Nieuws*, June 3, 1919.

114. Speeches at Petit's funeral referred to in this paragraph: at Schaarbeek City Hall, Prime Minister Léon Delacroix spoke, followed by the Schaarbeek alderman Raymond Foucart, and by Auguste Coppejans, a former secret intelligence agent now speaking for an association of political prisoners. At the church, Cardinal Mercier gave the eulogy. At the cemetery, the former resisters and present "memory agents" for political prisoners Chrétien Flippen and Albert "Fidelis" Van de Kerckhove spoke at length. The lawyer Lemmens spoke briefly on behalf of the Red Cross. The last speech was pronounced by the Brussels lawyer Léon Rycx, the president of a memory association (the *Ligue Nationale du Souvenir*) similar to Hennebicq's *Ligue des Patriotes*. For text of the speeches, see note 14 in Prologue.

115. SMA, Carton.

116. "Falcon", "En patrouille chez l'ennemi: l'activité de Gabrielle Petit," *La Dernière Heure*, May 29, 1919, p. 1.

117. Kirschen, *Devant les conseils*.

118. *Le Soir*, May 24, 1919, p. 3.

119. *La Gazette*, May 31, 1919.

120. *Enfance, jeunesse et martyre*, pp. 35–40; cf. May 28 editorial in *Le Vingtième Siècle*, reprinted in M.H., *La vie et la mort*, pp. 21–27. Also *Het Laatste Nieuws*, November 20, 1918; *La Libre Belgique*, February 3, 1919. Van De Kerckhove was secretary general of the Commission of National Gratitude (Commission de la Reconnaissance Nationale) created by royal decree on April 5, 1919.

121. Albert, "Du martyr à la star"; Todorova, *Bones of Contention*.

122. Michelet in 1872, quoted in Anderson, *Imagined Communities*, p. 198.

123. 1886 opera *Patrie* (Émile Paladilhe), based on Victorien Sardou's eponymous 1869 play. Postwar performances a.o. *Congrès National des ex-Prisonniers* [1921]; *La Nation Belge*, December 16, 1923, p. 3.

124. *Enfance, jeunesse et martyre*, pp. 29–31; court hearing, BSA, SPA, 173, HS, p. 40, 32.

125. Anderson, *Imagined Communities*, pp. 25–26, 36.

126. PA: S, 1918–1919, 2 July 1919, pp. 416–418.

127. Godelaine, *Monseigneur Keesen*; Gerard, *De christelijke arbeidersbeweging*, Part 2, p. 37; obituaries, *La Libre Belgique*, August 17, 1923, *Le Soir*, August 23, 1923; cf. "Les arguments de Mgr Keesen," *Le Féminisme chrétien de Belgique* 12:6 (June 1921), pp. 88–91.

128. Albert, "Du martyr à la star."

129. Charle, *La crise*, pp. 201–203. Cf. Datta, *Heroes and Legends*, pp. 14–15, and Chapter 4.

130. PA: S, 1918–1919, July 2, 1919, pp. 409–415.

131. *Enfance, jeunesse et martyre.*

132. "Jeanne d'Arc," in Allem, ed., *Michelet*, p. 117.

133. *Het Laatste Nieuws*, July 29, 1919, p. 2.

134. *Enfance, jeunesse et martyre*, pp. 21–22.

135. The booklet gave the author's name as "Dame Madeleine," a friend of Hélène Petit. No catalog, bibliography, or publication elucidates this alias. But d'Oultremont's presence at the court hearing and exhumation (see below) is a first clue; and an insert in *Het Laatste Nieuws*, July 29, 1919, p. 2, provides final corroboration: it mentions "the booklets by Mrs. d'Oultremont and Mr. Cyrille Van Overbergh." On Renée de Mérode-d'Oultremont see the entry in Gubin et al., *Dictionnaire des femmes belges*.

136. Sorgeloos and Veirman, "La guerre du silence."

137. BSA, SPA, 173, HS, p. 40.

138. *Le Drapeau*, June 28 through July 19, 1919.

139. *Le Soir*, May 29, 1919.

140. "À côté des funérailles de Gabrielle Petit—pénible incident," *Le Drapeau*, May 31, 1919, p. 2; "À côté des funérailles de Gabrielle Petit," *Le Drapeau*, June 14, 1919, p. 2; "Sur une Tombe," *Le Courrier de l'Escaut*, June 4, 11, and 18, 1919; Ronvaux, *Petit*, pp. 415–417, 441–443.

141. BSA, SPA, 173, HS, p. 40.

142. BSA, SPA, 173, HS, p. 14.

143. BRAM, PC, GP, Folder 2, postcards.

144. BRAM, PC, GP, item VIII 2993 (lock of hair, piece of coat, transcript of songs). Hélène Petit had given these to her counsel in the burial trial, the Brussels attorney Georges Dupont.

145. TMF, GP, Hélène Ségard to the Mother Superior at Brugelette, April 14, 1919.

146. Paquet, *Petit*, p. 12.

147. BRAM, CP.

Chapter 7

1. *Le Soir*, December 19, 1920; *Revue belge du cinéma*, January 2, 1921.

2. *La Libre Belgique,* May 22, 1919.

3. Sevens, *Petit.*

4. The film was produced by Hippolyte De Kempeneer who founded the *League of Moral Cinema* in 1913 (Collette, *Moralité*, pp. 47, 71, 74; Engelen, *De verbeelding*, pp. 66–71; entry on De Kempeneer in Belgium, *Biographie Nationale*, volume 41, 1979–1980; *Le Drapeau*, June 21, 1919, p. 2). The film received subsidies from the governor of Brabant province,

Émile Béco (cf. his *La croisade*): *Le Soir*, January 14, 1921. It was shot in October–November 1920 (Engelen, *De verbeelding*, p. 71); film censorship was introduced in Belgium in that year.

5. "À la mémoire de Gabrielle Petit," *L'Indépendance Belge*, December 2, 1919, p. 1; "La cellule de Gabrielle Petit," *Bulletin officiel de la Fédération nationale des prisonniers politiques de la Guerre* 2:10 (February, 1920), pp. 5–6; *L'Événement illustré*, 223 (January 31, 1920); plaques in storage, Saint-Gilles prison.

6. M.H., *La vie et la mort*, pp. 11, 14; Sevens, *Petit*.

7. *Le Drapeau*, July 12, 1919, p. 2; July 19, 1919, p. 2.

8. *Le Courrier de l'Escaut, La Dernière Heure, La Nation Belge, L'Événement illustré*, a.o. September 21, 1919; *Notre Pays*, December 12, 1919. Footage in Yser Journal, Cinematek, Brussels.

9. Ronvaux, *Petit*, p. 466.

10. Anonymous, *Petit* [1919].

11. Hans (Verbeke), *Petit*.

12. Van Ypersele and Debruyne, *De la guerre de l'ombre*, pp. 116–119.

13. Stocq, *Petit*.

14. Van Nieuwenhove, *Petit*.

15. G. Raal [Lode Opdebeek], *Gaby, het Vliegenierstertje*.

16. BSA, War Library, Hespel, *Petit*.

17. Hans (Verbeke), *Petit*.

18. Stocq, *Petit*; Van Nieuwenhove, *Petit*.

19. Datta, *Heroes and Legends*, p. 7.

20. Engelen, *De verbeelding*, p. 108.

21. Proctor, *Female Intelligence*, p. 99 and passim.

22. M.H., *La vie et la mort*.

23. Léon Rycx in *Le Soir*, May 31, 1919, p. 2.

24. *Enfance, jeunesse et martyre*, pp. 29–32.

25. Hespel, *Petit*.

26. Cf. De Schaepdrijver, "Death Is Elsewhere"; "Vile Times."

27. Christens et al., "Enlightened Tutelage," p. 64.

28. The clue is hidden in the old card catalog at the Royal Library in Brussels. The thematic card catalog covering themes from 1910 to 1959 reveals that "Jan Verbeke" was a pseudonym for Hans. The thematic card catalog covering pre-1910 themes—which, unlogically, contains many works on the First World War—reveals that "A. du Jardin," too, was a pseudonym for Hans. The electronic catalog does not mention A. du Jardin as a pseudonym of Hans, and it does not mention the Dutch-language Petit bibliography at all, though it is in the library's collections. But it does offer one further clue: one 1914 work on Robespierre is listed as written by "A. Du Jardin" and "A. Hans."

29. Horne and Kramer, *German Atrocities*, p. 38.

30. BSA, SPA, 173, Gobert to CAP, March 21, 1921.

31. Debruyne, "Sortir de l'ombre," p. 452.

32. Todorova, *Bones of Contention*, p. X.

33. Landau, *All's Fair*, pp. 188–217.

34. Debruyne, "Sortir de l'ombre," pp. 450, 473–478.

35. Van Nieuwenhove, *Petit*.

36. Colleaux interpellation, PA: CR, 1920, p. 162, January 15, 1920; p. 250, January 29, 1920; Debruyne, "Sortir de l'ombre."

37. *Congrès National des ex-Prisonniers*, pp. 68–75.

38. In response, Paul Tschoffen, "Leur sépulcre sera glorieux," *Le Soir*, May 18, 1922, p. 1; cf. Tschoffen bill, PA: CR, 1920, p. 358, February 17, 1920.

39. Tassier, *L'histoire*, pp. 62–64; Tallier, "Les Archives de la Guerre."

40. BSA, SPA, 173, Mussche calling-card.

41. BSA, SPA, 173, Mussche/Germain.

42. De Schaepdrijver, *"We who are so Cosmopolitan,"* pp. 130–131.

43. BRAM, CP, folder 4, Otto Becker to Hélène Petit, October 15, 1919.

44. "À la mémoire de Gabrielle Petit," *L'Indépendance Belge*, December 2, 1919, p. 1; BSA, SPA, 173, Mons 1921; Marin January 1921; Deloge, *Petit*, p. 190.

45. Deperchin, "Loos"; James Connolly, personal communication, January 21, 2011; BBL, AA, R 901/26415, Bloquet file.

46. Aurore François, personal communication, January 17, 2011.

47. Deloge, *Petit*, pp. 157, 192; BSA, SPA, 173, Marin January 1921.

48. BSA, SPA, 173, BM, carbon copy of the transcript dated March 2, 1920. Marin later claimed he had given his documents to Deloge (BSA, SPA, 173, Mons 1921). But Deloge only quoted the cut version of Petit's letter, which suggests he was never given the original; he criticized Marin's decision to "mutilate" this document (Deloge, *Petit*, p. 163).

49. BSA, SPA, 173, HS; Snoeck to Germain, November 30, 1920.

50. Manteleers, *Kroniek*; BSA, SPA, 196, Ball, report 1 p. 42.

51. Nysten, *Comment ils meurent*; on Nysten, BSA, SPA, 84 (*Mot du Soldat*), 81, 194 (*Libre Belgique*). Nysten-Leyendecker correspondence, May 1920—January 1921, in BSA, SPA, 90 (Aumôniers allemands).

52. BSA, SPA, 173, Leyendecker.

53. Nysten, *Comment ils meurent*, p. 125.

54. Horne and Kramer, *German Atrocities*; Horne, ed., *Démobilisations culturelles*.

55. Van Overbergh, *Petit*, 1919, p. 12; cf. Deloge, *Petit*, p. 136.

56. Manteleers, *Kroniek*, pp. 112–113.

57. BSA, SPA, 173, Germain.

58. Eriksen, "Être ou agir"; cf. Todorova, *Bones of contention*, p. 496.

59. BSA, SPA, 90 (Keurvers), Keurvers to "the Head of Security at Liège," February 22, 1920; see also folder "Police Allemande—Pièces diverses"; Deloge, Petit, 117.

60. Germain: "Autographe."

61. Unless otherwise indicated, all quotations in this paragraph are taken from Deloge, *Petit*.

62. Deloge, *Conduire les Hommes; Mannen aanvoeren*. It had sold 8,000 copies by 1922 (*Petit*, inside cover).

63. Deloge, *Trésignies*. It had sold 2,000 copies by 1922 (*Petit*, inside cover).

64. Paul Delforge, entry on Deloge in *Encyclopédie du Mouvement Wallon*; Paul Delforge, personal communication, March 11, 2011.

65. Deloge, *Nos P'tits*.

66. Deloge, *La Demoiselle de Magasin*.

67. BSA, SPA, 173, Mons 1921.

68. Publisher's leaflet.

69. Publisher's leaflet.

70. MW 1923.

71. MW 1923; quote from Maurice Barrès, "Discours."

72. *Le Soir*, July 22, 1923; *L'avenir du Tournaisis*, July 23–24, 1923.

73. BCA, IP, BA, 313. Unless otherwise specified, all of the details in this paragraph are taken from this file.

74. *Le Soir*, July 22, 1923; *La Métropole*, July 22, 1923.

75. Cf. BRAM, CP, letter from the French ambassador, Maurice Herbotte, to Hélène Petit, July 5, 1923.

76. Prost, "Les monuments aux morts."

77. BCA, IP, BA, 313; *Le Soir*, July 22 and 23, 1923; *La Métropole*, July 22, 1923; *L'avenir du Tournaisis*, July 23–24, 1923; *Le Matin*, July 22, 1923; pictures in *Le Patriote Illustré*, July 29, 1923.

78. *Le Drapeau*, May 1, 1919, p. 2; *Le Soir*, May 28 and 31, 1919; June 10, 1919; BCA, IP, BA, 313.

79. *Le Drapeau*, June 14, 1919, p. 1; June 28, 1919, p. 2 (Chrétien Flippen gave 5 francs); July 5, p. 2; July 12, p. 2; July 19, p. 4; August 15, p. 2 (this list brought in some 700 francs; the Stock Exchange Commission contributed 330 francs), September 1, p. 2; October 1, p. 1; October 15, p. 2; November 15, p. 2; December 1, p. 1; December 15, p. 4 (Gabrielle Petit Gala); January 1, 1920; January 15, p. 2; February 1, 1920; February 15; March 1; March 15; April 1, 1920; a very long 21st subscription list on May 1, 1920. On July 1—*Le Drapeau* had not appeared for a while due to an illness of Hennebicq's—the entire second page was devoted to the 22nd subscription list. Further, August 1, and November 15, 1920; April 5, 1921, p. 4, 25th list, featuring Cyrille Van Overbergh donating 50 francs; and the Employees' Union contributing too, for the eighth time. This brought the total to 66,444.64 francs. This was the last issue of *Le Drapeau*.

80. Van Reybrouck, *Slagschaduw*, pp. 44–50, 178, 192.

81. Van Reybrouck, *Slagschaduw*, p. 46. Critics, Claisse, *Ils ont bien mérité*, Chapter IV.

82. *Le Droit de l'Employé*, August 1, 1923, p. 1.

83. *Le Soir*, July 22, 1923; *La Métropole*, July 22, 1923.

84. Louise Birnbaum-Coens, "La crise des servantes," *Le Soir*, July 20, 1923.

85. *Le Droit de l'Employé*, May 1, 1920, p. 2.

86. Subscriptions opened in May 1920. The first lists came from Bruges, Ghent, and Sint-Niklaas, totalling 155 francs (*Le Droit de l'Employé*, May 16, 1920, p. 3). The second batch garnered almost 1,400 francs: 13 lists from Kortrijk, 3 from Charleroi, 5 from the mining region of the Centre, 2 from Arlon, 6 from Ghent, 12 from Brussels (*Le Droit de l'Employé*, 1 June 1920, p. 4). Another 400 francs had come in by mid-June: 5 Brussels lists, 2 from Charleroi, 2 from Waremme, 7 from Soignies, 1 from Ghent and 1 from Dendermonde (*Le Droit de l'Employé*, June 16, 1920, p. 3). Almost 700 francs a month later: 1 list from Aalst, 7 from Soignies, 3 from Brussels, 1 from Mons, 1 from Charleroi, one from the Syndicate of Female Employees

in Antwerp (25 francs), 11 from Mons, 4 from Renaix. This brought the total to almost 4,000 francs. (July 16, p. 5). *Le Droit de l'Employé*, September 1, 1920, p. 4, gave an update: 1 list from Ostend, 7 from Verviers, 2 from Charleroi, 7 from Brussels, 1 from Izegem, 5 from Soignies, 2 from Liège, 2 from Enghien, 2 from Antwerp, 6 from Mons, 2 from Nivelles, 1 from Bruges contributed altogether almost 1,500 francs. Sum total almost 6,400 francs.

87. *Le Droit de l'Employé*, April 16, 1922, p. 5.

88. *Le Droit de l'Employé*, August 16, 1923, p. 4.

89. *Le Droit de l'Employé*, August 1, 1923, p. 1.

90. Engelen and Sterckx, "Herinneringen."

91. *Le Soir*, July 28 and 31, 1923; October 13, 1923.

92. Van Ypersele and Debruyne, *De la guerre de l'ombre*, pp. 103–179.

93. Deloge, *Petit*, p. 72.

94. Paul Colin, "'Leur' fête," *Haro !* 3 (August 5, 1919), pp. 18–19; cf. Colin's later *La Belgique*. Colin (1895–1943) had spent the war in the occupied country. In 1919, he became editor-in-chief of the avant-garde and pacifist *L'Art Libre* and ran the modern-art gallery Giroux in Brussels. During the Second World War, Colin turned to collaborationist journalism and was murdered by the resistance. See also Waterlot-Jottrand and Lefebvre, *Haro!*

95. De Schaepdrijver, *La Belgique*, pp. 239–241, 307–309; "Occupation, Propaganda."

96. Eekhoud, "Des Hommes."

97. De Schaepdrijver, "An outsider inside."

98. BSA, SPA, 173, Leyendecker; BSA, SPA, 141, Lauwers, p. 7; BAAE, C-R, Brassinne.

99. Lucien, *Eekhoud le rauque*, pp. 185–186.

100. Van Ypersele and Debruyne, *De la guerre de l'ombre*, p. 285 note 364.

101. BCA, BC, 831, "soldats allemands fusillés"; BSA, SPA, 90(Aumôniers allemands) Leyendecker to Nysten, May 30, 1920; "La légende du soldat Rammler," *Le Peuple*, December 29, 1929; BSA, SPA, 141, Lauwers, p. 7; BAAE, C-R, Brassinne. On Rammler in Cavell lore, Robertson, "Dawn." Transferral of the German soldiers' corpses to Brussels municipal cemetery: BCA, Police Papers, Box 431, "Manifestation de piété nationale," letter by Brussels Central Division Police Commissar, May 30, 1919.

102. *Enfance, jeunesse et martyre*, pp. 29–31; BCA, BC, 831; Bailly, "La grande fusillée."

103. Lyr, "POST-SCRIPTUM", in id., *Nos héros*, Part Four, p. 36. This lavish tome of homage was subsidized by the King's cabinet.

104. De Schaepdrijver, "Occupation, Propaganda"; entry on Van den Reeck by Guy Leemans in *Nieuwe Encyclopedie van de Vlaamse Beweging* (1998).

105. *Het Laatste Nieuws*, May 24, 1919; cf. Hans' editorials on the parliamentary debate (May 19–21).

106. Van Everbroeck, *Borms*.

107. De Schaepdrijver, "Vile times."

108. Van der Fraenen, *Voor den kop geschoten*, pp. 317–384; Van der Fraenen and Lachaert, *Spioneren*.

109. Van Ypersele and Claisse chapters in Van Ypersele and Debruyne, *De la guerre de l'ombre*; cf. De Schaepdrijver, "Death is Elsewhere."

110. *La Libre Belgique*, August 5, 1921.

111. Claisse, *Ils ont bien mérité*, pp. 525–544; *La Libre Belgique*, August 5, 1922.

112. Souhami, *Cavell*, p. 420.

113. De Schaepdrijver, "Les dangers."

Chapter 8

1. Stéphany, *Les années '20–'30*, vol. II, pp. 28–29

2. Martin, who was 23 in 1928, had acted in the 1921 film; and he played Petit's fiancé in *Femme belge*. Engelen, *De verbeelding*, p. 119.

3. Hirschfeld, *Sittengeschichte*, p. 396.

4. Binder, *Spionagezentrale Brüssel*, pp. 16, 178.

5. Von Lettow-Vorbeck, ed., *Die Weltkriegsspionage*.

6. Pirenne, *La Belgique*; De Schaepdrijver, "Vile times"; id., "That Theory of Races."

7. PA: CR, 1927–1928, vol. 2, session of September 19, 1928, p. 2487.

8. Though others too stood to benefit from amnesty measures. Those who had fled abroad could return: 161 ex-activists, condemned in absentia, were still living in the Netherlands or Germany in 1928. Another 94 who had served their sentence would get their political rights back. Amnesty opened the door for yet wider revisions: a larger group of people had not been sentenced to prison but had lost official positions; they might eventually be reinstated.

9. PA: CR, 1927–1928, vol. 2, session of September 20, 1928, pp. 2491–2492.

10. De Schaepdrijver, "Les dangers."

11. De Schaepdrijver, "Occupation, propaganda."

12. The only in-depth study of it remains unpublished: Van Everbroeck, *L'activisme entre condamnation et réhabilitation*.

13. Cartoon signed "Clem," *'t Vlaamsche Land*, 5:12, June 6, 1937, front page; see also "By de plaat," p. 2. Archive sources: Brussels City Archive, Police Archives, Box D 21/47, "Manifestation des V.O.S." Press consulted for this paragraph: *Het Laatste Nieuws, La Libre Belgique, Le Soir, De Standaard* ("silly incident", May 24, 1937, p. 4), *De Volksgazet, Vooruit*.

14. On the different stages of First World War memory in interwar Belgium, See Van Ypersele and Debruyne, *De la guerre de l'ombre*, pp. 103–179.

15. BRAM, CP, file 5.

16. BRAM, CP, file 5 (October 1931).

17. Engelen, *De verbeelding*, p. 116.

18. Prud'homme-Malherbe, *Petit*.

19. On March 19, 1940, Walter Ravez, the curator of the Folklore Museum in Tournai, wrote to the daughter of Charles Bara to ask for information about Petit on Catulle-Mendès' behalf. The daughter, Madame Duphénieux-Bara, apparently wrote back with details, as a follow-up letter by Ravez shows. But her letter has not survived: on May 16 and 17, a series of Luftwaffe attacks destroyed the center of Tournai, and the Folklore Museum and Ravez' papers with it. On Catulle-Mendès before the war, Datta, "Sur les boulevards"; on her wartime lecture tours, Snider, "Patriots and Pacifists." Especially, Audoin-Rouzeau, "Stabat Mater" in *Cinq deuils de guerre*, pp. 211–261. There seems to be no trace of the Petit project in Catulle-Mendès' own correspondence in the public domain: Stéphane Audoin-Rouzeau, personal communication, May 2010.

20. TMF, GP, Walter Ravez to Madame Duphénieux-Bara, March 19, 1940.

21. TMF, GP, Petit to Bara, 1909 and 1910; Lucien Jardez to Pierre Ronvaux, November 19, 1988; Ronvaux, *Petit*, pp. 139–141, 147–151. The troops in question belonged to the 35th Infantry Division of the Wehrmacht.

22. Debruyne, *La guerre secrète*, p. 339.

23. Delandsheere and Ooms, *La Belgique sous les Nazis*, vol. I, p. 175, vol. II, p. 199.

24. Struye, *Journal*, p. 154 (November 6, 1940).

25. Delandsheere and Ooms, *La Belgique sous les Nazis*, vol. II, p. 304.

26. Debruyne, *La guerre secrète*, pp. 336–343; Debruyne and Van Ypersele, *De la guerre de l'ombre*, pp. 212–221.

27. Debruyne, *La guerre secrète*, p. 310.

28. RvO, Hélène Pilatte files; additional clarifications, Gerd De Prins, letter to the author, December 22, 2009.

29. BAAE, Gobert file.

30. Van Reybrouck, *Slagschaduw*, p. 185; Stéphany, *Des Belges très occupés*, p. 361.

31. From a 1946 clipping in Hélène Petit's papers, no title given: BRAM, CP, folder 1; cf. Debruyne, *La guerre secrète*, p. 310.

32. Cinematek, Brussels, Fox Movietone newsreel 1949.

33. Cf. Conway, *The Sorrows of Belgium*, pp. 368, 377.

34. Didden, *Een gehucht in een moeras*, p. 130.

35. The original design was by a 17-year-old student named Jean-Pierre Bodson, with the aid of a local sculptor, Louis Van Cutsem (1909–1992), whose 1951 monument to eleven resisters in a small town south of Brussels was similar to the one to Petit. The statue was completed by the sculptor Maurice Christiaens (1906–1985), known for his stylized renderings of the human body.

36. *Le Soir*, August 22, 1964. The *Libre Belgique* ran a picture of the 1919 funeral on the front page of its September 19–20, 1964 weekend edition.

37. *La Libre Belgique*, September 21, 1964; September 19–20, 1964.

38. The post-Armistice young were a baby boom generation: natality rates until 1900 were high, and the fighting-age males had not been decimated as in France or Germany. Olbrechts, "La population."

39. *La Libre Belgique*, September 21, 1964.

40. Sheehan, *Where have all the soldiers gone?*

41. Ronvaux, *Petit*, pp. 17–18, 458.

42. References for what follows: TMF, GP, 1966 anniversaire; *Le Courrier de l'Escaut*, April 2–3, 1966; materials in Hélène Petit's papers, BRAM, CP, folder 1.

43. Redier, *La guerre des femmes*, p. 53.

44. *Nord-Matin*, April 8, 1966.

45. *La Libre Belgique*, September 19–20, 1964.

46. I was alerted to this interview by two letters in Hélène Petit's papers: BRAM, CP, folder 4, Jacques Bredael to Hélène Petit, July and August 1966. RTB, *14–18*, episode of March 28, 1966. The interview was conducted by Jean-Marie Delmée, a distinguished journalist known for his sympathetic reporting on the Algerian war.

47. M.H., *La vie et la mort*, p. 11.

48. They were labeled "Célis papers" and so misfiled with the "Sélys papers" pertaining to the World War Two pilot Hubert de Sélys Longchamps. Ronvaux, *Petit*, pp. 16, 402–404. This has been cleared up since 2012.

49. Ronvaux, *Petit*, pp. 19, 263, 299, 325.

50. Ronvaux, *Petit*, pp. 391–393, 134.

51. The reference to the poems written by the French World War Two collaborator Robert Brasillach on the eve of his 1946 execution was involuntary.

52. Ronvaux, *Petit*, p. 392.

53. Ronvaux, *Petit*, pp. 20–21, 404.

54. Stéphane Detaille, "Gabrielle Petit, le mythe revisité," *Le Soir*, October 17, 1994.

55. *De Standaard*, April 7, 2005. In the event, Petit ranked 94th in the Flemish survey, behind soccer impresario Constant Vanden Stock, and 85th in the French-speaking one, behind hat designer Elvis Pompilio. Given the otherwise striking difference between the two linguistic top-hundreds, the relative similarity of Petit's ranking is not unimportant. *De Grootste Belg / Le Plus Grand Belge* was organized by the television networks VRT-Canvas and RTBf in conjunction with the daily press.

56. "L'ultime au revoir à Marie Trintignant," *La Dernière Heure*, August 7, 2003.

57. Reading by novelist Johanna Spaey, in VRT-Radio 1, "Een blauwe mantel," April 1, 2006.

58. Van Reybrouck, *Slagschaduw*, p. 155.

Conclusion

1. De Schaepdrijver, "Populations," p. 255.

2. Atkinson, *Life*, p. 445.

3. Eliot, *Middlemarch*, pp. 226 ("that roar"), 25 ("spiritual grandeur").

BIBLIOGRAPHY

Unpublished Primary Sources

N.B. This is a list of archive collections, not of the separate documents used; it only itemizes those separate documents that are abbreviated in the notes. The terms in brackets correspond to the abbreviations in the notes.

1. Brussels, Belgian State Archives (BSA)

(a) Services Patriotiques archives (SPA)
File 35
Folder "M.S.": Louis Loos, "Verslag der diensten aan het Vaderland bewezen door Mr. Laukens, Frans, van Neerpelt," September 3, 1919. (Loos)

File 39
Folder Baeckelmans:
—"Extraits du rapport de Mlle Doutreligne sur les débuts du service Wallinger," n.d., presumably 26 January 1921. (Doutreligne)
—"Extrait des notes concernant le service Wallinger et ses agents en Hollande," July 14, 1920. (Wallinger)

File 40
Folder Petit
Folder Daubechies
Folder "Alice"

File 46
Folder Adelin Colon: "Journal de Désiré Dufrasne." (Dufrasne)

Files 81, 193, 194
Folders *La Libre Belgique*
Folders *La Revue de la Presse*

Files 83, 84, 85; box 84bis
Folders *Le Mot du Soldat*

File 90
Folder Aumôniers allemands
Folder Keurvers
Folder Police Allemande—Pièces diverses

File 92
Folder Avocats belges

File 125
"Schéma général de l'organisation des services de renseignements officiels en Hollande"

File 141
Folder Bruxelles: typescript "La prison de Saint-Gilles pendant l'occupation—Récit de Monsieur Félicien Lauwers," a memoir by a warden at the prison, n.d. (Lauwers)

File 143

Folder Prison de Saint-Gilles

File 173

Folder Petit:

—Otto Becker to Xavier Marin, December 1, 1919 (BM)

—Georges Delmeule-Marlier testimony, April 12, 1920 (D-M)

— Doutreligne report, n.d., January 26, 1921 (Doutreligne)

—five-page carbon copy of a typescript, n.d., unsigned, starting with the words "Messieurs, ce n'est pas sans appréhension." Identified as a draft of a lecture by the archivist Jules Germain in mid-1921. (Germain)

—Hélène Ségard testimony, n.d., between July and December 1919 (HS)

—"Copie d'une lettre d'un aumônier allemand de la prison de St Gilles": letter by Chaplain Leonhard Leyendecker to Father Jan Nysten, January 7, 1921. At Leyendecker's request, his name is not mentioned. (Leyendecker)

—three-page typescript, unsigned, undated, starting with the words "À la suite d'un entretien avec Monsieur Marin." Identified as a transcript of an interview by the archivist Jules Germain with prison director Xavier Marin on January 24 or 29, 1921. (Marin January 1921)

—Marie Collet testimony, February 16, 1920. (MC (a))

—Marie Collet testimony, December 1920. (MC (b))

—Undated, unsigned internal note starting with the words "Mons qui étudie le service Daubechies." Identified as J. Durieu to Jules Germain, probably early 1921. (Mons 1921)

—Note on calling-card by Father August Mussche, addressee unidentified, probably the archivist Jules Germain; undated, but after February 16, 1920, and before May 2, 1921. (Mussche calling-card)

—five-page manuscript, undated, untitled, unsigned, partly illegible, starting with the words "Jour où la condamnation confirmée." Identified as the archivist Jules Germain's notes of a talk with Father Mussche in 1920 or 1921. (Mussche/Germain)

—"Extrait d'une lettre adressée par Gabrielle Petit à un soldat allemand," Gabrielle Petit to Otto Becker, n.d., probably late March 1916. Sent by Becker to prison director Xavier Marin on December 1, 1919. This document is a typescript copy of a partial transcript by Marin, with a short introduction by him, dated March 2, 1920. (Petit to Becker)

—"Renseignements recueillis par Monsieur Philippart, Secrétaire de la C.D.A. à Tournai sur G. Petit," n.d. but before March 5, 1920. (Philippart (a))

—Henri Philippart, "Remarques", April 13, 1920. (Philippart (b))

—Henri Philippart, "À propos des voyages de Gabrielle Petit à Tournai," July 2, 1920. (Philippart (c))

—Marie-Léonie Van Houte [sic] testimony, July 30, 1919. (Van Houtte)

—Emmanuel Van Tichelen, excerpt from report, March 15, 1920. (Van Tichelen)

File 195

Folder *GQG Français—correspondance Folkestone* (GQG Français)

Folder Contre-espionnage allemand: "Antar Cenobio," pseud. of Léopold Wartel, *La guerre secrète. Mémoires d'un policier de la Rue de Berlaimont*, undated typescript, n.d., 1920 or early 1921. Wartel compiled his report in Leuven prison. It is undated, but he probably wrote it in June 1920 to appeal his life sentence. He was condemned to death on May 4, 1920; the sentence was automatically commuted. His June 1920 appeal was rejected. There is no further information: Wartel's case file was destroyed along with others in a 1940 Luftwaffe bombing (cf. Baclin, *La répression*). (Wartel)

File 196

Folder Police Allemande: Fritz Ball testimony. Document provided by Jan Van der Fraenen. The report is in three parts and carries no date, but the second part is dated December 18, 1918 (Ball report 2 p. 70). Ball sent the reports from The Hague to a judge at the Brussels court of appeal in November 1919 in hopes of being admitted back into Belgium (note added to Ball report 2). On Ball's background, see the note "Rapport de Monsieur l'Abbé Philippot de Namur," n.d., added to report 2. (Ball)

File 248
Folder Police Allemande

(b) Leopold—Klein Papers (LKP)
Von der Lancken to Zimmermann, December 15, 1915. Document provided by Michaël Amara. (L-Z)

(c) War Library
Arthur Hespel, *L'héroïne martyre Gabrielle Petit*, stenciled manuscript with sketches of the sets, n.d., n.p., no publisher mentioned. (Hespel)

2. Brussels, State Archives Annex (depot Joseph Cuvelier) (BSAA)

Archives du tribunal de première instance de Bruxelles. Tribunal civil. Ordonnances, jugements sur requête et répertoires y afférents 1865/1871–1939, section *Jugements sur requête, 1871–1939*; interim injunction, May 23–27, 1919. Research support by Luc Janssen; documents provided by Pierre-Alain Tallier. (May 1919 injunction)
Cour militaire. Dossiers des arrêts 1915–1954, Box 157

3. Brussels, Royal Army Museum (BRAM)

Prints Cabinet (PC): Gabrielle Petit Papers (GP)
Célis Papers (CP)
Belgian GHQ. Document provided by Rob Troubleyn

4. Belgian Army Archives, Evere (Brussels) (BAAE)

Documents provided by Jeroen Huygelier, Rob Troubleyn and Jan Van der Fraenen.
Military file Maurice Victor Gobert, 57.593
Military file Joseph Marie Ange Ide, 242.309
Military file Jules Petit, 144.521
Cavell-Rammler file (C-R), letter by André Brassinne, November 1934. (Brassinne)

5. Brussels City Archives (BCA)

Burgomaster's Cabinet (BC)
File 831, "soldats allemands fusillés." Documents provided by Jan Van der Fraenen. (831)
Instruction Publique, department Beaux-Arts (IP, BA)
File 313 on Petit's 1923 monument (313)
Police 1914–1918 files. Research support by Jean Houssiau
Police Papers
Box 431
Box D 21/47
Population Registers 1910, 1920

6. Brussels, Archives et Musée de la Littérature (BAML)

Adrien Bayet Diary, ML 3546
Georges Eekhoud Diary, ML 2954

7. Brussels, archives of the Rijksdienst voor Oorlogsslachtoffers (RvO)

Documents provided by Gerd De Prins
Louise Pilatte-Petit files, VC 215961 and VC 212847
Hélène Pilatte files, d55232 and ppad54289

8. Brussels, Royal Palace Archives (BRPA)

King's Cabinet, Albert I, 1914–1918 (KC, A 14–18):
—Ministry of the Interior, 280bis, "Extraits des opinions exprimées par différentes personnalites
 de la Belgique occupée sur les principaux problèmes de l'avenir du pays. 1918" (1918 survey)
—Files "Secours accordés, dons"

9. Tournai, Musée du Folklore (TMF)

GP: typescript desciption of 1966 ceremonies, *1er avril 1966—cinquantième anniversaire—
Hommage Gabrielle Petit* (1966 anniversaire)

10. Molenbeek (Brussels) Municipal Archives (MMA)

Research support by Sven Steffens
Population Census 1910, card catalog
Population Registers 1910, *Registres par folio; Registres par rue*

11. Saint-Josse (Brussels) Municipal Archives (StJMA)

Excerpts provided by Robin de Salle
Population Registers 1910 and 1920

12. Schaarbeek (Brussels) Municipal Archives (SMA)

Documents provided by Rob Troubleyn
Typescript flyer, *Commune de Schaarbeek—Communiqué à la Presse. Funérailles solennelles des
Fusillés Gabrielle Petit, Mathieu Bodson & Aimé Smekens* (Communiqué)
"Carton distribué aux enfants des écoles de Schaerbeek," May 29, 1919 (Carton)

13. Institut Sainte Gertrude, Brugelette, Belgium

Documents provided by Pierre Ronvaux
Reverend Sister Marie-Walthère (Berthe Depaquier), Institut de l'Enfant-Jésus, Brugelette,
 unpaginated manuscript notes, two sets, photocopy. The first set is undated but was most
 likely written in the second half of 1923, because it quotes as "recent" a lecture by Maurice
 Barrès held in July 1923, and still refers to Barrès as a living author; he died in December
 1923. The second set of notes is dated April 8, 1940. (MW 1923 and MW 1940)

14. Antwerp, Openbaar Centrum voor Maatschappelijk Welzijn (OCMW)

Eugène Ségard file; summarized by Robert Van Hee

15. Centre d'Études Guerre et Société | Studiecentrum Oorlog en Maatschappij, Brussels (CEGESOMA)

British War Office, *The German police system as applied to military security in war*, unpublished typescript report, 1921. Document provided by Clive Emsley and Benoît Majerus

16. Imperial War Museum, London (IWM)

Walter Kirke Diaries

17. Intelligence Corps Museum, Chicksands, Bedfordshire (ICM)

Research by Jim Beach.
Payne Best Memoir (c1978)

18. Berlin, Bundesarchiv Berlin-Lichterfelde (BBL)

(a) Reichsamt/Reichsministerium des Innern (RI)
R 1501 / 119374 and R 1501 / 119375, *Das Polizeiwesen in den besetzten Gebieten Belgiens*, 2 parts (Polizeiwesen)

(b) Auswärtiges Amt (AA)
With thanks to Isabel Hull for helping me decipher the signatories' initials.
Rechtsabteilung (R 901), Akte R 901/26415: Rechtssachen Allgemein—Begnadigungsangelegenheiten Februar—April 1916 (R 901/26415)

19. Bayerisches Hauptstaatsarchiv München—Kriegsarchiv (BHMK)

Friedrich von Hurt Papers. Research by Ronnie P. Hsia
Personal file Eduard Stoeber. Research by Rainer Hiltermann

20. Author's personal collection

Éditions Veuve Ferdinand Larcier, Brussels, publisher's leaflet for Arthur Deloge's *Gabrielle Petit: Sa Vie et son Oeuvre*, n.d. [1922]. (Publisher's leaflet)

Published Primary Sources

Official documents

Arrondissement de Tournai. Liste des électeurs aux Chambres, Tournai: Casterman, 1883.
Les avis, proclamations et nouvelles de guerre allemands affichés à Bruxelles pendant l'occupation, Brussels: Brian Hill, n.d.
Belgium, *Parliamentary Annals: Senate, 1918–1919, 1920* (PA: S)
Belgium, *Parliamentary Annals: Chamber of Representatives, 1918–1919, 1920, 1927–1928* (PA: CR)
Commission d'enquête sur les violations des règles du droit des gens, des lois et des coutumes de la guerre, ed., *Rapports et documents d'enquête*, Part One, *Rapports sur les attentats commis par*

les troupes allemandes pendant l'invasion et l'occupation de la Belgique, Brussels-Liège: Dewit-Larcier-Thone, 1922, 2 vols

Werner Conze, ed., Quellen zur Geschichte des Parlamentarismus und der politischen Parteien 1. Reihe: Von der konstitutionellen Monarchie zur parlamentischen Republik, Vol. 6, Die Regierung der Volksbeauftragten 1918/19 (Susanne Miller et al., ed.)

"Liste des électeurs à Tournai en 1877," http://www.apis-tornacensis.be/ accessed November 15, 2009

Camille Rousset, ed., Annuaire de la verrerie et de la céramique, Paris, 1907

James Scott, ed., The Proceedings of the Hague Peace Conferences: The Conference of 1899 and 1907, New York: Oxford University Press, 1921

Vatican City, Archivio della Seconda Sezione della Segreteria di Stato, Rapporti con gli Stati: Belgio, 1904–1922, listed in http://www.vaticana.be/regesten/4760.php, accessed July 11, 2011. (VC, ASG, B)

Guido von Frobel, ed., Militär-Wochenblatt, vol. 89 (1904), part 1

Newspapers and periodicals

(a) Clandestine, 1914–1918
L'Âme Belge
La Libre Belgique

(b) After 1918
L'avenir du Tournaisis; research by Pierre Ronvaux
Bulletin officiel de la Fédération nationale des prisonniers politiques de la Guerre, 1919–1927
Le Courrier de l'Escaut; research by Pierre Ronvaux
La Dernière Heure, 1919
Le Droit de l'Employé 1918–1923; research by Florence Loriaux
L'Événement illustré, 1919–1920
L'Exploité, 1919
Le Féminisme chrétien de Belgique, 1919–1921
La Femme belge, 1919–1921
La Gazette, 1919
Haro! 1919–1920
L'Indépendance Belge, 1919
Het Laatste Nieuws, 1918–1923; 1937
La Libre Belgique 1918–1923; 1964
Le Drapeau 1919–1921
La Métropole 1923
La Nation Belge 1919; 1923
Le National Bruxellois 1919
Le Patriote Illustré 1923
Le Peuple 1919, 1929
Revue belge du cinéma 1921; research by Leen Engelen
Le Soir 1918–1923; 1964
De Standaard, 1919; 1937; 2005
Le Vingtième Siècle 1919
't Vlaamsche Land 1937

Chronicles and diaries

Anonymous [George Garnir], Pourquoi Pas? pendant l'occupation. Par un des Trois Moustiquaires. La vie bruxelloise de 1914 à 1918, Brussels: L'Expansion belge, 1919.

Michaël Amara and Hubert Roland, eds, *Gouverner en Belgique occupée: Oscar von der Lancken-Wakenitz—Rapports d'activité 1915-1918. Édition critique*, Brussels-Bern: P.I.E.-Peter Lang, 2004.

Jean-Paul De Cloet, ed., *1914-1918: Oorlog in België*, Ghent: Geschiedkundige Uitgeverij, 2010–2014 (compilation of articles from the Dutch daily *De Nieuwe Rotterdamsche Courant*).

Paul Delandsheere and Alphonse Ooms, *La Belgique sous les Nazis*, Brussels: L'Édition Universelle, n.d., 4 vols.

Charles Gheude, *Nos années terribles 1914-1918*, Brussels: Charles Lamberty, n.d., 3 vols.

Louis Gille, Alphonse Ooms and Paul Delandsheere, *Cinquante mois d'occupation allemande*, Brussels: Albert Dewit, 1919, 4 vols.

Benoît Majerus and Sven Soupart eds, *Journal de guerre de Paul Max: notes d'un Bruxellois 1914-1918*, Brussels: Archives de la Ville de Bruxelles, 2006.

C. Sorgeloos and G. Veirman, "La guerre du silence ou le journal de la Comtesse d'Oultremont," *Revue Belge d'Histoire Militaire* 29 (1991), 123–144 and 209–228.

Thea Sternheim, *Tagebücher 1903-1971*, Thomas Ehrsam and Regula Wyss eds, Vol. 1, Göttingen: Wallstein, 2002.

Paul Struye, *Journal de Guerre 1940-1945*, Thierry Grosbois ed., Brussels: Racine, 2004.

Jules De Thier and Olympe Gilbart, *Liège pendant la Grande Guerre*, Liège: Imprimerie Bénard, 1919, 4 vols.

Charles Tytgat, *Bruxelles sous la botte allemande, de la déclaration de guerre de la Roumanie à la délivrance. Journal d'un journaliste*, Brussels: Imprimerie scientifique Charles Bulens & Cie, 1919.

Auguste Vierset, *Mes souvenirs sur l'occupation allemande en Belgique*, Paris: Plon, 1932.

Karel Van De Woestijne, *Verzameld journalistiek werk*, Ada Deprez ed., Ghent: Cultureel Documentatiecentrum, 1992, Vol. IX.

Books and articles

Anonymous [Renée de Mérode], *Enfance, jeunesse et martyre de Gabrielle Petit, 20 février 1893-1er avril 1916*, Brussels, Veuve Ferdinand Larcier, 1919.

Anonymous ("M.H."), *La vie et la mort d'une jeune héroïne belge: Gabriëlle [sic] Petit*, Antwerp: Opdebeek, n.d. [1920].

Anonymous, *Gabrielle Petit*, Antwerp: Opdebeek, n.d. [1919].

Anonymous [Ferdinand Van Nieuwenhove], *Gabrielle Petit, onze nationale heldin. Geschiedkundige [sic] drama in drij bedrijven*, Geraardsbergen: Victor Van Nieuwenhove, n.d. [early 1920].

(No author named), "Les opérations: première sortie d'Anvers," *Bulletin Belge des Sciences Militaires* 10 (1921), pp. 803–814; 11 (1921), pp. 907–914.

(No author named), *Bruxelles, Louvain*, Clermont-Ferrand: Michelin & Cie, 1921.

(No author named), *Congrès National des ex-Prisonniers et Condamnés Politiques de la Guerre (11, 12 et 13 Novembre 1921): Livre des Comptes-Rendus*, Ixelles-Brussels: no publisher, n.d.

Maurice Allem, ed., *Jules Michelet: pages historiques*, Paris: Garnier, n.d.

José Akersen, *Geteisterd België, of de inval der Duitschers*, Antwerp: Patria, n.d. [1919].

Marcel Anciaux, *Un martyr national: Philippe Baucq*, Brussels: Cercle Saint-Jean de Capistran, 1920.

Kate Atkinson, *Life After Life*, New York-London: Little, Brown, 2013.

Albert Bailly, "La grande fusillée", *Notre Pays: Revue Panoramique Belge* 2: 9 (April 11, 1920), pp 138–140; 2: 10 (April 18, 1920), pp. 156–159.

Willem Ballings (Abbé), *Ter herinnering aan het overbrengen naar Neerpelt op 25 augustus 1919 der stoffelijke overblijfselen van onzen held Jaak Tasset*, Neerpelt: Jacobs & Vonckers, 1919.

Maurice Barrès, *La Glorification de Déroulède à Metz, 16 octobre 1921*, Paris: Ligue des Patriotes, 1921.

Maurice Barrès, "Discours prononcé à Clermont-Ferrand, au nom de l'Académie française, le 7 Juillet 1923," in *Troisième centenaire de Pascal*, Paris: Plon, 1923; special issue 28 of *La Revue Hebdomadaire*.

Émile Béco, *La croisade entreprise contre les mauvais cinémas pendant la guerre*, Turnhout: Brepols, 1919.

Gottfried Benn, "Wie Miss Cavell erschossen wurde", *Gesammelte Werke*, Vol. IV: *Autobiographische und vermischte Schriften*, Dieter Wellershoff ed., Wiesbaden: Limes, 1961, pp. 194–201.

Louis Bertrand, *Souvenirs d'un meneur socialiste*, Brussels: L'Églantine, 1927, 2 vols.

Heinrich Binder, *Spionagezentrale Brüssel. Der Kampf der deutschen Armee mit der belgisch-englischen Spionage und der Meisterspionin Gabrielle Petit*, Hamburg: Hanseatische Verlagsanstalt, 1929.

Victor Bonnevie, *La défense des Belges devant les tribunaux de guerre allemands*, Bruxelles: J. Lebègue & Cie, 1919.

André Brassinne, "Nos maîtres de la *Kommandantur*", *Bulletin Officiel du Touring Club de Belgique* 25: 5 (1919).

Gordon Brown, *Courage: Eight Portraits*, London: Bloomsbury, 2007.

Ernest Claes, *Ik was student* [1957], in id., *Claes Omnibus Drie*, Antwerp-Utrecht: Standaard, 1967.

Paul Colin, *La Belgique après la guerre*, Rome: Rassegna Internazionale, n.d. [1921].

Henri Davignon, *Souvenirs d'Un Écrivain Belge*, Paris: Plon, 1954.

Jeanne De Beir, *In The Eagle's Claws*, Bruges, n.d. [c. 1928].

Marie de Croÿ, *Souvenirs de la princesse Marie de Croÿ 1914–1918*, Paris: Plon, 1933.

Hippolyte Delehaye, *Les légendes hagiographiques* [1905], 3d edn, Brussels: Société des Bollandistes, 1927.

Louis de Lichtervelde, *Avant l'orage (1911–1914)*, Brussels: L'Édition Universelle, n.d. [1938].

Arthur Deloge, *Nos P'tits (chant du navire-école naufragé)*, n.p.: no publisher, n.d. [c. 1906].

Arthur Deloge, *La Demoiselle de Magasin. Roman*, Brussels: Imprimerie de la Centrale Sociale, 1914.

Arthur Deloge, *Conduire les Hommes: ce que tout gradé doit savoir*, Paris-Nancy: Berger-Levrault, "Librairie Militaire" series, 1917; reprinted Brussels: Jos van Melle, 1918; Dutch translation: *Mannen aanvoeren. Wat elke gegradeerde weten moet*, 1918.

Arthur Deloge, *Le caporal Trésignies, ouvrier d'usine, héros du Pont-Brûlé*, 1st edn. 1921; 2nd edn, 1922 (*Les âmes héroïques* Part 17).

Arthur Deloge, *Gabrielle Petit: Sa Vie et son Oeuvre*. Brussels: Veuve Ferdinand Larcier, 1922.

Paulo de Moffarts (Baroness), *Un enfant belge fusillé à Lille: Léon Trulin*, Paris-Brussels: Desclée-De Brouwer, n.d.

Marc Didden, *Een gehucht in een moeras: Brusselse verhalen*, Antwerp: Luster, 2013.

Jean d'Osta, *Dictionnaire historique et anecdotique des rues de Bruxelles*, Brussels: Le Livre, 1995.

Eloy Druart, *Franz Merjay et sa famille*, Brussels: Revue des Arts et des Livres, 1921.

Marie d'Ursel Spoelbergh de Lovenjoel (vicomtesse de), *La Belgique Charitable*, 1904.

Georges Eekhoud, "Des Hommes", *Clarté*, March 1, 1920, p. 1.

George Eliot, *Middlemarch* [1871], W.J. Harvey ed., Middlesex: Penguin, [1965] 1977.

Friedrich Felger, "Das Netz über Belgien," in Von Lettow-Vorbeck, *Die Weltkriegsspionage*, pp. 440–454.

René Foucart, "Les Oeuvres de Charité en 1914–1916," in *Almanach Rétrospectif 1917: Actualités 1914–1916, 2ième année*, Brussels: Les éditions Brian Hill, n.d.

Jean Francis, *La chanson des rues de Molenbeek-Saint-Jean*, Brussels: Louis Musin, 1975.

Henri Frick et al., *Histoire de la Commune de Saint-Josse pendant la Guerre Mondiale et l'Occupation allemande 1914–1918*, Brussels: A. Lesigne, 1920.

Jules Germain, "Autographe de Gabrielle Petit. Quatrième rapport au Grand Quartier Général anglais", *Bulletin de la Commission des Archives de la Guerre*, tome I, 1921–1924, pp. 136–138.

Hugh Gibson, *A journal from our legation in Belgium. A diplomatic diary*, New York: Doubleday, 1917.

C. Godelaine, *Monseigneur Keesen, een groot en populair limburger. 1841–1923*, Maaseik: Van der Donck-Robyns, 1928.

Pierre Goemaere, *Histoire de la Libre Belgique clandestine*, Brussels: La Libre Belgique, n.d. (2 editions in 1919).

Abraham Hans (writing as A. Du Jardin), *Gabrielle Petit, l'héroïne nationale*, Antwerp: L. Opdebeek, n.d. [1920 or 1921].

Abraham Hans (writing as Jan Verbeke), *Gabrielle Petit, onze nationale heldin*, Antwerp, Opdebeek, n.d. [1920 or 1921].

Adolphe Hardy, "Une héroïne ardennaise: Elise Grandprez," *La femme belge. Revue de questions morales, sociales, littéraires et artistiques* 3: 1 (May 1919), pp. 15–26.

Magnus Hirschfeld, *Sittengeschichte des Weltkrieges*, 1930, reprint as *Sittengeschichte des Ersten Weltkrieges*, Hanau a.M.: Schustek, 1966.

Georges Hostelet, "Nurse Cavell: the Story of her Trial told by One of the Condemned," *The XIXth Century and After* 35 (January–June 1919), pp. 523–547.

Sadi Kirschen, *Devant les conseils de guerre allemands*, Brussels: Rossel & Fils, 1919.

Henry Landau, *All's Fair. The story of the British secret service behind the German lines*, New York: Putnam, 1934.

Henry Landau, *Secrets of the White Lady*, New York: Putnam, 1935.

Laurent Lombard, *Zone de mort*, Stavelot: Vox Patriae, n.d. [1938].

Laurent Lombard, *Le drame de la villa des hirondelles*, Stavelot: Éditions Vox Patriae, Collection Historique 1914–1918, s.d. [February 1939].

René Lyr (pseudonym of René Vanderhaeghe, 1887–1957), *Nos héros morts pour la patrie. L'épopée belge de 1914 à 1918 (histoire et documentation). Tableau d'honneur des officiers, sous-officiers, soldats, marins et civils tombés pour la défense des foyers belges*, Brussels: Van Der Elst, 1920.

Fritz Masoin, *Après la Victoire*, Brussels: A. Breuer, 1919.

Fernand Mayence, *La Correspondance de S.E. le Cardinal Mercier avec le gouvernement général allemand pendant l'occupation 1914–1918*, Brussels: Albert Dewit, and Paris: Gabalda, 1919.

Gustav Mayer, *Erinnerungen. Vom Journalisten zum Historiker der deutschen Arbeiterbewegung*, Zürich: Europaverlag, 1949.

John McCain, with Mark Salter, *Character Is Destiny: Inspiring Stories Every Young Person Should Know and Every Adult Should Remember*, New York: Random House, 2005.

Oscar E. Millard and Auguste Vierset, *Burgomaster Max: the Epic Story of Brussels during the War*, London: Hutchinson & Co., 1936.

Jaime Mir, *Mémoires d'un condamné à mort (1914–1918)*, Paris: Plon, 1926.

Gem Moriaud, *Louise de Bettignies*, Paris: Tallandier, 1928.

Allan Nevins ed., *The letters and journal of Brand Whitlock*, New York-London: Appleton, 1936.

Walter Nicolai, *Geheime Mächte. Internationale Spionage und ihre Bekämpfung im Weltkrieg und Heute*, 2nd edn, Leipzig: F. Koehler, 1924.

Jean Nysten (Abbé), *Comment ils meurent*, Liège: H. Dessain, n.d. [1920].

Emile Paquet (Abbé), *Gabrielle Petit*, Tournai-Paris: Casterman, 1920.

Alex Pasquier (writing as Alix Pasquier), *L'occupation allemande. Dans les ténèbres*, Paris: Eugène Figuière et Cie, 1921.

Henri Pirenne, "Le pangermanisme et la Belgique," *Académie Royale de Belgique. Bulletin de la classe des lettres et des sciences morales et politiques* 5 (May 1919), pp. 339–373.

L. Pousset, *La geôle des détenus politiques pendant l'occupation 1914–1918. Dessins exécutés par L. Pousset pendant son séjour à la prison de St-Gilles, 1916–1917*, Brussels, n.d. [1919].

G. Preud'homme, "Un jésuite résistant à Tournai (1915–1918). Edition du rapport du P.H. Philippart", *Mémoires de la Société Royale d'Histoire et d'Archéologie de Tournai*, vol. 4, 1983–1984, pp. 367–427.

Madame Prud'homme-Malherbe, *Gabrielle Petit*, Averbode: Bonne Presse, 1940. (*Presto Film. Hebdomadaire pour la Jeunesse*, no. 286.)

G. Raal [Lode Opdebeek], *Gaby, het Vliegenierstertje*, booklet 2 in the series *Ons Heldenboek: Oorlogsverhalen* [Our Book of Heroes: War Stories], by Abraham Hans and G. Raal, Antwerp: 1919.

Antoine Redier, *La Guerre des Femmes. Histoire de Louise de Bettignies et de ses compagnes*, Paris, Les Éditions de la Vraie France, 1924.

Philip Scheidemann, *Memoiren eines Sozialdemokraten*, Dresden: C. Reissner, 1928.

Theodoor Sevens, *Gabrielle Petit. Vaderlandsch gedicht en levensschets*, Antwerp: Lode Opdebeek, 1920.

A.F. Stocq [abbé Adolphe Stocq], *Gabrielle Petit. Drame en 5 tableaux*, Nivelles: Impr. Louis Havaux-Houdart, 1st edn, 1919; 2nd and 3rd edn, 1920.

Eduard Stoeber, "Vier Jahre Feldjustizbeamter," in Von Lettow-Vorbeck, *Die Weltkriegsspionage*, pp. 384–397.

Charles Tytgat, *Acta Martyrum: Nos fusillés (recruteurs et espions)*, Brussels: Imprimerie scientifique Charles Bulens & Cie, 1919.

Jean Van Audenhove, *Les rues d'Anderlecht*, Brussels: Cercle d'Archéologie, Folklore et Histoire d'Anderlecht, 1990.

Louise Van den Plas, "Les rapports des enfants avec les domestiques," in *Memorie presentate al IIe congresso internazionale di educazione familiare, Milano, Settembre 1906*, Milan: L.F. Cogliati, pp. 23–26.

Louise Van den Plas, "Notre campagne suffragiste," *Le Féminisme chrétien de Belgique* 10: 1–2 (April–May 1919), pp. 7–17.

Louise Van den Plas and Jane Brigode, "Lettre ouverte adressée aux membres du Gouvernement par la Fédération belge pour le suffrage des femmes," December 1918; reprint in *Le Féminisme chrétien de Belgique* 10:1–2 (April–May 1919), pp. 17–20.

Louise Van den Plas, "Victoire suffragiste," *La femme belge* 3: 1 (May, 1919), pp. 12–14.

Cyrille Van Overbergh, *La Classe Sociale*, Brussels: Oscar Schepens, 1905.

Cyrille Van Overbergh, *Le vote politique des femmes*, Brussels: Albert Dewit, 1914.

Cyrille Van Overbergh, *Gabrielle Petit, héroïne nationale*, Brussels: Syndicat national des employés, 1919.

Cyrille Van Overbergh, "Gabrielle Petit, Martyre," *La femme belge* 3: 1 (May, 1919), pp. 4–11.

Cyrille Van Overbergh, *Le programme de l'électrice communale*, Brussels, 1921.

Paul von Lettow-Vorbeck, ed., *Die Weltkriegsspionage*, Munich: J. Moser, 1931.

Heinrich Wandt, *Etappe Gent: Streiflichter zum Zusammenbruch*, 2nd edn, Berlin and Vienna: Aegis, 1926.

Brand Whitlock, *Belgium: A Personal Narrative*, New York: Appleton, 1919, 2 vols.

Film, television, and radio

Feature films

Armand Du Plessy, dir., *La Libre Belgique et l'héroïque Gabrielle Petit*, Brussels: Compagnie Belge des Films Cinématographiques, 1921.

Francis Martin, dir., *Femme Belge: Gabrielle Petit*, Brussels: Les Productions Cinématographiques Belges, 1928.

Newsreels

Translation des restes de Gabrielle Petit, de Bodson & de Smekens (fusillés par les Allemands). Pathé newsreel, June 1, 1919.

Yser Journal, footage of Tournai ceremony, September 21, 1919 (Copy at Cinematek, Brussels).

Fox Movietone newsreel, footage of 1949 anniversary of Petit's execution (Copy at Cinematek, Brussels).

Television

Radio Télévision Belge (RTB), *14–18*, Henri Mordant, dir., co-presented by Jacques Bredael; episode "85e et 86e semaine de la guerre," March 28, 1966, episode directed by Michel Stamechkine.

Radio

VRT-Radio 1, "Een blauwe mantel en rijglaarsjes," episode in the series *Alaska* (Annick Lesage and Wim Vangrootloon, dirs.), April 1, 2006.

Secondary Sources

Books and articles

Maartje M. Abbenhuis, *The Art of Staying Neutral: the Netherlands in the First World War, 1914–1918*: Amsterdam University Press, 2006.

Jean-Pierre Albert, "Du martyr à la star. Les métamorphoses des héros nationaux," in Pierre Centlivres, Daniel Fabre, and Françoise Zonabend, eds, *La fabrique des héros*, theme issue 12 of *Cahiers d'ethnologie de la France*, Paris: Maison des Sciences de l'Homme, 1999, pp. 11–32.

Michaël Amara, *Les Belges à l'épreuve de l'exil. Les réfugiés belges de la Première Guerre Mondiale en France, au Royaume-Uni et aux Pays-Bas*, Brussels: Éditions de l'Université Libre, 2008.

Benedict Anderson, *Imagined Communities: Reflections on the Origin and Spread of Nationalism*, revised edn, London-New York: Verso, 1991.

Christopher M. Andrew, *Her Majesty's Secret Service. The Making of the British Intelligence Community*, New York: Viking, [1985] 1986.

Stéphane Audoin-Rouzeau, *Cinq deuils de guerre 1914–1918*, Paris: Noêsis, 2001.

Stéphane Audoin-Rouzeau and Christophe Prochasson, eds, *Sortir de la Grande Guerre. Le monde et l'après-1918*, Paris: Tallandier, 2008.

Judith Tydor Baumel-Schwartz, *Perfect Heroes: The World War II Parachutists and the Making of Israeli Collective Memory*, Madison: University of Wisconsin Press, 2010.

Jim Beach, " 'Intelligent civilians in uniform': the British Expeditionary Force's Intelligence Corps officers, 1914–1918," *War and Society* 27: 1 (2008), pp. 1–22.

Jim Beach, *Haig's Intelligence: GHQ and the German Army, 1916–1918*, Cambridge: Cambridge University Press, 2013.

Annette Becker, *Les monuments aux morts: patrimoine et mémoire de la Grande Guerre*, Paris: Errance, 1988.

Annette Becker, "Le culte des morts, entre mémoire et oubli" in Stéphane Audoin-Rouzeau and Jean-Jacques Becker, eds, *Encyclopédie de la Grande Guerre 1914–1918. Histoire et culture*, Paris: Bayard, 2004, pp. 1099–1112

Annette Becker, *Les cicatrices rouges. France et Belgique occupées, 1914–1918*, Paris: Fayard, 2010.

Edward Berenson, *Heroes of Empire: Five Charismatic Men and the Conquest of Africa*, Berkeley: University of California Press, 2011.

Henri Bernard, *L'An 14 ou la campagne des illusions*, Brussels: La Renaissance du Livre, 1983.

Marie-Thérèse Bitsch, *La Belgique entre la France et l'Allemagne 1905–1914*, Paris: Publications de la Sorbonne, 1994.

Bruno Cabanes and Guillaume Piketty, eds, *Sorties de guerre au XXième siècle*, theme issue of *Histoire@Politique* 3, Nov–Dec. 2007.

Pierre Centlivres, Daniel Fabre, and Françoise Zonabend, eds, *La fabrique des héros*, theme issue 12 of *Cahiers d'ethnologie de la France*, Paris: Maison des Sciences de l'Homme, 1999.

Christophe Charle, *La crise des sociétés impériales. Allemagne, France, Grande-Bretagne 1900–1940*, Paris: Seuil, 2001.

Ria Christens et al., "From enlightened tutelage to means of emancipation. The educational function of Catholic children's and youth literature in Flanders in the 19th and 20th centuries," in Jan De Maeyer et al., *Religion, Children's Literature and Modernity in Western Europe, 1750–2000*, Leuven: Leuven University Press, 2005, pp. 51–76.

Jenneke Christiaens, "Stoute kinderen achter slot en grendel: het vaderlijk tuchtigingsrecht in de ontstaansgeschiedenis van de 19de-eeuwse kinderbescherming," *Tijdschrift voor Sociale Geschiedenis* 2 (1994), pp. 149–169.

Stéphanie Claisse and Thierry Lemoine, eds, *Comment (se) sortir de la Grande Guerre? Regards sur quelques pays 'vainqueurs': la Belgique, la France et la Grande-Bretagne*, Paris: L'Harmattan, 2005.

Martin Conway, "Building the Christian City: Catholics and Politics in Inter-War Francophone Belgium," *Past and Present* 1990, pp. 117–151.

Martin Conway, *The Sorrows of Belgium: Liberation and Political Reconstruction, 1944–1947*, Oxford: Oxford University Press, 2012.

Alain Corbin, *Le monde retrouvé de Louis-François Pinagot: sur les traces d'un inconnu (1798–1876)*, Paris: Flammarion, 1998.

Margaret H. Darrow, *French Women and the First World War: War Stories of the Home Front*, Oxford: Berg, 2000.

Venita Datta, "Sur les boulevards: la représentation de Jeanne d'Arc dans le théâtre populaire," *Clio* 24: 2 (2006), pp. 125–147.

Venita Datta, *Heroes and Legends of Fin-de-Siècle France: Gender, Politics, and the Nation*, Cambridge-New York: Cambridge University Press, 2011.

Jos De Belder, "Socio-professionele structuren," in Jean Stengers, ed., *Brussel: groei van een hoofdstad*, Antwerp: Mercatorfonds, 1979, pp. 227–234.

Emmanuel Debruyne, *La guerre secrète des espions belges 1940–1944*, Brussels: Racine, 2008.

Emmanuel Debruyne, "Patriotes désintéressés ou espions vénaux? Agents et argent en Belgique et en France occupées, 1914–1918", *Guerres mondiales et conflits contemporains* 232 (October–November 2008), pp. 25–45.

Emmanuel Debruyne and Laurence Van Ypersele, "Le monument à Omer Lefèvre ou l'engagement clandestin sous les traits de l'hommage public." *La France et la Belgique occupées (1914–1918): regards croisés. Cahiers de l'IRHiS* 7 (2009), pp. 66–75.

Emmanuel Debruyne and Jehanne Paternostre, *La résistance au quotidien 1914–1918: témoignages inédits*, Brussels: Racine, 2009.

Emmanuel Debruyne, "Sortir de l'ombre. Des combattants clandestins en quête de reconnaissance," in Tallier and Nefors, *When the Guns Fall Silent*, 2010, pp. 449–480.

Emmanuel Debruyne and Laurence Van Ypersele, *Je serai fusillé demain. Les dernières lettres des patriotes belges et français fusillés par l'occupant, 1914–1918*, Brussels: Racine, 2011.

Elien Declercq and Saartje Vanden Borre, "Cultural integration of Belgian migrants in northern France (1870–1914): a study of popular songs," *French History* 27: 1 (March 2013), pp. 91–108.

Pierre Decock, *La Dame Blanche. Un réseau de renseignements de la Grande Guerre*, Raleigh, NC: Lulu, 2011.

Nel De Muêlenaere, "An uphill battle: campaigning for the militarization of Belgium, 1870–1914," *Journal of Belgian History* XLII, 2012, 4, pp. 144–179.

Annie Deperchin, "Un établissement pénitentiaire pendant la Grande Guerre: Loos", *Revue du Nord* LXXX, theme issue *1914–1918, guerre et occupation* 325 (1998), pp. 337–354.

Evelyn De Roodt, *Oorlogsgasten: vluchtelingen en krijgsgevangenen in Nederland tijdens de Eerste Wereldoorlog*, Amsterdam: Europese Bibliotheek, 2000.

René Deruyk, *Louise de Bettignies: résistante lilloise 1880–1918*, Lille: Éditions de la Voix du Nord, 1998.

Sophie De Schaepdrijver, "Regulated prostitution in nineteenth-century Brussels: a policy and its implementation," *Historical Social Research/Historische Sozialforschung* 37 (1986), pp. 89–108.

Sophie De Schaepdrijver, "Occupation, propaganda, and the idea of Belgium," in Aviel Roshwald and Richard Stites, eds, *European Culture in the Great War: the Arts, Entertainment, and Propaganda, 1914–1918*, Cambridge: Cambridge University Press, 1999, pp. 267–294.

Sophie De Schaepdrijver, "Death is elsewhere: the shifting locus of tragedy in Belgian First World War literature", *Yale French Studies* 102, *Belgian Memories*, Catherine Labio, ed., 2002, pp. 94–114.

Sophie De Schaepdrijver, "Les dangers de l'idéalisme: souvenirs contestés de l'occupation allemande en Belgique," in John Horne ed., *Démobilisations culturelles après la Grande Guerre*, Péronne: Historial de la Grande Guerre, 2002, pp. 114–127.

Sophie De Schaepdrijver, *La Belgique et la Première Guerre Mondiale*, Frankfurt, P.I.E.-Peter Lang, 2004.

Sophie De Schaepdrijver, "An outsider inside: the occupation diary of Georges Eekhoud," in Jaumain et al., *Une guerre totale*, pp. 79–95.

Sophie De Schaepdrijver, *"We who are so Cosmopolitan": The War Diary of Constance Graeffe, 1914–1915*, Brussels: Archives Générales du Royaume, 2008. (*Studies on World War One*, 14)

Sophie De Schaepdrijver, "Vile Times: Belgian interwar literature and the German occupation of 1914–1918," in Tallier and Nefors, *When the Guns Fall Silent*, pp. 535–554.

Sophie De Schaepdrijver, "Belgium," in Horne, ed., *A Companion to World War I*, London: Wiley-Blackwell, 2010, pp. 386–402.

Sophie De Schaepdrijver, " 'That Theory of Races': Henri Pirenne on the unfinished business of the Great War," *Revue Belge d'Histoire Contemporaine* 41 (2011), pp. 3–4, 533–552.

Sophie De Schaepdrijver, "Military Occupations, Political Imaginations, and the First World War," *First World War Studies* 4: 1 (March 2013), 1–5.

Sophie De Schaepdrijver and Emmanuel Debruyne, "*Sursum Corda*: the underground press in occupied Belgium, 1914–1918," *First World War Studies*, 4: 1 (March 2013), pp. 23–38.

Sophie De Schaepdrijver, "Populations under occupation," in Jay Winter, ed., *Cambridge History of the First World War*, Cambridge-New York: Cambridge University Press, 2013, vol. III, Chapter 10, pp. 476–504, 1280–1285.

Céline Detournay, *La Grande Guerre sous le regard de l'élite tournaisienne occupée: contribution à la culture de guerre*, Brussels: Archives Générales du Royaume, 2003 (*Studies on World War One*, 10).

Robert Devleeshouwer, *Les Belges et le danger de guerre 1910–1914*, Leuven: Nauwelaerts, 1958.

Jan De Volder, *Benoît XV et la Belgique durant la Grande Guerre*, Brussels-Rome: Institut Historique Belge de Rome, 1996.

Denise de Weerdt, *De vrouwen van de Eerste Wereldoorlog*, Ghent: Stichting Mens en Kultuur, 1990.

Renée Dresse, *La Centrale Nationale des Employés. Aperçu historique 1912–1980*, Brussels: Centre d'Animation et de Recherche en Histoire Ouvrière et Populaire (CARHOP), n.d.

Mathilde Dubesset and Michelle Zancarini-Fournel, "Le couvent-ouvroir, substitut de la puissance paternelle," in idem, *Parcours de femmes: réalités et représentations, Saint-Étienne (1880–1950)*, Lyon: Presses Universitaires de Lyon, 1993.

Anne Duménil, "De la guerre de mouvement à la guerre de positions: les combattants allemands," in John Horne, ed., *Vers la guerre totale: le tournant de 1914–1915*, pp. 53–76.

Michel Dumoulin, "L'entrée dans le XXe siècle, 1905–1918" in Dumoulin et al., *Nouvelle Histoire de Belgique* Vol. 2: *1905–1950*, Brussels: Complexe, 2006, pp. 3–167.

Leen Engelen and Marjan Sterckx, "Herinneringen in steen en op papier. Monumenten en prentbriefkaarten voor twee heldinnen van de Eerste Wereldoorlog: Gabrielle Petit en Edith Cavell," *Volkskunde* 111: 4 (2010), pp. 379–403

Anne Eriksen, "Être ou agir ou le dilemme de l'héroïne," in Centlivres et al., *La fabrique des héros*, pp. 149–164.

Frances Finnegan, *Do Penance or Perish: A Study of Magdalene Asylums in Ireland*, Piltown, Co. Kilkenny: Congrave Press, 2001.

Emmanuel Gerard, *De christelijke arbeidersbeweging in België 1891–1991*, Leuven: University Press, 1991, 2 vols.

Adrian Gregory, *The Last Great War. British Society and the First World War*, Cambridge: Cambridge University Press, 2008.

Éliane Gubin, "La grande ville, un lieu féminin. L'exemple de Bruxelles avant 1914," in id. and Jean-Pierre Nandrin, eds, *La ville et les femmes en Belgique*, Brussels: Publications des Facultés universitaires Saint-Louis, 1993, pp. 77–96.

Éliane Gubin and Leen Van Molle, *Femmes et politique en Belgique*, Brussels: Racine, 1997.

Éliane Gubin and Valérie Piette, "Les employées à Bruxelles (XIXe s.–1960) ou la victoire de la travailleuse indésirable," in Sylvette Denèfle, *Femmes et villes*, Tours: Presses Universitaires François-Rabelais, 2004, pp. 379–398.

Éliane Gubin et al., *Dictionnaire des femmes belges, XIX° et XX° siècles*, Brussels: Racine, 2006.

Éliane Gubin, *Choisir l'histoire des femmes*, Brussels: Éditions de l'Université de Bruxelles, 2007.

Jonathan Gumz, "Norms of war and the Austro-Hungarian encounter with Serbia, 1914–1918," in Sophie De Schaepdrijver, ed., *Military Occupations in the First World War*, special issue of *First World War Studies* 4: 1 (March 2013), pp. 97–110.

Henri Haag, *Le comte Charles de Broqueville, Ministre d'Etat, et les luttes pour le pouvoir (1910–1940)*, Louvain-la-Neuve-Brussels: Collège Erasme-Nauwelaerts, 1990, 2 volumes.

Camille Hanlet, *Les écrivains belges contemporains de langue française 1800–1946*, Liège: H. Dessain, 1946, 2 vols.

June Hargrove, *Les Statues de Paris. La représentation des grands hommes dans les rues et sur les places de Paris*, Antwerp: Fonds Mercator, 1989. English-language original: *The Statues of Paris: An Open-Air Pantheon. The History of Monuments to Great Men*, New York: Vendome Press, 1989.

John Horne and Alan Kramer, *German Atrocities 1914: A History of Denial*, New Haven and London: Yale University Press, 2001.

John Horne, ed., *Démobilisations culturelles après la Grande Guerre*, Péronne Historial de la Grande Guerre, 2002.

John Horne, "Public opinion and politics," in id., ed., *A Companion*, pp. 279–294.

John Horne, ed., *A Companion to World War I*, London: Wiley-Blackwell, 2010.

Isabel V. Hull, *Absolute Destruction. Military Culture and the Practices of War in Imperial Germany*. Ithaca-London: Cornell University Press, 2005.

Serge Jaumain et al., eds, *Une guerre totale? La Belgique dans la Première Guerre mondiale*, Brussels, Archives Générales du Royaume, 2005 (*Studies on World War One*, 11).

Serge Jaumain et al., *Brussel 14–18: Een stad in oorlog, dag na dag* (Brussels, CIRHIBRU, 2005).

Keith Jeffery, *MI6: The History of the Secret Intelligence Service 1909–1949*, London: Bloomsbury Academic, 2010.

Élise Julien, *Paris, Berlin. La mémoire de la guerre 1914–1933*, Rennes: Presses Universitaires de Rennes, 2009.

John Keegan, *The First World War*, New York: Knopf, 1999.

Thomas W. Laqueur, "Memory and Naming in the Great War," in John R. Gillis, ed., *Commemorations: the Politics of National Identity*, Princeton University Press, 1994, pp. 150–167.

Yvon Leblicq and Machteld De Metsenaere, "De groei," in Jean Stengers., ed., *Brussel: groei van een hoofdstad*, Antwerp: Mercatorfonds, 1979, pp. 167–177.

Fernand Lehouck, "De 'grote' vakbonden in België tijdens Wereldoorlog I", *Belgisch tijdschrift voor militaire geschiedenis* 25 (1983), pp. 149–166; 26 (1984), pp. 149–180.

Jean-Yves Le Naour, "Femmes tondues et répression des 'femmes à Boches' en 1918," *Revue d'Histoire Moderne et Contemporaine* 47: 1 (2000), pp. 148–158.

Jean-Yves Le Naour, "Le suffrage des morts ou l'impossible reconstruction politique," in Stéphanie Claisse and Thierry Lemoine, eds, *Comment (se) sortir de la Grande Guerre? Regards sur quelques pays 'vainqueurs': la Belgique, la France et la Grande-Bretagne*, Paris: L'Harmattan, 2005, pp. 77–88.

Mirande Lucien, *Eekhoud le rauque*, Villeneuve d'Ascq: Presses Universitaires du Septentrion, 1999.

Karl Mair, *Der Traum vom Glück: Die kühnen Projekte des Thomas Gillitzer in Rosenheim um 1900*, Stadt Rosenheim Stadtarchiv, 2002.

Michel Manteleers, *Kroniek van een Gesellenverein in de Pletinckxstraat 1888–1918: de Duitse missie in Brussel*, Brussels: Christelijke Sociale Werken, 2002.

Sally Marks, *Innocent Abroad: Belgium at the Paris Peace Conference of 1919*, Chapel Hill: University of North Carolina Press, 1981.

Kevin McAleer, *Duelling: The Cult of Honour in Fin-de-Siècle Germany*, Princeton: Princeton University Press, 1995.

Benoît Majerus, *Occupations et logiques policières. La police bruxelloise en 1914–1918 et 1940–1945*, Brussels: Académie Royale de Belgique, 2007.

Sarah Maza, *Violette Nozière: A Story of Murder in 1930s Paris*, Berkeley: University of California Press, 2011.

Ilse Meseberg-Haubold, *Der Widerstand Kardinal Merciers gegen die deutsche Besetzung Belgiens 1914–1918: ein Beitrag zur politischen Rolle des Katholizismus im ersten Weltkrieg*, Frankfurt am Main-Bern: Peter Lang, 1982.

George Mosse, *Fallen Soldiers: Reshaping the Memory of the World Wars*, New York-Oxford: Oxford University Press, 1990.

Karma Nabulsi, *Traditions of War: Occupation, Resistance, and the Law*, Oxford: Oxford University Press, 1999.

Philippe Nivet, *La France occupée 1914–1918*, Paris: Armand Colin, 2011.

Michael Occleshaw, *Armour against Fate. British Military Intelligence in the First World War*, London: Columbus Books, 1989.

Raymond Olbrechts, "La population", in Ernest Mahaim, *La Belgique restaurée: étude sociologique*, Brussels: Maurice Lamertin, 1926, pp. 3–66.

Mona Ozouf, *La fête révolutionnaire 1789–1799*, Paris: Gallimard, 1976.

Justine Picardie, *Coco Chanel: The Legend and the Life*, New York: HarperCollins, 2010.

Katie Pickles, *Transnational Outrage: The Death and Commemoration of Edith Cavell*, London: Palgrave Macmillan, 2007.

Valérie Piette, *Domestiques et servantes: des vies sous condition. Essai sur le travail domestique en Belgique au 19ième siècle*, Brussels: Académie Royale de Belgique, 2000.

Valérie Piette and Serge Jaumain eds, *Bruxelles en '14-'18: la guerre au quotidien*, Brussels: La Fonderie, 2005.

Henri Pirenne, *La Belgique et la guerre mondiale*, Paris-New Haven: Presses Universitaires de France—Yale University Press (Carnegie Series in the Economic and Social History of the War, James Shotwell ed.), 1928. Reprint in id., *Histoire de Belgique des origines à nos jours*, Brussels: La Renaissance du Livre, 1975, Part V.

Markus Pöhlmann, "German intelligence at war 1914–1918", *The Journal of Intelligence History* 5: 2 (Winter, 2005), pp. 25–54.

Tammy M. Proctor, *Female Intelligence: Women and Espionage in the First World War*, New York: New York University Press, 2003.

Tammy M. Proctor, *Civilians in a World at War, 1914–1918*, New York: New York University Press, 2010.

Antoine Prost, "Les monuments aux morts," in Pierre Nora ed., *Les Lieux de mémoire* vol. 1: *La République*, Paris: Gallimard, 1984, pp. 195–225.

Antoine Prost, "Les cimetières militaires de la Grande Guerre, 1914–1940," *Le Mouvement Social* 237 (October-December 2011), theme issue *Cimetières et politique*, Danièle Tartakowsky, ed., pp. 135–151.

Anson Rabinbach, *The Human Motor. Energy, Fatigue and the Origins of Modernity*, Berkeley: University of California Press, 1992.

James C. Robertson, "*Dawn* (1928): Edith Cavell and Anglo-German relations," *Historical Journal of Film, Radio and Television* 4: 1 (1984), pp. 15–28.

Hubert Roland, *La "colonie" littéraire allemande en Belgique 1914–1918*, Brussels: Labor, 2003

Pierre Ronvaux, *Gabrielle Petit: La mort en face*, Izegem: Illustra, 1994.

Rainer Rumold and O.K. Werckmeister, *The Ideological Crisis of Expressionism: The Literary and Artistic German War Colony in Belgium 1914–1918*, Columbia, SC.: Camden House, 1990.

Peter Scholliers and Frank Daelemans, "Standards of living and standards of health in wartime Belgium," in Richard Wall and Jay Winter, eds, *The Upheaval of War: Family, Work and Welfare in Europe, 1914–1918*, Cambridge: Cambridge University Press, 1988, pp. 139–158.

James J. Sheehan, *Where have all the soldiers gone? The transformation of modern Europe*, Boston-New York: Houghton Mifflin, 2008.

James M. Smith, *Ireland's Magdalen Laundries and the Nation's Architecture of Containment*, Notre Dame, IN: University of Notre Dame Press, 2007.

Christelle Snider, "Propagande, vandalisme et oubli: la statue d'Edith Cavell d'une guerre à l'autre," in Philippe Chassaigne and Jean-Marc Largeaud, eds, *Villes en guerre 1914–1945*, Paris: Armand Colin, 2004, pp. 285–295.

Christy Jo Snider, "Patriots and pacifists: the rhetorical debate about peace, pacifism, and internationalism, 1914–1930," *Rhetoric and Public Affairs* 8: 1 (Spring 2005), pp. 59–83.

Diana Souhami, *Edith Cavell*, London: Quercus, 2010.

Jean Stengers, "L'entrée en guerre de la Belgique," *Guerres mondiales et conflits contemporains* 179 (1995), pp. 13–33.

Pierre Stéphany, *Les années '20–'30: la Belgique entre les deux guerres*, Brussels: Legrain, 1983, 2 vols.

Pierre Stéphany, *Des Belges très occupés 1940–1945*, Brussels: Racine, 2005.

Pierre-Alain Tallier, *Service des prisons. Bureau allemand de la prison de Saint-Gilles 1914–1918*, Brussels: Archives Générales du Royaume, 1998.

Pierre-Alain Tallier, "Les "Archives de la Guerre" et les fonds associés conservés aux Archives Générales du Royaume," in Richard Boijen, eds, *La Belgique et la Première Guerre Mondiale. État des sources—État de la recherche*, Brussels: Archives Générales du Royaume, 2002 (*Studies on World War One*, 9), pp. 25–38.

Pierre-Alain Tallier and Patrick Nefors, eds, *When the Guns Fall Silent: Proceedings of the International Colloquium, Brussels, November 2008*, Brussels: Archives Générales du Royaume, 2010 (*Studies on World War One*, 18).

Maurice-Albert Tasnier and Raoul Van Overstraeten, *Les opérations militaires*, Brussels: Bertels, 1923 (*La Belgique et la Guerre*, III).

Suzanne Tassier, *L'histoire de la Guerre Mondiale. Pour un office de la guerre mondiale et un office de documentation contemporaine*, Brussels: Institut Solvay, 1944.

Jens Thiel, *Menschenbassin Belgien. Anwerbung, Deportation und Zwangsarbeit im Ersten Weltkrieg*, Essen: Klartext Verlag, 2007.

Maria Todorova, *Bones of Contention: The Living Archive of Vasil Levski and the Making of Bulgaria's National Hero*, Budapest and New York: Central European University Press, 2009.

Toon Toelen, *De grote en kleine geschiedenis van de kassei / La grande et petite histoire de la chaussée*, Brussels: Archief en Museum voor het Vlaams Leven in Brussel, 2004.

Jo Tollebeek, Geert Vanpaemel, and Kaat Wils, eds, *Degeneratie in België 1860–1940: een geschiedenis van ideeën en praktijken*, Leuven: Universitaire Pers Leuven, 2003.

Andreas Toppe, *Militär und Kriegsvölkerrecht: Rechtsnorm, Fachdiskurs und Kriegspraxis in Deutschland 1899–1940*, Munich: Oldenbourg Wissenschaftsverlag, 2008.

Jeffrey Tyssens, "Le monument Ferrer ou l'histoire d'une statue mal aimée," in Anne Morelli and J. Lemaire, eds, *Francisco Ferrer, cent ans après son exécution. Les avatars d'une image*, Brussels: La Pensée et les Hommes, 2011, pp. 199–222.

Volker Ullrich, *Die Nervöse Grossmacht 1871–1918: Aufstieg und Untergang des deutschen Kaiserreichs*, Frankfurt: Fischer, 2004.

Bernd Ulrich, Jakob Vogel, and Benjamin Ziemann, eds, *Untertan in Uniform. Militär und Militarismus im Kaiserreich 1871–1914: Quellen und Dokumente*, Frankfurt: Fischer, 2001.

Myriam Vanden Eede and Albert Martens, *De Noordwijk: slopen en wonen*, Berchem: Epo, 1994.

Jan Van der Fraenen, *Voor den kop geschoten. Executies van Belgische spionnen door de Duitse bezetter (1914–1918)*, Roeselare: Roularta Books, 2009.

Jan Van der Fraenen and Pieter-Jan Lachaert, *Spioneren voor het vaderland. De memoires van Evarist De Geyter 1914–1918*, Kortrijk: Groeninghe, 2011.

Christine Van Everbroeck, *August Borms: zijn leven, zijn oorlogen, zijn dood*, Antwerp: Meulenhoff/Manteau, 2005.

Alex Vanneste, *Kroniek van een dorp in oorlog. Neerpelt 1914–1918*, Deurne: Universitas, 1998, 2 vols.

Alex Vanneste, "Le premier 'Rideau de fer'? La clôture electrisée à la frontière belgo-hollandaise pendant la Première Guerre Mondiale," *Bulletin de Dexia Banque*, 214: 4 (2000), pp. 39–82.

David Van Reybrouck, *Slagschaduw*, Amsterdam-Antwerp: Meulenhoff-Manteau, 2007.

David Van Reybrouck, *Congo: een geschiedenis*, Amsterdam: De Bezige Bij, 2010.

Guy Vanschoenbeek, "Leger en socialisme voor de Eerste Wereldoorlog", *Belgisch Tijdschrift voor Militaire Geschiedenis*, September 1979, pp. 219–262.

Hubert P. Van Tuyll van Serooskerken, *The Netherlands and World War I: espionage, diplomacy and survival*, Leiden: Brill, 2001.

Laurence Van Ypersele and Emmanuel Debruyne (with Stéphanie Claisse), *De la guerre de l'ombre aux ombres de la guerre. L'espionnage en Belgique durant la guerre 1914–1918. Histoire et mémoire*, Brussels: Labor, 2004.

Laurence Van Ypersele and Xavier Rousseaux, "Leaving the war: popular violence and judicial repression of 'unpatriotic' behaviour in Belgium (1918–1921)," *European Review of History* 12: 1 (March 2005), pp. 3–22.

Laurence Van Ypersele, "Héros, martyrs et traîtres: les fractures de la Belgique libérée," in Audoin-Rouzeau and Prochasson, eds, *Sortir de la Grande Guerre*, pp. 213–236.

Vincent Viaene, "Reprise-remise: de Congolese identiteitscrisis van België rond 1908," in Viaene et al., eds, *Congo in België: koloniale cultuur in de metropool*, Leuven: University Press, 2009, pp. 43–62.

Véronique Waterlot-Jottrand and Daniel Lefebvre, eds, *Haro! Une revue belge d'avant-garde 1913–1928*, Mons: L'Oiseau-Lire, 1995.

Thomas Weber, *Hitler's First War: Adolf Hitler, the Men of the List Regiment, and the First World War*, New York: Oxford University Press, 2010.

Hayden White, *Metahistory: the Historical Imagination in Nineteenth-Century Europe*, Baltimore-London: Johns Hopkins University Press, 1973.

Jay Winter, *Sites of Memory, Sites of Mourning: The Great War in European Cultural History*, Cambridge: Cambridge University Press, 1995.

Jay Winter and Emmanuel Sivan, "Setting the framework," in Winter and Sivan, eds, *War and Remembrance in the Twentieth Century*, Cambridge: Cambridge University Press, [1999] 2000, pp. 6–39.

Theses and unpublished papers

Guillaume Baclin, *La répression de l'incivisme dans le Hainaut après la Grande Guerre. Pratiques judiciaires et presse montoise (1918–1925)*, licenciate thesis, Université Catholique de Louvain, 2005.

Jim Beach, *British Intelligence and the German Army, 1914–1918*, Ph.D. diss., University College London, 2005.

Stéphanie Claisse: *Ils ont bien mérité de la Patrie! Monuments aux soldats et civils belges de la Grande Guerre. Mémoire(s) et reconnaissance (1918–1924)*, Ph.D. diss., Université Catholique de Louvain, 2006, 3 vols.

Arnaud Collette, *Moralité et immoralité du cinéma belge de 1910 à 1920*, licenciate thesis, University of Liège, 1992–1993.

James Connolly, *Encountering Germany: Northern France and the Experience of Occupation during the First World War*, Ph.D. diss., King's College London, 2012.

Pierre Decock, *La Dame Blanche: Un réseau de renseignements de la Grande Guerre 1916–1918*, licenciate thesis, Université Libre de Bruxelles, 1981.

Leen Engelen, *De verbeelding van de Eerste Wereldoorlog in de Belgische speelfilm (1913–1939)*, Ph.D. diss., Katholieke Universiteit Leuven, 2005.

Aurore François, *Guerres et délinquance juvénile (1912–1950). Un demi-siècle de pratiques judiciaires et institutionnelles envers des mineurs en difficulté*, Ph.D. diss., Université Catholique de Louvain, 2008, 2 vols.

Benoît Majerus, *Occupation et logiques policières: la police communale de Bruxelles pendant les Première et Deuxième Guerres mondiales*, Ph.D. diss., Université Libre de Bruxelles, 2005, 3 vols.

Jérôme Niset, *Le quotidien d'information "La Belgique": organe belge de collaboration, censuré par les autorités allemandes durant la Première Guerre Mondiale*, licenciate thesis, Université Libre de Bruxelles, 2002–2003

Ruth Robinson Perry, *Clandestine publications issued in Belgium during the German occupation, 1914–1918, with a checklist of clandestine serials in the Hoover Library*, M.A. thesis in Librarianship, University of California, 1939.

Christoph Roolf, "Deutsche Besatzungsbeamte in Belgien 1914–1918 und die Selbstdeutungen ihrer neuen biographischen Rolle als Besatzer," unpublished paper, workshop *Besatzungserfahrungen in Europa (1914–1945)*, Technische Universität / Centre Marc Bloch, Berlin, September 10–11, 2004.

Russell A. Spinney, *A Nation in Peril? Rethinking how Fear influenced Everyday Life and Politics in the Weimar Republic*, Ph.D. diss., The Pennsylvania State University, December 2009.

Jan Van der Fraenen, *Voor het Duitse vuurpeloton. Executies in bezet België tijdens de Eerste Wereldoorlog. Tussen realiteit en mythe*, licenciate thesis, University of Ghent, 2005.

Christine Van Everbroeck, *L'activisme entre condamnation et réhabilitation. Influence de l'activisme et des activistes sur le développement du nationalisme flamand dans l'entre-deux-guerres. Contribution à l'histoire du nationalisme flamand*, Ph.D. diss., Université Libre de Bruxelles, 1998, 2 vols.

Sofia Vergara, *Le culte Francisco Ferrer en Belgique*, licenciate thesis, Université Libre de Bruxelles, 1987.

Miet Verhamme, *Cyrille Van Overbergh. Een bijdrage tot de studie van de christen-democratie*, licenciate thesis, Katholieke Universiteit Leuven, 1989.

Marc Walckiers, *Joseph Cardyn [sic] jusqu'avant la fondation de la J.O.C. Vicaire à Laeken 1912–1918, directeur des œuvres sociales de Bruxelles 1915–1927*, Ph.D. diss., Université Catholique de Louvain, 1981.

INDEX

Page numbers in italics refer to illustrations.